Counseling and Educational Research

Third Edition

To my lifelong best friend and spouse, Carmen, my cherished daughter Clarissa, who epitomizes resilience, my grandchildren, Ian and Soraya, and my cherished daughter Serena, a sensitive, creative, and thoughtful colleague.

Counseling and Educational Research

Evaluation and Application

Third Edition

Rick A. Houser
The University of Alabama

Los Angeles | London | New Delhi
Singapore | Washington DC

Los Angeles | London | New Delhi
Singapore | Washington DC

FOR INFORMATION

SAGE Publications, Inc.
2455 Teller Road
Thousand Oaks, California 91320
E-mail: order@sagepub.com

SAGE Publications Ltd.
1 Oliver's Yard
55 City Road
London, EC1Y 1SP
United Kingdom

SAGE Publications India Pvt. Ltd.
B 1/I 1 Mohan Cooperative Industrial Area
Mathura Road, New Delhi 110 044
India

SAGE Publications Asia-Pacific Pte. Ltd.
3 Church Street
#10-04 Samsung Hub
Singapore 048763

Acquisitions Editor: Kassie Graves
Associate Editor: Maggie Stanley
Editorial Assistant: Carrie Baarns
Production Editor: Jane Haenel
Copy Editor: Pam Schroeder
Typesetter: Hurix Systems Private Ltd.
Proofreader: Kate Peterson
Indexer: Judy Hunt
Marketing Manager: Shari Countryman

Printed in the United States of America

Library of Congress Cataloging-in-Publication Data

Houser, Rick.

Counseling and educational research : evaluation and application / Rick A. Houser, the University of Alabama. — 3rd edition.

pages cm

Includes bibliographical references and index.

ISBN 978-1-4522-7702-8 (alk. paper)

1. Research—Study and teaching. 2. Statistics—Study and teaching. I. Title.

Q180.A1H595 2015

001.4—dc23

2013038718

This book is printed on acid-free paper.

15 16 17 18 10 9 8 7 6 5 4 3 2

CONTENTS

FOREWORD

The growing national movement toward evidence-based practice has created a need for psychologists, counselors, and educators to be competent consumers of research. The delivery of services must be based on the most up-to-date evidence-based practices, and *Counseling and Educational Research: Evaluation and Application* (3rd edition) by Dr. Rick Houser is essential reading toward this goal.

Building on the second edition of this classic text, Dr. Houser continues to refine and improve what is already an outstanding contribution to the field. His enthusiasm and passion for conducting research are inspiring and contagious. Dr. Houser's extensive years of practice doing and teaching evaluation and research are clearly evident. It is rare to find a researcher and teacher equally facile in both arenas; Dr. Houser is equally adept in both roles and demonstrates a breadth and depth of knowledge that is truly remarkable. For example, he is equally versed in issues that are general and specific to education, family therapy, and counseling, and therefore, students are exposed to and grapple with a range of broadening and expanding diverse research readings. New chapters focus on qualitative data analysis, single-subject research, and technology and research; additional helpful and clarifying examples to illustrate key points can be found throughout the text.

Dr. Houser is a masterful, engaging teacher and writer. Using language that is easy to comprehend but never compromises complexity, Dr. Houser presents research concepts with superb examples that allow readers to apply what they have read in multiple contexts that address cross-cultural issues. He is thorough, systematic, and comprehensive in his approach. For example, most chapters are written such that the reader has multiple opportunities to develop mastery. A predictable structure is presented by Dr. Houser, often with clarifying tables that provide the reader with relevant and up-to-date material and examples and critical questions to consider, followed by opportunities to master and critique other works of research.

Ongoing feedback is given by Dr. Houser such that the reader can ascertain the degree to which he or she has mastered the material. Finally, summaries at the ends of chapters, with engaging exercises that allow the reader the opportunity to consolidate the skills covered, are invaluable.

It is difficult to improve upon a text that has proven to be effective, relevant, and one of the best in the field of research and evaluation. Yet, Dr. Houser has met this challenging goal. It is an honor to review a truly exceptional text.

Varda Konstam, PhD
Professor Emerita
Department of Counseling and School Psychology
University of Massachusetts, Boston

PREFACE

The intent of this text is to prepare students in counseling and educational graduate programs to be good users and consumers of research. Our society holds science and decisions based on sound information as crucial and even uses such standards in determining culpability for malpractice. It is imperative that practitioners embrace research and the research process, which can provide the best and most current practices. This means using the research literature in one's area of expertise, whether it is counseling, education, or both, and systematically evaluating whether the information presented in professional journals is valid and appropriate for the populations for which it is intended. Acquiring necessary skills for systematically evaluating professional scientific literature is critical in functioning as a practitioner. The majority of this text focuses on preparing readers to be good consumers and evaluators of scientific literature published in professional journals.

In addition, a practitioner should engage in small-scale research on the job site to test out new ideas. The practitioner is in a unique position to see problems confronting those whom he or she serves and can systematically develop new strategies to test. The second purpose of this book is to prepare readers to engage in small-scale research projects that are field based and can be practically implemented.

I have taught research and evaluation to students in counseling and education programs for more than 25 years, and I am acutely aware that the majority of students does not look forward to taking a research course. However, I truly believe it is critical that those entering the counseling and educational fields must have a solid background as consumers in reading the professional literature. This means developing the skills to systematically evaluate the professional literature with a critical eye and to use the literature in a responsible fashion. I have found that, at the end of a research course, students generally have a more positive attitude toward research and, most important, feel more competent in reading research from the professional literature. Also, I have had students who, at the beginning of a research course, state that they shy away from research but, at the end of the research, reported that they actually enjoyed the experience. I believe that learning should be relatively enjoyable, and this typically occurs when there is in an interest in the topic. This textbook is organized in such a way that students are encouraged to evaluate articles in the professional literature using a systematic approach, with specific questions to address. Therefore, I would recommend that students choose articles to evaluate that are of significant interest to them and not just find any article to analyze.

I see this text being used as an introduction to the research process and useful for those who plan to be practitioners and consumers of research. There are numerous texts that teach students to be primarily researchers, but that is not the intent of this book. Research and the research process are public phenomena, and consequently, I have found that allowing students to engage in discussions in reviewing articles, typically in small groups, facilitates the learning process. Also, participating in small-group discussions with student peers and potential future colleagues will, I hope, promote habits that will carry over into professional practice—for instance, discussing research in the professional literature among professional colleagues.

NEW TO THIS EDITION

New to this third edition are several important chapters that are increasingly relevant in counseling and educational research. Qualitative research is increasing in our fields, and there is a chapter addressing an overview of qualitative research that has been in the previous editions. A chapter describing analyses of qualitative research has been added. This information should help the reader gain a better understanding in the interpretation of articles in professional journals. A second new chapter is focused on single-case and single-subject research. Counseling and education have used single-case and single-subject research for some time; however, with advances and ease of concise measurements (e.g., electroencephalography [EEG] and other measures), the uses of such designs are conducive to research in our disciplines. Additionally, the increased emphasis on evidence-based practice and field-based research lends itself to using single-case and single-subject research designs. Realistically, practitioners in counseling and education are more likely to use single-case or single-subject research design than larger-scale group comparison studies due to time constraints and costs. A third chapter focuses on the use of technology in counseling and educational research. There are a number of technologies that provide unique opportunities to increase the quality and design of counseling and educational research. Rapid advances in use of the Internet, interactive video, iPads and iPhones (smartphones), virtual reality, and neuroscience allow for innovative applications and assessments. An understanding of these technologies is important for practitioners, both in reading such research and considering the use of technology in one's own research (and potentially one's practice). I have included additional examples to illustrate concepts and demonstrate how to interpret research published in professional journals. Also, chapters in Section II: Evaluating Articles in the Professional Literature include examples of single-case and single-subject research. Finally, there are additional examples of professional ethical violations illustrating the importance of maintaining professional standards in the practice of research.

I enjoyed writing this third edition of the book, as I did the first and second editions, because I like the scientific approach, and I enjoy discussing new ideas and using creative problem solving to address practical issues. I have added a number of new examples to this edition along with introduction to single-subject research. I hope students find this text a readable and practical guide that will facilitate the practice of their exciting and challenging professions of counseling and education.

ACKNOWLEDGMENTS

I have been fortunate in my academic career to work with dedicated and thoughtful students. Students have provided comments and feedback over the past several years about the first and second editions of *Counseling and Educational Research: Evaluation and Application*. I want to acknowledge the insightful comments of prior students, and I hope the changes that have been made reflect the needs of other students taking courses in research.

Completion of this book required significant effort, and there are a number of others who have made essential contributions that I want to acknowledge. First, Kassie Graves, the Acquisitions Editor–Human Services for Sage Publications, carefully selected reviewers to assist in the revision of the text. Her supportive efforts and expertise are greatly appreciated. I have worked with Kassie for almost 15 years, and she has been exceptionally helpful. Also, Maggie Stanley, Associate Editor, Sage Publications, provided significant assistance and professional expertise in completing this third edition. Her comments and feedback have been timely and important in focusing on the new additions to the text. I want to acknowledge the reviewers who provided insightful and thoughtful comments. The reviewers included Rhonda M. Bryant, Capella University; Jo Ann Jankoski, Pennsylvania State University; Mankato Lakitta Johnson, Jackson State University; Karin Linstrom Bremer, Minnesota State University; Annette F. Nelligan, University of Maine; Delila Owens, Indiana Wesleyan University;

Ja'net M. Seward, Midwestern University; Shon D. Smith, Argosy University Sarasota; and Scott Snyder, University of Alabama Birmingham. Elizabeth Luizzi, Editorial Assistant, facilitated the submission process and moved the book through production efficiently and in a timely fashion. Jane Haenel, Project Editor, assisted in setting up copy editing and provided important feedback. Pam Schroeder, copy editor, provided timely copy editing. She provided exceptional review and diligently reviewed the manuscript and suggested valuable changes. Dr. Varda Konstam, a well-respected colleague, graciously wrote the foreword, which provides a thoughtful summary of the text. Her efforts are greatly appreciated. I enjoy the writing process, and it is made more enjoyable with the assistance of the highly skilled individuals mentioned above.

SECTION I

INTRODUCTION TO THE
RESEARCH PROCESS

1

SCIENCE AND THE RESEARCH PROCESS

There typically are a wide variety of attitudes (and emotions) associated with reading about research and potentially conducting research by graduate students. You may be excited about taking a research course, or you may have considerable concern and apprehension. Also, you may place considerable faith in scientific knowledge, or you may question reports of research outcomes. The variety of attitudes and emotions that students in education and counseling have mirrors the general population in many respects. Across the centuries, there have been frequent attempts to improve the plight of humankind, and frequently, these efforts have focused on the use of research to do so. However, most recent advances in science have been most dramatic. Little (2006) stated, "During the last fifty years science and invention have led us further and further from the world that was; deeper and deeper into a new environment. The process of change has been so rapid that readjustment has been difficult. Yet readjust ourselves we must" (p. 54). Science and scientific advances have been purported to be critical in promoting the well-being of individuals and in societal functioning (Frye, 1965; Mendelsohn & Nowotny, 1984). Padgett (2004) noted that "faith in the scientific method has been the rock solid foundation of technological advances" (p. 1).

The words *science* and *research* have significant meaning in our current world. According to Padgett (2004), our society has had a love–hate relationship with science. This love–hate relationship may be found in various aspects of our lives. The entertainment industry provides good examples of this conflicted relationship. Science and research have been depicted both positively and negatively in movies and on television. Star Trek, the Six Million Dollar Man, Ian Fleming's James Bond books and movies, and other media presentations have frequently portrayed science in a positive light. Conversely, Frankenstein and even Jurassic Park are examples of science and research being presented as potentially out of control and creating problems. Al Gore's movie *An Inconvenient Truth* presents how human efforts in science (creating a greenhouse effect through technology) have impacted our world and potentially may lead to major changes in Earth's ability to sustain life. The debate over the greenhouse effect also demonstrates the range of societal views on the value of science (Nisbet & Myers, 2007). For example, trust and acceptance of research on global warming are mixed (Nisbet & Myers, 2007). Nisbet and Myers (2007) cite recent surveys that U.S. public opinion shows that about 60 percent believe that global warming is real, whereas another 40 percent do not share this view and question the research on this topic.

Modern science has a long history, more than 400 years, starting in the mid-1600s with scientists such as Isaac Newton and Galileo introducing major advances in scientific knowledge and methods (Okasha, 2002). More recently, the advent of the telephone, electricity, and computers (the Internet), along with advances in medicine (genetic engineering), are examples of how science has changed and (theoretically) improved our lives. In fact, today, there are probably few places you can go or activities you can engage in and not come into contact with advances achieved through science and research. Most recent scientific advances have occurred in neuroscience and cognitive sciences (Okasha, 2002). In fact, recent advances in neuroscience and cognitive sciences have resulted in specific applications to education and counseling (Goswami, 2006; Patton & Campbell, 2011). Decisions in our society made by government and other social institutions are typically based on scientific research outcomes. Finally, you cannot read a newspaper on a daily basis without coming across reports of scientific advances.

DEFINITIONS OF RESEARCH

The terms *science* and *research* have been defined in various ways, but there are common elements to the definitions. Best and Kahn (2003) defined science as "an approach to the gathering of knowledge rather than a field or subject matter" (p. 6). They further described science as consisting "of two primary functions: (1) the development of theory and (2) the testing of substantive hypotheses that are deduced from theory" (p. 6). Gay, Mills, and Airasian (2012) defined the scientific method as "an orderly process entailing a number of steps: recognition and definition of a problem; formulation of hypotheses; collection of data; analysis of data; and statement of conclusions" (p. 5). The connection of science to research is found in the application of the scientific method (Ary, Jacobs, & Sorensen, 2010; Gay et al., 2012). Creswell (2012) defined research as "a process of steps used to collect and analyze information to increase our understanding of a topic or issue" (p. 3). Common elements of science and research include acquisition of knowledge, a systematic approach, and an objective analysis with opportunities for conclusions about how our world may function. The ultimate goal of research and science is to obtain knowledge useful in understating how our world operates. Cooper (2012) discussed five ways humans tend to make decisions about what is true. These include information about truth given by authority, tradition or history, personal observation, the use of rational analysis, and the scientific method. Cooper suggested that the first four methods may lead to errors in detecting truth, whereas the scientific method is based on a combination of rational analysis and observation that make the process more objective and likely to lead to discovering truth.

Moore (1983) described different approaches we use in obtaining knowledge that is not based on the scientific method such as personal experience, tradition, expert opinion, authority, and church–state scholarship. He noted that the use of these methods of obtaining knowledge is fraught with subjective bias. The conclusion he suggests we reach is that using the research method reduces such subjective bias. Ary and colleagues (2010) also have identified similar sources of knowledge that do not use the scientific method. One frequently used source of knowledge is experience (Ary et al., 2010). We may even trust our experience more than what may be presented in scientific journals. A second source of knowledge, according to Ary and colleagues (2010), is authority, and we frequently seek out the advice of those who have particular expertise, such as lawyers, physicians, and others who hold high levels of expertise in a specified body of knowledge. In our everyday lives we make decisions, some of which are based upon scientific information and some that are based on personal experiences and other sources. In fact, there are decisions we make that do not call for an objective systematic approach (the scientific method), for example, what cereal to eat in the morning or what color to paint a bedroom. However, most in the fields of education and counseling believe that use of the scientific method is critical in the practice of our professions (Spencer, Detrich, & Slocum, 2012).

Salkind (2006) proposed that there are a number of elements of quality research. For example, he noted that quality research (1) can be replicated, (2) is generalizable to other settings, (3) is based on a reasonable rationale and linked to a theory or theories, (4) is not based upon political beliefs, and (5) is objective. Gall, Gall, and Borg (2002) suggested that there are four different types of knowledge, and these various types of knowledge can be clearly linked to certain research approaches. The four are description, prediction, improvement, and explanation. Knowledge viewed from a descriptive approach may be interpreted to consist of attempts to describe natural, social, or psychological events. The key to descriptive knowledge is a focus on assessment, which allows descriptions of identified events to be made. In counseling, this may involve, for example, a description of the specific characteristics of an emotional condition, such as obsessive–compulsive disorder. In education, an example of knowledge from a descriptive view might be how a teacher interacts with children based upon gender in a classroom.

Knowledge based on a predictive view involves developing ways to predict identified outcomes (Gall et al., 2002). For example, in education, we may want to predict success in a particular type of educational program, such as an advanced placement course in biology. In counseling, we may want to predict who may benefit most from a particular treatment approach, such as a posttraumatic stress treatment, for example, a virtual reality technique; we need objective knowledge that allows us to predict effectively.

Another type of research knowledge, improvement, involves developing information designed to determine the effectiveness of interventions (Gall et al., 2002). For example, in education, we may be interested in knowing the effectiveness of mainstreaming students with disabilities. An example from counseling might be an interest in the effectiveness of a specific counseling approach—the cognitive behavioral approach, for example—with a condition such as a posttraumatic stress.

The fourth and final type of research knowledge, according to Gall and colleagues (2002), is explanation. This type of knowledge may be the broadest of all and subsumes the others. Typically, researchers frame questions and problems in terms of theories or explanations of phenomena. For example, behavioral theory may be a basis for explaining a child's tantrum behavior and the reinforcement sequence developed within a particular environment. Researchers would use the theory to establish research studies to support or refute components of the theory.

Although the research method clearly, inherently does reduce subjective bias, I want to caution against complete acceptance of the notion that research is always objective and never biased. Babbie (2011) suggested that there are four types of errors in inquiry. The four are inaccurate observation, overgeneralization, selective observation, and illogical reasoning. Inaccurate observation can occur easily when humans are asked to use their senses to document outcomes. For example, inaccurate observation may occur in research investigations, especially if the investigators are not careful in their procedures. Overgeneralization may occur particularly when conclusions are based on limited information, small sample sizes, and not larger samples from the population (Babbie, 2011). These conclusions are made with the intent of suggesting the findings are general patterns and insight into explaining a general pattern or explanation for an outcome. For example, an educational researcher may make conclusions about an innovative math program using expensive technology tested on a small sample, a sample that is characterized by selection from an upper-middle-class community. The researcher may overgeneralize and conclude this math program could be used with any population of children, for example, lower-income communities that may have limited technology resources.

Gall and colleagues (2002) suggested that another potential criticism of research is that, inevitably, the researcher's own biases and selection of what to observe create problems. This is the error of selective observation (Babbie, 2011). Babbie noted that, when one bases research on broad theories, it may be possible that the researcher seeks to confirm research outcomes based on the theory. Consequently, the research may seek evidence to support the theory even when the results do not actually fit the theory. Researchers have found that we, as human beings, have a tendency to quickly decide upon a hypothesis and then gather information to confirm it rather than seek alternative hypotheses (Pottick, Kirk, & Hsieh, 2007; Strohmer, Pellerin, & Davidson, 1995). The last error in inquiry, illogical reasoning, concerns conclusions that may be based on individual idiosyncratic views or interpretations (Babbie, 2011). For example, an individual may interpret results from a counseling study on teaching a stress-reduction method and conclude it is effective because of the time of day of the training.

The important question to address is whether the research method does provide more objectivity in gaining knowledge about our world. Kelly (1955), a personality theorist, stated that a major motivation for human beings is to be a good scientist, and being a good scientist involves making accurate predictions about events. A major tenet of psychology is that we, as human beings, inherently like to predict and control our lives. Scientific and research methods may ultimately provide one of the better ways to be a good scientist and make good predictions, particularly when we make professional decisions. Being a good scientist professionally may be achieved in part through our ability to systematically evaluate the efficacy of the scientific and research process and the information present in professional journals used in practice.

PRACTITIONER–SCIENTIST

In counseling and psychology, there has been a relatively long tradition of graduate-level training from a scientist–practitioner orientation (Forsyth & Leary, 1997; Gelso, 2006; Hinkin, Holtom, & Klag, 2007; Hoshmand & Polkinghorne, 1992; Kram, Wasserman, & Yip, 2012; Lane & Corrie, 2006; Leong & Zachar, 1991; Nelson & Neufeldt, 1996; Stoltenber, McNeil, & Elliott, 1995; Vespia, Sauer, & Lyddon, 2006). Goldfried (1984) suggested that a profession based on a scientific approach is in a better position to be considered legitimate. The scientist–practitioner model was developed by the American Psychological Association (APA) in 1947 (Bernstein & Kerr, 1993). The basic concept is that those practicing the profession of psychology, and also counseling (Bernstein & Kerr, 1993), would split their time and focus rather evenly between research and practice. However, as Heppner, Kivlighan, and Wampold (1992) noted, the reality may be a much different ratio, more like 75 percent practice and 25 percent research, based on need and interest. Most practitioners have been dissatisfied with heavy emphasis on scientific methods and knowledge, using the ideal model of 50 percent research and 50 percent practice. Love, Bahner, Jones, and Nilsson (2007) discussed the relevance of research in psychology or counseling: "Research advances knowledge in the field of psychology and often guides clinical practice, yet very few psychologists conduct research after graduate school" (p. 314). Gelso (2006) noted that students entering graduate programs typically are interested in practice and not in conducting research, and this is manifested in the low productivity of research by those who complete graduate counseling and psychology programs.

Education has not had the history with the scientist–practitioner model, but recently, there have been efforts to consider how such a model can be implemented in education (Apel, 2011). Kamhi (2011) suggested that school personnel cannot truly use the scientific approach and model because they function and practice based upon a perspective of certainty. Essentially, Kamhi noted that practitioners who hold consistent and certain views of how they should practice are not using a scientific approach. He contends that a scientific approach involves the careful balance between certainty and uncertainty. We know what we know because of experience, but can one be open and consider other options to explain events? Science is based to a certain degree of uncertainty, and as Kamhi noted, being in a state of uncertainty causes individuals to pursue additional knowledge and information, possibly collected based on the scientific method. We want to have questions answered, and science provides a good model to answer questions, particularly in a systematic way. However, Apel (2011) argues that educators can use the scientific model in practice if they embrace an attitude of uncertainty. This attitude of uncertainty is characterized by a desire to seek to solve a problem. An attitude of uncertainty in science is defined by a problem with a hypothesis. A hypothesis is a tentative guess about phenomena or events. What this means is that, rather than knowing with certainty how to set up discipline in the classroom, a teacher using an attitude of uncertainty establishes or thinks in terms of a hypothesis. As Apel noted, most practitioners do not like to admit they are uncertain or do not know; many times, educators (and counselors) are encouraged during preservice training (academic preparation) to behave and act definitively. An alternative approach, the scientific approach, is to treat difficult situations (where one does not know) by using a hypothesis. In essence, the educator or counselor develops hypotheses to test out in practice to solve problems and attempts to employ systematic methods (gather data and evaluate particular interventions or instructional methods).

Manicas and Secord (1983) attempted to differentiate the tasks of the scientist and the practitioner by stating, "The former practices science by creating at least partially close systems; the latter uses the discoveries of science, but . . . also employs a great deal of knowledge that extends beyond science" (p. 412). They were stating that practitioners use not only science but other forms of information, such as personal information, in the practice of their professions. Consequently, I like the term *practitioner–scientist* to more appropriately reflect the realities of how many master's-level-trained counselors and educators use and participate in research. The emphasis is on practice first, with the use of research as a foundation for conducting practice. Others also have used the term *practitioner–scientist/ researcher* (Bernstein & Kerr, 1993). As Heppner and colleagues (1992) noted, the use of science in practice does not need to be evenly split. Practitioners will most likely choose to emphasize practice with science as a source of knowledge for treatment decisions rather than conducting research or being the researchers who gather the knowledge. Hunsley (2007) noted the different terms utilized from the original scientist–practitioner view to include *practitioner scholar* or *clinical scientists.*

Heiman (1995) stated that "psychology is as much a science as the natural sciences of physics, chemistry, or biology because they all employ the scientific method" (p. 5). This statement by Heiman can be applied to education also, as long as the scientific method is employed. So, what differentiates a scientific approach from a nonscientific approach? The definition of science and several assumptions about science provide this answer.

ASSUMPTIONS ABOUT SCIENCE AND RESEARCH

assumptions are that science & research are predictable & explainable?

Heiman (1995) cited several important assumptions about science that may be helpful in understanding the difference between scientific activity and nonscience. A basic premise of research and science, according to Heiman, is that one can find lawfulness in the subject studied (e.g., psychology or counseling and education). Lawfulness in our disciplines, counseling and education, is determined by the extent to which we can find ways to predict and control events. For example, we may hypothesize that, when a client in counseling describes a certain psychological reaction, such as an obsession with cleanliness, and is always washing his or her hands, the client has an obsessive–compulsive personality. Consequently, we can hypothesize and predict to some degree how the person will react in the future. In education, an example may be teaching a child reading with certain methods of instruction, for instance, phonics or whole word, and we may predict that one method of instruction will be better than another based on research outcomes.

A second important assumption, according to Heiman (1995), is that nature is understandable. This means that the laws of nature are understandable, and we

Predictable outcomes and ability to manipulate

can explain them in some way based on a theory. Understanding from a research perspective refers back to an explanation, which is a major goal of the scientific approach (Gall et al., 2002). Gall, Gall and Borg (2006) proposed that researchers employ different theoretical orientations in the search for explanations. Three orientations may be used by investigators in their attempt to explain natural or social and psychological phenomena: mechanistic, postpositivistic, and scientific realism. The mechanistic approach has been a major orientation of scientific research since the 1800s and consists of developing scientific explanations from a cause-and-effect relationship. If a bowler rolls a bowling ball down a bowling alley and it hits the pins, the assumption is that the ball caused the pins to fall. There is a direct relationship between two or more events: the ball rolling and hitting the pins and the pins falling. An example in education may be an adolescent taking an advanced placement course, and consequently, he or she does well on college entrance exams.

The postpositivist approach, according to Gall and colleagues (2002), involves an assumption that individual perceptions of the social environment and an event influence how they behave: There is an interaction between the person's perception and certain phenomena. To concretely illustrate this orientation, we can go back to the example of encouraging a child to study and complete his or her work, and the result is a high grade. According to the postpositivist view, the child's interpretation and the meaning attached to getting a high grade will have a significant impact on the outcome. Consequently, the explanation for a particular event or phenomenon is not a simple cause-and-effect relationship. Children may interpret a high grade in a different ways; some may consider a B a good grade, whereas others may be satisfied only with an A.

The scientific realism view for explaining events states that the world is composed of layers of causal structures. Some of the causal structures are easy to observe, while others are not as easy to observe (Gall, Borg, & Gall, 1996). The job of the researcher is to identify the various causal structures and how they interact to produce an effect. The following interpretation may be made if we again return, using the scientific realism view, to an example of a child studying to receive a high grade. Not only does the grade influence the outcome, but the events prior to studying have influence as well. For example, did the child's parents have a fight prior to the child starting to study? The student may have just received a high grade in another subject, and this motivates him or her to work hard on the current topic. The job of the researcher using the scientific realism approach is to identify the relevant causal structures influencing the event or phenomenon being studied. The scientific realism view is an attempt to move research beyond a laboratory and into the real world, where events are complex and not based on simple cause-and-effect relationships.

Relevance of Using and Applying Skills in Evaluating Research

The importance of using and applying skills in evaluating research is founded on the classic view of the scientist–practitioner model. As I mentioned earlier, if you read a large daily newspaper on any given day, you will find reports and summaries of scientific research studies. However, the newspapers do not publish specifics of the studies or information about how the study was conducted. An important question is this: How much credence should you place on the information you read in such sources? Additionally, if you have a copy of the study, do you accept the results unequivocally because they are published in a professional journal? I would suggest that accepting the results of a scientific study without systematically evaluating the methods is analogous to buying something, for instance a car, without ever test-driving it. Few of us would buy a car or a house without first systematically evaluating the quality of the item being purchased. Consequently, I believe we as professionals have an obligation to carefully evaluate knowledge and research results that may be used in the practice of our professions. I am not suggesting that you evaluate each piece of knowledge presented to you in a comprehensive fashion (this would be extremely tedious and probably impossible), but I believe that acquiring the skills to evaluate how knowledge was generated is a key to functioning as a professional and differentiates those with advanced graduate degrees from those who are not so trained. Most recently, counseling and psychology influenced by medicine has introduced the use of evidence-based practice (American Psychological Association, 2006; Tanenbaum, 2003). Evidence-based practice is focused on the identification and use of the best research available in the implementation of services. Love and colleagues (2007) concluded that "one of the most important goals of psychological research is to provide guidance and answers for clinicians with practical, relevant, and useful information that will enhance their ability to practice effectively, ultimately providing more sound services to clients" (p. 315). The use of evidence-based practice as a model provides counselors with a foundation for decision making and services that are more systematic and theoretically more ethical. Few people want to see a physician who does not use the most current research to guide his or her practice.

STEPS IN THE SCIENTIFIC PROCESS

Science and research are based on a systematic approach and proceed according to specific rules. I want to describe the generally accepted steps in the scientific research process and relate these steps to the sections of a journal article. I also want to note that an important step in the research process is that, ultimately, the procedures used in a study will be presented in a public arena such as a professional

Table 1.1	Steps in the Scientific Research Method

Step 1. Identify a problem.

Step 2. Define the problem operationally.

Step 3. Develop hypotheses or research questions.

Step 4. Identify and develop the research design (procedures).

Step 5. Develop and identify techniques or instruments that can be used to gain knowledge about the identified problem.

Step 6. Collect data.

Step 7. Analyze the data collected.

Step 8. Generate conclusions about the data.

Step 9. Report the data in a public arena such as a professional journal or presentation.

journal or a professional presentation, so the methods can be evaluated as to their efficacy. The steps to scientific research are depicted in Table 1.1.

PURPOSE AND OVERVIEW OF THE TEXT

A major purpose of this text is to provide a framework for practitioners in the fields of counseling and education to use in systematically evaluating the efficacy of scientific research reported in professional journals so that the information may be used and applied in practice. In other words, one goal of this book is to prepare counselors and educators to be good consumers and users of scientific research. This will be partly accomplished by relating the scientific research method to journal articles and providing a guide for evaluating counseling and educational research. The format of a research article may easily be related to the scientific method through the steps described earlier (Table 1.1). A research article is typically composed of four major sections: introduction, methods, results, and discussion (Table 1.2).

A second purpose of this text is to provide the basic skills necessary to professionally practice as a practitioner–scientist from a systematic and, when appropriate, a scientific approach. The completion of this purpose involves a discussion of how to conduct research. A basic overview of how to participate in and conduct research is presented. Contributing to the professional counseling and educational

Table 1.2 Relating Sections of a Journal Article to Steps in Scientific Research

Sections of Journal Article	Steps in Scientific Research
Introduction	Identify the problem.
Review of the literature	Define the problem operationally.
Purpose statement	Develop hypotheses or research questions.
Methods sample	Identify and develop the research design (procedures).
Procedures	Identify techniques or instruments that can be used.
Instruments	Collect the data.
Results	Analyze the data collected.
Discussion	Generate conclusions about the data. Report the data in a public area.

research literature is an exciting and important role of graduate-level-trained practitioners. This discussion includes coverage of conducting both quantitative and qualitative research.

Another goal of this book is to provide an introduction to program evaluation. Also, I provide information about program evaluation—how to systematically evaluate interventions used. Steps in conducting program evaluation are discussed, as are various types of program evaluation, such as formative and summative evaluation. There is a presentation of an example of a program evaluation to illustrate the process.

The last goal is to inform the reader of current and future issues confronting those conducting and using research in the fields of counseling and education. As was mentioned earlier, there is a controversy over the designation of training graduate-level practitioners as scientist–practitioners or as practitioner–scientists. Another issue (and this is discussed in early chapters) is the use of quantitative versus qualitative research. The last issue addressed is the use and conduct of research sensitive to cultural diversity. We live in an extremely diverse society, and the use of research in a responsible and sensitive manner based on cultural and diversity issues is critical. Ignoring culture and diversity is irresponsible in research and may result in its misuse.

To accomplish the goals cited, this text (the third edition) is organized around three major sections: Introduction to the Research Process, Evaluating Articles in the Professional Literature, and the Application of Research and Evaluation.

Section I: Introduction to the Research Process, includes the first 10 chapters. The first chapter is an overview of the research process and the third involves updating references and the scientific process. An example is a discussion of the value of science in our current society. Chapter 2 is an introduction to searching for journal articles and the use of electronic online databases. Additionally, there are additional examples of plagiarism and an addition of a section on professional writing and use of APA format. The third chapter is a basic overview of statistical methods. It includes a discussion of descriptive, inferential, correlation, and regression methods. Students have commented to me that the examples are helpful and they would like more examples, so more are included in this third edition. Chapter 4 is an overview of a certain category of research, quantitative research, which is defined in terms of results and data being quantifiable. Most standard research designs may be categorized as quantitative research, and most professional journals publish primarily quantitative research rather than other types, such as qualitative research. As part of this chapter, there is a presentation of various research designs that may best characterize this type of research. There are limitations to the quantitative approach, and these are presented. Chapter 5 is a discussion of qualitative research methods and includes research approaches such as case study, phenomenological, grounded theory, and ethnographic methods. Qualitative methods provide opportunities for investigators to do more naturalized observations of the actual object of study versus the more experimentally controlled approach used in quantitative methods. Limitations of the qualitative approach are discussed in this chapter. Additional examples of qualitative research studies are provided in this third edition. Chapter 6 presents the basics of qualitative research data analysis. There is discussion of the sequence of how researchers systematically analyze qualitative data.

Chapter 7 involves a discussion of mixed research methods. The development of mixed research has provided a link between qualitative and quantitative research methods. These two traditions, quantitative and qualitative, have had significant differences over the past 100 years. There have been recent efforts to develop systematic mixed methods designs, which have led to more integration of the approaches. I discuss the benefits of employing mixed methods in research. There are additional examples of mixed methods studies to illustrate the various approaches here. Chapter 8, a new chapter for the third edition, is focused on single-case research designs. There are discussions of the strength and limitations of single-case study. Additionally, there are discussions of when to use single-case study designs. Both the threats to internal and external validity are covered. Also discussed are specific single-case study designs such as multiple baseline, ABAB designs, between-group designs, and multiple treatment designs. Subsequent chapters involving critique of articles, including new examples of single-subject studies. Chapter 9 is a focus on evidence-based research practice. As was mentioned earlier, the importance of using evidence-based practice as a model is increasingly being acknowledged as a critical component of becoming an effective counselor (Slocum, Spencer, Detrich, 2012; Tanenbaum, 2003) or educator (Spencer et al., 2012). There is a discussion of the strengths and limitations in using an evidence-based practice approach. Last, there is a discussion of the best way to practice using an evidence-based model (Davison & Lazarus, 2007). Chapter 10 focuses on ethics in the research process. The primary focus of the discussion is on the appropriateness of interpreting and applying results from one specific sample in the literature to a different group of subjects or in practice. Guidelines for interpreting the impact of research results on the population are presented, and studies from the research literature are used to illustrate how to evaluate ethical concerns. For example, there is an evaluation of the Tuskegee Syphilis Study with African American males, using the proposed guidelines. The purpose of the Tuskegee study was to determine the natural course of untreated syphilis. The researchers in this study used 400 African American males who were left untreated for syphilis, even when effective treatment was available. The third edition involves an update of examples of current ethical research issues and an expansion of discussion of ethical misconduct in research. Examples such as manipulation of data will are provided, for example, Anil Potti and manipulation of cancer research data.

Chapters 11 through 17 comprise Section II: Evaluating Articles in the Professional Literature and provide a foundation for systematically evaluating the efficacy of articles presented in the professional counseling and educational literature. The section of evaluating articles involves updating examples used in illustrating how to effectively evaluate articles. As stated earlier, students have reported that additional examples are always helpful. Chapters 11 through 17 are focused on evaluating articles, and new examples illustrating how to evaluate the articles have been added to each chapter. Also, each chapter includes a qualitative study that was not provided in previous editions. Finally, there are examples from single-case research in each chapter and discussion on how to evaluate the studies based on the criteria provided. Chapter 11 is the beginning of the major focus of this text: a presentation of guidelines for evaluating the efficacy of research reported in journal articles. Methods for evaluating each section of a journal article are presented, starting with an article's introduction. To clearly illustrate how to evaluate the various sections of a journal article, there are examples taken from the counseling and educational research literature. The introduction section of an article includes the development of the argument or the rationale for conducting the study cited; this is frequently accomplished through a review of the relevant literature. Methods for evaluating the literature review are presented here. Chapter 12 is a discussion of how to evaluate the purposes and hypotheses statements that are also a part of the introduction section. The purpose statement and hypothesis (or hypotheses) are typically found toward the end of the introduction section, after the literature review. The purpose statement should be clear and concise as to what the study and researchers are investigating, whereas the hypothesis is more specific and gives information about any predictions the researcher is making. The next chapter, Chapter 13, focuses on the second section of a journal article, the methods section, beginning with samples or subjects used in the study. A discussion is included on how to evaluate the selection procedures used and the appropriateness of the particular sample based on the purpose of the study. Chapter 14 is an examination of how to evaluate the procedures used and described in the methods section. The procedures are a step-by-step description of how the study was conducted. Chapter 15 is a discussion of how to evaluate the third part of the methods section, the instruments. Investigators must decide how to assess the outcomes of the focus of the study and use valid and reliable methods. Guidelines for evaluating the results sections are the focus of Chapter 16. The results section generally involves the presentation of statistical methods used in the analysis of the study. It is not unusual for students in counseling and education to skip or skim over this section because of an aversion to numbers and math or statistics. The ability to evaluate the results section is not based solely on knowledge of statistical methods, and the evaluation approach introduced here is rooted in general concepts and assumptions that can be reviewed without significant expertise in statistics. Chapter 17, the last chapter in the discussion of the evaluation process of a research journal article, is the discussion section. This is where the researchers summarize the results of the study in descriptive form and attempt to generalize and relate the results to actual practice in counseling and education.

Section III: Application of Research and Evaluation is a discussion of how to develop and use research in actual practice for those in the fields of counseling and education. The discussion is presented from the practitioner–scientist approach. In Chapter 18, I provide a brief overview of how one goes about developing a research proposal. The discussion includes how to conduct small research studies as a practitioner, with particular emphasis on using the professional literature as a basis of design and implementation. Both quantitative and qualitative research designs are discussed. The chapter is updated with relevant references. As with other chapters, additional discussion of using single-case research is introduced as an option particularly relevant for practitioners interested in conducting such research. Chapter 19 addresses program evaluation. Counselors and educators may be asked to interpret and develop program evaluation. Program evaluation is quite useful to practitioners because the focus is on evaluating the effectiveness of the programs they are implementing and providing justification for continuing such programs. Program evaluation knowledge and skills seem particularly important in recent times of fiscal conservatism and accountability. The purpose here is to provide only an overview of the process of program evaluation and not to provide and in-depth review; there are other texts designed to provide a more detailed explanation (Padgett, 2004; Sanders, 1994; Thyer, 2005; Wholey, Hatry, & Newcomer, 2004). The third edition involves updates that include adding new examples of program evaluations in various settings, for example, schools, agencies, and higher education institutions (Hernandez, 2012).

Chapter 20 is new in the third edition and is focused on the use of technology in research. Advances in technology provide interesting and significant opportunities for conducting research that has not been available in the past. There is a range of technologies that enhance the opportunities for research. For example, one is the use of virtual worlds such as Second Life. Second Life is a virtual environment that allows for the virtual experience of social and educational experiences. The benefits of using a virtual world in research is that one can control the environment in much greater detail than in real life involving humans. Also, research participants can engage in social interactions that would be more challenging in real life, for example, visiting another country and interacting with residents from that country. Another example of using technology in research is the use of low-current electrical stimulation to treat many conditions such as learning disabilities, stroke, depression, posttraumatic stress disorder (PTSD), schizophrenia, and so on. A third technology is the use of "bug in the ear" for supervision of teachers in a classroom. Current technology allows for video streaming into a classroom and supervision at a central site. Such technology can be particularly helpful in training teachers and supplement faculty contact with student interns.

The last chapter, Current and Future Issues in Counseling and Educational Research (Chapter 21), is a discussion of the current and future issues confronting those conducting, and particularly those using, counseling and educational research (Brunoni, Nitsche, Bolognini, et al., 2012; Schwartz & Revicki, 2012). For example, the issue of conducting research that is sensitive to cultural diversity is a current dilemma in the field. Another controversial issue is accountability in counseling and education. How can research be done to address such issues?

2

SEARCHING ARTICLES IN PROFESSIONAL JOURNALS AND ONLINE DATABASES

A basic skill in the research process, which you may have already mastered, is to conduct searches through various sources. As a user—and even a producer—of research, you need to develop skills for searching various sources. An understanding of the search process can facilitate your searching. Search sources include hardbound journals, electronic journals, databases, online search engines, and meta-search engines. There are strategies that can be used to expedite and refine your search. Once you have identified what you want to search, you must decide how you will search and what sources you will use. After obtaining the search information, you must determine how you will use the information and how you will cite or reference the information you obtained. A key component of using information is the fair and accurate citation of the information. There is a discussion of appropriate methods of citation, issues of plagiarism, and ways to avoid plagiarism.

One of the first steps in using and conducting research is to access sources of information. A starting point in accessing information is to first identify what you want to search. This sounds simple, but if you do not have a clear search topic, you will struggle to find usable information that meets your needs. Once you have identified a topic, or someone (an instructor) has identified one for you, you should conduct a brief initial investigation of the topic to find out how broad it is. You can do an initial search through a search engine such as Yahoo or Google Scholar or databases such as PsycInfo or EBSCOhost. There will be a discussion later in the chapter giving more information about using a database like PsycInfo or EBSCOhost and various search engines. You also can go to your class textbook or various encyclopedias to select your topic (see www.lib.umb.edu/newtutorial/module1.php). Your initial investigation gives you information about how large the topic is and what may be some variations within it. Once you complete this initial search, you likely will need to refine your search because it may be either too large or not quite what you wanted. Keep in mind that you want to be able to manage the information, and if your search topic is too large, you may have trouble covering all the information available. After refining your topic, you want to generate key search terms. The selection of your search terms is important because it may result in the search being too large or too narrow, thus missing your topic altogether. Various strategies have been suggested, such as organizing a search using a Boolean approach (see http://www.lib.ua.edu/content/tutorials/WebTutorial/module1/Module1-4.html). A Boolean search involves the use of the following terms: *and, or,* and *not.* The use of *and* results in connecting two or more words in your search.

The result is a narrowing of your search based upon the terms used. The use of *or* expands your search because either term can be used alone. The use of *not* results in the exclusion of identified terms. You may be aware of a topic that is connected to your search that you want to eliminate, so you use *not* to narrow your search.

DATABASE SEARCHES

Once you have identified key search terms, you are ready to proceed with your search strategy. I do not suggest jumping to use search engines such as Yahoo but using a more scientifically based source such as PsycInfo or EBSCOhost and initially conducting a database search. Databases like PsycInfo and EBSCOhost are useful because they contain primarily citations of original research that typically are peer-reviewed (peer-reviewed refers to publication in a journal where the articles have been critiqued by professionals in the field before publication or acceptance for publication), so the quality is good. If you go to the university library's Web site and click on *database search,* you can begin the process. The databases are listed by topic and alphabetically. The major databases you would search include PsycInfo, Academic Search Primer, Expanded Academic, Journal Storage (JSTOR), EBSCOhost, PsycArticles, PsychCritiques, Sociological Abstracts, and Biological Abstracts. Once you determine the database, you type in your search terms and the Boolean search strategy. Typically, the Boolean search strategy gives you options from a drop-down box. If you receive too many results to manage, you may want to restrict your search. If you receive too few, you may want to expand. For example, you may restrict your search by reviewing sample citations and identifying those that closely match your interests and then using the specific terms found in the citation to further focus your search. Once you find your citations in the database, you may have a choice of an article abstract or full-text option. Most often, you want full-text options, so you can access the full article. The full-text options may be in either PDF or HTML format. Periodically, an article is available in both PDF and HTML formats. You can restrict the years of your search. You also may search by author and publication date.

Another good source of finding scientifically based sources is through Google Scholar. Google describes its database this way:

> Google Scholar provides a simple way to broadly search for scholarly literature. From one place, you can search across many disciplines and sources: articles, theses, books, abstracts and court opinions, from academic publishers, professional societies, online repositories, universities and other web sites. Google Scholar helps you find relevant work across the world of scholarly research. (http://scholar.google.com/intl/en/scholar/about.html)

Based on the search term, Google Scholar can provide a list of relevant sources ranked according to the source of the publication and where it was published. Also, Google Scholar provides information about the frequency of citation by other authors and researchers, which commonly is viewed as a good indication of the quality and relevance of a publication.

ELECTRONIC JOURNALS

Another format for a search is through electronic journals. If you know the journal title and the publication year, you can locate an article through your university's electronic journals. Electronic journals are alphabetized, so you can easily find what you are looking for. Also, there is the option of abstracts or full-text articles (not your choice but the library's and publisher's). Electronic journals are organized by date and publication volume. Once you have an article that fits your interest and topic, you may use the references in the article to gather further journal publications that may be of interest. You may want to determine the impact of a particular topic or an article or research, and you can do this through citation searching. There are several Internet databases that provide information about the number of times an article or publication is cited in a particular database. Such citations give evidence of the impact of a publication on the field—the view is that others are using the article or study information as documentation in their work. A primary source for determining the impact of a study is the Web of Science database. A search of the Web of Science database provides information about citations listed in the sciences, social sciences, and arts and humanities. As noted earlier, Google Scholar is another source that can be used to determine the citation frequency of a particular article.

SEARCH ENGINES

Before I discuss how to conduct a search through a search engine, I want to review how to evaluate the source in regard to quality. The information on the Internet (aside from that found in electronic professional journals) may or may not be accurate. There is no systematic evaluation of information posted on a Web site, and essentially, accuracy of information may be very weak or strong depending on the originator's knowledge and intention (a contributor to a Web site may intend to mislead readers). Consequently, you as the reader must determine whether the information posted is credible. Guidelines for evaluating Web-based information include a determination of accuracy, authority, objectivity, and currency (see www.lib.ua.edu/tutorials/ WebTutorial/module7/Module7-2.html and www.lib.umb.edu/tutorials/Evaluate Info/GuidelinesEvalInfo.pdf). One question is whether the information is accurate and is factual. Another question—what is the source of the information? Are there any citations of objective data presented, such as refereed journal publications? Recall that refereed publications are defined as those publications whose documents are evaluated by experts, and their review is an anonymous review. Another question is whether the information presented is peer-reviewed and sources are documented. A second criterion for evaluating the source of information concerns authority and whether there is an author identified and what his or her credentials are. Does the author have an expertise and background on the topic addressed on the Web site? It is not often that an author is listed on many Web sites on the Internet, so this is an important consideration in using such information. If you were discussing an issue with a colleague in person and they noted that others have said something in particular, would you accept such a statement as a strong argument? You probably shouldn't unless your colleague indicated who the others were. A third criterion is a determination of objectivity of the source. Is there any bias expressed in the information provided, or is the site affiliated with a group (e.g., a political group) that has a specific agenda (see www.lib.umb.edu/tutorials/EvaluateInfo/ GuidelinesEvalInfo.pdf)? The fourth criterion to consider when evaluating a Web site is the currency or recentness of the information. Materials several years old may not have current information, and the information may not be accurate as a consequence (see www.lib.ua.edu/tutorials/WebTutorial/module7/Module7-2.html and www.lib .umb.edu/tutorials/EvaluateInfo/GuidelinesEvalInfo.pdf). The last question concerns relevancy and addresses the appropriateness of the material for your topic (see www .lib.ua.edu/tutorials/WebTutorial/module7/Module7-2.html).

Once you have completed a search through traditional formal methods such as databases and electronic journals, you may want to expand your search and use a search engine such as Yahoo, HotBot, AltaVista, AllTheWeb, or Google. You also can use a search engine when you have narrowed your search and you are looking for a specific site and specific information. You may find important information through search engines, such as government Web sites that provide information about state, national, and international statistics. Additionally, brief government reports may be available through these Web sites identified through the search engines.

Broader search engines are the meta-search engines such as Dogpile, Mamma, and Vivisimo. These search engines are designed to link to multiple single-search engines, and they can provide a large base of information. These meta-searches are fast and can find large amounts of information (see www.lib.ua.edu/tutorials/WebTutorial/module7/Module7-2.html). However, you need to use search terms that fit their configurations, or you may miss relevant topics in your search.

PLAGIARISM

Because the topic of this chapter addresses searching topics and the use of database citations, it is important to discuss academic honesty or, rather, what is considered academic dishonesty. One type of academic dishonesty that relates to searches and citation of references is plagiarism. Plagiarism is committed when someone presents another's ideas or writings as his or her own. In essence, the plagiarist is not giving the person who actually wrote the material credit and is attempting to take credit himself or herself. An alternate form of plagiarism is called cybercheating and refers to taking another's work from the Web, copying it, and pasting it into your own work (see www.lib.ua.edu/tutorials/WebTutorial/module7/Module7-2.html). Marsh (2007) concluded that "plagiarists commit acts of petty larceny, trying to steal or pass off the words or ideas of another as if they were their own" (p. 31). One may consider using another's words without appropriate acknowledgment and citation as not a big issue, but in academia, it is tantamount to stealing. In essence, thoughts and ideas are owned by the originators, and not providing appropriate citation takes something from them.

Researchers have noted the frequency of cheating and plagiarism among college student, particularly undergraduates (Belter & du Pre, 2009). Belter and du Pre (2009) noted that use of cheating (purchasing papers) and other types of plagiarism (inappropriate or lack of citing a source) ranges from 50 to 80 percent of all college students. Park (2003) identified several reasons why college students plagiarize: lack of understanding, efficiency gain, time management, personal values or attitudes, defiance, attitudes toward teachers, denial, and lack of deterrence. College students may intentionally or unintentionally plagiarize. Certainly, it may seem more expedient to use others' work and purchase a paper or copy word for word another's work, but this is cheating and potentially stealing from others. Also, students may unintentionally plagiarize; researchers have found that college students have difficulty knowing what plagiarism is (Landau, Druen, & Arcuri, 2002; Roig, 1997). Undergraduates in the Landau and colleagues (2002) study could not identify acts of plagiarism in a text sample. Also, plagiarism may be unintentional and be a consequence of the person's memory of the source material (Bredart, Lampinen, & Defeldre, 2003). Bredart and colleagues (2003) termed plagiarism that was unintentional and a result of not remembering that one obtained the information from another source as *cryptomnesia*. Despite there being a controversy over the ability to detect or know if one is plagiarizing or whether it is a case of cryptomnesia, colleges and universities have increasingly focused on stopping such practices (Roig & Caso, 2005).

Roig and Caso (2005) stated, "Many in academia now believe that with the advent of computers and the internet 'copy and paste' plagiarism has increased dramatically in recent years" (p. 485). In most instances, the discovery of plagiarism results in a negative consequence for the student that may involve lowering a course grade or dismissal from the university (Robinson-Zanartu, Pena, Cook-Morales, et al., 2005). So, it is important for students to be aware of what plagiarism is and how to avoid it. There are several ways to avoid plagiarism (Landau et al., 2002). One way is to provide appropriate and accurate citation of the work used in your search. It is acceptable to quote a source based on the accuracy of the citation. The citation should include the author, title, date of publication, and location (see www .lib.umb.edu/tutorials/EvaluateInfo/GuidelinesEvalInfo.pdf). Another approach is to use methods of reporting on an article or publication through summarizing or paraphrasing, so you do not use the exact words used by others, unless you are using a quote. You still need to cite the source of your information; ideas are considered property, and giving credit for ideas is important. Practice summarizing and paraphrasing can help with reducing or stopping plagiarism, along with appropriate and accurate citation of the work. A review of a few samples of paraphrasing and direct quotes may help understand how to avoid plagiarism.

An example of a direct quote is: Olvera, Steward, Galindo, and Stephens (2007) stated, "Group (particularly familial) goals are emphasized by most Latinos; however, American culture emphasizes individual goals" (p. 225). A paraphrase of the same quotation could be: American culture generally highlights individual goals over group goals, whereas Latinos tend to highlight group goals (Olvera, Steward, Galindo, & Stephens, 2007). Note that the paraphrase results in the use of different words to provide the same meaning.

Another example of a direct quote is: "Students in our science classes were sending us mixed messages. On the one hand, they didn't see the content of our science classes as relevant to them. They didn't engage with the content of the class, and they let us know that they saw classwork as busy work and homework as optional" (O'Neill, Yamagata, Yamagata, & Togioka, 2012). A paraphrase of this quote might be: One study on teaching science found that students informally communicated that they perceived science as not very relevant to them. They also communicated that homework was a choice and not a requirement. Finally, the students indicated that classwork was in essence busy work (O'Neill, Yamagata, Yamagata, & Togioka, 2012). You can see the meaning of the paraphrase is similar to the direct quote and conveys the findings of the authors from the study cited.

SUMMARY

Conducting a search involves first using a relatively reliable source through databases. Further searches may be done through various search engines to help focus your topic and the information you are collecting. An even broader approach to gathering information on your topic is the use of a meta-search engine, which combines the search power from single-source search engines. Once you have obtained the information, you want to be sure that you cite the source of the information accurately and give credit for information that you have accessed in order to avoid plagiarism. The search procedures you use will determine how useful the information is, so it is important to employ systematic and effective search strategies.

3

BASICS OF STATISTICAL METHODS

The basics of quantitative research methods were discussed in the previous chapter, and to understand and systematically evaluate quantitative research, it is imperative to have an understanding of several basic statistical methods and related terminology. Gravetter and Wallnau (2008) referred to statistics as "a set of mathematical procedures" (p. 3). Bluman (2012) defined statistics as "the science of conducting studies to collect, organize, analyse, and draw conclusions from data" (p. 3). Mendenhall (1983) described statistics as "an area of science concerned with the extraction of information from numerical data and its use in making inferences about a population from which data are obtained" (p. 6). Important in these definitions are ideas about extracting information through the use of mathematical procedures and making inferences about a population. Statistics is primarily focused on making inferences about the population. Before we start a detailed discussion of statistics, I want to point out that whole courses are presented on various quantitative statistical methods, such as analysis of variance and multiple regressions. This chapter will consist of a discussion of (1) different measurement scales, (2) descriptive statistics, (3) inferential statistics, and (4) correlational and regression methods.

MEASUREMENT SCALES

All quantitative research can be characterized in terms of the types of measurement scales used (mathematical quantification) of the variables, dependent variables, and at times, independent variables (measurement types of independent variables). Four different measurement scales have been identified that are used in quantitative research: (1) a nominal scale, (2) an ordinal scale, (3) an interval scale, and (4) a ratio scale (see Table 3.1). Researchers generally differentiate between numerals and numbers. *Numerals* are defined in terms of symbols, such as letters or words (e.g., male and female), and the interval between units cannot be assumed to be equal. Nominal and ordinal scales are considered numerals. *Numbers* are values on which one can perform certain mathematical operations such as adding, subtracting, and so on, and the distance between units is even (e.g., the interval between 101 and 102 is the same as that between 104 and 105). Interval and ratio scales are based on the use of numbers. These measurement types of scales are considered to be somewhat hierarchical in regard to the different mathematical operations that can be performed on them. Nominal scales are considered to be the simplest and ratio scales the most complex. This means that the most mathematical operations (statistical calculations) may be performed on ratio types of data and the least on nominal types of data.

A nominal scale refers to one in which the researcher has assigned differences in observations or measurements to distinct categories. It is the least complex scale, one in which the fewest mathematical operations may be performed. Examples of nominal data are gender status (male or female) and ethnicity (African American, Asian, Caucasian, etc.). Nominal scale data, therefore, involve counts for each category. Researchers do at times assign values to nominal scales to compute a limited number of mathematical operations. For example, a researcher may assign a value to different ethnic groups (e.g., Latino = 1, African American = 2, Caucasian = 3) to perform basic mathematical operations such as determining probabilities, but they cannot calculate means or averages because the value assigned is artificial and a different assignment of values would result in a different calculation of averages. Another example of nominal data is religious affiliation. Again, an example may be (assigning numerical values somewhat arbitrarily) Christian = 1, Jewish = 2, Muslim = 3, Hindu = 4. One exception is where one can do more sophisticated analyses with logistical regression (this method will be discussed later in the chapter) with nominal scales.

Ordinal scales involve assigning values to data based on rank or order. This is the second-least precise scale of measurement. One example of ordinal data is ranks in the military (private, corporal, sergeant, etc.). Ranks are not overly precise and do not differentiate by equal units. For example, a sergeant is not twice as good as private, but a sergeant outranks a private. Essentially, ranks are not equidistant between points. A second example might be ranking brands of ice cream by taste. If we rank brands A, B, and C, we know that ice cream brand A tastes better than brand B, but we do not know if brand A is twice as good as brand B. Brands A and B may be only slightly different, or they may be significantly different. So, we would assign ranks as numerical values: brand A = 1; brand B = 2, and brand C = 3. A third example may be ranking of teachers by a principal for merit review. The principal may rank 10 teachers according to the quality of their teaching. Each teacher would receive a numerical rank, 1, 2, 3, 4, and so on.

Interval scales are the third type of measurement in quantitative research and involve the use of numbers with equal units of measurement. However, even though numbers are used, there is no true zero point on the scale. For example,

Table 3.1   Types of Scales

Scale	*Description*	*Numeral or Number*	*Mathematical Operations*
Nominal	Represents nomination to categories for variables	Numeral	Minimal calculating expectancies
Ordinal *to rank*	Represents position or order for variables	Numeral	Minimal calculating expectancies
Interval *true zero has no measurable value*	Represents equal units or intervals	Number	Most statistical operations
Ratio *zero represents, something that is measurable*	Represents equal units and has a true zero	Number	Any statistical operation

(handwritten annotation above Description column: "to choose")

most psychological and educational tests are based on an interval type of scale. An individual can obtain a range of scores on an IQ test, for example, from 20 to 200, but can an IQ of zero be measured? Someone could theoretically score a zero, but the true score will not be known, or cannot be measured, because of the limitations of the instrument. Other examples of interval scales are test scores, even standard test scores such as national exams (ACT and SAT tests). There is the National Counselor Exam (NCE), for counselors and the Praxis II tests for teachers, both of which are based on an interval scale. Both tests are used to measure level of knowledge in their respective disciplines.

(handwritten annotation in right margin: "because range goes from 0–20, –3, etc., zero has no measurable value")

Ratio scales are the fourth type of measurement scale and are defined in terms of equal numbered units, similar to interval scales, but there is a true zero. Weight is an example of a ratio scale, and the measurement starts at zero. Another example is temperature based on a Kelvin temperature scale. The ratio is the most precise of all the scales and the one in which the greatest number of concise mathematical operations can be done. A research study using weight loss as a dependent variable is based on a ratio scale. A study can be considered quantitative only when the variables have been operationalized into one of the four scales mentioned above.

COMMON STATISTICAL DEFINITIONS

Data set refers to the scores found in a specific collection of scores, generally from a sample of the population. So, an example of a data set might be scores of 100 respondents in a sample from a particular study.

Descriptive statistics refers to a collection of data that is representative of a sample of the population. It typically refers to reporting means, standard deviations, and tables in summarizing and explaining sample data.

Distribution refers to how scores are distributed across a data set.

Frequencies refer to the number of times a score is found in a distribution.

Inferential statistics refers to the generalizing of data from a sample back to a population using probabilities and hypothesis testing to make inferences about the population from a sample.

Median refers to the middle point, where 50 percent of the scores fall above and 50 percent fall below this point.

Mode is the most frequent score in a distribution.

Nonparametric statistics refers to characteristics of the population that are not based upon a normal distribution.

Normal curve refers to a symmetrical, bell-shaped curve.

Parametric statistics refers to population parameters such as means and standard deviations, which are based on normal distributions.

Range refers to the distance between the highest and lowest scores in the distribution.

Scales of measurement refer to the types of scales used in measuring the identified variables.

Standard deviation is the way scores vary around the mean and are stated as standard units or standard deviations.

Tables refer to methods of summarizing data through graphs, charts (bar charts), frequency polygons, and so on.

Variance is how scores vary from the mean in a distribution.

DESCRIPTIVE STATISTICS

Descriptive statistics are used to describe the sample on which the study was conducted (not the population). Descriptive statistics are not synonymous with descriptive research designs; they are separate concepts, and they have separate purposes. It was stated earlier that the intent of statistics is to make inferences back to the population. However, descriptive statistics are used to first describe the sample of the study. Lomax and Hahs-Vaughn (2012) defined descriptive statistics as "techniques which allow us to tabulate, summarize, and depict a collection of data in an abbreviated fashion" (p. 6). The statistics associated with descriptive statistics are in part presented based on the normal curve and are identified as measures of central tendency. A good place to start this discussion is a focus on the normal curve. A normal curve is a bell-shaped curve that is evenly distributed on both sides of the mean (and mode). The normal curve is characterized by a specific distribution across a normal curve with related percentages of scores associated with each standard deviation (see Figure 3.1). The distribution is based on establishing a corresponding standard deviation above and below the mean. For example, a mean in a study may be 100, and the standard deviation is found to be 20. One standard deviation above the mean is 120, and one standard deviation below the mean is 80. Just over 68 percent of the scores in a normal curve will fall within these two standard deviations, one standard deviation below and one standard deviation above the mean.

Descriptive statistics have been characterized as efforts by researchers to systematically summarize the data collected (Lomax & Hahs-Vaughn, 2012: Urdan, 2005). The idea is for researchers to present data descriptively in a way that is easy to understand and that conceptualizes general characteristics of the sample's responses. Descriptive statistics address the sample only and are in no way connected to understanding or generalizing back to the population. Generally, descriptive statistics are presented first in the results section, followed by inferential statistics. The actual calculation of descriptive statistics can be easily accomplished using statistical software. I do provide the statistical formulas for calculating basic description statistics (see Table 3.2). Typically, four major types of descriptive statistical measures are used in reported research results: central tendency, variability, tables and graphs, and relationships or correlations (see Table 3.3).

The most commonly used measure of central tendency is the mean, which is the arithmetic average of all of the scores in a frequency. The mean is calculated as the sum of all scores divided by the total number of scores. Another measure of central tendency, but not used as often as the mean, is the mode. The mode is simply determined by counting the most frequent score in a distribution. The median is calculated by adding one to the total number of

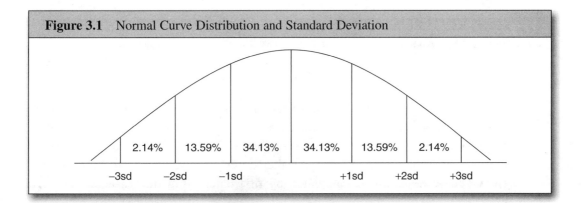

Figure 3.1 Normal Curve Distribution and Standard Deviation

	2.14%	13.59%	34.13%	34.13%	13.59%	2.14%	
−3sd		−2sd	−1sd		+1sd	+2sd	+3sd

Table 3.2 Measures of Central Tendency and Variation

Statistical Procedure	Calculation
Mean	$\mu = \dfrac{\sum x_i}{N}$
Mode	The most frequent value in the distribution
Median	The midpoint in a distribution, the 50th percentile
Standard deviation	$\sigma = \dfrac{\sqrt{\sum (x-\mu)^2}}{N}$
Variance	$\sigma^2 = \dfrac{\sum (x-\mu)^2}{N}$
Range	Highest value minus the lowest value in the distribution

Table 3.3 Characteristics of Descriptive Statistics

Statistical Procedure	Characteristics
Measures of central tendency (mean, median, and mode)	Statistical methods that are used to describe the frequency distribution of scores or the sample. The most frequently used measure of central tendency is the mean.
Measures of variability (standard deviation, variance, and range)	Statistical methods that are used to describe or summarize how scores are dispersed. The most frequently reported measure of variability is the standard deviation.
Tables and graphs (histograms, bar graphs, frequency polygons, stem-and-leaf displays, etc.)	Visual methods that are used to describe the frequency distribution of a data set.
Measures of relationship (Pearson correlation and Spearman rho)	Methods that are used to determine the relationship between two variables. To what degree do the two variables covary?

observations and dividing by two. Based on this calculation, you find the midpoint in the distribution. It is not the actual score but a score where 50 percent fall above and 50 percent below. So if a researcher has 11 scores, the median is the sixth score in the distribution (when the scores are arranged from high to low). The standard deviation is calculated by first calculating the variance, which is the sum of differences between each score in the distribution and the mean. The sum of differences is then divided by the total number of scores. This calculation gives the variance, but the variance is not helpful as a statistic because one cannot compare a variance in one distribution to another. Taking the square root of the variance gives a standard score, which can be converted to a score that can be interpreted on a normal curve.

Tables and graphs are other methods that researchers use to describe the sample (see Table 3.3). Tables and graphs are visual and can provide the reader with quick summaries of certain descriptive results. Tables and graphs may be used to display frequencies of participant responses, percentages, means, standard deviations, and so on. Various types of graphs (e.g., bar graphs) may be used within nominal and ordinal data to illustrate results (see Figure 3.2).

Measures of relationships (e.g., central tendency and variation) are a type of descriptive statistics researchers use to present results from the sample (see Table 3.2). Relationships are descriptions of the extent to which two or more variables covary. A relationship between two or more variables is generally defined in linear terms. Correlations may be understood as potentially ranging from a positive 1.0 (a perfect positive correlation) to a –1.0 (a perfect negative correlation). Figure 3.3 depicts a positive correlation but not a perfect one. Figure 3.4 illustrates a negative correlation. Note that, when there is a high correlation, either positive or negative,

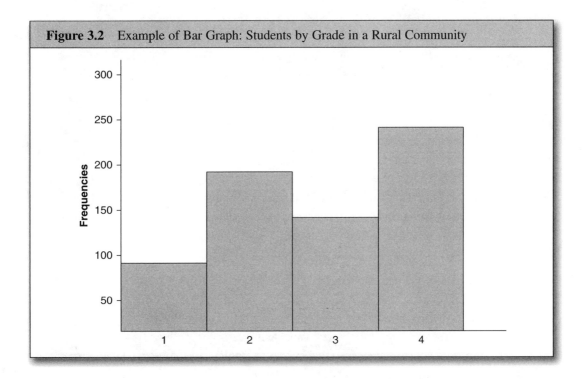

Figure 3.2   Example of Bar Graph: Students by Grade in a Rural Community

the variables covary closely. For example, a high score on one variable is correlated in a positive correlation with a high score on a second variable. When there is no relationship between variables, the correlation is closer to zero. It is most important to remember that a strong correlation, or relationship, is never an indication of a cause-and-effect relationship; it simply means that the variables of interest vary together.

The most frequently used correlation statistic is Pearson's Product–Moment Coefficient, or a Pearson *r*. The Pearson *r* can be used only with interval or ratio data. The Spearman rho, or rank–order coefficient, is used with ordinal data but is used much less frequently than the Pearson *r* statistic because the Pearson *r* is more sensitive to finding significant correlations. The Spearman Rank Correlation Coefficient is used at times to determine correlations or relationships between two variables when one of the variables is based on rank-ordered data.

Worley, Tate, and Brown (2012) provide an example of reporting means and standard deviations. The purpose of the study was to "examine if group differences in depression were mediated by 12-step involvement and if the effects of 12-step involvement on future alcohol and drug use were mediated by reduction in depression" (p. 1974). The researchers use a table to report means and standard deviations on the sample studied. For example, they reported attendance at a 12-step program over a 6-month period. In the table, they report the means .48(.31), .34(.31), and .25(.27) for intake, 3 months, and 6 months.

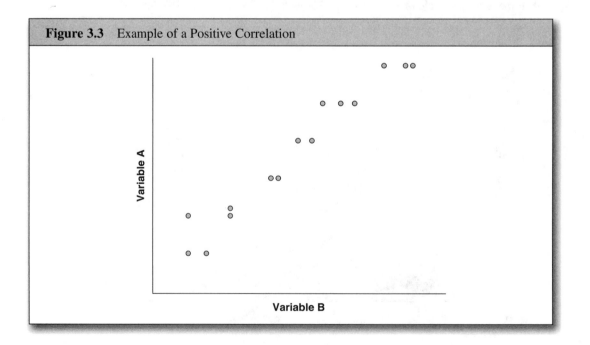

Figure 3.3   Example of a Positive Correlation

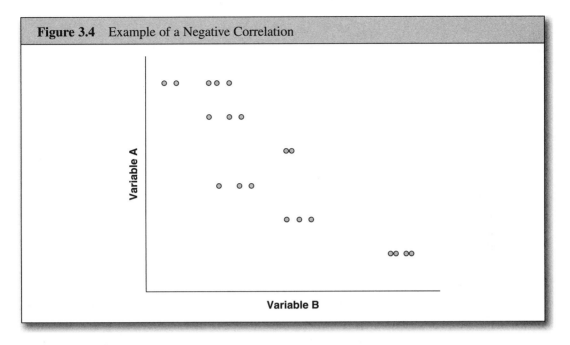

Figure 3.4 Example of a Negative Correlation

INFERENTIAL STATISTICS

Lomax and Hahs-Vaughn (2012) defined inferential statistics as "techniques which allow us to employ inductive reasoning to infer the properties of an entire group or collection of individuals, a population, from a small number of those individuals, a sample" (p. 6). Key in this definition is the use of methods to make inferences based on a sample (a small representation of the population) back to the population. This is the core of inferential statistics and in many ways the intention and goal of statisticians.

Before beginning our discussion of inferential statistics, we must understand several important concepts: (1) four basic assumptions of inferential statistics, (2) the differences between parametric and nonparametric statistics, and (3) level of significance (Coolidge, 2006; Cooper, 2012; Lomax & Hahs-Vaughn, 2012; Moore, 1983). In considering which statistical methods to use, researchers have determined that it is best to maintain four basic assumptions about the data. The four assumptions of inferential statistics are normality, linearity, independence, and homogeneity of variance. Moore (1983) defined normality as the extent to which a distribution of scores approximates the standard normal curve. Essentially, the assumption for normality states that a set of scores (the scores of a sample) does not significantly differ from a normal curve. There are statistical methods, such as the chi-square goodness-of-fit test (Cooper, 2012; Moore, 1983), to determine if these scores do significantly deviate from the normal curve. Also, one can use a graph to check visually for a violation of this assumption (Lomax & Hahs-Vaughn, 2012). A violation of this assumption—scores that deviate significantly from the normal standard curve—theoretically indicates that certain statistical methods should be used and not others, typically nonparametric statistics if a normal curve is not represented.

Linearity, a second assumption to consider when determining which statistical methods need to be used, particularly when the researcher is interested in how variables relate, concerns the extent to which two variables correlate in a linear fashion. Some relationships between variables may be more curved or circular and violate this assumption; therefore, the researcher is required to use appropriate statistical methods, that is, a nonparametric statistical method. Lomax and Hahs-Vaughn (2012) suggested that one can evaluate linearity through reviewing scatterplots.

A third assumption, independence, is concerned with whether each score is independent of every other score. Basically, this assumption states that scores must be independent of each other and that individual scores must not influence each other in any way. Violation of this assumption, as with others, requires researchers to use certain statistical methods. For example, if a group serves as its own control and completes pretesting and posttesting, the scores are not independent of each other because the same individuals are responding pretest and posttest. If researchers compare the pretest and the posttest, this violates the assumption of independence. There are nonparametric statistical tests that can be used in cases where independence is violated, that is, paired t-tests.

The fourth assumption, homogeneity of variance, is the extent to which the variances of the groups are homogeneous. There are statistical tests to determine whether the assumption of homogeneity of variance is violated: the F Maximum test for homogeneity of variance or Levine's test for homogeneity (Brayer, MacKinnon, & Page, 2003; Gall et al., 2002). A general rule of thumb is that, if standard deviations are three times larger for one group than any of the others, it is likely that this assumption has been violated, but statistical tests should be calculated to be sure. Again, if this assumption is violated, the researcher likely should use certain statistical methods, that is, a nonparametric.

No specific number of violations of assumptions has been associated with the decision to use particular statistical methods, parametric or nonparametric. Recently, researchers have noted that the violation of one or several of these assumptions does not necessitate using less powerful statistical methods (Coolidge, 2006). When all these assumptions are met, researchers can typically use statistical methods that are more sensitive to differences and thus more powerful in detecting differences. Parametric statistics are more sensitive to detecting differences, whereas nonparametric statistical methods are more robust and stable.

Consequently, nonparametric statistics are less impacted by significant variance in scores that may occur with violation of the assumption noted above, for example, significantly skewed data (Metfessel & Greene, 2012).

To interpret inferential statistics, it is important to understand levels of significance. Levels of significance refer to the probability of accepting or rejecting a null hypothesis. A null hypothesis refers to a conclusion that there are no differences between compared groups. The level of significance is typically referred to as a p (probability) value or alpha level. Basically, the level of significance is the chance of an error occurring in the rejection of the null hypothesis, a Type I error. A Type I error is defined as when there is a decision (based on collected data) to reject the null hypothesis when it is actually true. For example, a researcher might compare the effects of a stress training program (the independent variable) on reported levels of stress (the dependent variable). The researcher basically wants to know if the program brought about the differences in generalized stress scores between the group that experienced the program (intervention) and the group that did not. The null hypothesis states that there is no difference between the groups on generalized stress scores. In this situation, the researcher sets an alpha (p) value, which reduces the chance of rejecting the null hypothesis but at the same time detects the real differences between the groups as a consequence of the program. So, if a researcher conducted 100 studies using the same methods and randomly selected the subjects from the population of interest, he or she is by chance going to make an error in the actual outcome based upon the p value. Specifically, if all 100 studies were conducted, there is a probability that a certain percentage, for example, 5 percent ($p = .05$) would result in outcomes not consistent with what actually should be found, or the chance of error.

There are several explanations for why this occurs. One of the major reasons is that the sample chosen in any one group is not representative of the actual population, and therefore, their responses on the dependent variable are not based upon the influence of the independent variable but more likely based on personal characteristics that make them different from the population. The chance of making an error in the acceptance or rejection of a null hypothesis has been defined in terms of Type I and Type II errors. A Type I, as stated above, is where the researcher rejects the null hypothesis, although there are in actuality no real differences between the groups. A Type II error is that in which the researcher accepts the null hypothesis, although there is in actuality a difference. A curious phenomenon is that increasing the chances of making a Type I error decreases the chances of making a Type II error. That is, raising the p or alpha value from .01 to .05 increases the chance of making a Type I error, while it reduces the chance of making a Type II error. Typically, researchers have determined that an acceptable level of error is .05, or five chances out of 100, of making an error and rejecting the null hypothesis when it should not be rejected, a

Type I error. The important issue in setting a low level of significance, .05, is that, if the researcher finds a difference, he or she is publicly stating so and is creating new knowledge. Consequently, researchers generally would rather make a Type II error, not rejecting the null hypothesis when in reality it should be rejected, than a Type I error, rejecting the null hypothesis when it should not be rejected. Basically, the researcher is testing whether the group means (from data dealing with the dependent variable) are significantly different, taking into account the variances within and between the groups compared.

The setting of a level of significance at .05 or .01 is connected to tabled values that are compared to statistical calculations based on the data obtained. Whatever the statistical calculation, numerical values that relate to the levels of significance have been established. The established values are also connected to what is referred to as degrees of freedom. The number of degrees of freedom has been defined as the number of observations that cannot be clearly determined. Specifically, if there are five respondents and there are five scores having to do with the dependent variable, then only one score can be clearly identified once the other four are known. This is a difficult concept to explain and understand. For example, suppose that you know the IQ scores for four participants: 111, 101, 116, and 97. There is only one score left, and you know which participant had the missing score. If there were two scores left, you could not be sure which score was related to which participant. Degrees of freedom are used in the calculation of several inferential statistics and in reading tabled values for levels of significance.

Inferential statistics are used to make decisions or reach conclusions about whether results obtained from a sample can be applied to the target population. All the methods discussed as applications of inferential statistics are associated with quantitative research methods. There are a number of types of inferential statistics, but I want to address the most frequently used parametric tests: *t*-test, analysis of variance (ANOVA), multivariate analysis of variance (MANOVA), analysis of covariance (ANCOVA), multiple regression, chi-square and structural equation modeling (SEM; see Table 3.4). The majority of the methods used in inferential statistical procedures involve making comparisons between groups.

One statistical procedure, the *t*-test, is intended to compare the differences of a dependent measure between two groups. Data analyzed must be either interval or ratio scale scores. Basically, calculation of the *t*-test concerns differences between the groups compared to within-group differences. The between-group differences must be significantly larger than the within-group differences (within the two comparison groups) before the researcher can conclude that the scores on the dependent measure show a significant difference. The calculation of the *t*-test focuses on determining whether the groups in the sample score are more like each other compared to the comparison group or that there is no difference in dependent measure scores between groups. Gortmaker and Brown (2006) conducted a study focusing on the perceptions of out-of-the-closet versus not-out-of-the-closet gay and lesbian college students in a campus climate. The researchers used *t*-tests to determine if there were any differences between the perceptions of the campus climate. The specific question they addressed was this: "Is level of outness related to students' perceptions and experiences on campus?" They described the results as follows:

> Perceptions and experiences of an anti-LG climate. The first variable consisted of a total score of perceptions of an anti-LG climate and sightings of anti-LG graffiti. The perceptions of anti-LG attitudes item used a 1–5 response format (1 = "very little extent," 5 = "very great extent"). Students noted the number of times they saw anti-graffiti on campus using a "0" to "four times or more" response format. Using an independent *t*-test and nonoverlapping 99 percent confidence intervals, our students perceived the environment significantly more negatively than did closeted students ($t[78] = 3.56$; $p = .001$). (p. 610)

In this example, the calculated *t* value is 3.56, and it is significant at the *p* value of .001. This means that the two groups, those who were out of the college closet versus those who were not, reported significantly different experiences in a college climate. Specifically, those who were out of the college closet reported a more negative climate than those who were not out of the college closet. There is only a 0.1 percent chance of making a Type I error, rejecting the null hypothesis, when in fact there are no differences between the groups' perceptions of the college climate, which is a quite small chance of error. The researchers in this study can be relatively confident that there are significant differences in perceptions and attitudes given the small chance of a Type I error.

Resendes and Lecci (2012) provide another example of the use of the *t*-test. They described their purpose as to "whether parental competency and child custody samples are in fact similar with respect to their MMPI-2 profiles" (p. 1055). More than 600 parents were included the study, those who had parent competency evaluations versus those who had child custody hearings. They wanted to know if there were differences in personality profiles that could be used in the future in making court decisions. The researchers stated, "We used a series of independent samples *t* tests to determine whether there are significant differences between the MMPI-2 scores of the present competency sample and a child custody sample" (p. 1056). The researchers reported *t*-test values in a table. An example of one *t*-test outcome is $t(642) = 15.48$ with a $p < .003$.

A second frequently used inferential statistical procedure is ANOVA, which is used to compare groups (it also is referred to as an *F* test). Two or more groups can be compared with this approach (see Table 3.4). It is used when there is one independent variable and, typically, three or more groups. The dependent variable must be in interval or ratio scale. As with the t-test, the basic function of the ANOVA is to determine whether there are significant differences between groups versus within groups. The larger the difference between groups versus within groups, the more likely significant differences will be found. Luszcyznska and Sobczyk (2007) provide an example of the use of ANOVA in a study on obesity. They describe the results of their ANOVA analysis as follows:

> Our first hypothesis concerned the effects of the IIP on weight loss and BMI. An ANOVA revealed a main effect of time for body weight, $F(1, 49) = 84.92$, $p < .001$ ($\eta^2 = .67$), as well as a Time × Group interaction, $F(1, 49) = 9.08$, $p < .01$ ($\eta^2 = .18$; post hoc observed power test 0.84). On average, IIP participants lost 4.2 kg (95% confidence interval [CI] = 3.19, 5.07), whereas control group participants lost 2.1 kg (95% CI = 1.11, 3.09). (p. 510)

Calculation of the F ratio is achieved by computing the mean square between divided by the mean square within. The mean square between is determined by calculating the sum of squares between. The sum of square between is generated by calculating the total mean for all groups and dividing it by the degrees of freedom for between. To obtain a significant F value and the difference among groups, the researcher must find that the means differ and the variances between and within the groups do not account for this difference.

Frein (2011) studied how undergraduate college students preferred taking tests. There were three categories (levels) of the independent variable: in-class tests, out-of-class computer-based tests, and computer-based tests at each student's choosing. They described their data analysis as follows: "A one-way ANOVA indicated that there was no difference in test performance among the three groups, $F(2, 169) = .139$, $p = .87$" (p. 285). The researchers concluded there was no difference in student preference of how they took tests, with p value of .87 (needed to be less than .05 to reach level of significance).

Another type of ANOVA is the factorial ANOVA, which allows the researcher to compare different levels of several independent variables and determine if there are any interactions between the independent variables and the dependent variable (see Table 3.4). For example, a researcher could use a factorial ANOVA to compare the effects of a teaching intervention compared to a control group and also compare the students by gender. Such a study would be characterized as a 2 × 2 factorial design, 2 (experimental intervention and control group) × 2 (male and female).

An example of a factorial ANOVA (Bishop, Barry, & Hardiman, 2012) focused on language learning abilities in children with learning disabilities and those without learning disabilities. The researchers compared age and family history of learning disability (specific language impairment [SLI]). The researchers described the study as follows: "In the current study, we wished to test whether short-term and long-term learning of new words is compromised in children with SLI. We tested the hypothesis that children with SLI and their adult relatives would show poor retention of phonological material over a delay" (p. 2). The researchers included comparisons based on families with a child with SLI and those without. Also, it included adults with SLI and those adults without SLI (parents). The researchers used a 2×2 factorial analysis, comparing those children with SLI and those with typical language and parents of the children with SLI and age, those below 18 and those above 18 years of age. The dependent variable was word retention. The researchers stated some of the results as follows: "For difference scores the main effect of Age band was significant, $F(1, 55) = 8.87$, $p = .004$, $\eta^2 = .139$, whereas the main effect of Family status was not, $F(1, 55)$, $= .20$, $p = .889$, $\eta^2 = 0$. The interaction between these factors was also nonsignificant, $F(1, 55)$, $= 2.36$, $p = .130$, $\eta^2 = .041$" (p. 3). There are two main effect comparisons, one focused on age and a second based on family status. Only one main effect was found and that was the age of the child. There was no effect on the dependent variable (word retention) based on family status. Additionally, there was no interaction effect between age and family status.

The repeated-measures ANOVA allows the researcher to compare the dependent variable to be measured and compared over several different observations or measurements (see Table 3.4). This statistical procedure addresses the threat to external validity of novelty or disruption effects (ecological validity; Bracht & Glass, 1968). A researcher can use a repeated-measures design to assess the effects of the dependent variable over time and determine whether the effects are short-term or long-term changes. Iverson, Brooks, Collins, and Lovell (2006) conducted a study and utilized a repeated-measures ANOVA. The purpose of the study was to determine the changes in neuropsychological functioning after a brain injury over time. Participants were 30 athletes who each experienced a concussion during a sporting activity. They described in their results section the statistical calculations, one using a repeated-measures ANOVA: "Repeated measures ANOVAs were used to determine if mean cognitive and symptom scores differed across the four assessments. . . . For the verbal memory composite score, there was a significant main effect for time" (p. 248). The repeated-measures ANOVA gave the researchers the opportunity to determine the impact of a concussion from a sports brain injury over time and four observations.

Painter (2012) utilized a repeated ANOVA in studying the use of wraparound services in the treatment of those with severe emotional disturbance. The researcher described the purpose of the study as "to evaluate outcomes for children ages 5–18 experiencing serious emotional disturbances who received wraparound in a system of care community" (p. 407). The dependent variables were clinical levels of improvement in behavior and emotional functioning and mental health symptoms. The researcher was interested in changes over time, and therefore, she used a repeated-measures ANOVA. More than 300 children participated in the study. The researcher described wraparound services as such: "A family team is developed based on the desires of the youth and family. Team members include both formal service providers and informal support persons such as friends, school teachers, family, coaches, or other persons important to the family" (p. 409). The researcher described her results using a repeated-measures ANOVA as follows: "A statistically significant level of change in youth behavioural and emotional strengths was found on the parent completed BERS-2, $F = 16.76$ (4, 399), $p < .001$" (p. 417). The results show that there was a difference over time as a consequence of the wraparound services with a small chance of a Type I error, a chance of less than one in a 1,000, $p < .001$. For most researchers, this is good evidence that the sample is representative of the impact of the wraparound services if it were used with all in the population.

Table 3.4 Characteristics of Parametric Inferential Statistics

Statistical Procedure	*Characteristics*
T-tests (independent), *t*-tests (correlated)	Involves testing the differences between the means of two groups.
Analysis of variance (ANOVA)	Involves testing the extent the means differ based upon the degree that variances differ among the means of three or more groups with one independent variable.
Factorial ANOVA	Involves the use of two or more independent variables and two or more levels. Allows for researcher to determine if there is an interaction between independent variables.
Repeated measures of ANOVA	Allows the researcher to compare differences over several different observations or times.
Multivariate analysis of variance (MANOVA)	A statistical procedure to calculate difference among the variances of means of two or more groups with two or more dependent variables. The analysis of the dependent variables is conducted simultaneously.
Analysis of covariance (ANCOVA)	A statistical procedure to calculate differences among the variances of means of two or more groups and simultaneously control for the effects of an extraneous variable on the dependent variable.

Table 3.4   (Continued)

Statistical Procedure	Characteristics
Multiple regression	A statistical procedure used to calculate the relationship between a predicted variable and several predictor variables.
Chi-square	A statistical procedure designed to determine whether there is a significant difference between observed versus expected scores.
Structural equation modeling	A statistical technique that is used in theory testing. Relevant constructs are operationalized and instruments identified to test the model. Correlational techniques are used in theory testing.

MANOVA is another type of inferential statistic (see Table 3.4). MANOVA is similar to the ANOVA, which involves comparison among groups, but includes comparisons for more than one dependent variable simultaneously. There are situations in which dependent variables have strong interrelationships and should be analyzed together, such as when the individual item scores that related to a particular dependent measure are compared between two or more groups. Results reported in the literature using MANOVAs are similar to the way in which ANOVAs are expressed. Henry, Anshel, and Michael (2006) studied various types of aerobic and interval circuit training programs on fitness and body image. They used MANOVA in their study and compared groups and time. They described their results:

> Table 3 presents the pretest and posttest scores for each body image subscale. A 3 (group) × 2 (time) MANOVA with repeated measures on the last factor yielded a significant main effect for time ($F[9, 61] = 3.54$, $p = .001$) and for time × group interaction ($F[18, 122] = 2.02$; $p = .013$). The group × time interaction indicates that the three groups differed on changes in body image during the training program. Univariate analyses of variance were then performed to detect which physical fitness variables were responsible for the significant interaction in the overall MANOVA. (p. 294)

ANCOVA is a statistical procedure for calculating differences among the variances of means of two or more groups and simultaneously controlling for the effects of an extraneous variable on the dependent variable. Moore (1983) described the ANCOVA as adjusting the scores on the dependent variable based on the effects of one or more extraneous variables (the use of ANCOVA changes it to a control variable). A study by Culatta, Reese, and Setzer (2006) illustrates the use of ANCOVA in a research study. They described their study as focusing on the effectiveness of an early literacy program that uses skill-based instruction to improve literacy. In the results section, they state: "To contrast performance on the trained versus untrained rhyme and alliteration skills, two-way ANCOVAS (2[Class: AR, RA] × 2[Time: Posttest 1, Posttest 2]) were conducted using each group's pretest performance as a covariate to control for entering performance for each of the literacy measures" (p. 74). So, the researchers compared trained and untrained rhyme and alliteration skills. They controlled for beginning performance because they could not randomly assign to groups; they had to take an intact classroom.

Multiple regression is a statistical method that involves the use of statistical procedures that allow one to predict scores on one variable based on those from one or more variables (Rosenthal, 2001; Toothaker & Miller, 1996). The underlying concept in regression is that the variables of interest may covary together in either a positive or negative way. It does not mean that one variable causes the other but that they vary or covary together. A common example of the use of regression is the prediction of success in college. There may be several predictors of college success, but a few that have been used include high school grade point average (GPA), admission test scores such as the ACT or SAT, success in advanced placement courses, and high school rank. A college admissions officer may want to know the relationship between college success and these high school sources of information. College admissions officers want to make the best predictions for success, and so a good regression equation would give them valuable information. A researcher may find that high school GPA and success in advanced placement classes are the best predictors of college success, not SAT or ACT scores. It does not mean that high school GPA causes the success in college but only that one can predict the other. Figure 3.5 illustrates how high school GPA can predict college GPA. A high GPA in high school is related, or varies in a positive way, to predicting college GPA.

Klomegah (2007) provides an example of the use of multiple regression. His study focused on predictors of academic performance in college students. He was particularly interested in understanding how variables such as ability, self-efficacy, and goal setting were predictive of course grades. He described his multiple regression results:

> To explore the research questions posed above, standard multiple regression was utilized. First, a check of the assumption of multicollinearity showed that none of the independent variables were correlated highly. The collinearity diagnostics performed by SPSS did not show any low value of tolerance in the diagnostic table indicating that the independent variables did not correlate among themselves; therefore the assumption of multicollinearity was not violated. With regard to the normality and linearity of the residuals, the Normal Probability Plot was inspected and found to be in a reasonably straight line, suggesting no major deviations from normality. Upon examining the scatterplot, no cases of outliers were detected as cases had a standardized residual of less than 3.3 or –3.3.

As indicated in the table, the R^2 equals .44 meaning that the model (which includes ability, self-set goals, self-efficacy, and assigned goals) was able to explain 44% of the variance and the dependent variable (academic performance). (p. 414)

An important point in reviewing Klomegah's results is the statement that 44 percent of the variance was explained by the predictor variables. This means that the predictor variables are able to predict almost half of the scores on the outcome variable, academic performance. This leaves 56 percent unexplained and results in other factors influencing the outcome that are unknown to the researcher. The explained variance in this example is quite high. The larger the R^2 value, the greater the explained variance.

Chi-square is another statistical procedure, and it is considered both a parametric and a nonparametric statistic. However, most calculations with chi-square use nominal data, and therefore, it is used in cases such as a nonparametric statistic. The underlying principle of chi-square is that there is a comparison between observed and expected frequencies. The intention is to determine if any significant differences exist between these scores. The calculation is determined by first identifying the expected frequency. Expected frequency is calculated by summing the total number of responses and dividing by 2. So, if a researcher wants to know the ice cream preferences of choices between chocolate and vanilla and there are 250 respondents, he or she would divide 250 by 2, and the expected frequency would be 125. The expected frequency would then be compared to the observed, or actual, frequency.

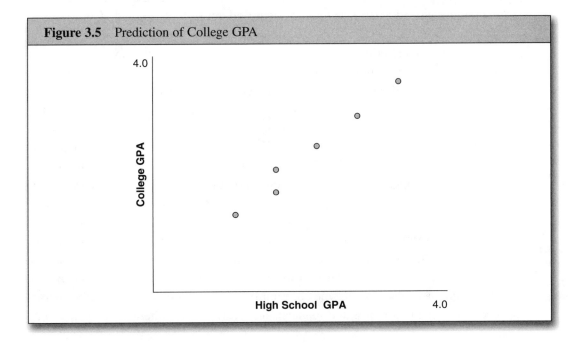

Figure 3.5   Prediction of College GPA

Odaci and Kalkan (2010) conducted a study focused on problems with Internet use, loneliness, and dating anxiety among college students. The researchers stated the following purpose: "This study investigates problematic Internet use in young adult university students and examines the relation between problematic Internet use and loneliness and dating anxiety" (p. 1092). Almost 500 students were included in the study. The researchers collected data using a loneliness scale, a dating anxiety scale, and an online cognition scale. The online cognition scale included measuring feelings with being online. The researchers used chi-square to answer the research hypothesis: "There is a significant association between length of Internet use and how individuals feel when not online" (p. 1092). The researchers described the use of chi-square as follows:

> Chi-square results reveal a significant association between Internet use duration and how students feel when not going online (chi-square = 116.543, $p < .001$). As shown on Table 7, none of those using Internet for more than 5 hours a day felt "very unhappy" when not online, and 2.6% felt "very unhappy; 2.2% of those using the Internet 1–5 hours a day felt "very happy." (p. 1094)

The researchers used the categories, for example, very unhappy, in the chi-square analysis. They were comparing expected versus actual scores with the chi-square analysis.

Another statistical method is structural equation modeling. Structural equation modeling is a statistical technique that is used in theory testing. Relevant constructs are operationalized and instruments identified to test the model. Correlational techniques are used in theory testing. Raykov and Marcoulides (2006) noted several different methods of structural equation modeling: path analysis models, confirmatory factor analysis models, structural regression models, and latent change models. Path analysis models may be understood in terms of the models for explaining adolescent aggression, for example. Components of this particular model may also include participation in aggressive video games, experiencing bullying, and experiencing child abuse. The path analysis would seek to find correlations between these variables in explaining the variance of the outcome, in this case adolescent aggression. Also, it would attempt to show how these variables relate to each other—for example, does experiencing bullying interact with playing video games? A confirmatory factor analysis model is focused on discovering patterns of interrelationships among several variables (Raykov & Marcoulides, 2006). For example, multiple intelligences have been identified, and there may be numerous factors that contribute to these different intelligences (Shearer, 2004). For example, two theoretical types of multiple intelligence that potentially interact are kinesthetic intelligence and musical intelligence. Kinesthetic intelligence may include abilities in movement, such as dance or athletic activities. Variables related to kinesthetic intelligence that may contribute to this intelligence may be peripheral vision and eye–hand coordination. Musical intelligence may involve a relationship between pitch and rhythm. Also, these two intelligences may interact; for example, pitch and rhythm may interact with movement and dance abilities and intelligence. So, these variables may be assessed, and a confirmatory factor analysis may be used to look at the relationships and how they interact. A latent change approach is characterized by using repeated assessment over time (Raykov & Marcoulides, 2006). The intent is to discover that pattern of change over time on the identified variables.

Structural regression models are somewhat similar to confirmatory factor analysis models, but there are indications of directions and relationships that the research has identified and that can be tested (Raykov & Marcoulides, 2006). So, if we return to the previous example of multiple intelligences, it may have been found that kinesthetic intelligence is related to the abilities of dance and that musical intelligence of pitch and rhythm is more closely linked to pitch. The structural regression equation would seek to further understand that relationship.

The last structural equation model is the latent change model. This model involves analyzing change over time with repeated measures; it is referred to as latent change analysis (Raykov & Marcoulides, 2006). This model is particularly helpful in determining effects over time, both increases and decreases.

Sellbom, Lee, Ben-Porath, Arbisi, and Gervais (2012) used structural equation modeling and focused on developing models of PTSD in those with disabilities. The purpose of the study was described as "to explore models of assessing various forms of Post-Traumatic Stress Disorder (PTSD) symptomotology that incorporate both broad and narrowly focused affective markers" (p. 172). The researchers further described their data analysis and noted, "We conducted structural equation modelling (SEM) that focused on examining MMPI-2 scales in predicting latent variables representing PTSD symptoms globally, as well as individual PTSD symptom clusters." The results using SEM were described as follows:

> We first tested a model that focused on predicting the global second-order latent PTSD variable on which the DAPS, DTS, and IES total scores loaded. We regressed this variable onto RCd (demoralization), RC2 (low positive emotions), RC7 (dysfunctional negative emotions), and RC8(Aberrant Experiences). The model had acceptable fit, $SB - \chi^2 = 132.19$, d.f. $= 43$, $p < .001$, CFI $= .95$, TLI $= .92$, RMSEA $= .078$ (90% CI $.062 - .094$), SRMR $= .048$. (p. 175)

They report several models of fit evaluation, or fit to the model that is identified. The first analysis is based on a chi-square (χ^2) goodness of fit for the data to a model.

The next analysis of evaluating fit is comparative fit index (CFI), which focuses on comparing the identified model with alternative models, including a null hypothesis in describing the variable relationships. Another fit assessment, the Tucker Lewis Index (TLI), may be interpreted an any score over .90 as providing good fit for the model identified. Root mean square error of approximation (RMSEA) is another form of assessing model fit. Finally, standardized root mean residual (SRMR) is another method of assessing model fit. Scores below .05 suggest a good fit model, and it was .048 in this study.

NONPARAMETRIC STATISTICS

Parametric statistics are used when the data are essentially based on normal distributions and meet the four basic assumptions discussed earlier. Data must be interval or ratio for parametric statistical methods to be used. Nonparametric statistical methods are used when ranks or ordinal types of data are used, and this involves violations of the assumptions cited earlier (e.g., normality, homogeneity of variance). Several nonparametric tests are used in inferential statistical methods. Generally, nonparametric tests are used with nominal and ordinal data or when there is a violation of one or more of the four assumptions cited earlier. The correlated t-test is similar to the non-correlated t-test, except that it is used when there is a violation of independence. A researcher may choose to compare the same participants on a pretest and posttest, and the scores are not independent of each other. Consequently, the research must use a nonparametric statistics.

Other examples of nonparametric tests include the Wilcoxon signed rank test and the Mann–Whitney U Test (Koronyo-Hamaoui, Danziger, Frisch, et al., 2002). Both are designed to test differences between groups. These tests are used rather infrequently because most comparisons made by researchers are based on interval or ratio data. Koronyo-Hamaoui and colleagues (2002) studied anorexia nervosa and genetic factors like chemical imbalance. In the results section, they stated, "The non-parametric two-tailed Wilcoxon signed rank test was used to compare the distribution of transmitted and non-transmitted alleles derived by HRR (haplotype relative risk) from the family trios" (p. 84). Essentially, the researchers were attempting to determine if there was a higher rate of transmission of certain genes to those who had anorexia nervosa and those who did not, a form of nominal data. They also stated, "In the case-control study, allele frequencies and distribution were compared between anorexia nervosa and control groups with the two-tailed Mann–Whitney test" (p. 84). Using the Mann–Whitney U Test, they compared those with anorexia nervosa and a healthy control group.

Table 3.5 Characteristics of Nonparametric Inferential Statistics

Statistical Procedures	*Characteristics*
Wilcoxon signed rank test	A statistical procedure used to compare differences between paired ranks with ordinal data.
Mann–Whitney U test	A statistical procedure used to compare differences between groups when the data violate one or more of the assumptions underlying inferential statistics (e.g., normality or homogeneity).

Linder and Bauer (1983) conducted a study focusing on agreement between males and females on their value systems and their understanding of the opposite gender's value systems. They used a Wilcoxon signed rank test in their analysis. They stated in the results section that "comparisons of males and females at different levels of perspective were made for each terminal value using the Wilcoxon rank-sum statistics. The probability level accepted was .05. The results are presented in Table 2" (p. 60). In Table 2 in their article, the researchers listed different values, such as a comfortable life, an exciting life, and so on. The Wilcoxon rank statistic was reported for differences between males and females based on ranks, and the researchers found, for example, values of 364.5 (a comfortable life) and 528.5 (an exciting life). A difference in rankings by males and females was found for the value of having an exciting life at the .05 level of significance, Wilcoxon rank order = 528.5. (See Table 3.5.) This statistic is not used very often, and there are not many examples from the research literature.

Aljughaiman and Ayoub (2012) provided an example of the use of the Mann Whitney U Test in a study focused on the effect of an enrichment program on certain outcomes (analytical, creative, and practical abilities in elementary gifted children. The study purpose was described as follows: "The current study investigated the effects of a school enrichment program on the analytical, creative, and practical abilities of elementary gifted student students" (p. 153). There were 42 students who served as participants in the study. The researchers described the analysis for the study: "The Mann-Whitney U test for two independent samples was applied. Results showed there were no statistically significant differences between the medians of the mental and control groups in the pretest ($z = -.40$, $p > .05$ for analytical" (p. 164). Interpretation of these results shows that there was no significant difference, $p > .05$.

SUMMARY

Statistics are used to understand and make inferences about the population. The underlying principles of statistics concern determining the probability of obtaining data that are representative of the population of interest. Measurement scales are used in collecting data about the dependent variable, and each type of measure allows the researcher to make calculations based upon the data collected. Descriptive statistics are best understood as a summary of the data obtained from the sample. No attempt is made with descriptive statistics to make inferences back to the population. Descriptive statistics are concerned only with describing the results from the sample.

Inferential statistics are those that are used to make inferences back to the population of interest. Inferential statistics are based on probabilities of the data being representative of the population. There are several different types of inferential statistics, and these include *t*-tests, ANOVA, MANOVA, ANCOVA, multiple regression, structural equation modeling, and chi-square.

In cases where the data, particularly the types of data (nominal and ordinal), are not based upon the normal curve, the researcher must use nonparametric tests. Nonparametric tests are most appropriate for certain types of data and where there are violations of assumptions, such as normality, homogeneity of the variance, and so on. Nonparametric tests include the correlated *t*-test, the Mann-Whitney U Test, and the Wilcoxon signed rank test.

4

QUANTITATIVE RESEARCH AND RESEARCH DESIGNS

A basic understanding of research designs and the research process is necessary to understand and systematically evaluate research. This chapter will consist of a discussion of (1) strengths and weaknesses of quantitative research, (2) types of variables used in quantitative research, (3) typical research designs used in quantitative research, and (4) examples of quantitative research designs from the counseling and education literature. Quantitative research is defined as research that is based on measurement and the quantification of data. Whatever the dependent variable of interest in quantitative research, the data must be transformed into numbers or numerals.

STRENGTHS AND WEAKNESSES OF QUANTITATIVE RESEARCH

Quantitative research has been associated with the philosophical paradigm of positivism (Walker, 2005). Streubert and Carpenter (1995) noted that a positivism approach is characterized by objectivity and efforts at prediction and control. Walker (2005) also proposed that quantitative research is focused on obtaining quantifiable information. The strengths and weaknesses of quantitative research are complex. One reason for this complexity is because, as with all research, the use of various designs is dependent on the types of questions the researcher is attempting to address. A researcher who wants to describe a phenomenon or condition using quantitative information or data would likely use descriptive types of research methods (descriptive research designs are described in more detail later in the chapter). An example of an effective use of descriptive methods can be found in discovering the existence of what now is known as PTSD. Prior to the Vietnam War and the 1960s, the existence of PTSD was unknown or unidentified. Through descriptive research methods, the phenomenon of PTSD was determined to be a real experience. Another example is the frequency of child sexual abuse. In the 1960s, child sexual abuse was not seen as a significant issue, but through collection of descriptive data, it was determined that this was a significant issue. It would be inappropriate (and ineffective) to attempt to answer a research question using descriptive research about the effectiveness of two reading programs or a comparison of two reading programs. There are other quantitative research methods that are better suited to answer such a question, such as a quasi-experimental or true experimental design. These designs allow for the collection of quantitative or numerical data to compare the two reading methods. The most important point to remember here is that matching a research question to a research design reduces weaknesses and increases the strength of quantitative methods.

As was already mentioned, quantitative research by definition is associated with increased control by the researcher. Control over the variables being studied increases the predictions a researcher can make. Control over the variables studied has been noted to be a strength of quantitative research (Walker, 2005). Control may be understood to be based on the reading example given previously about comparing two reading methods. Control over which individuals or group receives the intervention (assignment to groups) and exactly how the reading interventions are administered are examples of experimenter control.

There are weaknesses to the use of quantitative research beyond the inappropriate selection of a design. Campbell and Stanley (1966) provided a detailed discussion of the weaknesses of various quantitative research designs. I discuss in great detail these weaknesses, including threats to internal and external validity, with each design later in this chapter. Ultimately, a researcher who uses quantitative methods wants to reduce any such threats to the validity of the results.

One final comment on weaknesses with quantitative research is that it requires the use of larger sample sizes (there are a few exceptions with single-subject designs, but here, multiple assessments provide larger data). Additionally, with the use of larger sample sizes, one typically investigates broader issues that may be theoretically characteristic of a population. A researcher wants to find common reactions or characteristics of the population. The intention is not to provide an in-depth understanding of what the investigator is studying. Generally, when a researcher chooses a research question about in-depth understanding he or she employs qualitative methods.

TYPES OF VARIABLES

Before I begin discussing research designs, it would be helpful to understand the relevant variables that have been identified as important in research, and they include (1) independent variables, (2) dependent variables, (3) extraneous variables, and (4) control variables. Creswell (2012) defined a variable as "an attribute or characteristics of individuals that researchers study" (p. 13). An independent variable is an event, condition, or measured attribute or characteristic that the researcher for the most part controls (there is no manipulation or control of an independent variable that is measured). Manipulation refers to the researcher's having some control over or the ability to alter an event or condition of interest for an individual or group (the sample). Ary, Jacobs, and Razavieh (2002) described the independent variable in this way: "the manipulation of an independent variable is a deliberate operation performed by the experimenter" (p. 279). There are different degrees to which a researcher can manipulate or control an event, and this affects the quality of the study, which will be discussed in greater detail in subsequent chapters. Additionally, an independent variable must have two or more levels or groups to compare.

Attributes, or measured independent variables, have been defined as those characteristics about a person that the researcher cannot manipulate but are of interest to the research as it affects a dependent variable. Examples of attributes or measured independent variables include socioeconomic status, age, gender, IQ, race, marital status, religious affiliation, and living arrangements. More specifically, a researcher may be interested in a causal relationship that IQ has with coping behaviors during stress. Clearly, the researcher cannot manipulate IQ; he or she wants to understand a causal relationship between an individual's coping and IQ. As independent variables, measurement-type variables must be categorized so that they become specific categories and not continuous numbers. For example, IQ can range from the 50s to the mid-140s. A researcher using IQ as a measurement-type independent variable would need to group the scores because raw scores would make it difficult to use such data—there would be too many groups. The researcher may use average IQ as one category.

The dependent variable is defined in terms of changes in the subject as a consequence of the independent variable. In essence, dependent variables are influenced by and dependent on independent variables. Returning to the stress and coping example, the dependent variable is the subject's level of stress at any one moment of interest.

Extraneous variables are considered to be either uncontrolled or unknown factors that can potentially affect the results or the response to the dependent variable. These are not variables controlled by the researcher, and the results of a study may be called into question if significant extraneous variables are identified and not controlled for in the design. For example, in a study on stress and coping, extraneous variables might be socioeconomic status, age, and health of the subjects (Gallo, Bogart, Vranceanu, & Matthews, 2005). They are extraneous variables because they may impact the dependent variable, which could be the amount of stress reported.

The fourth type of variable is the control variable. This is an extraneous variable that the researcher has identified, and he or she has developed ways to control for its effects. There are several methods of addressing extraneous variables so that they become control variables. One method is to build the extraneous variable into the design and thus control its effects. For example, if socioeconomic status is hypothesized to influence stress levels, the researcher may want to select subjects from different, specific socioeconomic groups and assess the effects of IQ on stress levels. The researcher can include analysis of socioeconomic status on stress levels; thus, in this situation, a previous extraneous variable becomes an independent variable.

A second method of making an extraneous variable a control variable is to remove the possible effects of the extraneous variable. This may be accomplished by selecting subjects from only one socioeconomic group, for instance, the middle class or lower class. All other socioeconomic groups would be excluded from this particular study. However, the researcher could only generalize the results back to the specific socioeconomic group selected. A third method of controlling an extraneous variable is through statistical methods after the study has been conducted. For example, as mentioned in Chapter 3, there is a statistical method called ANCOVA that factors the effects of the identified control variable into the analysis.

RESEARCH DESIGNS

Quantitative research can also be distinguished, for the most part, by the type of research design used and by the type of data collected (quantitative data). There have been several different ways proposed to categorize research designs, but there is still some common agreement (Cooper, 2012; Gall et al., 2006; Heppner et al., 1992; Moore, 1983). Different designs are frequently associated with either quantitative or qualitative research, but some designs actually may be used in both methods and are then differentiated by the types of data collection done and how the data are analyzed (e.g., when quantitative data are analyzed with the use of numerals or numbers, and in qualitative research, it is with words). Major categories of research designs include true experimental, quasi-experimental, preexperimental, descriptive, and correlational (see Table 4.1). Typically, true experimental, quasi-experimental, preexperimental, and correlational designs are more closely associated with quantitative research (Charles, 1995). Ethnographic and historical research are more closely associated with qualitative research (Charles, 1995). In this chapter, I will address all four types of research designs (see Table 4.1).

TRUE EXPERIMENTAL DESIGNS

Experimental design is essentially a map or systematic plan for conducting the collection of data. Each design results in more or less clarity in the plan or more or less control over the relevant variables (Heppner et al., 1992). I will address the amount of control the researcher has over the various methods and the strengths and weakness of each design in Chapter 14, Evaluating the Methods Section: Procedures.

It is important to keep in mind, as we review the various research designs, that these traditional designs may be modified to fit the purpose of a study. For example, many traditional research designs have had a control group or a comparison group. However, variations may include changing the comparison group to a group exposed to a more traditional intervention, which is then compared to a new, innovative method. A study may or may not have a traditional control group but still have a comparison group. Also, a study may have multiple experimental groups and interventions and still have a similar design to a study with one intervention.

Two criteria are used in distinguishing true experimental designs from other designs: random assignment to groups and manipulation of the independent variable. True experimental designs include a pretest–posttest equivalent group, a posttest-only group, and the Solomon Four-Group Design.

Researchers have developed methods of representing research designs with symbols (Campbell & Stanley, 1966). The symbols used include the following designations:

R = random assignment of participants to groups

X = exposure of the group to treatment or manipulation of a targeted condition

O = observation or measurement of the dependent variable

The pretest–posttest equivalent group design is then denoted like this:

Group 1: $R\ O_1\ X\ O_2$

Group 2: $R\ O_3\ O_4$

In the pretest–posttest equivalent group design, there is random assignment of subjects to groups, and a pretest is given. The pretest is a measurement of the dependent variable or variables. Group 1 is the experimental group, and the *X* denotes an intervention or manipulation of a condition or experience of the subjects. The second group, the control group, in this case receives no manipulation. Both groups receive a posttest, again measuring the dependent variable or variables.

Table 4.1 Categories of Quantitative Research Designs

Type of Design	*Purpose*	*Amount of Control by the Researcher Over Extraneous Variables*	*Characteristics*
True experimental (e.g., pretest–posttest or posttest-only equivalent group)	Comparisons of treatment groups to control or traditional approaches	High amount of control	Manipulation of the independent variable and random assignment to groups
Quasi-experimental (e.g., time series or ABAB)	Comparisons between groups or the same group at different times	Moderate amount of control	Manipulation of the independent variable; no random assignment to groups; typically multiple assessments of the dependent variable
Preexperimental (e.g., one-shot pretest–posttest)	Comparisons between groups or within a group but generally not over time	Minimal control	Manipulation of the independent variable or measurement of an event that has occurred for one group over which the researcher has no control; no random assignment to groups
Descriptive (e.g., survey, causal comparative or observational)	To describe an event or phenomenon	No control over the event or phenomenon	No manipulation of an independent variable; no random assignment to groups

As mentioned earlier, there can be variations of the general designs. For example, the design can be slightly altered and be denoted as such:

Group 1: $R\ O_1\ X_1\ O_2$

Group 2: $R\ O_3\ X_2\ O_4$

Group 1 in this altered design may be subjected to a traditional intervention, whereas Group 2 may possibly experience a new intervention. For example, if you wanted to determine the effectiveness of a new cognitive approach (X_2) to treating anxiety, you might compare it to a group that received a traditional behavioral approach (X_1). The design still involves the pretest and posttest for both groups, along with random assignment to groups and a manipulation. However, there is no control group, a group that does not receive any intervention.

Another variation of the pretest–posttest research design involves adding additional groups but still retaining the major steps, including random assignment, manipulation, and pretests and posttests. This is the symbolic representation of such a design:

Group 1: $R\ O_1\ X_1\ O_2$

Group 2: $R\ O_3\ X_2\ O_4$

Group 3: $R\ O_5\ X_3\ O_6$

In this variation of the pretest–posttest design, the researcher is comparing three different interventions. Group 1 may again receive the traditional behavioral approach to treating anxiety. The second group may receive a new, innovative intervention, such as a cognitive approach. Finally, Group 3 may receive a combination of a cognitive approach and medication.

Driver, O'Connor, Lox, and Rees (2004) conducted a study using a true experimental design, pretest–posttest (see Table 4.2). The study focused on understanding the effects of an aquatic exercise on the physical fitness of people with brain injuries. The experimental condition was the aquatic exercise. The control condition was simply those who had brain injuries but did not participate in an aquatic exercise program. The researchers stated, "A stratified random sampling technique was used. A pool of participants was created from individuals who were outpatients at a local rehabilitation centre, who were above level six (confused-appropriate) on the Ranchos Los Amigos Scale of Cognitive Functioning" (p. 850). They further described the experimental group: "The experimental group completed an 8-week exercise programme that consisted of 24 exercise sessions (three times a week) each lasting 1-hour" (p. 850). This study met the two criteria for being a true experimental design: random assignment and a manipulation.

Table 4.2 Pretest–Posttest Research Design, Example 1

Aquatic exercise (experimental)	R	O_1	X_1	O_2
		Body composition	8-week exercise program that consisted of 24 exercise sessions	Body composition
		Flexibility— sit and reach		Flexibility— sit and reach
		Modified curl test		Modified curl test
Vocational class (control)	R	O_3	*Control*	O_4
		Body composition	Vocational class was a reading and writing program for instructional and safety reasons.	Body composition
		Flexibility— sit and reach		Flexibility— sit and reach
		Modified curl test		Modified curl test

Source: Structure taken from Driver, O'Connor, Lox, and Rees (2004).

Wikles, Marcus, Bright, Dapelo, and Psychol (2012) investigated how emotion affected eating disorder symptoms among those with anorexia nervosa (see Table 4.3). They employed a pretest–posttest design. They described their study purpose as "to evaluate the effect of experimentally induced negative emotion on self-reported eating disorder symptoms and objectively-measured eating behavior in women with anorexia nervosa" (p. 877). Twenty-eight adult females who were diagnosed with anorexia nervosa participated in the study. They were randomly assigned to either a negative or neutral mood induction condition. Those in the experimental condition viewed a negative-emotion film, one that included violence and conflict. The control group, neutral-emotion condition, viewed a film focused on nature that depicted no significant emotional stimuli. Both groups were administered a pretest, the Positive and Negative Affect Schedule (PANAS) and self-reported symptoms of the eating disorder. After viewing the films, both experimental (negative emotion) and control (neutral emotion) completed posttest measures, the same as those administered during pretest. The research design may be depicted as such:

Experimental group: $R \ O_1 \ X_1 \ O_2$

Control group: $R \ O_3 \ O_4$

A second design is the posttest-only equivalent-groups design, which is denoted in the following way:

Group 1: $R \ X_1 \ O_1$

Group 2: $R \ X_2 \ O_2$

In this design, there is random assignment to groups, and then, the intervention is presented to the experimental group. Note that no pretest is given. After the intervention for the experimental group, both groups are given a posttest. The purpose of using the posttest-only equivalent-groups design is to reduce the effects of pretesting sensitivity. I will further explain the effects of pretesting on the validity

Table 4.3 Pretest–Posttest Research Design, Example 2

Negative-emotion film (experimental)	R	O_1	X_1	O_2
		Positive and Negative Affect Schedule (PANAS)	Viewed negative-emotion film	Positive and Negative Affect Schedule (PANAS)
		Self-reported symptoms of eating disorder		Self-reported symptoms of eating disorder
Neutral-emotion film (control)	R	O_3		O_4
		Positive and Negative Affect Schedule (PANAS)	Viewed neutral-emotion film	Positive and Negative Affect Schedule (PANAS)
		Self-reported symptoms of eating disorder		Self-reported symptoms of eating disorder

Source: Structure taken from Wikles, Marcus, Bright, Dapelo, and Psychol (2012).

of a study in Chapter 14, Evaluating the Methods Section: Procedures. As with the previous design, there can be variations of the posttest-only equivalent-groups design. For example, two or more treatment groups may be used:

Group 1: $R\ X_1\ O_1$

Group 2: $R\ X_2\ O_2$

Group 3: $R\ X_3\ O_3$

In the above design, the researcher is comparing three different treatments using the posttest-only equivalent-groups design. To maintain the essential format of the posttest-only equivalent-groups design, the researcher must have random assignment to groups and use only a posttest to measure the dependent variable or variables. The posttest-equivalent group design is not used as often as other designs, such as the pretest–posttest design.

Park, Chang, and Chung (2005) conducted a study on the effects of a cognitive intervention program on health beliefs in Korean women. The study design was described as follows: "This study used non-equivalent, control group, post-test only design to test the effects of a cognition–emotion focused program. The post-test only design was used because repeated measures of variables such as knowledge and attitudes can result in a testing effect" (p. 291). They further defined their procedures: "After random assignment of the participants to the two groups, the experimental group met to schedule attendance for the group program" (p. 293). (See Table 4.4.)

Table 4.4 Posttest-Only Equivalent-Group Design

Group 1	R_a	X_1	O_1
		Cognitive intervention program	Knowledge of cervical cancer
			Health belief
			Self-efficacy
Group 2	R	X_2	O_2
		No treatment	Knowledge of cervical cancer
			Health belief
			Self-efficacy

Source: Structure taken from Park, Chang, and Chung (2005).

Houser, Thoma, Stanton, O'Connor, Jiang, and Dong (2013) conducted a study on the use of low-current brain stimulation on math and statistical calculation. They employed a posttest-only design (see Table 4.5). The purpose of this study was to determine if different levels of low-current brain stimulation affected undergraduate students' learning statistics. They described their study design as "a posttest only research design with random assignment to one of, three groups was used. There were three conditions used in the study, two experimental and one control. The control group, group 1, was connected to the tDCS stimulator with the sham condition. The exact same montage and procedures used with the control group as was used with the other two groups (experimental groups) who received 1 or 2 mA" (p. 1). The dependent variable was performance on a statistical calculation, calculation of a non-parametric statistic (a Kruskal–Wallis).

Researchers are hesitant to use the posttest-only design because, without the pretest, they do not have information at the beginning of the experiment as to whether the groups used are truly equivalent. However, when the sample is large enough, significant characteristics should be adequately distributed, ensuring equivalence across the groups with random assignment (Moore, 1983). (Random assignment involves randomly assigning participants to experimental and control groups.)

The Solomon Four-Group Design is the last true experimental design I want to discuss. It may be denoted symbolically:

Group 1: $R\ O_1\ X_1\ O_2$

Group 2: $R\ O_3\ O_4$

Group 3: $R\ X_1\ O_5$

Group 4: $R\ O_6$

Table 4.5 Posttest-Only Equivalent-Group Design

Group (1 mA)	R	X_1	O_1
		1 mA low-current brain stimulation	Statistics calculation
Group 2 (2 mA)	R	X_2	O_2
		2 mA low-current brain stimulation	Statistical calculation
Group 3 (control group)	R	Control group, no brain stimulation	Statistical calculation

Source: Structure taken from Houser and colleagues (2013).

A Solomon Four-Group Design is a <u>combination</u> of the pretest–posttest equivalent-groups and the posttest-only equivalent-groups designs. There is random assignment to each of the four conditions, and two groups receive the intervention or manipulation. Use of this design is an attempt to control for the effects of testing or the subjects' becoming sensitive to what the researcher is investigating through repeated administration of the dependent variable or variables. Possible variations here include the control groups simply receiving a traditional method of treatment rather than receiving no treatment. A Solomon Four-Group Design is not used often, mainly because it is expensive to conduct: Four groups, and thus more subjects, are required (Bohon, Santos, Sanchez-Sosa, & Singer, 1994; DeTienne & Chandler, 2007; Reid & Finchilescu, 1995; Sawilowsky & Markman, 1990). (See Table 4.6.)

Table 4.6 Solomon Four-Group Design, Example 1

Control group 1 (15 males, 15 females)	R_a	O_1		O_2
		Mental task: mathematical computation		Mental task: mathematical computation
Exertion group 1 (experimental; 15 males, 15 females)	R	O_3	X_1	O_4
		Mental task: mathematical computation	Exertion: walking as exercise	Mental task: mathematical computation
Control group 2 (15 males, 15 females)	R	O_3		O_5
		Mental task: mathematical computation		Mental task: mathematical computation
Exertion group 2 (experimental; 15 males, 15 females)	R		X_1	O_6
			Exertion: walking as exercise	Mental task: mathematical computation

Source: Structure taken from McNaughten and Gabbard (1993).

Beck, Boys, Rose, and Beck (2012) studied how video games impacted acceptance of rape (see Table 4.7). Their specific purpose was to "expand research on media violence by being the first study to use actual video games to explore the influence of the negative, sexist portrayal of women in video games on rape-supportive attitudes" (p. 3020). Participants were undergraduates at a Midwestern university. They stated that they used a Solomon Four-Group Design because "the Solomon four-group design controls for the possible effects of a pretest on participants' subsequent performance and can help determine both the main effects and interactions of testing" (p. 3022). Participants were assigned to one of four groups: two control and two experimental. The experimental groups watched a video, *Grand Theft Auto IV,* while the control groups did not see any video. The two dependent variables were: the Illinois Rape Myth Acceptance Scale and a video game survey (amount of time spent on video games).

Table 4.7 Solomon Four-Group Design, Example 2

Control group 1 (15 males, 15 females)	R	O_1		O_2
		Illinois Rape Myth Acceptance Scale and video game survey		Illinois Rape Myth Acceptance Scale and video game survey
Exertion group 1: viewed video	R	O_3	X_1	O_4
		Illinois Rape Myth Acceptance Scale and video game survey	video *Grand Theft Auto IV*	Illinois Rape Myth Acceptance Scale and video game survey
Control group 2 (15 males, 15 females)	R			O_5
				Illinois Rape Myth Acceptance Scale and video game survey
Exertion group 2 (experimental)	R		X_1	O_6
			video *Grand Theft Auto IV*	Illinois Rape Myth Acceptance Scale and video game survey

Source: Structure taken from Beck and colleagues (2012).

QUASI-EXPERIMENTAL DESIGNS

A number of different quasi-experimental designs have been proposed (Campbell & Stanley, 1966). The definition of a quasi-experimental design is one in which there is a manipulation that is controlled by the researcher but no random assignment to groups. I want to review three of the more common quasi-experimental designs: the pretest–posttest nonequivalent-groups design, the time series design, and the multiple time series design. The pretest–posttest nonequivalent-group design consists of no random assignment to groups. Because of the characteristics of the situation, the groups cannot be separated (for instance, intact treatment groups may be used, such as two different day treatment programs for those with chronic mental illness). In this design, a pretest and posttest are administered to all groups involved. The typical design is a comparison between an experimental group and a control group, but as with other designs, there can be alterations with more than two groups used. A symbolic representation of the design would be as follows:

Experimental group: $O_1 \, X_1 \, O_2$

Control group: $O_3 \, O_4$

When the researcher is unable to use random assignment to groups, there are more threats to the internal validity of the study because there are possible differences between the group members prior to the intervention. (Internal validity refers to the reduction of the effects from extraneous variables on the study; this concept will be defined more thoroughly in Chapter 14.)

Farynaiarz and Lockwood (1992) employed a pretest–posttest nonequivalent-group quasi-experimental design in a study focusing on the impact of microcomputer simulations on environmental problem solving. Subjects for the study were 59 community college students who were enrolled in environmental science and biology courses. The experimental group comprised those registered in the environmental sciences course, and the control group consisted of those in the biology course. No random assignment to groups was possible because students made their own selection of courses. The investigators stated, "Because there were similar environmental concepts included in both course curricula, the samples were considered to be from a single population" (p. 457). The intervention that the experimental group received involved computer simulations of environmental problems. Students were provided with information indicating the relevant variables to consider in problem solving. The design is depicted symbolically in Table 4.8.

Hersch, Hutchinson, Davidson, et al. (2004) also used a quasi-experimental pretest–posttest nonequivalent-groups design to study the effects of cultural heritage experience on quality of life of those in a long-term elder-care facility (see Table 4.9). The purpose of the study was described this way: "We investigated the effectiveness of an occupation-based cultural heritage intervention to facilitate adaptation to relocation into long term care as measured by quality of life, activity engagement, and social participation" (p. 224). The participants were from long-term care facilities, and they all were older than 55 years of age. The research design was described as follows: "We used a quasi-experimental nonequivalent control group design with pre- and posttests" (p. 224). The dependent variables were: quality of life, activity engagement, and social participation. Note that there is no random assignment to groups in this study.

Table 4.8 Pretest–Posttest Nonequivalent-Group Quasi-Experimental Design, Example 1

Group 1 (comparison)	O_1		O_2
	Tests of integrated science		Tests of integrated science
Group 2 (experimental)	O_3	X_1	O_4
	Supervised home-based exercise training, high intensity	Environmental simulations (e.g., wastewater treatment)	Tests of integrated science

Source: Structure taken from Farynaiarz and Lockwood (1992).

Table 4.9 Pretest–Posttest Nonequivalent-Group Quasi-Experimental Design, Example 2

Group 1 (control group)	O_1		O_2
	Quality of life Activity engagement Social participation		Quality of life Activity engagement Social participation
Group 2 (experimental)	O_3	X_1	O_4
	Quality of life Activity engagement Social participation	Cultural heritage intervention	Quality of life Activity engagement Social participation

Source: Structure taken from Hersch and colleagues (2004).

A third example of a pretest–posttest nonequivalent-group design was conducted by Ernst and Monroe (2006). The study focused on the effects of environment-based education on students' critical thinking skills (see Table 4.10). The authors stated that "this study examined the relationship between environment-based education and high school students' critical thinking skills and disposition toward critical thinking" (p. 429). The participants for this study were 165 ninth-grade high school students. The dependent variable was a critical thinking test (Cornell Critical Thinking Test) and a test to measure disposition for critical thinking (California Measure of Mental Motivation). The intervention or independent variable was the use of local environments for students' educational experiences. The control group was taken from schools and classrooms that used traditional instructional strategies (did not use local environments for educational experiences).

A second type of quasi-experimental design is the time series design. In this design, there is again no random assignment, but there is a manipulation. One group is used with assessment or observations taken over a period of time. No comparison group is used. The design may be symbolized as such:

$$O_1 \, O_2 \, O_3 \, O_4 \, X_1 \, O_5 \, O_6 \, O_7 \, O_8$$

Table 4.10 Pretest–Posttest Nonequivalent-Group Quasi-Experimental Design, Example 3

Group 1 (control group)	O_1		O_2
	Critical thinking test (Cornell Critical Thinking Test) Disposition for critical thinking (California Measure of Mental Motivation)	Traditional instructional method	Critical thinking test (Cornell Critical Thinking Test) Disposition for critical thinking (California Measure of Mental Motivation)
Group 2 (experimental)	O_3	X_1	O_4
	Critical thinking test (Cornell Critical Thinking Test) Disposition for critical thinking (California Measure of Mental Motivation)	Instruction in local environment	Critical thinking test (Cornell Critical Thinking Test) Disposition for critical thinking (California Measure of Mental Motivation)

Source: Structure taken from Ernst and Monroe (2006).

In the time series design, the researcher is looking for changes that occur between observations or assessments four and five (O_4 and O_5) or after the intervention has occurred. Variations of this design may include more observations or measurements. As with the previous quasi-experimental design, there are some problems with controlling for extraneous variables and more threats to the validity of the study.

Mastel-Smith, Binder, Malecha, et al. (2006) provide an example of a time series design. The purpose of the study was to investigate therapeutic life review procedures to determine the effects on depression among senior women. The subjects for the study were 14 older women who received home health services. The treatment or intervention involved the use of a therapeutic life review. A single group was used, and the design is symbolically represented in Table 4.11.

A third type of quasi-experimental design is the multiple time series design. The time series design uses multiple observations with multiple groups. There is no random assignment to groups, but the independent variable or variables are manipulated. The design may be symbolized like this:

$$O_1\ O_2\ O_3\ O_4\ X_1\ O_5\ O_6\ O_7\ O_8$$
$$O_9\ O_{10}\ O_{11}\ O_{12}\ X_2\ O_{12}\ O_{13}\ O_{14}\ O_{15}\ O_{16}$$
$$O_{17}\ O_{18}\ O_{19}\ O_{20}\ X_3\ O_{21}\ O_{22}\ O_{23}\ O_{24}$$

The multiple time series design typically involves two or more groups, all of which receive some form of manipulation of the independent variable. Felce, de Kock, Mansell, and Jenkins (1984) conducted a study that illustrates the use of a multiple time series design. The study focused on evaluating the effects of systematic teaching to severely disturbed and profoundly mentally handicapped adults in residential facilities. Subjects for the study were 24 residents of four community-based programs serving individuals with mental handicaps. Felce and colleagues (1984) described the intervention as follows:

A behavioral assessment is made of the current skill repertoire of the client by care staff, who then meet to decide a realistic goal. The programme-writer

Table 4.11   Time Series Design

Group	O_a	X	O
14 women over 65	$O_1\ O_2$	Therapeutic life review	$O_3\ O_4$

Source: Structure taken from Mastel-Smith and colleagues (2006).

O_a = observation of sharing

Table 4.12   Multiple Time Series Design

Group: Skill	Assessment of Skill Demonstrated					Skill Training	Assessment of Skill Demonstrated
Group 1: client touches cradle	O_1	O_2	O_3	O_4	O_5	X_1	O_6
Group 2: client picks up striker and hits xylophone	O_1	O_2	O_3	O_4	O_5	X_1	O_6
Group 3: client works a jigsaw	O_1	O_2	O_3	O_4	O_5	X_1	O_6
Group 4: client washes hands	O_1	O_2	O_3	O_4	O_5	X_1	O_6
Group 5: client colors pictures	O_1	O_2	O_3	O_4	O_5	X_1	O_6
Group 6: client copies name	O_1	O_2	O_3	O_4	O_5	X_1	O_6

Source: Structure taken from Felce and colleagues (1984).

(a senior member of the staff) plans a sequence of weekly teaching steps that take the client by small increments from their current skill repertoire to the long-term goal. The teaching strategy is derived by analyzing the target skill into component behaviors and by teaching each with varying conditions of help. (p. 302)

A multiple time series design was employed (see Table 4.12) with six groups. The groups were identified by the goals set with a skills training method.

PREEXPERIMENTAL DESIGNS

Preexperimental designs have been described as having no random assignment to groups with an intervention (Ary et al., 2010; Campbell & Stanley, 1966). Furthermore, preexperimental designs typically do not allow for detection of differences through comparisons with other groups or with multiple assessments of baseline. Baseline is defined as the starting point prior to the presentation of the independent variable or the condition of the dependent variable before intervention. Two types of research designs have been categorized as preexperimental (Ary et al., 2010): the one-group pretest–posttest design and the static group comparison.

The one-group pretest–posttest design is composed of a single group receiving an intervention with a pretest and posttest for minimal comparison purposes. Again, in this design, there is no random assignment because there is only one group. This design is rarely found in the professional literature because of the many threats to validity (see Chapter 14). The design may be depicted symbolically as such:

$$O_1 \, X \, O_2$$

Matheny and Edwards (1974) provide an example of a one-group pretest–posttest design. Matheny and Edwards "attempted to bring about certain changes in pupil behavior through specified changes in teacher behavior. The desired changes in pupil behavior were increased proficiency in reading, an increased sense of control over the environment, and improved school attendance" (p. 224). Twenty-five elementary classroom teachers and 757 students in Grades 1 through 7 participated in the study. The intervention was a weeklong teacher-training session in contingency management. In addition, two in-service training sessions were held during the school year to reinforce skills. The dependent variables were reading achievement, a sense of control over one's environment, and school attendance. Note that only one group, elementary school students, was used in the study, with no comparison group. (See Table 4.13.)

Salloum, Avery, and McClain (2001) provide a second example of a one-group pretest–posttest study (see Table 4.14). The researchers asked the following question: "Can brief, time-limited, grief and trauma groups for inner-city African-American adolescents of homicide victims reduce symptoms of trauma?" (p. 126). The independent variable was the group treatment intervention focusing on dealing with grief after experiencing a murder or homicide by a close family member. The dependent variable was the stress reaction (the Child Posttraumatic Stress Reaction Index).

Table 4.13   One-Group Pretest–Posttest Design, Example 1

Group 1	O_1	X_1	O_2
	Reading achievement Sense of control over environment School attendance	Classroom management approach: contingency management	Reading achievement Sense of control over environment School attendance

Source: Structure taken from Matheny and Edwards (1974).

Table 4.14   One-Group Pretest–Posttest Design, Example 2

Group 1	O_1	X_1	O_2
	Stress reaction (Child Posttraumatic Stress Reaction Index)	Group treatment focused on grief associated with a homicide	Stress reaction (Child Posttraumatic Stress Reaction Index)

Source: Structure taken from Salloum and colleagues (2001).

The final preexperimental research design, the static group comparison, involves a condition that a control group has not experienced. There is no random assignment to groups and no attempt to determine whether the groups are similar or are matched on relevant demographic or extraneous variables. For practical reasons, the comparison generally involves an intervention or experience that has already occurred, so the groups cannot be randomly assigned to an experimental or control condition. Thus, the use of the term *static* refers to existing groups remaining intact because the intervention has occurred. The static group comparison design may be symbolically represented as such:

$$X\,O_1$$
$$\overline{\hspace{3cm}}$$
$$O_2$$

The line between indicates that the groups are not randomly assigned, not equivalent, and intact prior to participation in the study.

Lynch and colleagues (2001) conducted a study using a static group comparison design in which they focused on participants in a rural scholars program for physicians. Subjects for the study were 52 medical students who enrolled in the rural scholars program and a comparison group of 318 medical students who did not participate in this program. The authors described their methods: "A static-group comparison design where post-intervention comparisons are made between one group who participated in an intervention and one group who did not, was used to compare scholars with their peers" (p. 38). The independent variable in this study was an enrichment program for encouraging general medical practice in rural settings. The groups are considered static because the researcher cannot assign individuals to medical student groups. The measurement variable or dependent variable was placement of students in specific settings, such as family practice and community hospitals. (See Table 4.15.)

Brooks, Lewinson, Aszman, and Wolk (2012) used a static group comparison to study those who used housing vouchers versus those who lived in public housing and satisfaction with their housing, material hardships, and economic well-being. The authors described their research design as follows:

> Since funding for the present study was received 3 years after Harris Homes was torn down, a pretest–posttest quasi-experimental was impossible to construct. Although in the discussion section we made some comparisons between the 2006 data and the previous two waves of data collection, the current study. . . . Therefore, the present research design is a static group comparison. (p. 12)

The researchers compared those who used vouchers and those who lived in public housing. The independent variable was the housing program. The dependent variables were resident perception of housing satisfaction, perception of economic well-being, and material hardships (ability to pay rent). (See Table 4.16.)

Table 4.15   Static Group Comparison Design, Example 1

Group 1	X_1	O_1
52 medical students	Enrichment program	Practice choice
Group 2	X_1	O_2
318 medical students	Traditional medical school training	Practice choice

Source: Structure taken from Lynch, Teplin, Willis, et al. (2001).

Table 4.16   Static Group Comparison Design, Example 2

Group 1	X_1	O_1
	Those who used housing vouchers	Perception of housing satisfaction Perceptions of economic well-being Material hardship (ability to pay rent)
Group 2	X_1	O_2
	Those living in public housing	Perception of housing satisfaction Perceptions of economic well-being Material hardship (ability to pay rent)

Source: Structure taken from Brooks and colleagues (2012).

DESCRIPTIVE DESIGNS

Descriptive research has been noted to include four different approaches: survey, observational, correlational, and causal comparative (Ary et al., 2010; Moore, 1983). Descriptive designs involve no random assignment to groups, nor is there any manipulation of an independent variable. Generally, descriptive research is an attempt to describe characteristics or the effects of events for an identified population. A significant portion of published psychological research may be categorized as descriptive (survey, observational, correlational, and causal comparative).

A survey of descriptive design involves the use of self-report to clarify the perceptions, attitudes, or behaviors of a target group. In survey research, there is no independent variable. Manning and Cheers (1995) provide an example of survey descriptive research. The purpose of their study was to identify how strongly residents of a small country town felt about child abuse and how likely they were to notify authorities when abuse was suspected. In the methods section, the researchers described the design in the following way: "In a cross-sectional survey design, semistructured interviews were conducted in 1989 with a simple random sample of all people over 18 years in 60 non-Aboriginal living groups in a small remote town in central western Queensland, Australia" (p. 389). The purpose of this study was not to determine the effects of a treatment or an intervention. The methods were designed to gather information about the attitude of a target group, individuals living in a small rural town.

Eaves, Rabren, and Hall (2012) provide a second example of a survey study; they were interested in the success of those who received special education services in high school (had an individualized education plan) and their obtaining competitive employment postgraduation. More than 900 students completed the survey, and the researchers gathered information about the participants' types of disability and types of diploma obtained. No manipulation was completed, but data were collected about the relevant identified variables of interest by the researchers.

Observational descriptive research is an attempt to avoid problems with self-report (problems with self-report approaches will be discussed further in Chapter 15) and still clarify personal characteristics through observations by others or raters. The sole domain of interest is behaviors of the target group; clearly one cannot observe another's attitudes or feelings. Shore, Lerman, Smith, Iwata, and DeLeon (1995) conducted a study using an observational descriptive design. The purpose of the study was described as an attempt to examine and identify the quality of care in a geriatric setting. Subjects for the study were 104 residents of a proprietary nursing home and the staff who provided their care. In the journal abstract, the researchers stated, "Direct observation was used to examine multiple aspects of care provided in a proprietary nursing home" (p. 435). Furthermore, the researchers stated in the methods section:

> Upon entering the facility, the observer proceeded to each observation area and scored categories of environment condition, resident condition, and staff activity using a time-sampling procedure in which observers recorded the event of interest at the "moment" of observation. (p. 438)

The researchers in this study were interested in systematically identifying certain variables of interest, such as quality of care. The methods used were based solely on observations made by trained observers.

Ballespi, Jane, and Riba (2012) provide another example of observational research. The focus of this research was the use of an observational behavioral scale to measure young children's temperamental disposition toward social anxiety. The scale was completed by parents and teachers on a sample of 365 children. They used the Behavioral Inhibition Scale, which was designed for children 3 to 6 years of age. There was no manipulation of an independent variable, and the researchers were interested in describing specific behaviors of children, that is, temperamental disposition toward social anxiety.

A third type of descriptive design is a correlational approach. Human beings are complex, and oftentimes, it is difficult to separate important variables that influence behaviors, attitudes, and perceptions. Consequently, researchers use correlational methods to identify and understand the relationship between multiple variables or how several variables of interest covary. The use of correlational research may be particularly relevant in education and counseling given that there is a need to study complex human issues and understand their relationships.

Preechawong, Zauszniewski, Heinzer, et al. (2007) conducted a correlational study investigating the relationship between family functioning, self-esteem, and coping in adolescents with asthma. The researchers described the purpose of their study: "This study examined the relationships of both self-esteem and family functioning to resourceful coping in Thai adolescents with asthma" (p. 25). The researchers used a sample of convenience and adolescents who had asthma, taken from outpatient clinics in four hospitals.

McNaught, Lam, and Cheng (2012) investigated the relationships between online learning and student outcomes. The study purpose was described as "to examine possible relationships between features of online learning designs and student learning outcomes" (p. 271). A good indication that this is a correlational study is the statement in the purpose that the intention was to examine the relationship. Correlational studies are designed to explore relationships between variables. There is no intention of finding a cause-and-effect relationship (e.g., through a manipulation) as with other types of research, for example, true experimental designs. The researchers further clarified the type of study by describing the results, that is, "the findings of this correlational study indicate . . ." (p. 271).

Causal-comparative descriptive research concerns attempting to identify the effects of an independent variable after the fact. The independent variable is not under the control of the researcher but is of interest. The researcher therefore compares two or more groups who have had different experiences (the identified independent variables). Hollowood, Salisbury, Rainforth, and Palobaro (1994) investigated the use of teacher and student time when the classroom had students with mild and severe disabilities. The researchers described the research design as follows:

> A causal-comparative between groups design was used. Group membership (independent variable) was determined by the presence or absence of a child with a severe disability or whether a classmate evidenced a severe disability. Students in Group 3 constituted a post-hoc control group. The major dependent variables were allocated time, used time, and engaged time. (p. 245)

Eighteen elementary school students with severe and mild disabilities served as subjects for the study. Group 1 was composed of six students in Grades 1, 3, and 4 with severe disabilities who were enrolled in four different classrooms. Groups 2 and 3 were composed of students without disabilities who were randomly selected from students in Grades 1, 3, and 4. For this study, then, the comparisons were made between three groups, and the researcher had no control over the independent variable, that is, the type of disability.

Liang, Fulmer, Majerich, Clevenstine, and Howanski (2012) employed the use of a causal-comparative approach in their study focusing on a physics curriculum. The researchers described the purpose of their study as "to examine the effects of a model-based introductory physics curriculum on conceptual learning in a Physics First initiative" (p. 115). The research design is described as follows: "Given the empirical nature of our inquiry that explores differential effects of two science programs within their real-life contexts, a causal-comparative research design was adopted for this study" (p. 117). There is no manipulation in a causal-comparative study, but there is an attempt to compare two or more levels of a variable, for example, in this case, different methods of teaching physics. The key here is that the comparison was made after implementation of the teaching models. If there researchers had collected the data after a manipulation controlled by the researcher, then this would have been a different design, either a true experimental or quasi-experimental design.

Locicero (2002) used a causal-comparative research method to compare noncertified and certified grief counselors with respect to education, experience, credentials and supervision. The researcher described his study like this: "This study utilized a causal-comparative research design to explore the similarities and differences between non-certified and certified grief counselors of education, training, experiences, credentials, and supervision" (p. 5). The researcher, again, with this study did not manipulate the independent variable, that is, type of counselor—noncertified or certified. Comparisons were made on dependent variables of education, training, and so on.

SUMMARY

Quantitative research methods, the traditional approach to conducting research, may be defined in terms of converting the results into measurable quantifiable units for analysis. Additionally, the researcher in true experimental and quasi-experimental designs has control over the variables of interest. There are other designs, such as preexperimental and descriptive designs, where the researcher does not have control over the independent variable. Measurement amounts may be categorized as four different scales: nominal, ordinal, interval, and ratio. Four different types of variables are of interest to researchers using the quantitative method: independent, dependent, extraneous, and control.

Research designs most closely associated with quantitative research are true experimental designs, quasi-experimental designs, preexperimental designs, and descriptive designs. True experimental designs always include random assignment to groups and manipulation of the independent variable. Quasi-experimental designs involve no random assignment but a manipulation of the independent variable. Preexperimental designs also involve no random assignment with a manipulation; however, the amount of control by the researcher over extraneous variables for preexperimental designs is the least among the four designs.

Descriptive designs, the fourth general category of research methods used in quantitative approaches, include survey, observational, correlational, and causal comparative. Descriptive designs involve no random assignment, nor is there a manipulation of an independent variable. Typically, descriptive designs are an attempt by the researcher to characterize events or conditions of an identified population.

5

Qualitative Research Methods

The initial use of qualitative methods was first introduced by philosophers René Descartes and Immanuel Kant in the 1600s and 1700s (Hamilton, 1992). Hamilton noted that Descartes was responsible for founding the qualitative research approach. Qualitative research approaches have been used in more recent history since the early part of the 20th century by sociologists and anthropologists (Pistrang & Barker, 2012; Rosaldo, 1989). However, the term *qualitative research* is a fairly recent one and first appeared in the 1960s (Bogdan & Biklen, 2007). The 1980s and 1990s saw an interest in qualitative research beyond anthropologists and sociologists (Gergin, 1985).

Denzin and Lincoln (2000) described qualitative research as follows:

> An emphasis on the qualities of entities and on processes and meanings that are not experimentally examined or measured (if measured at all) in terms of quantity, amount, intensity, or frequency. Qualitative researchers stress the socially constructed nature of reality, the intimate relationship between the researcher and what is studied, and the situational constraints that shape the inquiry. (p. 8)

Pistrang and Barker (2012) described the strengths of qualitative research and stated they "give in-depth, textured data; are particularly useful for investigating personal meanings; are valuable for inductively generating theory and are therefore often used in underresearched, undertheorized areas in which exploratory work is needed . . . and give research participants freedom to describe their own experiences in their own language" (p. 6). Creswell (2012) suggested the qualitative research is best suited for investigating variables that are unknown and need to be discovered. The goal of qualitative research has been described as "to gain an in-depth, holistic perspective of groups of people, environments, programs, events, or any phenomenon one wishes to study by interacting closely with the people one is studying" (Farber, 2006, p. 368).

In this chapter, I will first address the strengths and weaknesses of qualitative research and its basic characteristics. Second, several approaches or traditions of conducting research within a qualitative orientation will be presented, including the case study method, ethnographic methods, grounded theory, phenomenological methods, participatory action research, narrative analysis, historical descriptive methods, and mixed methods.

Researchers in the social sciences have long struggled with achieving a sense of respectability for the methods that are used (Padgett, 2004). This struggle has been associated with perceptions of how objective and measurable results are. Guba and Lincoln (1992) noted that the social sciences have long been considered "soft" sciences and less quantifiable compared to "hard" sciences like mathematics, chemistry, and physics. This struggle and the desire to be viewed both externally and within the social science fields as closer to "hard" sciences have resulted in qualitative methods of inquiry being perceived as less desirable. Sells, Smith, and Sprenkle (1995) have described the historical antagonism between quantitative and qualitative research methods. They noted that, in many investigators' views, the traditional quantitative approaches were the only ethically responsible way of conducting research. An added issue for those conducting qualitative research is that the way qualitative data are organized and reported in professional journals is different from the ways used for traditional quantitative research (e.g., the methods section in particular may differ).

ADVANTAGES AND DISADVANTAGES OF QUALITATIVE RESEARCH

Several advantages and disadvantages of qualitative research have been proposed (see Table 5.1; Gall et al., 2006). One advantage is that the researcher can gain a more detailed understanding of the phenomena of interest than with quantitative research. Second, qualitative research is helpful in understanding or explaining unusual situations that could not be identified through large-scale quantitative methods. A third advantage is that the researcher can adjust data-collection procedures during the process, based on the issues that arise.

The major difficulty with qualitative methods concerns the validity of generalizing results to the larger population (Gall et al., 1996). By focusing on specific phenomena, the researcher increases the understanding of those phenomena but loses a broader perspective. A second limitation of qualitative research involves ethically maintaining the privacy of the individuals studied when the information presented is so specific.

Bogdan and Biklen (2007) have identified five characteristics of qualitative research: a naturalistic approach, the use of descriptive data, an emphasis on process, an inductive approach, and a focus on meaning. A naturalistic approach involves the collection of data from the natural environment. Contrary to traditional quantitative methods, which attempt to control the extraneous variables in the natural environment, qualitative research enters the natural setting to study its complexity. An understanding of the context is critical to observing and being in the natural setting. The second characteristic of qualitative research is the use of descriptive data, which is collected and presented through language and pictures (Bogdan & Biklen, 2007). Bogdan and Biklen (2007) noted that such data may be in the form of interview transcripts, videotapes, notations made, and photographs. Such data collection may be done with exceptional detail and focus on small elements of the context. A third characteristic of qualitative research, with its emphasis on the process, is to some degree an investigation that is more interested in the way things are done rather than the outcomes or the accomplishments (Bogdan & Biklen, 2007). The emphasis is on how things happen and an understanding of how events or conditions occur. A fourth characteristic is an inductive approach, which is an attempt to explore in a more organic way what comes up rather than hypothesizing what is there and looking to find support for the hypothesis, which is the deductive approach. The orientation of the qualitative researcher is one of entering the naturalistic environment with an openness to discovering what can be found but with a focus on elements of the environment. The last characteristic is the meaning of the experience to those in the context and environment (Bogdan & Biklen, 2007). The researcher is interested in understanding the participants in that environment, perspective, and view of the experience. In essence, the question is what meaning certain things in that environment have for the person or participant.

Table 5.1   Advantages and Disadvantages of Qualitative Research

Advantages	*Disadvantages*
1. Able to obtain a detailed understanding of a person, event, or phenomenon	1. Limitations in generalizing the results to the larger population
2. Flexibility in responding to events or phenomena (e.g., can alter flow of interview to address uniqueness of an event or phenomenon)	2. Potential for bias in interpreting data
	3. Lack of consistency in methods of data collection

(Continued)

Table 5.1   (Continued)

Advantages	Disadvantages
3. Generally does not require extensive resources to conduct	4. Potential for loss of privacy for individuals studied because of intensive description of individual cases
4. Helpful in understanding unusual or exceptional situations	
5. Helpful in the initial exploration of individuals, events, or phenomena	

Table 5.2   Comparison of Qualitative and Quantitative Research

Comparison Points	Qualitative Research	Quantitative Research
Focus	Quality, which includes the nature and essence	Quantity, which includes amounts
Philosophical orientation	Phenomenology and interaction	Empiricism and logical positivism
Approaches	Fieldwork, ethnographic, naturalistic, and grounded	Experimental, empirical, and statistical
Goals	Understanding, describing, discovery, and hypothesis generating	Prediction, control, and hypothesis testing
Design characteristics	Flexible and evolving	Fixed and predetermined
Sample	Generally a small sample, which is nonrandom, is used	A large, random sample of the population is used
Data-collection approaches	Research achieved through interviews and observations	Administration of structured instruments, surveys, and questionnaires
Method of analysis	Inductive and use of language	Deductive and use of statistics

Source: Adapted from Sorin-Peters (2004).

Sorin-Peters (2004) differentiated qualitative research and quantitative research on specific comparison points. For example, the focus of qualitative research is quality, and the focus of quantitative research is quantity. (See Table 5.2.)

TRADITIONS OR PARADIGMS IN CONDUCTING QUALITATIVE RESEARCH

As has been mentioned, there are several different approaches for conducting qualitative research. One major approach is the case study. Although all case study research is not qualitative, some case study methods may be (Yin, 2003). Case study research has long had an important history and influence in psychology and education; Sigmund Freud and Jean Piaget used this approach to develop many of their theories. Case study is an intensive investigation of a single individual in an effort to treat or intervene with that person or to make inferences about others. For example, Freud (Spurling, 1989) developed much of his theory of personality development using case study methods (e.g., the cases of Dora and Little Hans). Piaget employed his own children as case studies, using this method to develop his insights into cognitive development during infancy (Daehler & Bukatko, 1985).

Case Study Approach

The case study approach of qualitative research may be defined in terms of the intensity of focus on a particular case or set of cases and specific phenomena of the case or cases. Case study research is typically, although not always, conducted in a natural setting. Stake (2000) noted that qualitative case study requires establishing boundaries and units of analysis to study in the environment, so it is not totally open or undefined. As Stake (2000) stated, "Case study is not a methodological choice but a choice of what is to be studied" (p. 435). Gall and colleagues (1996) stated that case studies serve three purposes: to achieve detailed descriptions of phenomena of interest, to develop possible explanations of phenomena, and to evaluate the phenomena of interest. To understand the case study as a qualitative approach, it may be best to have a description of the characteristics of the approach. As Stake (2000) stated, "Perhaps the simplest rule for method in qualitative case work is this: Place the best brains available into the thick of what is going on. The brain work ostensibly is observational, but more basically it is reflective" (p. 445). This refers to the use of strong observational methods in the naturalistic setting to understand the case of interest. Yin (2003) proposed that several different approaches to case study may be distinguished and that there may be single or multiple case studies. A single case study clearly involves focusing only on one case. A multiple case study is composed of several single-case studies.

Another way to characterize case study research is by the manner in which the data are collected and analyzed. Data in case study research are typically collected in the form of summaries and extensive note-taking of the researcher's observations. Researchers may use triangulation in data collection, which refers to using multiple data-collection methods, sources, or observers (Stake, 2000). For example, the researcher might use several other researchers to observe the same phenomena, or use a variety of sources to understand a particular phenomenon or meaning. They engage in continuous contact with the case or environment and revise meanings and understandings over time (Stake, 2000).

The qualitative researcher is generally interested in particular phenomena that may shed light on processes of events, persons, or things (Gall et al., 1996). Qualitative researchers identify a focus of their attention in regard to the phenomena of interest; they also define the unit of analysis to be studied. If, for example, researchers are interested in understanding the counseling relationship as the focus, they might choose the relationship unit of analysis. The case study then would be of single client–counselor interactions. Researchers might choose to study more than one counseling relationship, but the unit of analysis still remains the same, and the researcher in qualitative research uses the case study approach. The researcher may observe the counseling relationship over several sessions and record or describe the process. Recall that qualitative research is generally conducted in the natural setting, so the researcher might observe through a one-way mirror. Also, the counselor may choose multiple case studies and study several counselor–client relationships.

An example in educational qualitative research might be an interest in the process of interaction between a teacher and his or her students. The unit of analysis might be a group (all those in the classroom). The researcher might enter the classroom as an observer over several days, weeks, or longer. Detailed descriptions would be made of the interactions between the class and the teacher. A multiple case study would involve studying several classrooms.

Stake (2000) described the selection of case study as being unique, and this is based on the particular interest in the specific cases to be studied. He goes on to propose that selection of the case is of critical importance and that a researcher may choose to randomly select from a certain population that is of interest. Despite the limitation of generalizability of qualitative research, there remains the intent of offering some effort at generalization. Stake proposes six steps in using a case study approach: (1) establishing the boundaries of the case, (2) identifying themes of emphasis, (3) focusing on specific patterns of data, (4) the use of triangulation in data interpretation, (5) considering alternative views, and (6) determining appropriate generalizations from the case.

Erickson, Hatton, Roy, Fox, and Renne (2007) conducted a qualitative case study to investigate the leaders in the field of early intervention for children with visual impairments promoting literacy. The researchers described the procedures as follows:

The qualitative case study was selected for its strength as a means of exploring, explaining, and describing the contexts within which particular practices are employed. When the unique features of each case are compared with the experiences of others, each of the three cases has important atypical features, relationships, and situations that may be generalizable to other cases (Stake, 2000). Because of the dynamic nature of home visits and the lack of empirical information on this topic, the case study methods were deemed the most appropriate for the research question. The combination of participant observations, teacher interviews, and document reviews provided multiples sources of information, and supported the extraction of as much information as possible about the early intervention practices employed by the participants in the study. (p. 83)

One can see from this description that the researchers used several approaches to gather data, including triangulation of data gathered from several participant observers and interviews.

Sandage (2012) also conducted a case study and focused on the case of an individual who committed suicide. The study involved focusing on a single case and one individual. Sandage described one of the research questions of the study as "seeking to identify and understand the following: (a) tragic and ironic narrative themes in the subject's writing, documents" (p. 20). The research described in detail the subject of the study or the case. For example, the subject was described as such:

Jim was a Euro-American male who grew up in a metropolitan area of the Southeast region of the United States. He was the fifth of six children in a lower middle-class Irish-Catholic family. Jim started drinking heavily early in his marriage and developed alcohol dependence. . . . In his late 40s, Jim was charged with a robbery-related homicide to which he pled "not guilty." He was convicted and spent several years in prison before his conviction was overturned. . . . After Jim was released from prison, he continued to live at a considerable distance from his children and had minimal contact with them. . . . In his midfifties he died by suicide via exsanguination (i.e. cutting his wrists with a knife). (p. 20)

Sandage (2012) used a number of sources to gather information about the subject's suicide and life leading up to the suicide. For example, the researcher worked with Jim's daughter, who shared letters and other correspondence. The researcher had 103 letters that Jim had sent to his daughter while he was in prison. Also, there were 35 letters that Jim sent to other relatives. Sandage described the initial review of the data analysis: "Data analysis started with reading and rereading the documents several times to become immersed in the data and to allow patterns of themes to emerge" (p. 22). A major theme that emerged in review of the data was one of tragedy and fatalism. The researcher quoted several excerpts from the data (the subject's letters) illustrating this theme. Sandage linked the results and interpretation to theory, specifically Heinz Kohut's theory of personality, and the use of the term *tragic man.*

Ethnographic

Ethnographic research methods involve intensive study of the characteristics of a given culture or distinct group with its own worldview from naturalistic, firsthand experience (Tedlock, 2000). Silverman (2011) provides an interesting description of ethnography and states, "Ethnography puts together two different words: ethno means 'folk' while 'graph' derives from 'writing'. Ethnography refers, then, to social science writing about particular folks" (p. 114). Like many other qualitative methods, the ethnographic approach was initially developed by anthropologists. Tedlock (2000) described the benefits of an ethnographic approach as "ethno-graphers can better understand the beliefs, motivation, and behaviors of their subjects than they can by using any other approach" (p. 456). Shimahara (1988) identified three characteristics of ethnographic research: (1) focusing on investigating cultural patterns in behavior and commonalities of a given culture, (2) determining how members of a culture define and derive meaning from the experiences and events occurring within that culture, and (3) studying these cultural behaviors and patterns in their natural environment. Thus, for those using the ethnographic approach to research, defining characteristics are to focus on culture or a particular group. Gall and colleagues (1996) provided an interesting perspective of ethnographic research and concluded that it is to look at "cultural phenomena from the perspective of an outsider, and then [seek] to understand the phenomenon from the perspective of an insider" (p. 612). The life history approach or biography is one used in ethnography (Tedlock, 2000). A common approach to ethnographic research is as a participant observer (Silverman, 2011). The investigator enters the social system and lives among those he or she is studying. Another strategy in an ethnographic approach is the use of memoir, or the ethnographic genre. The ethnographic genre has been described as a combination of both memoir and life history approaches (Tedlock, 2000). The researcher, based on his or her experience as a participant observer, writes about the experience as if it were a memoir. Data-collection methods have ranged from the participant observer to the observer participant. Both counseling and education have adopted these approaches to conducting research. They offer an effective new paradigm for understanding major concepts and practices in our fields.

Brown (2006) conducted a study in which she used an ethnographic research approach. The focus of her study was to attempt to understand the culture and perceptions about the quality of mothering by African American women in rural areas. The methods are described as follows: "A holistic ethnographic approach informed the design and data collection method of this study" (p. 22). She further described her methods: "Interview topics included drug use; social networks; values; employment history; childhood experiences; sexual behavior; and HIV/AIDS-related knowledge, beliefs and perceptions" (p. 22). The respondents for this qualitative study were 30 African American women who reported using cocaine at the time of participation. The actual data collection is described in detail: "Multiple data collection strategies (in-depth audiotaped interviews, participant observation, and information interviews) over a prolonged period (four years), monthly peer debriefing between the PI and project director, and member checks were used to enhance the validity/credibility of the data" (p. 23).

Jones (2011) also conducted a qualitative study using an ethnographic approach. The study involved an in-depth analysis of how a Black Baptist community constructed Christian media and how it impacted their religious practices. The researcher described the methods as follows: "This ethnographic study was conducted with a predominantly African-American Baptist church in a mid-sized city in Southeastern Pennsylvania" (p. 3). Jones noted that he used purposeful sampling and recruited participants who represented different ages, income levels, and ethnic groups. Data were collected through direct observation of church activities, such as Bible study groups and various church meetings. Additionally, the researcher reviewed basic church documents that included church flyers and programs. Jones reviewed the data and identified three major themes. One theme concerned feelings of remorse or regret for watching media that depicted violence and sex. A second theme concerned watching media that was uplifting and inspirational. The last theme concerned the development of social bonds and media outlets focused on sharing and positive relationships. Finally, Jones noted that he returned to the church community and shared his results with members of the community. He provided a written summary to those attending the meeting. He requested feedback from the members, and the community confirmed Jones's interpretation and findings. Based on the description, Jones did use a naturalistic approach to gather data and completed direct observation of the participants in an effort to collect his data. The group he studied was unique, and he studied in depth the lives of those in the community.

Grounded Theory

Grounded theory is a qualitative research approach that was originally developed by two sociologists, Barney Glasser and Anselm Strass (Charmaz, 2006). The primary approach to grounded theory is the dynamic interaction of identifying categories, which are analyzed and reconstituted into more complex ones with each continuous level of analysis. Willig (2001) provides the example of identifying initial categories described by participants as anger and anxiety into a broader category of emotions. Each level of analysis may lead to a higher level of abstraction (Willig, 2001). In essence, the more abstract categories are grounded on earlier ones, which are more basic. Theory is built on a systematic analysis and reanalysis of the data. This approach gives the researcher a significant amount of flexibility in adjusting the investigation to the information collected. Isaksson, Lexell, and Skar (2007) used a grounded theory approach in studying how social support affects motivation for those with spinal cord injuries. The participants were 13 women with spinal cord injuries, ages 25 to 61. The authors described the data collection as "using repeated in-depth interviews and field notes. The first interview focused on how the women perceived the importance of the current social support from their social network members. The interview consisted of open-ended questions, and field notes were taken after the interview" (p. 24). The researchers went on to describe their procedures using grounded theory: "The interview data were analyzed using a grounded theory approach. . . . Grounded theory was chosen because it uses an interactional approach and contributes to an improved understanding of relationships and interactions between individuals" (p. 24). The interactional approach allows for discovery of the more abstract categories and elements of the situation or the broader categories of support and motivation.

Ellis and Chen (2013) also conducted a study using grounded theory; they studied identity development for undocumented immigrant college students. The researchers described the purpose of the study:

> First, given that existing research focuses on the legal challenges and risks associated with being undocumented, we explored how cultural and contextual factors affect the process within which undocumented immigrant college students navigate their educational and career pursuit. Second, we aimed to understand the dynamic relationship between career identity and ethnic identity formation in undocumented immigrant college students. (p. 252)

The researchers described their methods like this: "The data were analysed using a version of grounded theory. . . . The researcher is guided by the analysis of data to develop an understanding of phenomena grounded in empirical observation." (p. 252). The researchers reported using a purposive method of sampling, and they included 11 undocumented college students. Participants were originally from Mexico, Central and Latin America, South Korea, and Poland. Data were collected from interviews, field notes, and journals. The researchers first immersed themselves in the data before analysis. They coded the data and verified the coding and interpretation through checks with the subjects. Participants could remove information they did not want to have included. The researchers also included in the analysis their own personal biases through reflexivity. Ellis and Chen discovered four themes. One theme involved an enhancement of positive attributes achieved through struggles as an undocumented immigrant. A second theme was how being an undocumented immigrant changed self-perceptions. A third theme involved the long-term development of identity formation. The final theme involved an understanding of a bicultural identity. The researchers discussed how they completed analyses and how they used an iterative process to engage in a continuous process of interpretation.

Phenomenological

A third method of conducting qualitative research is through a phenomenological approach. Willig (2001) noted that the phenomenological approach was developed by Edmund Husserl in the early 1900s. The focus of the phenomenological approach is to understand how humans develop a way of knowing the world. What is the human perception of events or things? It is focused on the perceptual phenomena of the world or an event. The intent is to describe phenomena as they occur. In essence, the phenomenological researcher attempts to understand an individual's personal perspective (his or her feelings and reactions) to events under study. A phenomenological method of research is particularly helpful when a researcher wants to identify relevant issues and concepts in the context of a particular event and possibly conduct quantitative research or other types of qualitative research to further understand the event.

Brunelle, Cousineau, and Brochu (2005) used a phenomenological approach to study youth perceptions of their juvenile drug use. The purpose of the study is described as follows: "Our study has the particularity of focusing on the processes of juvenile deviance, specifically drug use and delinquency, from a phenomenological point of view" (p. 722). The researchers further describe the methods of their study:

> In keeping with the study's phenomenological character, a qualitative approach was used. It has already been established that this type of approach offers a better understanding of the specificity and complexity of the processes at work by providing an insider's point of view. . . . Data were collected using the autobiographical life account method. . . . Beginning with a very open-ended instruction, this method leaves room for participants to deliver their accounts spontaneously and allows them to lead the interview. Life accounts are usually incomplete because participants can omit, voluntarily or not, certain aspects of their lives or their interpretations. Phenomenology focuses on the social actors' (conscious) reading of their own realities. (p. 723)

As the researchers noted, the process of the phenomenological approach is to understand the perceptions and realities of the participants from their points of view.

Historical

Historical research is a fourth method of conducting qualitative research, the purpose of which is to systematically understand past events and phenomena to obtain a clearer understanding of current issues. Historical research may involve the use of systematic methods, such as diaries, oral records, and relics (Gall et al., 1996). Gall and colleagues (1996) proposed these steps in historical research: (1) Define the problem or develop a hypothesis, (2) identify potential sources of historical data, (3) evaluate the historical sources, and (4) report and summarize results.

Morawski (1992) provided an example of historical research when she studied the place of introductory textbooks in American psychology. She addressed the following questions in her investigation:

> Because so little historical appraisal has been done on the topic, it is difficult to assess the function of psychological textbooks. Are they significant artifacts of psychology's place in American culture, or are they the products of ill-conceived educational programs, financial desires, or the discipline's efforts to fit itself into social institutions? Have they made a difference to the discipline or to people's lives, and, if so in what ways? What makes an introductory text, and how has the literary genre evolved over the last century? These questions guided my historical study of introductory textbooks, a study that progressively raised new questions about his ubiquitous yet mysterious literary form. (p. 162)

Her historical study of early psychology textbooks was accomplished through a focus on textual strategies used by the authors. Morawski (1992) defined the problems of interest in her research questions. She focused on a specific time period, the late 1800s and early 1900s, and the introductory psychology textbooks written at that time, and described the texts she reviewed (p. 166). Finally, she summarized her findings and attempted to make conclusions. For example, she stated in her summary, "By examining psychologists' work, such as textbooks, we can see more closely the macro- and micropolitics of transforming human welfare" (p. 168). As an aside, it is interesting to note the language used by researchers based on their particular approach. Morawski stated, "My sojourn into this realm of deprecated relics necessarily required a mapping of the literary terrain and compilation of a bibliography" (p. 162). The use of the word *relics* is informative as to the approach used by the researcher.

SUMMARY

Qualitative research provides the researcher with opportunities to study phenomena, events, and experiences in great detail and in a more natural way. Additionally, qualitative methods allow for flexibility in addressing the needs of the situation: The researcher can adjust his or her focus and approach to meet the characteristics of the situation. There has been considerable debate about the validity of conducting research based on qualitative methods, and various attempts have been made to remove some of the identified concerns (Onwuegbuzie & Leech, 2005).

Investigators using qualitative research methods have developed systematic categories for data collection, such as the categories of relationship and groups. Additionally, specific methods or traditions for research procedures have been identified for those conducting qualitative research. There clearly has been an increase in qualitative research reported in the professional literature in counselling and education. In subsequent chapters, there will be examples of qualitative research and the identification of relevant questions to address in analyzing and evaluating such research.

6

BASICS OF QUALITATIVE RESEARCH DATA ANALYSIS

Creswell (2012) noted that "qualitative analysis is messy and nonlinear" (p. 513), which is considerably different from quantitative analysis, which is more specific and at times linear. Hogan, Dolan, and Donnelly (2009) proposed three phases of qualitative data analysis: generating data, management of data, and analysis of data. Others have suggested similar phases or stages (Creswell, 2012; Marshall & Rossman, 2006; Maxwell, 2009). Creswell (2012) added to the Hogan and colleagues (2009) phase model and suggested three stages: organizing and familiarizing, coding and reducing, and interpreting and representing. I want to integrate both models in this discussion, where there are four phases or stages: generating data, organizing data, coding and reducing data, and interpreting and representing data (includes reporting data).

The first phase in qualitative research analysis is generating data (Hogan et al., 2009). The question here is how will the data be collected: interviews, natural observation, focus groups, review of archival data such as diaries, and so on? One important consideration that frequently is left out of this process is determining what the unit of analysis is (Lofland, Snow, Anderson, & Lofland, 2006). Prior to deciding on how to collect the data, there needs to be a decision on the units of data gathering.

GENERATING DATA: UNITS OF DATA COLLECTION

Lofland and colleagues (2006) proposed a common approach to understanding and interpreting qualitative research through units of data gathering. They proposed that there are nine units of analysis or data collection (gathering) for qualitative research: social practices, episodes, encounters, roles (roles and social types), relationships, groups and cliques, organizations, settlements, and lifestyles or subcultures.

According to Lofland and colleagues (2006), units are arranged hierarchically and increase in social complexity from practices to lifestyles. Social practices are defined as the smallest unit of analysis in social settings and are characterized by repetition of communications and behaviors in interactions. Additionally, social practices are identified by being routine or unnoticeable (Lofland et al., 2006). For example, rituals may be classified as practices. One ritual that might be studied in counseling is that of initial greetings, such as a handshake or the client calling the counselor *Ms., Doctor,* and so on.

A second type of data unit analysis, episodes, has been characterized as unusual dramatic experiences. Examples of episodes are significant events such as going through a divorce, experiencing a natural disaster such as a hurricane, or experiencing a violent crime. Episodes, according to Lofland and colleagues (2006), may involve only a few people, such as a violent crime in which one individual robs another, or may include thousands of people, such as all those experiencing an earthquake. The important issue is that the unit is episodic and not long term. Researchers in the field of counseling might be interested in a number of psychological events that affect a client and have the potential to bring a client into counseling, such as rape, divorce, or the death of someone close. The effects or experience of the terrorist attacks of 9/11 is another example of an episode.

The third category for unit of analysis in qualitative research is encounters, which are defined in terms of there being two or more individuals sharing social space and who are focused on maintaining a mutual interaction (Lofland et al., 2006). Encounters are well defined and generally involve specific roles and boundaries between participants. The key point is that there is a mutual focus among the participants. An example of an encounter in counseling is a client and counselor meeting for the first few sessions. The interaction is based to a large extent on the social roles each brings to the relationship, and there is a common focus: identifying and understanding the client's problem. Researchers in counseling might be interested, for example, in the meaning ascribed by the client to early counseling experiences (e.g., the client's knowledge of the process of counseling and the roles client and counselor are to play).

A fourth type of unit of analysis in qualitative research is composed of two subcategories: roles and social types. Roles are composed of clusters of behaviors that are connected to a specific position. So, a teacher is expected to behave in a certain way in a classroom, for example, stand in front of the class and impart information, give tests, ask questions, and so on. Social types are considered to be a subcategory of roles and are somewhat more general. Examples of social types may be a bully or class clown (Lofland et al., 2006).

The next relevant unit of analysis is the relationship, which has been defined as involving two individuals who are relatively connected and to some degree interdependent over a period of time (Lofland et al., 2006). Examples of relationships are spouses, friends, and supervisors and employees. For counseling researchers, the counseling relationship (beyond the first few sessions) may be interpreted as this kind of analytic unit.

Groups are another type of unit of analysis; they are defined as a number of individuals who interact over a period of time and form a social structure (Lofland et al., 2006). Work groups and families are examples of groups as units of analysis. Counseling researchers might be interested in how families cope with changes, such as those that occur when a young child attends school for the first time.

Organizations are the next level of social unit analysts suggest for conducting qualitative research. They are defined as systematically formed collectives of individuals with specific purposes and goals (Lofland et al., 2006). Organizations are established with specific rules and entrance restrictions. An example of an organization is a student club. A counseling researcher might be interested in studying an informal treatment organization, such as Alcoholics Anonymous (AA). There are formal goals for AA, such as maintaining sobriety, and rules for participating in the organization, such as maintaining the anonymity of members (Alcoholics Anonymous, 1952).

Settlements or habitats are another unit of analysis, identified by Lofland and colleagues (2006), and these are defined as "complexly interrelated sets of encounters, roles, groups, and organizations, existing within a socially defined territory and performing a range of life-sustaining functions" (p. 129). Concrete examples of settlements are neighborhoods, towns, and villages. The counselor researcher might be interested in investigating the effects of a drug-prevention program on a town or a neighborhood.

Lifestyles or subcultures are the last social unit of measurement category in qualitative research. Lofland and colleagues (2006) defined lifestyles as "a mixture of behavioral, normative, and cognitive elements that together characterize the way of life or orientation of a set of similarly situated individuals and that distinguishes them from other groups or aggregations within or across other social units" (p. 131). A counseling researcher might, for example, be interested in discovering how different health lifestyles affect psychological well-being, whereas an educator might be interested in how socioeconomic background influences motivation for learning.

GENERATING DATA: INTERVIEWS, NATURAL OBSERVATIONS, FOCUS GROUPS, AND DIARIES

Interviews

Interviews are a common approach to data collection for those conducting qualitative research. Different from quantitative interview methods, which typically use close-ended questions, qualitative research involves the use of open-ended questions (Creswell, 2012; Silverman, 2011). Creswell (2012) noted that there are several different types of interviews: unstructured, semi-structured, and structured; all three may be used in qualitative research. An unstructured interview is essentially wide-open and left to the interviewer to determine the direction. A specific set of questions is not generated prior to the interview, but there are general beginning questions based upon the focus of the study. Creswell (2012) suggested that basic questions such as who, what, why serve as categories. Not every participant may be asked the same questions. Structured interviews are planned, and every participant is asked the same set of questions. The questions are still posed as open-ended. Questions typically cannot be answered in a yes–no format (Creswell, 2012). Semi-structured interviews are a combination of unstructured and structured formats. A semi-structured interview includes a predetermined set of questions, but the interview has the latitude to explore areas in more detail if it appears warranted.

Natural Observations

Natural observation is another key tool in data collection in qualitative research (Creswell, 2012; Silverman, 2011). Natural observation does require thoughtful consideration of the role a researcher takes in collecting data (Marshall & Rossman, 2010). According to Creswell (2012), a qualitative researcher may take on the role of complete participant, participant as observer, covert participant, or complete observer in naturalistic observation. Each role has benefits and limitations. A complete participant actually functions as a member of the community under study. There have been instances where a graduate student entered a psychiatric hospital (with a few outside the institution who knew the role) and became a patient to understand the experience and to determine whether diagnosing was accurate (Rosenhan, 1973). Another role a qualitative researcher may take is as a covert participant (Creswell, 2012). In such instances, the researcher does not inform the group or community of his or her status. Certainly, in such cases, careful consultation with the Institutional Review Board (IRB) is necessary to protect those being studied. An example may be entering an online community such as Second Life (an online social community) and not disclosing that others are being studied while functioning with an avatar (Boellestorff, 2010). The role of participant observer is more open, and others in the community are aware of the observer's role. There have been several instances where a researcher has entered an Amish family as a participant observer. In such cases, the researcher does participate in daily life, attends church, and so on. The last type of observer is the complete observer. Generally, the complete observer is unknown to those being observed (Creswell, 2012). This role, the complete observer, is completed in a public setting such as supermarket or a sports facility. For example, a researcher may want to study fan reactions at a University of Alabama football game. He or she would not inform those being studied, and to maintain the role, the researcher would not support the team (or the opposing team).

Focus Groups

Focus groups are another approach to data collection in qualitative research (Creswell, 2012; Silverman, 2011). Creswell (2012) stated that a focus group may be thought of as a group interview. There can be structured, semi-structured, or unstructured questions for the group to address; a difference is the researcher attending to the interaction that occurs from the discussion within the group. A focus group also may function as a way to save time, for example, interviewing more than one person at a time. Typically, focus groups are recorded, so the researcher can later transcribe the discussions. Also, recording the session allows the researcher to focus on the comments and the interaction and not be distracted by taking notes. Creswell suggested that a focus group generally include six to 12 members. A group too large does not allow enough talk time for each member, and in a group too small, there may not be enough conversation. Focus groups may involve more than one session depending upon the methodological approach used; for example, grounded theory involves an iterative process.

Diaries

Silverman (2011) described the use of diaries in qualitative research: "Diaries can be rich sources of data which detail how people make sense of their everyday lives" (p. 250). Recall the example in Chapter 5, involving a suicide (Jim), where diaries and written communications were used. There have been many diaries analyzed of soldiers about their war experiences dating back to the Revolutionary War and including the Civil War. Yi (2008) used diaries in a qualitative study investigating teachers' evaluation of rating students' work. Three teachers participated in the study, and they were involved in scoring more than 100 student papers. It was revealed that, despite having rating schemas for student work, the teachers infused their own perspectives in the rating process; the information was obtained from review of the diaries.

ORGANIZING DATA

A first step in organizing data is to become familiar with the data (Creswell, 2012). In quantitative data analysis, one may review basic descriptive statistics to become initially familiar with the data. Qualitative data can involve a large amount of information and an initial review, and understanding of what has been collected is important. Also, organizing data includes linking the data to the sources of data collection, for example, interviews or diaries. Creswell noted that organizing data is tedious and involves reading and rereading data collected. A researcher may choose to transcribe interviews and focus group conversations. Transcription is time-consuming, but it gives a researcher additional opportunity to become familiar with the data. A qualitative researcher may choose to organize the data or use computer programs that are designed to organize such data (Creswell, 2012). There are several computer programs that can be used during organization of data: Atlas.ti (http://www.atlasti .com/qualitative-software.html) and QSR NVivo (http://www.qsrinternational.com), for example. There are benefits and limitations of organizing the data oneself or using a computer software program. Use of a computer program requires additional cost and time to learn the program but allows for organizing and managing a large of amount of data. Many qualitative researchers like the hands-on experience of organizing the data themselves because they feel they become more familiar with it. However, organizing the data without a computer software program is more time-consuming.

MANAGEMENT OF DATA: CODING AND REDUCING

The next step in data analysis is management of data (Creswell, 2012; Hogan et al., 2009). Management of data includes developing themes, categorizing, coding, and identifying patterns (Marshall & Rossman, 2006; Maxwell, 2009; Wolcott, 1994). This step has been described as the core of qualitative analysis (Ary, Jacobs, Sorensen & Walker, 2014). Initial coding may involve, kind of in a brainstorming fashion, setting up many categories that can be reduced later once the researcher has completed the first pass at the data. This may involve considerable detailed analysis and involve assigning a code to words (establishing elements), sentences, or paragraphs (Ary et al., 2014). Silverman (2011) suggested using memos to keep track of categories. Several investigators have proposed strategies for coding (Ary et al., 2014; Creswell, 2007, 2012; Silverman, 2011). Another major part of the data analysis process in qualitative research is the use of triangulation. Creswell (2012) defined triangulation as "the process of corroborating evidence from different individuals, methods of data collection in description of themes" (p. 259). In essence, the researcher attempts to corroborate a theme through different sources (e.g., different individual's reporting similar information or convergence of the sources of data collection or different sources of data collection such as interviews and diaries; Creswell, 2012).

Creswell (2012) described three different approaches to organizing and coding qualitative data: through description, identifying themes, and layering and interrelating themes. The intent of organizing data through description is to provide the reader with detailed information that "transport[s] the reader to the research site" (p. 247). The idea, according to Creswell, is to provide the reader with extensive, detailed information about the person or individuals, their situations or environments, and their experiences. The idea is to allow the reader to experience what the researcher experienced in the research site and to develop a deeper understanding.

A second approach to coding data, or data analysis, is through the identification of themes. Creswell (2012) described themes in qualitative research as "similar codes aggregated together to form a major idea in the database" (p. 248). Typically, these themes are stated in two to four words, and it is not usual to identify five to seven themes in a study (Creswell, 2012). Creswell also further separates themes into different categories: ordinary themes, unexpected themes, hard-to-classify themes, and major and minor themes. Ordinary themes are defined as ones the researcher would expect to find (Creswell, 2012). Unexpected themes are defined as those that surprise the researcher and arise during the data analysis (Creswell, 2012). Hard-to-classify themes refer to data (qualitative data) that does not easily fit into a particular category and may overlap other themes (Creswell, 2012). Last are major and minor themes, which can be defined simply as each term indicates: major and minor themes (Creswell, 2012).

The third type of categorizing and organizing qualitative data is through layering and interrelating themes (Creswell, 2012). The intent of a layering type of data analysis is to interconnect between themes (Creswell, 2012). The interconnection is developed first with more simple themes and progresses to more complex relationships and connected themes. The more complex themes are generally "broader levels of abstraction" (Creswell, 2012 p. 250).

Miles and Huberman (1994) suggested three steps in the analysis of qualitative data or coding data: data reduction, data display, and drawing conclusions. Data reduction involves describing the circumstances or context or units of the analysis or the data segments to code. Data display is how the researcher presents examples of the data collected, which may include graphs and charts. Last, the researcher wants to provide conclusions, and this may be achieved through concrete examples of the data that demonstrate the themes, concepts, or theories identified. The reader of qualitative research is most often interested in this last step, drawing conclusions, because this is where the researcher attempts to compose understanding of the data collected and come up with conclusions.

Miles and Huberman (1994) suggested the following systematic tactics for developing meanings and drawing conclusions in qualitative research: counting, noting patterns or themes, determining plausibility, clustering, creating metaphors, differentiation or splitting, noting relationships between variables, and making conceptual theoretical coherence. Counting, according to Miles and Huberman (1994), involves counting the number of times a theme or pattern emerges from data analysis. There are decisions made as to whether the number of times a particular theme or construct emerges in analysis is consistent and frequent enough to state that it is important or significant. The number of times a theme or construct is expressed may then be reported in a qualitative research article. A second approach to analyzing data is noting patterns or themes, and this involves identification of commonalities among data collected (Miles & Huberman, 1994). Certainly, when studying human beings in counseling or education, there may seem to be chaos in the information collected. The qualitative researcher may review pages of transcripts of interviews or review notes on observations to identify common patterns that consistently emerge. We as human beings have the ability to see patterns, and to predict and control our lives and environments, we use information from identified patterns.

Another strategy for analyzing qualitative research data is determining plausibility (Miles & Huberman, 1994). Basically, this refers to determining whether data collected and constructs formulated make sense. A researcher may conclude that the data make sense or appear to be plausible in explaining certain phenomena. For example, if a researcher interviewed several people who reported seeing unidentified flying objects (UFOs), that researcher might consider whether or not the experiences reported are plausible.

Clustering is the fourth strategy for analyzing qualitative research data (Miles & Huberman, 1994). This strategy involves clustering together experiences or phenomena that have common characteristics. It is an attempt to go beyond identifying patterns and may place similar patterns into larger categories. Miles and Huberman stated that clustering may be interpreted to be movement to higher levels of abstraction. An example might be young children, for example, 2-year-olds, showing outbursts that might be interpreted as patterns of temper tantrums. Clustering several common patterns or experiences together may result in identification of "characteristic" 2-year-old behavior; specifically, in addition to tantrums, the behavior may involve the expression of need for control and exercise of control over the child's environment.

Creating metaphors is another strategy for analyzing qualitative data (Miles & Huberman, 1994). Keeping in mind that analysis of qualitative data is based on a linguistic model, you may consider the use of metaphors as an attempt to describe and organize data beyond simply literal interpretations.

A sixth strategy for analyzing qualitative data is differentiation, or splitting (Miles & Huberman, 1994). Differentiating involves dissecting variables into smaller parts to further clarify concepts and themes. This is, in a sense, an attempt at moving from simple to more complex variables by noting variability and differences. Differentiation is used when a researcher wants to understand and break larger concepts and variables into component parts. An example in counseling might be an attempt to clarify conflict in a marital therapy. The general theme might be identifying conflict, and differentiation might address types of conflict, such as conflict over finances.

Another tactic is noting relationships between variables, which involves discovering any relationships between two or more variables (Miles & Huberman, 1994). Teachers, for example, may develop feelings of powerlessness with certain administrative approaches (e.g., authoritarian or criticism based). The relationship between these two processes may be analyzed (e.g., the relationship between the teacher's feelings of powerlessness and the administrator's critical and authoritarian behaviors).

An eighth tactic in analyzing qualitative research is making conceptual, theoretical coherence of variables of focus (Miles & Huberman, 1994). This tactic is one of the more frequently used and involves attempting to make sense of data in relation to concepts and theories. Data are analyzed, and there is an attempt to discover examples from the data that support concepts theories. The theory of attachment (infant attachment) might be a focus in a qualitative study. The researcher would focus on videotapes of interactions between an infant and his or her mother, comparing it to videotapes of interactions between an infant and a stranger. Detailed descriptions of the interactions in the two types of dyads would be developed based on this tactic.

INTERPRETING AND REPORTING

The next phase or stage, interpreting and reporting results, is the last step. Once the qualitative researcher has identified themes through extensive coding, he or she wants to make sense of the data, certainly one of the primary purposes of conducting research. A major consideration in making any interpretation is answering and responding to the intent or purpose of the study. Ary and colleagues (2014) noted that this also may be connected to the qualitative approach used (ethnographic or grounded theory). Theory development as a purpose of the study may involve the use of grounded theory in how the data are collected and interpreted. Interpretation therefore may involve linking the themes and results to the theory being developed.

Similar to quantitative research, the reporting of results is an important part of the research process. The literature review and even purpose statement may be similar to a quantitative study. As has been noted, often hypotheses are not used in qualitative research, and this may be one difference reported in the article. The methods section likely includes description of the sample, the procedures used, and how data were collected. The results section involves sharing the major themes and results through words. Specific examples that illustrate the themes are provided. There is no specific number of examples that are required to illustrate the themes, but they should be adequate and clearly presented. There are several benefits of providing such concrete examples: (1) The reader can develop a good understanding of the theme or concept, and (2) the reader can determine if the example and theme are consistent. Last, the researcher summarizes the results in the discussion section. The discussion should include identification of limitations and future recommended research.

SUMMARY

Data analysis in qualitative research is considerably different from the methods used quantitative methods. Data analysis may be understood through four phases or stages: generating data, organizing data, coding and reducing data, and interpreting and representing data (including reporting data). There are several methods for collecting data, such as interviews, focus groups, diaries, and natural observations. Analysis of the data is complex and time-consuming. Careful and repeated review of the data is required. Similar to quantitative research, a final product is an article, sharing the results publicly through professional journals. The format of such a journal article also is similar to a quantitative study. One area where there are significant differences is in the results section, where data are presented through words and language.

7

MIXED METHODS RESEARCH

The previous four chapters have addressed quantitative and qualitative research methods. You may have gotten the impression that these two methods are totally exclusive and are never mixed. However, recently, there have been efforts to identify the commonalities and use the strengths of each (Castro & Coe, 2007; Clark & Creswell, 2008; Creswell, 2012; Curlette, 2006; Todd, Nerlich, McKeown, & Clarke, 2004). The integration and mixing of qualitative and quantitative methods have not been easy. In fact, many researchers have noted that discussions of which method is best have resulted in philosophical wars (Tashakkori & Teddlie, 2008).

Creswell (2012) discussed the similarities and differences between quantitative and qualitative research methods. As we have discussed, there are basic steps in the research process, for example, identifying a problem, reviewing the literature, determining the purpose of the study, collecting data, analyzing the data, and reporting the data (see Chapter 1). Creswell noted that one similarity between quantitative and qualitative research is the use of the six steps in these research process. Both research methods use similar types of data collection, although the type of data collected is different. The type of data collection is similar with the use of interviews and observations. A difference is that quantitative research is much more closed-ended in the data collection; for example, rate your stress level on a scale of 1 to 100. Whereas qualitative data collection is more open-ended and might involve asking the research participant to describe his or her level of stress through words. Last, a major difference is in how the data are reported. In quantitative research, the data are reported through numbers, and in qualitative research, the data are reported through words.

In this chapter, I want to give a brief historical overview of the development of mixed methods research. Second, I want to discuss several proposed paradigms for mixed methods. Third, there will be a discussion of the use of triangulation in mixed methods, which is a key component of the mixed methods research paradigm. We will also examine examples of several research studies that employed mixed methods.

HISTORY OF MIXED METHODS RESEARCH

The history of mixed methods probably needs to start with a review of how both quantitative and qualitative methods developed as paradigms for research. Before I go into the history of mixed methods, I want to discuss the definition of a paradigm because the traditions of qualitative and quantitative research are founded on paradigms of research. Tashakkori and Teddlie (2008) defined a research paradigm as "the worldviews or belief systems that guide researchers" (p. 7).

In terms of the earlier history of quantitative methods or research paradigms, quantitative research originated out of experimental psychology from the late 1800s (Todd et al., 2004). Such early research was based on data collection at the individual level or single case, and quantitative methods were introduced when more advanced statistical methods were introduced that allowed for aggregating data (Todd et al., 2004). Quantitative research developed as a positivist paradigm. Lincoln and Guba (1985) identified several characteristics of a positivist research paradigm. One characteristic concerns the nature of reality. A positivist paradigm is based on the view that there is one reality (Lincoln & Guba, 1985). As Lincoln and Guba (1985) stated, "The basic belief system of positivism is rooted in a realist ontology, that is, the belief that there exists a reality out there, driven by immutable natural laws" (p. 19). A second characteristic, according to Lincoln and Guba (1985), is that research and inquiry are not based on any personal values. Another characteristic is that positivism holds that generalizations may be made across situations and contexts rather easily (Lincoln & Guba, 1985). There is a linear relationship between the antecedents to events and the consequences or outcomes, a Newtonian–Cartesian model (Lincoln & Guba, 1985). Todd and colleagues (2004) suggested another characteristic, namely, that there is deductive logic, progressing from the general to the specific in focus. During the 1950s and 1960s, the positivist paradigm and tradition became less accepted, and the postpositivist paradigm began to replace it. Postpositivism is a variation of positivism but is based on critical realism (Guba, 1990). The postpositivist position holds that research can be influenced by the personal values of researchers and that reality is constructed, not a unitary reality (Todd et al., 2004). Objectivity in a postpositivism paradigm is still valued, and it is believed that one may not obtain total objectivity but that one can strive to achieve it by using a critical perspective (Guba, 1990).

The qualitative research paradigm can be traced back to the social constructionists of the early 1900s (Tashakkori & Teddlie, 2008). The characteristics of qualitative research are almost directly the opposite of those from the positivist paradigm. Qualitative researchers hold that there are potentially a number of different constructed realities and that information is value laden; that is, the researcher interprets data from a personal perspective. Another characteristic of the qualitative research paradigm is that one cannot easily differentiate the cause-and-effect relationship between variables. Last, the qualitative research paradigm uses an inductive logic view, and the intent is to interpret from the specific to the general (Tashakkori & Teddlie, 2008).

One can see from the cited characteristics that these views did not hold promise for bringing together these two different research paradigms. Tashakkori and Teddlie (2008) describe the attempts by different researchers to criticize the other view. This resulted in the paradigm wars, or debates over which research tradition, quantitative or qualitative, was better. Tashakkori and Teddlie (2008) provide a clear sequence of the evolution of research methodology approaches since the early 1900s. The first period they characterized as the Purist Era because both qualitative and quantitative researchers advanced their views as being the better approach. This initial period lasted from the early 1900s to the 1950s and 1960s. The second period, Period II, according to Tashakkori and Teddlie (2008), started in the 1960s and extended until the 1980s. The focus of this period was a beginning attempt to find commonalities between the research paradigms and to begin to use mixed methods. The research designs were hypothetically viewed as being equal, and the result was models that used parallel methods simultaneously and sequentially—but equally. The 1990s saw a more advanced approach to mixing methods, with the use of different stages of implementing the methods. Based on the purpose of the study, there may be a single research paradigm used, for example, qualitative, and later, based on a series of studies on the same topic, another method might be used, for example, quantitative research. Tashakkori and Teddlie (1998) stated that the introduction of mixed methods research models essentially ended the significant debates and wars over which research method was superior.

Denzin and Lincoln (2011) noted that one way to understand the history and development of qualitative research is through a reflection of the paradigm wars during the 1970s through the 1990s. Essentially, differences began emerging along with a gradual increased use of qualitative methods in the 1970s. Quantitative research simultaneously provided pressure to those pursuing qualitative research through criticism of the rigor that was used. There were many journals that would not publish qualitative research. Qualitative research was in its infancy, and as with many such disciplines, there were efforts to legitimize the methods but not necessarily agreement on how to do so. By the 1990s, there were increased publications, both journal publications and books, on how to conduct qualitative research. Denzin and Lincoln further noted the problems qualitative research experienced after the 1990s, and they stated, "Politicians and hard scientists call qualitative researchers journalists or soft scientists" (p. 2). They explained that this criticism was based on attempts to maintain the more traditional approaches to science and not open up to new ideas and approaches. The expansion of qualitative research continues, and there are increases in the number of articles published and books written about qualitative research. Acceptance has been slow but continues within the scientific community, although not by everyone.

Alise and Teddlie (2010) conducted a study on the prevalence of using quantitative, qualitative, and mixed methods across the social and behavioral sciences. They were particularly interested in identifying the prevalence or percentage rates of quantitative, qualitative, and mixed methods research reported in professional journals. Additionally, they reported on use of these methods in applied versus pure social and behavioral science journals. The researchers found that pure social and behavioral sciences (psychology and sociology) used quantitative approaches much more frequently than others methods; they found that 85 percent used quantitative methods as reported in professional journals. In the applied disciplines of education, health, and medical sciences, such as nursing, they found that 42 percent of the articles published utilized quantitative methods. Alternatively, it was found that 24 percent used mixed methods, and 34 percent used qualitative methods solely. The researchers concluded that the applied social and behavioral sciences such as education and nursing used mixed methods and qualitative methods much more frequently than the pure social and behavioral sciences (sociology and psychology). As was mentioned previously, there has been increasing use of mixed methods and qualitative methods over the past 30 years, but there remain differences and acceptance in use by disciplines.

TRIANGULATION

Triangulation in mixed method research is defined in terms of the combined use of methods to investigate and understand the same phenomena (Jick, 2008). Creswell (2012) described the term *triangulation* as originating from the naval practice of using multiple reference points to locate a specific point. Essentially, a researcher uses multiple methods to focus on particular phenomena or events. There are several approaches to triangulation, such as scaling, reliability, and convergent validation (Jick, 2008). Scaling is accomplished with the conversion of qualitative data into scaling outcomes or quantitative data. There needs to be some sort of approach for converting qualitative data into quantitative data. The next type of triangulation is reliability. Reliability involves the use of similar methods of data collection, or a within-methods approach, such as multiple reviewers interpreting the same data (Jick, 2008). In this approach, the researcher may use interview methods for both quantitative and qualitative methods. The quantitative approach would employ the use of an interview with well-defined questions and responses, and the qualitative approach may use a more open-ended interview. The last triangulation method is convergent validity (Jick, 2008). This approach involves the use of different but complementary methods of data collection across methods, for example, qualitative and quantitative. For example, a researcher may use a survey to collect data about marital satisfaction and combine the results with an interview.

MIXED RESEARCH MODELS

It has been noted there are approximately 40 types of mixed methods research designs that have been used and reported in the research literature (Ivankova, Creswell, & Stick, 2006). However, there are six primary designs that are used most often. The six variations of mixed models that have been identified are convergent parallel, explanatory sequential, exploratory sequential, embedded, transformative, and multiphase designs (Creswell, 2012). Creswell described the purpose of convergent parallel design as "to simultaneously collect both quantitative and qualitative data, merge the data and use the results to understand the problem" (p. 540). This is probably the design most think of when considering a mixed methods design, equally and simultaneously combining methods. Creswell suggested that this design essentially involves combining both methods, which moderates the weaknesses. The process of data collection is accomplished through separate data collection (separating the qualitative and quantitative methods), and once this is accomplished, the researcher compares the results from both sources. Consequently, the researcher converges the data after the separate collection (parallel) method into one report or analysis.

Creswell (2012) suggested a second type of mixed method design, explanatory sequential, which is characterized by initially using quantitative methods followed by collecting data with qualitative methods. The intention is to use the qualitative methods to further explain in much more depth findings from the initial quantitative results. Creswell described the reasoning behind using this approach and stated, "The rationale for this approach is that the quantitative data and results provide a general picture of the research problem, more analysis, specifically through qualitative data collected" (p. 942). Use of this design provides the researcher with an opportunity to explore in greater detail typical cases found from the quantitative results, but the researcher needs to select what to address with the qualitative methods.

The next type of mixed method design is the exploratory sequential approach (Creswell, 2012). This design is characterized by first collecting data using a qualitative method. The second step is based on the qualitative data collected, and the researcher attempts "to explain the relationships found in the qualitative data" (Creswell, p. 543). The idea is to start by understanding in detail a particular phenomenon (gathering information in depth) and then seeking to discover whether the data is characteristic of a large sample or population through quantitative data collection. A strength of this approach, according to Creswell, is that the researcher does not need to predetermine and limit the focus of the study by starting with the qualitative approach, for example, keeping it open-ended. A limitation is that is a design that may take considerable time and effort (Creswell, 2012).

A fourth approach, according to Creswell (2012), is the embedded design. Creswell described the purpose of this design as "to collect quantitative and qualitative data simultaneously or sequentially, but to have one form of data to play a supportive role to the other form of data" (p. 544). In essence, the researcher collects data using both qualitative and quantitative methods and analyzes the results separately. He or she then determines which data to use as the primary or a major source and which to use as supporting data. He or she uses the supportive data to further explain the findings of the primary data collection methods. An example may be study where the researcher implements a new teaching method of math for fifth-grade students, and the data collected may be their scores on standardized tests, quantitative data. Simultaneously, the researcher collects qualitative data on students' personal reactions to the new teaching intervention. The researcher then determines to use the qualitative data, for example, interviews with the students, to explore in more depth the reactions of the students. The strength of this design is that it combines both qualitative and quantitative methods and tailors the study to the research questions addressed. The difficulty with this design is how to carefully integrate the data because each approach produces different information, that is, qualitative and quantitative data.

A fifth mixed methods approach is the transformative design (Creswell, 2012). Creswell noted that, in this design, the researcher employs one of the four previous designs (convergent, explanatory, exploratory, or embedded) combined with interpreting and setting up the study from a marginalized group perspective. The typical marginalized group perspectives include, for example, feminist, racial, ethnic, disability, and so on. Consequently, the researcher interprets and collects the data, both qualitative and quantitative, from a particular lens (an identified marginalized group) determined before collecting began. Creswell noted that the use of this approach is relatively new, and the strengths and limitations are not yet clear.

The last mixed methods approach is the multiphase model (Creswell, 2012). The process of the multiphase model is focused on a researcher studying a complex issue and using phases to gather and collect data. In essence, the purpose is to study a series of research questions that are theoretically built on each other. The phases are linked to the sequence of questions that are to be answered. The various phases may involve the use of any of the four major categories of mixed methods (convergent, explanatory, exploratory, or embedded). Typically, this approach is accomplished with a team of researchers because of the complexity involved and the various phases employed in the research process. An example of how a multiphase mixed method approach could be employed may be a study on school shootings (e.g., Columbine or Newtown) and the identification of a number of research questions focused on issues such as the mental health system, public policies such as gun control, influence of violent video games, and so on. The various phases may include studying student, family, and community reactions to the shootings. The complexity of this issue may be best suited through employment of a multiphase mixed method design.

RESEARCH STUDY EXAMPLES OF MIXED METHODS

There has been a significant increase in the number of published research articles using mixed methods research over the past 15 years (Alise, & Teddlie, 2010; Castro & Coe, 2007; Kartalova-O'Doherty & Doherty, 2008; Messersmith, Garrett, Davis-Kean, Malanchuk, & Eccles, 2008; Nicholson, Knapp, & Gardner, 2011; Strasser, Binswanger, Cerny, & Kesselring, 2007). Strasser and colleagues (2007) conducted a study to understand the effects of eating related distress (ERD) for males with cancer and the effects on their partners. The researchers described their design thusly: "Due to the paucity of research relating to concrete elements of ERD, we selected an approach using qualitative methodology supported by related quantitative data" (p. 130). The researchers used a concurrent nested design. Data were collected simultaneously, but the quantitative data were collected to support the qualitative methods.

Castro and Coe (2007) conducted a study with the intent of exploring beliefs and attitudes among rural women in regard to the use of alcohol during pregnancy. They were particularly interested in understanding how traditions, family, and rural lifestyle impacted the use of alcohol during pregnancy. The researchers employed a mixed methods research design. The researchers described their concurrent triangulation design:

> Figure 1 presents a paradigm for an integrative mixed-methods approach to such research. This integrative process begins with conceptualizing information as research evidence, which can take the form of verbal text narrative evidence

(qualitative) or numeric data evidence (quantitative). Based on theory, a core construct (e.g. traditionalism) can be featured as a central concept examined under each of six stages within a parallel process that facilitates data conversions (e.g. axial coding) to encode thematic categories into numeric thematic variables.

The greater the qualitative–quantitative parallelism in the study design and its implementation, the easier it is to compare and contrast textual and numeric forms of evidence in an integrative manner. (p. 270)

The researchers give a good example of a concurrent triangulation design with a focus on a parallel process of data collection with equal emphasis given to each method.

Nicholson, Knapp, and Gardner (2011) conducted a study using a mixed methods design. They described their study as follows: "This explanatory study combined four concurrent usability methods (user testing, think aloud protocol, observation and tracking the participant's online actions), with a sequential interview to examine five websites" (p. 25). The focus of the research was on evaluating the usability of Web sites designed to provide information about medicines. The researchers collected quantitative data in a first phase, for example, through observations and tracking online activities. The second phase of the study involved interviews with those using Web sites focused on providing information about medicines.

Another study that utilized mixed methods was conducted by Barclay-Goddard, Ripat, and Mayo (2012) that focused on developing a model of participation by poststroke patients. The researchers described their study methods as "an explanatory sequential mixed-methods design" (p. 417). The initial step in the study involved the use of quantitative data collection, specifically through observational methods. More than 400 participants were studied, and specific stroke symptoms were recorded for the quantitative data collection. Focus groups were used to collect the qualitative data. They also used photo–voice methods in collecting the qualitative data. The focus groups discussed participation poststroke.

SUMMARY

The development of the mixed methods research paradigm has provided a bridge between qualitative and quantitative research methods. The two traditions have had significant differences over the past 100 years. Recent efforts to develop systematic mixed methods designs have led to more integration of the approaches and potentially better research outcomes and utility using the strengths of each paradigm and tradition.

8

SINGLE-CASE AND SINGLE-SUBJECT RESEARCH DESIGNS

Single-case and single-subject research is a specific methodology that differs from the other approaches we have discussed to this point, that is, quantitative between-group differences and qualitative research (Barlow, Nock, & Hersen, 2009; Kazdin, 2011). Also, as has been noted, there is no one best research approach—quantitative between group, qualitative, or single subject—but potentially a best method of answering specific research questions. Kazdin suggested that single-subject research is best suited to applied research. He suggested the goal of applied research is "to develop, treat, educate, change, help or have impact in some immediate way" (p. 3). Based on being an applied approach, single-subject research methods are appropriate to use in counseling, education, psychology, social science, rehabilitation, and medicine (Kazdin, 2011). Wendt and Miller (2012) suggested that a review of professional literature shows that single-subject designs have been used with "individuals with autism spectrum and other developmental disorders, behavior disorders, communication disorders, learning disabilities, mental health disorders, and physical impairments" (p. 236).

GUIDELINES AND PROCEDURES IN SINGLE-SUBJECT DESIGN

The guidelines and procedures in single-subject research are slightly different from other quantitative research approaches (Barlow et al., 2009). The first step is selection and identification of the target behavior. Key in this identification is selection of the goal and outcome desired. Typically, the outcome or goal is written or expressed in terms of behavioral outcomes (Barlow et al., 2009). Often in applied disciplines such as counseling and education, there is an interest in changing specific problematic behaviors, for example, aggressive behaviors such as hitting or depressive symptoms such as behavioral lethargy or poor appetite. Consequently, it is generally not too difficult to identify the target or outcome. The most important issue is to state the outcome concretely and in behavioral terms so that the researcher and professionals involved in the intervention can clearly determine when the goal or outcome is achieved. There are instances in single-subject research where the goal or outcome is not observable behavior but may involve cognitive outcomes such as reduction in obsessive thoughts. One can still identify clear outcomes and goals with efforts to change cognitions including attitudes and beliefs.

A second step is the clarification of the baseline and measurement. Barlow and colleagues (2009) stated that there are two purposes of establishing a baseline in single-subject research: descriptive and predictive. The baseline provides a clear description of the condition of the target behavior. Second, the baseline can be used to predict future behavior unless something is done to change it, for example, the introduction of an intervention. It is important that the baseline demonstrate stability (Barlow et al., 2009). If the baseline is not stable, it is difficult to move forward with introduction of the intervention because any change is not easily identified. Figure 8.1 shows a stable target behavior. Barlow and colleagues suggested that a cardinal rule in single-subject research is to focus on one variable to change at a time before moving on to the next behavior. The primary reason for focusing on one variable is to avoid confusion over whether the intervention changed the targeted behavior versus how the behavior interacted with other behaviors that might be targets.

Analyzing the data includes both similar and different methods from traditional quantitative research. Methods of identifying trends such as charts are key methods of displaying study results. Additionally, inferential statistics such as t-tests may be used in single-subject research.

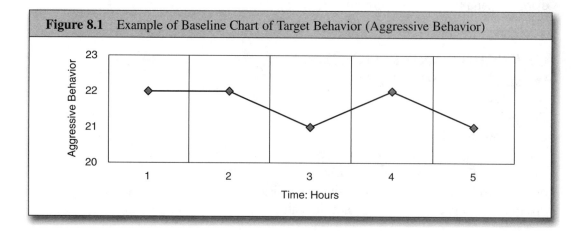

Figure 8.1 Example of Baseline Chart of Target Behavior (Aggressive Behavior)

RESEARCH DESIGNS IN SINGLE-CASE AND SINGLE-SUBJECT RESEARCH

A number of different single-case and single-subject research designs have been proposed (Barlow et al., 2009; Kazdin, 2011). I want to discuss the AB design, the ABA design, the ABAB design, and the multiple baseline design used in single-case and single-subject research. Also, there are examples illustrating all four types of design. Prior to beginning a single-subject study, there is a need to identify the target behavior to observe or change. Clearly defining the target behavior is essential. For example, target behaviors may include observable behaviors (e.g., aggressive behaviors, prosocial behaviors), attitudes of participants (e.g., self-efficacy beliefs, thoughts about perfection), or cognitive thoughts (e.g., self-defeating thoughts, ruminations).

The most basic single-subject design is the AB design. This design starts with a baseline A, which is then followed by an intervention B (see Figure 8.2). Storlie (2012) provided an example of an AB single-subject research design. The purpose of the study was to determine if using a presleep self-suggestion would enhance dream recall. The researcher presented the methodology and described the baseline phase as follows: "During phase A of this experiment, baseline data was collected according to the above instructions over 11 consecutive days" (p. 149). The researcher subsequently described the intervention phase this way: "On day 12, phase B was initiated and the invention was employed for an additional 11 consecutive day" (p. 149). It was reported that there was no increase in dream recall as a consequence of the intervention, that is, presleep self-suggestion.

Another basic single-subject design is the ABA design. This design begins with a period of baseline A, followed by an intervention B, which is then followed by a return to baseline A. All assessment phases, baseline or intervention, in single-subject research involve multiple or continuous assessments. For example, an initial baseline may involve continuous assessment and include four or more observations of the targeted behavior (see Figure 8.3). Hall, Verheyden, and Ashburn (2011) provide an example of an ABA single-subject research design. The study involved determining the impact of yoga on an individual with Parkinson's disease. They described their study design as follows: "A single subject ABA design was used. The participant entered a baseline, phase A, where measurements were taken but no intervention given. The yoga intervention was introduced during phase B, over an 8-week period, during which measurements were taken before the start of the intervention, at week 5 of the 8-week programme and at the end of the 8-week yoga programme. A further 5-week control phase (A) was then applied to observe any changes when the intervention was withdrawn" (p. 1484). The intervention was 60-minute yoga sessions with a trained instructor. One of the dependent

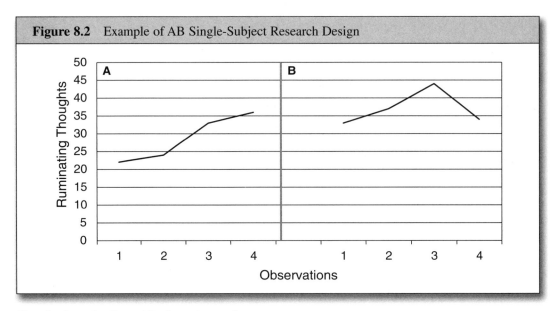

Figure 8.2 Example of AB Single-Subject Research Design

Note: A refers to baseline and B refers to intervention.

variables or outcome measures was range of movement. Range of movement was determined for hip flexion and extension, ankle plantar flexion, and dorsiflexion. All range of motion was calculated with a handheld goniometer. Other dependent measures were: a measure of activity limitations and a disease severity scale. All measures were administered at each point in the baseline and intervention phases. Results from the study are in part reported through figures showing changes in the target behavior over the various phases, that is, baselines and interventions. Figures and charts are typical to use in reporting single-subject designs along with other statistical calculations.

Another basic design is the ABAB design (see Figure 8.4). The primary format for this design is the introduction of a clear baseline setting or environment followed by introduction of the intervention or independent variable, ABAB. The A refers to baseline assessment, and the B refers to the intervention. Kazdin (2011) noted that a key component of this design is a continuous assessment over a period of time. It does not involve a one-time assessment but frequently multiple assessments during the baseline period. The intention is to obtain a clear understanding of the baseline. Most importantly, the researcher is attempting to identify a pattern of the target behaviors. It is typical to start a single-case or single-subject study with this design through an initial observation that may take place over a period of time, for example, several days or even weeks. Kazdin proposed that data from the baseline be used to predict future behavior, and the intent is to find stability in making such a prediction; the idea is that any change in the future from baseline is a consequence of an intervention. One looks for a baseline to remain relatively constant over time, whereas an introduction of an intervention should result in the behavior going up or down after introduction of the intervention.

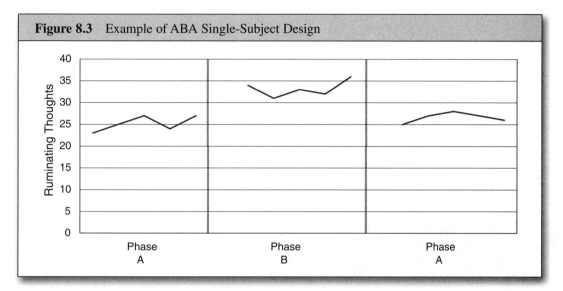

Figure 8.3 Example of ABA Single-Subject Design

Note: A refers to baseline and B refers to intervention.

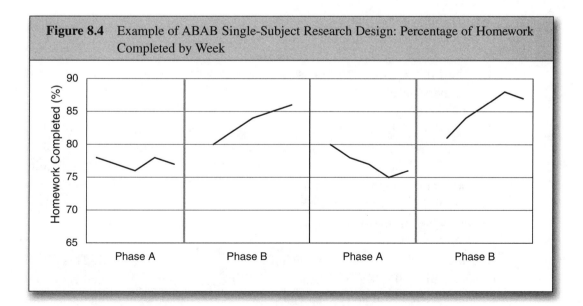

Figure 8.4 Example of ABAB Single-Subject Research Design: Percentage of Homework Completed by Week

Bernard, Cohen, and Moffett (2009) conducted a study using a single-subject ABAB design. They focused their research on increasing exercise compliance using a token economy with children who have cystic fibrosis. They had three children who served as participants. All three children were school age, had medically recommended exercise, and had not been compliant with the exercise recommendations. The researchers described the research design as follows: "The single-subject reversal (withdrawal) design, specifically the ABAB design, was used in this study" (p. 356). There were several outcome measures used: One measure was a self-report measure of perceived exertion during exercise; minutes of exercise were recorded day by parents and the child–participant; and a pedometer verified the exercise recorded each day. The phases of the research design were reported. Phase one, baseline one, is described as such: "The baseline of the study began with an initial visit to the cystic fibrosis center. The experimenter met with the child and parent(s) to explain the procedures of the study and obtain informed consent and child assent. They were given brief definitions of the type of exercise targeted in this study and explanations on how to complete the exercise diaries and properly use the pedometer" (p. 357). The intervention phase, B, involved two parts: training in exercise activities and introduction of a token reinforcement upon completion of exercise. The phase was described by the researchers as follows:

> The first hour of the first session consisted of training the parent(s) to set up a token economy to reinforce the child's exercise behavior. The target exercise amount was approximately four times per week for 20 minutes. Both the child and parent(s) participated in the session. The token economy was designed so that the child earned a small, immediate reward (e.g. special snack, small amount of money) each time the child exercised." (p. 357)

The third phase, A (return to baseline), was described as a reversal phase, and the researchers stated,

> The experimenter went to the participants' homes and removed the token economy and the information about problems associated with the token economies. A rationale for the return to baseline was provided. Specifically, parents were told that it is important to see if the token economy was necessary for the child to continue exercising. The parents were instructed to return to their typical behavior before the token economy was introduced. (p. 358)

The last phase of the research design was a return to treatment, B. This phase was described by the researchers as such: "During this phase the token economy materials were returned and the parent(s) were instructed to begin using the system again" (p. 358). The researchers also completed a follow-up, both after one-month and after three-months. The researchers did find that the token economy effectively increased exercise.

Kazdin (2011) described a third single-subject design, a multiple baseline design. In a multiple baseline design, there are still sequence of baselines and interventions. The primary difference is in the use of different baselines, different behaviors, different settings, or different individuals. The idea is to determine if the intervention is consistent across baselines and different behaviors, individuals, or settings. Using only one baseline raises questions about whether there are reinforcers or circumstances that are unique to one behavior or individual and which may not generalize to other circumstances (baselines). Similar to other single-subject designs, the dependent variable is measured and compared from baseline to intervention. One important consideration, according to Kazdin, is the length of time between administering one behavior and introduction of a second behavior or subsequent behaviors. He suggested that one criterion to determine the time between introducing different behaviors is a decision about stability in the behavior during a phase of the study; once stability is achieved, move to the next behavior. An important consideration when using individuals as the multiple baseline is introducing the intervention sequentially. A researcher starts one participant, and once the behavior is established, he or she proceeds to the next participant. All other participants continue with the baseline during the introduction of each individual to the intervention (see Figure 8.5). A third use of multiple baselines is across settings. Kazdin proposed that use of settings with multiple baselines begins with the measurement of each situation during baseline. Introduction of the intervention sequentially to each setting is an important step in this process.

Kang and Oh (2012) provide an example of using a multiple baseline single-subject design. The focus of the study was treatment of stroke patients using a body-tilt exercise and mental practice. The researchers used three participants who were diagnosed with poststroke hemiparesis (weakness on one side of the body). The research design is described as follows:

A single-subject research design (i.e. an alternating design with multiple baselines across individuals) was used to investigate the effects of mental practice incorporated into the whole-body tilt exercise. In general, a multiple baseline experimental design has different numbers of baseline sessions among subjects in order to have different treatment start times and compares the therapeutic effects between experimental conditions (i.e. with or without mental measurement). Subject 1, 2 and 3 began treatment in their 5th, 8th and 11th sessions respectively. (p. 199)

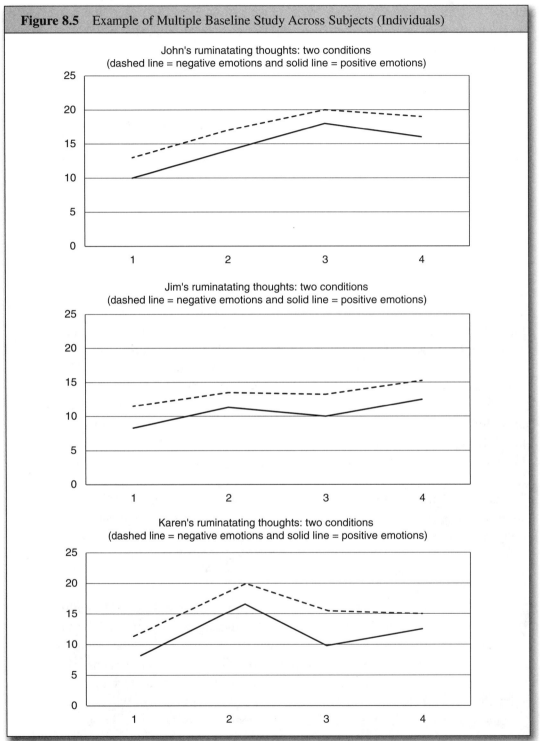

Figure 8.5   Example of Multiple Baseline Study Across Subjects (Individuals)

The dependent variables were balance and hemispatial neglect (awareness and ability to perceive one side of one's body). Participants were requested to practice a balance exercise with and without mental practice, which was the independent variable. All three participants showed changes in the dependent variables balance and hemispatial neglect.

Another type of single-subject design is the alternating treatment designs or the multiple treatment designs. When researchers introduce multiple treatments, it becomes more difficult to know which intervention made the impact, that is, multiple treatment interference (Barlow et al., 2009; Barlow & Hayes, 1979). Barlow and colleagues (2009) described alternating treatments involving the introduction of two or more interventions, typically with the same participants. A key aspect of this design is to alternate the introduction of treatments so that the researcher can determine the effects of sequencing the interventions. An example of single-subject design may be denoted as A B_1 B_2 A A B_1 A B_2 A (the subscripts with the intervention denote different interventions).

Maas, Butalla, and Farinella (2012) conducted a study that employed a single-subject alternating treatment design. The purpose of the study involved feedback frequency in the treatment of children with apraxia of speech, that is, difficulty with the connection of cognitive thoughts to motor production of speech. Maas and colleagues (2012) described the purpose of their study as follows: "The present study was to test these opposing predictions by comparing the effects of high- and low-frequency feedback on speech motor learning in four children with CAS (Childhood Apraxia of Speech)" (p. 241). Four children served as participants in this study, children diagnosed with CAS. The research design was described as such:

> We used an alternating treatments design with multiple baselines across behaviors over two phases. The independent variable was the amount of feedback, with two conditions: high-frequency feedback (HFF; feedback on all trials) and low-frequency feedback (LFF; feedback on 60% of trails). Both conditions were administered every treatment session, with order of conditions counterbalanced across sessions. . . . An initial baseline period with a minimum of three probe sessions over 2 weeks was implemented before any treatment. To assess retention, a 2-week maintenance period followed each treatment phase. A final probe was administered 1 month after the last treatment session. Thus, the total study duration from baseline to follow-up was 16 weeks. (p. 245)

The researchers reported varying results; for example, some children showed improvements, and some did not. The benefit of using a single-subject alternating design is that the researcher can review the impact of each treatment and compare it to the baseline, therefore determining the impact of different interventions with the same participants.

DATA INTERPRETATION IN SINGLE-CASE AND SINGLE-SUBJECT RESEARCH

As with other methods of research, single-subject research seeks to determine whether any changes are a consequence of the intervention or a consequence of chance (Kazdin, 2011). Kazdin (2011) noted that visual inspection of the data, typically achieved through review of charts and figures, is a common method of data analysis in single-subject research. A problem with visual inspection concerns the reliability of interpretation. Inferential statistics are based on reducing the possibility of Type I error (rejecting the null hypothesis when it should not be rejected), and the same level of scrutiny is not available with visual inspection. Visual inspection of graphs is not difficult when there are readily identifiable changes; however, if the changes are not as distinct from baseline through intervention, any conclusions become tenuous and unreliable. Kazdin noted that those using single-subject research have suggested using and reporting only large, easily identifiable changes, but in reality, this is not the outcome in a large amount of single-subject research.

Another method of analyzing single-subject research data is through formal statistical analysis. Recall the major assumptions of inferential statistics, which include independence of scores and normality of data. Both of these assumptions raise questions about statistical analyses with single-subject research. For example, Barlow and colleagues (2009) discussed the relevance of autocorrelation in single-subject research. They noted the use of repeated measurement results in similarity of scores over time simply because of the dependence between observations, what is termed *autocorrelations*. A key characteristic of autocorrelations is that scores similar in time are more closely related than those found at a distance.

Barlow and colleagues (2009) noted that some have used *t*-tests and *F* tests in analyzing single-subject designs. However, they noted that such approaches create significant problems with violations of assumptions such as independence and normality. The use of an interrupted time series analysis (ITSA) is a more commonly accepted statistical method (Barlow et al., 2009). Barlow and colleagues noted that ITSA statistically involves an attempt to analyze change in the slope and level of the dependent variable over time. A determination can be made about the changes in slope and level related to the independent variable. The method attempts to control for autocorrelations and generally involves a number of observations over time, sometimes recommended to be more than 50 observations. A related statistical approach is the autoregressive integrated moving average (ARIMA) model. It involves a three-stage process designed to remove autocorrelations.

EVALUATION CRITERIA FOR SINGLE-CASE AND SINGLE-SUBJECT RESEARCH

Kazdin (2011) noted that single-subject research designs have been criticized because they do not allow for comparison between subjects, a key element of traditional research. Wendt and Miller (2012) discussed a method for evaluating the quality of single-subject research designs, an effort to address questions of the scientific merit of single-subject research designs and how the research can be interpreted in regards to evidence-based practice. Wendt and Miller discussed a detailed analysis of various elements of the methods section of a single-subject study such as: description of the participants (so the study can be replicated), methods of selection of the sample, and operationalization of the dependent variable. All of these elements are discussed later in this text and are important in determining the efficacy of research that you read and want to apply in practice. The one area that is different and unique to single-subject research is the use of a baseline. Recall one of the major limitations of single-subject research is the lack of between-group comparison, that is, the opportunity to compare any impact of an independent variable on two or more independent groups of individuals.

Wendt and Miller (2012) proposed several questions to address when determining the quality of a single-subject research study and address the limitation expressed, that is, not having a between-subjects comparison. One question concerns whether the baseline provides for repeated measurement of the dependent variable. The use of multiple measurements at baseline provides a comparison within subjects, for example, within the participants where they become their own control. A second question proposed by Wendt and Miller states whether the baseline provides information about a pattern of performance so that one can determine the impact of the independent variable. If there is no pattern at baseline, it is difficult to make conclusions about the effect of the independent variable when it is introduced.

SUMMARY

Single-case and single-subject research involves a methodology that is somewhat different from quantitative between-group differences and qualitative research. The comparison in single-subject research is more focused on within-subject differences. Single-subject research is best suited to an applied research approach, for example, as with counseling and education (Kazdin, 2011).The goal of applied research may include treatment, educating, changing, or helping. Single-subject designs have been used with a range of individual and problems, for example, behavioral disorders, communication problems, mental health issues, and so on (Wendt & Miller, 2012). There is a slightly different approach to single-subject research, starting with an emphasis on assessment and the use of specific research designs. Typical research designs include AB, ABA, ABAB, and multiple baseline designs. Finally, there are questions that are helpful to consider in determining the quality of single-subject research, such as the number of times the dependent variable is measured, which is used for comparison within subjects.

9

EVIDENCE-BASED RESEARCH METHODS

Counseling and education are both practitioner based and involve professional preparation. Key in the preparation of the counseling and educational professional is exposure to and training in research, as has been discussed in this book. Recently, there has been a greater emphasis on linking practice and outcomes. Political and social expectations have changed, and there is pressure for both counseling and educational institutions to show how effective their activities are (Slocum et al., 2012). In fact, the No Child Left Behind Act (NCLB) requires educational professionals to utilize research-based evidence in their practice (Odom, Brantlinger, Gersten, et al., 2005). Evidence-based practice is an attempt to address the concern over demonstrating effectiveness.

Evidence-based practice originated within medicine and health care (Sackett, Straus, Richardson, Rosenberg, & Haynes, 2000). It has expanded to include counseling, psychology, business, and education (American Psychological Association Presidential Task Force on Evidence-Based Practice, 2006; Pring & Thomas, 2004; Rousseau & McCarthy, 2007; Slocum et al., 2012). The benefits and arguments of evidence-based practice have been identified (Kettlewell, 2004). Kettlewell (2004) suggested that one benefit is that "evidence-based treatments (EBT) provide guidance to better serve our patients or clients" (p. 190). He points out that most people expect their health care professionals to provide the best known treatment. A second argument for using evidence-based treatments/evidence-based practice (EBT/EBP), according to Kettlewell (2004), is as follows: "Using the scientific approach to evaluate treatment is the best way to advance our knowledge so that we can provide even better care in the future" (p. 190). Developing a fund of information about best practices enhances the status of the field. Another rationale for using EBT/EBP cited by Kettlewell (2004) is that "we need to use wisely the limited resources for mental health services" (p. 190). Currently, society and politicians want evidence about outcomes in making funding decisions. An evidence-based practice approach can provide opportunity to educate these constituencies about the effectiveness of the practices. A fourth argument presented by Kettlewell (2004) for using EBT/EBP is as follows: "We have treatments that work and most practitioners do not use them" (p. 190). Whether in education or counseling, practitioners have a tendency not to use the research literature to guide their practice but make decisions based upon personal beliefs and values. Providing clarity about the effectiveness of practice can be passed along to improve outcomes. A final argument for using EBT/EBP is founded on the question: "Is there a better alternative than to use science to guide practice?" (p. 191). Our society values science and the benefits that science has provided, and this provides credibility to EBT/EBP. The alternative is shifting the focus to making education and counseling an art or based upon one's personal experience. This may be similar to thinking about training in trades, where one simply learns a trade through observing and working with a master practitioner. Certainly, this had its benefits, but the limitations are that education and counseling are much more complex than learning a trade and therefore require more objectivity. The profession of education has developed enough evidence to develop a comprehensive source for accessing relevant information. One major source for evidence-based research in education is the What Works Clearinghouse (2011; http://ies.ed.gov/ncee/wwc/). It is a good source for identifying relevant evidence-based practice.

DEFINITIONS OF EVIDENCE-BASED PRACTICE

Several different definitions of evidence-based practice have been proposed (American Psychological Association Presidential Task Force on Evidence-Based Practice, 2006; Hunsley, 2007; Whaley & David, 2007). As previously mentioned, evidence-based practice originated in medicine. One of the earliest definitions is from medicine. Mayer (2004) defined evidence-based practice as "the conscientious, explicit, and judicious use of the best evidence in making decisions about the care of individual patients" (p. 9). The American Psychological Association Presidential Task Force on Evidence-Based Practice (2006) concluded evidence-based practice is "the integration of the best available research with clinical expertise in the context of patient characteristics, culture, and preferences" (p. 273). Slocum and colleagues (2012) summarized a definition of evidence-based practice as using the best available evidence, the use of professional judgment, and last, consideration of the client (children, parents, and clients) and context where the intervention is applied. Horner and Kratochwill (2012) suggested that evidence-based practice should consider the following components: (1) an operational definition of the procedure, (2) clarification of the competency of those providing the intervention, (3) identification of the situation and context where the intervention is implemented, (4) identification of the population for which the intervention is used, and (5) identification of the expected outcomes as a consequence of the intervention. Common among these definitions are statements about the best available research and thoughtfulness in selecting the practices to be used. The interesting point about the use of evidence-based practice is the perspective that, in medicine, previously, a physician would consult a senior, more experienced physician for answers to problems. The evidence-based approach does not exclude the use of this approach but encourages the use of more scientific evidence in decision making. As Slocum and colleagues suggested, the use of evidence-based practice is more than attempting to use the best evidence but does require good professional judgment, particularly with an understanding of one's client (client or student) with a particular context. Professional judgment may be enhanced through discussion with peers and through supervision. Additionally, consultation with peers and supervisors may enhance an understanding of the context and how and when to use the intervention.

STANDARDS AND STEPS IN EVIDENCE-BASED PRACTICE

Mayer (2004) suggested six steps in the evidence-based practice approach. Step one is the development of a question that needs to be answered. Part of the issue with this question is the identification of the outcome desired. A second step is the review of the professional literature that is relevant and will give the professional the best information available. The third step is the identification of a study that most closely resembles the issue to be addressed and a review of the outcomes. The fourth step is an analysis and critique of the study to determine how useful it is. Step five is to determine how the study findings can be applied to the current situation. The last step is to evaluate the results of what was used in practice—was it successful? What Works Clearinghouse (2011) suggests standards of evidence-based practice. It stated, "Only well-designed and well-implemented randomized controlled trials (RCTs) are considered strong evidence, while quasi-experimental designs (QEDs) with equating may only meet standards with reservations" (p. 11). What is important in these criteria is the conclusion that strong evidence should be based on true experimental designs that are based upon solid scientific methods.

PRINCIPLES OF EVIDENCE-BASED PRACTICE

Rousseau and McCarthy (2007) proposed several principles in the use of evidence-based practice. The first principle is this: "Focus on principles where the science is clear" (p. 85). What are the basic principles of the discipline? For example, one set of basic principles in counseling involves findings about human development. A second principle stated by Rousseau and McCarthy (2007) is as follows: "Develop decision awareness in professional practice" (p. 87). The idea here is to focus awareness and be open to critiquing how one practices professionally. It is suggested that there is a sharing among colleagues in evaluating and critiquing practices (Rousseau & McCarthy, 2007). A third principle is the diagnosis of underlying factors, which are related to practice decisions (Rousseau & McCarthy, 2007). The basic premise here is that the practitioner develops questions designed to diagnose the problem or identify the problem to be addressed with evidence-based practice. One needs to understand that there is an issue with how students, clients, and others are functioning and determine whether something can be done to improve their functioning in the classroom (education) or in their lives (counseling). The next principle concerns the practitioner's understanding the context of the situation and adapting the knowledge to the setting (Rousseau & McCarthy, 2007). This may include developing an awareness of how to adapt the scientific knowledge to the context or situation based upon cultural or environmental issues. The fifth principle states that there should be evidence-based practice decision supports (Rousseau & McCarthy, 2007). For example, in schools, it may make sense to discuss evidence-based practices among teaching faculty on a regular basis. In counseling settings, it may be beneficial to regularly discuss evidence-based practices among colleagues and how they have been tried in particular settings. The last principle is the ongoing acquisition of new information and ways to stay current in evidence-based practices (Rousseau & McCarthy, 2007). This may involve attending conferences on a regular basis and subscribing to professional journals.

CRITICISMS OF EVIDENCE-BASED PRACTICE

There has not been total acceptance of evidence-based practice, and there have been some critiques of the approach (Wampold, Goodheart, & Levant, 2007). Wampold and colleagues (2007) suggested caution in using and interpreting evidence-based practice information. The caution centers on the view that not enough is known to suggest that there is evidence that can be used to guide practice. The authors point out that one may miss the importance of the subjective experience of counseling or therapy. Counseling has been called an art, and losing subjectivity of the experience may interfere with this aspect of the process (Nystul, 1999). Wampold and colleagues (2007) pointed out that the evidence in psychology and counseling is not unambiguous: "Evidence is not data, nor is it truth" (p. 616). Several important questions arise with these criticisms. One question is this: How much of the subjective aspect of counseling or education should be part of the practice? Professions have been identified and defined in terms of having a basis of knowledge (Weikel & Palmo, 1996). Despite the practices of counseling and education having a subjective component, both fields need to substantiate their practices on a basis of knowledge and specifically a research basis. Another question is this: What level or amount of evidence is needed to use evidence-based research in practice? What has been suggested is to select the best available evidence and use it but, most important, evaluate the impact or effect.

EXAMPLES OF EVIDENCE-BASED PRACTICE

There have been a number of writings and summaries of evidence-based practice focusing on specific issues in counseling and education (Gowers, 2006; Kaiser, 2007; Stenhoff & Lignugaris-Kraft, 2007). Gowers (2006) provides evidence-based practice information for counseling adolescents with eating disorders using cognitive behavioral therapy. It is interesting to note that Gowers (2006) states that the research evidence for the treatment of bulimia nervosa using cognitive behavioral therapy is relatively good, and it is considered to be the gold standard treatment for this condition. However, he notes that the research evidence for using cognitive behavioral therapy with anorexia nervosa is less clear, and there needs to be further research before this can be considered the gold standard. What this means for practitioners using evidence-based practice is that there needs to be a careful investigation into what methods work in what situations. This does not mean that one cannot use a particular intervention, particularly if there is no other gold standard available. It is where there is a commonly accepted and well-documented intervention or approach that the educator or counselor should choose the best available one and use it.

Bryan, Stone, and Rudd (2011) reviewed evidence-based practice for means-restriction counseling with suicidal patients. They noted the issue surrounding counseling those who attempt or consider suicide. Certainly, identifying the best practices and founding interventions on evidence-based research is important in addressing this concern and problem. Means-restriction counseling involves working a client's social support system and identifying ways to restrict access to lethal methods of committing suicide. The authors stated in describing evidence-based research, "A large number of studies support the effectiveness of means restriction as a suicide prevention strategy when targeting methods that are highly lethal and common within a population" (p. 340). Additionally, the researchers noted that research supports the use of means-restriction efforts by family members of those considering suicide results in increasing the use of these methods.

Kaiser (2007) reviewed the evidence-based practice for addressing challenging behaviors in early childhood interventions. For example, Kaiser noted that "training parents to implement systematic behavioral interventions is an important example of a strategy in which there is sufficient research for it to be regarded as an evidence-based practice" (p. 116). Despite there being evidence that training parents is supported through research, the actual training of parents and methods to do so are not well developed. She noted that this area of research and evidence needed further study before conclusions could be made about evidence-based practice in training parents.

Stenhoff and Lignugaris-Kraft (2007) provide a review of peer tutoring with students with mild disabilities in secondary schools. They noted that peer tutoring is designed to help students with educational learning through other, more advanced students or peers. Stenhoff and Lignugaris-Kraft reviewed four different types of peer tutoring for effectiveness based on an evidence-based practice approach. These tutoring models included reverse role, heterogeneous, homogeneous, and cross age. Of the four tutoring models, only the heterogeneous approach was supported through evidence-based practice. The other three did not have sufficient research support to include in evidence-based practice at this point. Essentially, what this means is that a practitioner should likely use a heterogeneous tutoring approach rather than any of the other three. Additionally, researchers may continue to gather evidence on the efficacy of the other three methods. Stenhoff and Lignugaris-Kraft provide a good example of how evidence-based practice can be used by practitioners whereby they clearly identify the gold standard of practice in a particular area and demonstrate the criteria for their evaluation.

Spooner, Knight, Browder, and Smith (2012) discussed evidence-based practice for teaching academics to students with severe developmental disabilities. In an effort to identify adequate evidence-based research, Spooner and colleagues reviewed published research over an 8-year period in the professional literature, from 2003 through 2010. They include 18 studies as part of the evidence, studies that met criteria proposed by Horner, Carr, Halle, et al. (2005), which included: clear description of participants and the settings used, clear description of the dependent variable, the use of experimental control, and repeated confirmation over several research studies. The researchers described their findings of evidence-based practice for teaching academics to those with severe developmental disabilities:

Systematic instruction uses principles of behavior analysis in planning and implementing interventions. In systematic instruction, an observable, measurable response, set of responses, or response chain is targeted. In this review, we found that both the use of chained response (task analysis) and a discrete response are evidence-based practices. (p. 384)

For example, once a task analysis is identified, the professional determines a method of systematic prompting for responding and demonstrating academic learning.

Kamps and Abbott (2007) used evidence-based practice to inform decision making on the use of small-group reading instructions for English language learners in elementary grades. First, these researchers identify the specific reading skills that have been found to be essential for learning to read. They further noted that a systematic approach to teaching students how to learn to read is important. According to Kamps and Abbott, evidence-based research also has demonstrated that the instructional environment and the instructional intensity and duration affect learning outcomes. So, how long learning instruction occurs and the frequency of learning instruction impact outcomes or student learning (reading instruction for English language learners).

Baban and Craciun (2007) provided a comprehensive overview of research and evidence-based practice research on changing health-risk behavior. Examples of health-risk behaviors included smoking, sexual behavior, alcohol abuse, eating habits, screening behaviors, and medication adherence. They discussed different approaches to changing health-risk behavior, such as the Health Action Process approach and the Transtheoretical Model of Change approach. The authors provide a table outlining the approaches with various health-risk behaviors and the effectiveness of each, based upon research outcomes. For example, the Transtheoretical Model of Change approach was cited as being effective with smoking, alcohol abuse, and screening behaviors. However, it is not cited as effective with sexual behavior or with medication adherence. There could be several reasons that it was not found to be effective; for example, there may not be enough research to support a conclusion. Baban and Craciun provided an interesting view of the use of evidence-based approach with linking theories and approaches to specific conditions.

SUMMARY

The pressure for education and counseling to be grounded in evidence-based practice has increased with the passage of federal legislation, such as NCLB and societal requirements and expectations for documented effects. This may be considered good news for these professions because it suggests that we are arriving at a point that there is beginning to be adequate research to support the use of certain interventions and strategies. Such an approach encourages more research to build support for particular interventions or activities. Also, the use of evidence-based practice provides the practitioner with information about what does not work in certain circumstances or conditions. The use of evidence-based practice in education (Odom et al., 2005) and counseling (Gowers, 2006) is increasing and provides practitioners with criteria to use when engaging in their professional practices. Increasing high-quality research in education and counseling will continue to give these professionals information needed to be effective and provide the best services possible. Mozdzierz, Peluso, and Lisiecki (2011) provide three guidelines or suggestions for using evidence-based practice information for professionals. One suggestion is there should be caution in applying evidence-based research as a panacea for providing interventions. The standards for determining what is solid evidence is not consistent, and further efforts need to be made to identify clear guidelines. Second, practitioners should use solid clinical judgment in applying evidence-based information and research. Ultimately, the professional practitioner must use his or her own clinical judgment to apply evidence-based research. Third, the professional practitioner, educator, and counselor should consistently evaluate the impact of any evidence-based intervention and make adjustments.

10

ETHICS AND RESEARCH

This chapter involves a discussion of ethics and research. An important question is this: Why study ethics and research? A researcher must be aware of how ethical his or her procedures are in conducting research. There are federal laws that protect human subjects against potentially harmful research practices. However, this book is designed to prepare you to be a thoughtful consumer of research. What difference does it make to consider ethical issues in the articles you read in the professional literature? The answers to these questions are the foci of this chapter.

The purpose of this chapter is threefold: first, to introduce you to ethical guidelines helpful in understanding ethics and research; second, to discuss examples of ethical research violations, and third, more important for you as a practitioner, to provide a method of evaluating the ethics of a research design as ethics apply to your use in actual practice of the information from the research. Therefore, this chapter includes (1) discussion of basic principles that may be used to consider and understand ethics and research, (2) a foundation and set of criteria for evaluating research reported in the literature, with a particular focus on the ethics of the research design as the results apply to using the information in actual practice, and (3) a discussion of examples from the current literature, which illustrate how to use the criteria presented earlier in evaluating research for violations and problems from an ethical perspective for the practitioner in counseling and education.

ETHICAL PRINCIPLES AND GUIDELINES

When one considers ethical issues in research, it is helpful to conceptualize the guidelines available in the form of an inverted triangle (see Figure 10.1). At the top of the inverted triangle are general theories of ethics, and the space represents the number of situations that can be addressed with the theories. Conversely, the space may also represent the amount of ambiguity in decision making because there is not the specific clarity that some of the other guides provide. Next are general principles such as autonomy, nonmaleficence, and so on. These general principles allow for a somewhat clearer interpretation than the general theories but do not allow the same number of situations to be addressed. The third type of guide is the professional ethical code, such as that of the APA or the American Counseling Association (ACA). As we move down the triangle with the codes of ethics, there is an increased clarity in how and when to use the guidelines and a decrease in the number of situations to which they can be applied. Finally, at the bottom of the triangle are laws and federal or state statutes and regulations. These are the most specific and clear-cut guides for ethical decision making, but they apply (generally) to the fewest situations and circumstances.

Starting at the top of the triangle, you can see that two major types of theories have been proposed in ethical decision making: utilitarian and deontological approaches (Beauchamp & Childress, 2001). There are a number of other ethical theories that could be included in ethical decision making (Houser & Thoma, 2012; Houser, Wilczenski, & Ham, 2006). However, this book is not solely focused on ethics, so I will cover these two broad theories (utilitarian and deontological). Beauchamp and Childress (2001) defined utilitarian theories in terms of the end

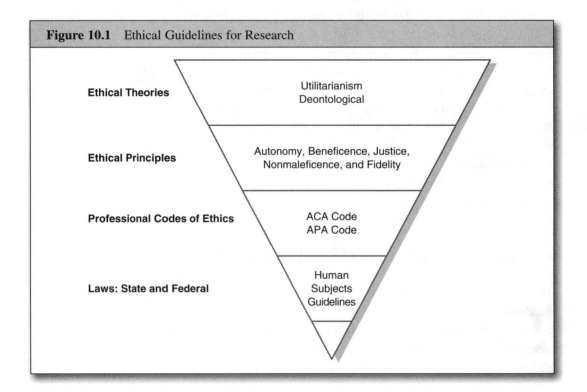

Figure 10.1   Ethical Guidelines for Research

Ethical Theories
Utilitarianism
Deontological

Ethical Principles
Autonomy, Beneficence, Justice,
Nonmaleficence, and Fidelity

Professional Codes of Ethics
ACA Code
APA Code

Laws: State and Federal
Human
Subjects
Guidelines

what is good for most

justifying or legitimizing the means and the promotion of the greatest good for the greatest number of people. Certainly, ethical decision making can be applied to a great number of situations, but how to proceed is not that clear. Beauchamp and Childress defined the deontological approach in terms of decisions about right and wrong. There are rules or principles of right and wrong. For example, one rule within this theory is the Golden Rule (treat others as you would like to be treated) that guides actions (Beauchamp & Childress, 2001). In this theory, the outcome is less important than following the rule or principle.

What is the right or wrong thing to do?

The next level of ethical guidelines is that of general principles. These include autonomy, beneficence, nonmaleficence, justice, and fidelity (Beauchamp & Childress, 2001). Autonomy, according to Beauchamp and Childress (2001), involves the concept of self-rule and self-choice. Self-choice includes full disclosure of information, which makes it possible to make an informed choice. Beneficence refers to doing what is best for another or looking out for another, whereas nonmaleficence is complementary to beneficence and concerns doing no intentional harm. Justice involves the fair distribution of resources. Finally, fidelity refers to keeping one's promise or commitment (Beauchamp & Childress, 2001).

The next level of ethical guidelines is that of professional codes of ethics (American Counseling Association, 2005; American Psychological Association, 2010). The ethical codes for the ACA address the following areas under research: (1) research responsibilities of the counselor, (2) the importance of informed consent, (3) reporting of results, and (4) issues of publication. For example, in obtaining informed consent for research purposes, counselors must use language that is clear and understandable to participants. There are exceptions when deception is required in a study, but deception is used only when no other methods are available. The APA ethical codes address (1) informed consent, (2) communication of risks possible when participating in research, (3) research with special populations, (4) providing participants with results of a study, (5) use of deception, (6) minimizing the invasiveness of data-gathering methods, (7) socially sensitive research, and (8) protection for withdrawing from research.

Finally, there are ethical guides that address specific procedures for the protection of human subjects (Office of Protection From Research Risks [OPRR], 1993). Federal legislation (OPRR, 1993) requires that investigators who are associated with institutions that receive federal funds must submit their studies to an extensive review by peers before the studies can be conducted. The primary focus is on ensuring that adequate protections for research subjects are in place. The peer review is done through a formally established institutional body, the human subjects IRB. Guidelines for reviewing research proposals include requirements for informed consent, an evaluation of risks and benefits, and confidentiality. The IRB must evaluate the risks as being reasonable in relation to anticipated benefits.

ETHICAL RESEARCH VIOLATIONS

Ethical violations or scientific misconduct has been defined in several different ways; there has been disagreement on what constitutes scientific misconduct (Habermann, Broome, Pryor, & Ziner, 2010). The Office of Research Integrity, U.S. Department of Health and Human Services, monitors and sanctions scientists who engage in ethical violations or scientific misconduct. Habermann and colleagues (2010) noted that federal guidelines for defining scientific misconduct as "fabrication, falsification, and plagiarism, as well as other practices that deviate seriously from those commonly accepted within the scientific community" (p. 52). Redman and Merz (2008) reviewed the public records for outcomes and consequences for investigators who were found to have engaged in scientific misconduct. They identified 106 individuals over an 8-year period, 1994 to 2001, that were reported publicly by the Office of Research Integrity. These individuals include those with PhDs or MDs. The scientific misconduct was identified as data falsification or plagiarism. Consequences for those engaging in scientific misconduct were found to be removal from grant funding opportunities and institutional oversight. Finally, some were required to correct scientific papers that included the falsified or plagiarized information.

A random selection of examples of misconduct from the Office of Research Integrity provides insight into how decisions and outcomes are applied. One example reported by the Office of Research Integrity states that a researcher was found to have engaged in research misconduct by falsifying or fabricating data. The data were discovered to be falsified or fabricated in several National Institutes of Health (NIH), National Institute of Child Health and Human Development, or National Institute on Aging grants. A consequence of the findings was a recommendation that all publications resulting from the falsified or fabricated studies be retracted with a notification in each journal. Six publications were identified for retraction. Additionally, the researcher voluntarily agreed to exclude himself from contracting or subcontracting with any federal grant for a period of 3 years.

A second case of misconduct reported by the Office of Research Integrity again involved falsifying data that were included in a grant application and in a publication in a research journal. The intention of the falsification was to show greater significance than was actually found. The consequence for the researcher, who signed a voluntary settlement agreement, included requiring the researcher to be supervised by any institution that receives U.S. Public Health Service (USPHS) grant funding. Additionally, if the researcher submits a grant application, the institution that employs her must include a supervision plan to ensure scientific integrity. One can see from a review of these two examples of scientific misconduct that in fact there are consequences for researchers who engage in such practices.

Another high-profile example of scientific misconduct is found in the research of Anil Potti. Dr. Potti, who was a medical researcher and oncologist at Duke University, was accused of falsifying his credentials, for example, that he was a Rhodes Scholar. Most importantly, statisticians, after a review of his work done in 2007, questioned the reliability of his results (Coombes, Wang, & Baggerly, 2007). An investigation into his research led to stoppage of his studies, and grant funds from the American Cancer Society were returned by Duke University. Additionally, efforts to obtain retractions of journal article publications were put under review.

GUIDELINES FOR EVALUATING THE RESEARCH LITERATURE

As has been shown, there are several approaches and guides for interpreting ethical issues in counseling research, but which methods are most useful for you as a consumer of research? The answer must be based on the focus and purpose you have. Researchers are most concerned with the protection of the human subjects used in their studies; therefore, the federal guidelines and professional codes addressing the protection of human subjects are most relevant. However, consumers of research are interested in the ethics of research that focuses on interpreting results and the implications for those for whom they provide services in the practice of their professions.

Gostin (1991) suggested guidelines to consider when conducting and applying research to populations (population research). He defined population research as "all research and practice, performed on, or which affects groups of people or populations" (p. 192). Gostin linked the application of ethical principles to populations and stated,

> Ethical principles applied to larger groups of people or populations are designed to protect the human dignity, integrity, self determination, confidentiality, rights, and health of populations and the people comprising them. The kinds of social groupings encompassed in this definition include communities, cultures, social orders, and other minorities. (p. 191)

The concern for practitioners providing counseling and educational services is that research results must be interpreted and implemented based on ethical guides that protect the populations we serve. Several of the previous ethical guides are pertinent to understanding and interpreting counseling research. The ethical principle of nonmaleficence states, "Do no harm." *Do no harm* can be interpreted in regard to population research based on the results and conclusions from research studies as to whether the outcomes harm the welfare of the populations studied.

As Gostin (1991) stated, this means protecting the dignity, integrity, and health of the populations. Neither the APA nor the ACA includes ethical codes that specifically address population research ethics. The focus of professional codes has been on the ethical treatment of research participants and not so much on the ethics of population research. A question that consumers of research want to ask in reviewing research is this: What negative implications or harm is possible based on the results from a particular study on the population of interest? Harm may include, as Gostin noted, an effect on the population's dignity, rights, integrity, or self-esteem.

A second ethical consideration in regard to population research can be found in the general ethical principle of beneficence. The question here is this: What are the possible benefits of the research results for the population? Certainly in our professional capacity, we are most concerned with research results that will be useful to those receiving counseling and educational services.

A third ethical guide that is applicable to population research is justice and the fair distribution of research outcomes. A question based on this ethical principle is this: Is the sample and population studied fairly representative of the general population that could benefit from the research results? More specifically, did the researcher or researchers present a reasonably clear argument for studying the population if the research was restricted to a particular group? Certainly, we cannot expect that a researcher will be able to study every possible group because of cost and time, but the exclusion of certain groups from the benefit of research results may bring the ethics of a study into question. For example, the NIH, which in part funds medical research, has historically approved mostly studies involving white males to the general exclusion of women. Fortunately, this issue of justice and fairness in funding medical research has changed over the past several years, and NIH now requires researchers to justify the sole use of males in a study (National Institutes of Health, 1994).

A restatement of the questions that consumers of counseling and education research might ask to determine the ethical quality of research published in professional journals could include the following:

1. What possible negative implications can be applied or harm can come to a population due to the results of a particular study?

2. What are the possible benefits of the research results for the population?

3. Are the sample and population studied fairly representative of the general population that could benefit from the research results? More specifically, did the researcher or researchers present a reasonably clear argument for studying the population if the study was restricted to a particular group?

EVALUATION OF RESEARCH PRESENTED IN THE PROFESSIONAL LITERATURE

There have been studies that were conducted and involved ethical violations, and these studies serve as illustrations of the significance of the impact they have on populations. I want to review two examples, the Tuskegee Syphilis Study and the Milgram Study. Next, I want to review some more current examples that provide illustrations of how a population may be impacted through certain research.

TUSKEGEE SYPHILIS STUDY

The Tuskegee Syphilis Study was intended to follow the natural course of syphilis, specifically in African American males. The study spanned 40 years, beginning in 1932 and ending in 1972. It was originally hypothesized that there were differences by race in the natural progression of syphilis (Thomas & Quinn, 1991). The study was designed to last for 6 to 9 months and was conducted in Macon, Alabama. The Alabama state health officer solicited assurance from the USPHS that participants would eventually receive treatment (Thomas & Quinn, 1991). However, the participants in this study never received treatment, even though treatment was available as early as 1943, when the USPHS began administering penicillin as a treatment for syphilis across the country. One reason given for not providing treatment was that of the attitudes of the officials who were overseeing the study. For example, Dr. John Heller, Director of the Division of Venereal Diseases, stated that "the men's status did not warrant ethical debate, they were subjects not patients, clinical material, not sick people" (Jones, 1981, p. 179).

The Tuskegee study was ended in 1972 when it became public that these men had had standard, effective medical treatment withheld. Numerous other reasons were cited for the treatment these men received (or did not receive), and many centered on the attitudes of the medical community toward those of different races, particularly African Americans (Gamble, 1993; Thomas & Quinn, 1991). For example, Gamble (1993) stated that certain assumptions about African Americans led to the unethical treatment of subjects in this study, such as beliefs that African Americans are promiscuous, lustful, and generally do not seek out medical treatment. Consequently, not providing medical treatment was justified in the minds of the study officials. It has been estimated that 28 to 100 of the participants died as a consequence of their untreated syphilis (Gamble, 1993).

The first question addresses concerns as to whether there were any negative implications based on the way the study was conducted and the results obtained for the population. Gamble (1993) described a legacy of mistrust among African

Americans toward medical research. She stated, "The Tuskegee Syphilis Study symbolizes for many African Americans the racism that pervades American institutions including the medical profession" (p. 37). Thomas and Quinn (1991) suggested that the Tuskegee Syphilis Study has resulted in such distrust of the medical profession that it hampers acquired immunodeficiency syndrome (AIDS) education and acceptance of treatment among African Americans. Mason (2007) stated, "Historically, African Americans have resisted participation in clinical trials and other research projects because of distrust of the mostly white research establishment" (p. 296). It would not be a stretch to conclude that the effects of this study have had a negative impact on the population of the study, African American males, and their attitudes toward seeking medical treatment.

Are there any potential benefits from this study for the population? It is difficult to identify any. I am not aware of any special knowledge gained from the results that has benefited the treatment practices for syphilis in African American males. One of the few benefits may be broader, in that the exposure of the Tuskegee Syphilis Study to Congress resulted in improved oversight of human subject research by the federal government.

The third question we are interested in addressing is this: Is there a clear argument for using this particular population for the study? Initially, there was speculation in the medical literature on racial differences in the natural course of syphilis (Thomas & Quinn, 1991), but there was no attempt to compare the target group with other racial groups, such as Caucasian males. Gamble (1993) has noted that African Americans historically have been considered by the medical and scientific community to be inferior and, consequently, good sources for medical experimentation. Gamble (1993) cited physicians' use of black women for medical experimentation during the late 1800s, prior to the use of treatments for white women.

In summary, it appears that the Tuskegee Syphilis Study is of questionable ethical quality where population research is considered. There appear to be no benefits to the population from the study, and in fact, the study appears to have harmed the population, in this case African American males, causing distrust of the medical profession and possible reducing their chances of seeking necessary medical treatment.

MILGRAM STUDY

A classic study in psychology that has received significant criticism over violations of ethics is the Milgram Study on obedience (Baumrind, 1964; Kelman, 1967; Milgram, 1963). Milgram (1974) described the aim of the study as "to find when and how people would defy authority in the face of a clear moral imperative" (pp. 3–4). The methods involved the use of deception with the subject involved.

Subjects were led to believe by the experiment that they were participating in a learning study. Subjects were requested to train or teach another through the systematic use of electrical shock. In reality, the learner was an actor who did not actually receive a shock. The "teacher" in this experiment (the actual subject) was instructed to administer an electrical shock whenever the learner responded with an incorrect answer. With each incorrect answer, the teacher was informed that he or she should increase the intensity of the shock. The electrical shocks were presented on a board to the teacher, starting at 15 volts and rising to 450 volts at 14-volt intervals. Also, there were designations on the shock board indicating slight shock to "danger: severe shock" (Milgram, 1963). Milgram described his experiments with obedience in the following way:

> The man receiving the shock, begins to indicate he is experiencing discomfort. At 75 volts, the "learner" grunts. At 120 volts he complains verbally; at 150 he demands to be released from the experiment. His protests continue as the shock escalate, growing increasingly vehement and emotional. At 285 volts his response can only be described as an agonized scream. (p. 4)

When the "teacher" (subject) expressed reluctance at continuing with the experiment, the investigator urged him to complete the study and administer up to the maximum shock in the severe range (Milgram, 1963).

Milgram (1963) noted subjects' ("teachers'") behaviors; several of the initial study's participants exhibited unusual reactions: "nervous laughter and smiling. . . . Full-blown, uncontrollable seizures were observed in 3 subjects" (p. 375). Additionally, Milgram described in detail one subject's reaction: "Initially [this subject was a] poised businessman . . . smiling and confident. Within 20 minutes he was reduced to a twitching, stuttering wreck, who was rapidly approaching a point of nervous collapse" (p. 377).

A key consideration in evaluating this study from a consumer's perspective is the use of deception. To answer the first question of harm to the population, I want to cite studies on the use of deception. Sharpe, Adair, and Roese (1992) found that subjects participating in psychological research expressed more negative views of psychological research after participation. Studies like Milgram's may contribute to mistrust in participating in psychological research or may influence participation in future research. Conversely, it is difficult to find more concrete negative effects on the population as a consequence of these results and research methods being published. The APA (2003) Code of Ethics states,

> Deception in Research (a) Psychologists do not conduct a study involving deception unless they have determined that the use of deceptive techniques

is justified by the study's significant prospective scientific, educational, or applied value and that effective nondeceptive alternative procedures are not feasible. (8.07a)

A possible benefit to the population is an understanding and realization of the vulnerability of humans in reacting to and complying with authority. Milgram's initial interest in studying obedience centered on compliance with authority and participation in aggressive acts, like those conducted by some Germans during World War II. These results may provide insights into why humans may engage in horrendous acts against others, and consequently, prevention measures may be developed.

The population studied was obtained from several universities and generally involved males. The use of the specific subjects in the study was not clearly defended in the introduction. What effect would it have had on the results to have included subjects not affiliated with a university? However, there does not seem to have been bias toward a particular group.

Overall, the Milgram study provides somewhat mixed results for ethical violations affecting the population. The study may more likely have violated the rights of participants than affected the intended population of the study.

OTHER STUDIES

To illustrate the practical application of ethics and counseling research literature, there will be application of several studies to address these three questions. Pandiani, Banks, and Schacht (2001) conducted a study addressing the effects of various children's services on outcomes like incarceration, hospitalization, and pregnancy among young adults. Participants were those over 17 who were receiving one of three services: special education, child protection and juvenile justice, or mental health services. The researchers found that those young males who received either child protection and juvenile justice or special education services had higher incarceration rates than those receiving mental health services and those not having involvement with any of the identified services. Also, those females who received state child protection and juvenile justice services had higher rates of pregnancy than those receiving mental health services or special education. This was a longitudinal study and thus had information on the long-term effects of services on the outcomes of young adults. These findings allow for an interpretation of the impact on the population or a review of ethics for population research.

The first question is whether there is any possible harm to the population. In the study presented here, the population is those receiving state child services such as special education, mental health services, or child protection and juvenile justice. What potential impact do the study results have on the reputation or dignity of the population? The results suggest that those males receiving special education and child protection and juvenile justice are more likely to be involved with the criminal justice system. One might interpret that someone going through these systems is more inclined to engage in criminal activities.

The benefit of the results from this study for the population is that such an at-risk group can be systematically addressed. Interventions can be focused on this population in an effort to change the outcomes of incarceration or pregnancy. Participants were primarily white and from a specific region, the New England area, and the results do not provide information on other populations, such as those from racial groups other than Caucasian.

In another study, Blanton and Dagenais (2007) investigated whether those with language-skills deficits had more incidents of criminal behavior and court involvement compared to those who did not have language-skills deficits. They included males and females who were either court involved or not court involved. Also, they categorized them as having language impairments or not. The authors provide a review of the literature, which noted that language acquisition is a critical issue during preschool years and the development of language. The authors found that language problems in children predicted later male criminal activity. The first question to address ethically is whether these results have a negative impact on or harm the population, that is, young males with language problems. Certainly, if an educator working with young males reads these article results, he or she would need to carefully understand the implications and that not every male with a language disorder is going to engage in criminal activity as he gets older. The ethical use and interpretation of these results is that young males with language disorders are more likely to engage in criminal activities in later life, but it is not an absolute, and these students should not be treated differently, for example, not be trusted because they may engage in criminal behavior in the future. The potential positive use of the outcomes from this study is that educators and school personnel could target interventions to help young males, first with their language disorders and second to develop interventions to address possible future criminal behavior and encourage prosocial behavior. The study was conducted in Alabama, and only Caucasian and African American youth were included. Latino, Asian, Native American, and other racial groups could potentially benefit from being studied in this area.

SUMMARY

As a consumer of research, it is important to consider ethical principles in interpreting and applying study results from population research. Three ethical principles seem particularly relevant: nonmaleficence, beneficence, and justice. Nonmaleficence concerns determining whether the results of a study, when interpreted and implemented, may harm the population. This includes how those interpreting the results use the results.

Beneficence is almost diametrically opposed to nonmaleficence and concerns whether study results benefit a population when implemented and made public. Researchers have the intention of finding results that benefit others, particularly in counseling and education. However, those using research results need to consider the benefits and how they can best be applied in practice. Finally, justice concerns the extent to which study results may be applied to all those in the population of interest and not just a select group.

A review of public records shows that researchers do engage in scientific misconduct, and there are consequences. Consequences may include a ban on submission of proposals to federal grants and institutional monitoring of scientific activity. Both represent significant impact on a researcher's activities and career. A review of examples of how to evaluate current research as it applies to population research show that, even today, there can be significant impact on those being studied. Researchers and those applying research in practice should be aware of how research results can negatively impact a population.

Exercise

Directions: Locate an article in the professional literature addressing a topic you are interested in exploring. Evaluate ethics and population research based on the questions addressed in this chapter. Try to explain and justify your answers based on specific examples from the article.

1. What are some possible negative implications that could be applied to the population or harm that could come to it from the results of your chosen study?

2. What are the possible benefits of the research results for the population?

3. Are the sample and population studied fairly representative of the general population that could benefit from the research results? More specially, did the researcher or researchers present a reasonably clear argument for studying the population if the study was restricted to a particular group?

SECTION II

EVALUATING ARTICLES IN THE PROFESSIONAL LITERATURE

11

EVALUATING THE LITERATURE REVIEW

The previous chapters have provided you with basic concepts you need to begin to be an effective consumer of counseling and educational research. Chapters 11 through 17 are focused on ways to evaluate research published in professional journals. Students have frequently commented to me, after receiving instruction in evaluating research, how surprised they are at the limitations of studies reported in the professional literature. Generally, they have accepted what was presented in the professional literature as basic truths.

The methods and guidelines for evaluating professional journal articles are fairly detailed. At first, the guidelines may seem tedious to use, but as with learning any new task, it becomes easier with practice. Certainly, once you have acquired the knowledge and skills to be an effective consumer of counseling and educational research, you will not need to evaluate each article you read in such detail. The intention is that, after in-depth practice, you will be able to note areas of potential problems and focus on these more specifically rather than on every single detail of the research article. It is important to remember that research with humans is complex, and every study will have some (or many) limitations. The purpose of developing a critical eye in reading and using research is to become a more effective consumer and user of research. Generally, no one error or limitation of a study should cause you to totally reject the findings. The evaluation approach suggested in this text is a guide for consumers and users of research. It may be used to systematically determine which components of a study are more valid and what needs to be accepted with caution.

A beginning point for evaluating a research article is the characteristics of a literature review. Guidelines and questions for evaluating counseling and educational research are discussed. Finally, examples are provided from the literature to illustrate how to use the guidelines to evaluate research.

The general purpose of the literature section is to provide an argument for conducting the study. Consequently, researchers attempt to systematically cite previous, related research to frame the problem dealt with in their own study. In addition, they attempt to identify any gaps in the current literature. It is helpful if the literature review summarizes the gaps in previous research on the topic and a link is provided to how the current study will address this gap. Typically, primary sources (other research conducted on the topic and reported in the professional literature) are used to develop the argument. The researchers should present a rationale or identify the significance of their own research in light of how it will add to current knowledge. The literature review should be thorough and comprehensive enough to develop the argument for conducting the study. You may find that a literature review varies in length depending on the intent and purpose of the particular journal in which the study is published. The majority of journals encourage researchers to present a thorough and comprehensive argument for conducting a study. A few journals, particularly journals where brief reports are published, may not require, or even allow, a longer literature review. It is important to first identify whether an article is intended to be a brief report before engaging in your detailed analysis of the literature review.

Researchers typically conduct a study because they are interested in the topic. Also, how they frame the study is influenced by their personal views and expectations about the possible results. This seems a contradiction to the idea of objectivity in research, but a researcher typically does not conduct a study unless he or she has a particular interest, and potentially a particular hypothesis, in mind. Many researchers have commented that they conduct studies because of the interest the subjects hold for them. A researcher's interest could be influenced by some personal events that could slant the way the study is presented. Additionally, the study could be a follow-up to a previous study, and thus certain outcomes might be expected. Because of researcher expectations and personal experiences, it is important to note any biases in the literature review.

Even though anyone reading a study reported in a professional journal is generally familiar with the field, the researcher needs to define any new or relatively unknown concepts in the literature review. Another intent of those writing the literature review may be to describe new or common research methods in a particular area of study that may be of interest in the current reported study.

GUIDELINES AND QUESTIONS FOR EVALUATING RESEARCH

As mentioned earlier, the major purpose of the literature review is to develop an argument for conducting the study. Several related questions may be asked concerning this argument: (1) Do the researchers present an adequate rationale for conducting the study, and are gaps in the literature clearly identified? (2) So what? Or a related question is this: What difference will the study make to the fields of counseling or education?

As has been noted, science and research have an intent of pursuing objectivity, but researchers may potentially include personal biases in the construction of a study. A relevant question then is this: Do the researchers present any potential biases in the literature review? For example, does the researcher cite only his or her own prior research? A related question is whether the researcher presents only one side of a theory or view. Generally, an issue or research topic has more than one viewpoint.

Previously, it was suggested that the literature review should include relevant definitions and descriptions of unknown concepts. A question to address here may be this: Are all important concepts clearly defined by the researchers?

Another area of concern is whether the literature is thorough and comprehensive enough to develop the argument for conducting the study. It is relevant to note whether important researchers and theorists are cited in the review. For example, if a researcher was addressing self-efficacy, he or she would want to acknowledge the works of Bandura (1977), who developed the concept. So, the question to address may be this: Is the literature review thorough and comprehensive?

Another question to address in the literature review is whether there is a description of any new methods in a particular area of study that relate to the current study. The question to ask is this: Do the researchers clearly describe previous methods that are relevant to understanding the purpose for conducting this study?

To review, here are the questions to address when analyzing a literature review:

1. Do the researchers present an adequate rationale for conducting the study, and are gaps in the literature clearly identified?

2. So what? What difference will the study make to the fields of counseling or education?

3. Is the literature review thorough and comprehensive?

4. Do the researchers demonstrate any potential biases in the literature review?

5. Are all important concepts clearly defined by the researchers?

6. Do the researchers clearly describe previous methods that are relevant to understanding the purpose for conducting this study?

EVALUATION OF EXAMPLES FROM THE RESEARCH LITERATURE

Quantitative Research

Henderson, Rosen, and Mascaro (2007) studied the effectiveness of using mandalas in working with those with posttraumatic stress. The literature review is cited below:

The expression and disclosure of previously experienced traumatic events is associated with better subsequent physical and mental health (Esterling, L'Abate, Murray, & Pennebaker, 1999; Smyth & Helm, 2003).

Extensive attention has been given to the efficacy of written expression of traumatic events in promoting physical and psychological well-being and various studies have resulted in a body of research supporting a written disclosure paradigm (see Pennebaker, 1997a, 1997b for a review). According to this paradigm set forth by James Pennebaker, writing about traumatic or stressful events in an emotional way for as little as 15 minutes over 3 to 4 consecutive days brings about improvements in physical and mental health (Pennebaker & Seagal, 1999).

The principle of therapeutic exposure posits that repeated exposure to aversive conditioned stimuli leads to the extinguishment of negative emotions associated with such stimuli, resulting in beneficial outcomes (Foa & Rothbaum, 1998). Some researchers contend that written disclosure serves as a context in which individuals are repeatedly exposed to traumatic memories (i.e. exposure to aversive stimuli and the negative emotions associated with it), which allows for the gradual extinction of negative emotional associations across sessions (Kloss & Lisman, 20020; Pennebaker, 1997b; Sloan & Marx, 2004a, 2004b). This is theorized to be one of the mechanisms underlying the overall effectiveness of the written disclosure paradigm.

Another theory regarding the effectiveness of written disclosure on physical and mental health has to do with the cognitive changes associated with this type of writing. Once a meaningful and integrated narrative is formed, it is hypothesized that the traumatic event can then be summarized, stored, and allowed to become a nonthreatening memory rather than a ghost that chronically haunts consciousness, subsequently leading to a decrease in psychological distress (Msyth, True, & Souto, 2001).

Although the innovative work of Pennebaker and other researchers has supported the utility of the written disclosure paradigm and the numerous benefits associated with the disclosure of trauma, the written disclosure paradigm has been found to be ineffective among individuals with disordered cognitive processes of relatively severe depression (Gidron, Peri, Onnonly, & Shaley, 1996; Stroebe, Stroebe, Schut, Zech, & van den Bout, 2002).

The vast majority of written disclosure studies involve only written expression; however, Judith Pizarro (2004) performed a recent study that examined whether art therapy was as effective as writing therapy in improving the outcomes of psychological and health measures.

Pizzaro sampled 41 participants using two experimental groups (expressive art therapy or writing therapy) and a control art condition.

Consistent with Pennebaker's findings, there was a significant decrease in social dysfunction within the writing group, however, the participants in the art groups did not have similar health benefits. Although the art groups did show a greater enjoyment of the experience, the researcher surmised "generating art" may not provide sufficient cognitive organization and therefore may not be able to provide the same positive health benefits as writing therapy (Pizarro, p. 10). A combination of the two was suggested in which writing could heal while art could make the process more enjoyable, thus increasing therapy compliance.

Rather than completely dismissing art therapy as an effective means of processing trauma, an artistic task that lends itself particularly well to the symbolic expression and disclosure of a traumatic event is mandala drawing.

A mandala, used as a meditative tool in various religions but most famously in Tibetan Buddhist [sic], is a circular design that is thought to promote psychological healing and integration when created by an individual. The use of the mandala as a therapeutic tool was first espoused by Carl Jung, who suggested that the act of drawing mandalas had a calming and healing effect on its creator while at the same time facilitating psychic integration and personal meaning in life (Jung, 1973), which serves as the rationale for using them for traumatic disclosure tasks. The mandala functions as a symbolic representation of emotionally laden and conflicting material, yet at the same time provides a sense of order and integration to this material.

In this manner, drawing a mandala is similar to a written disclosure in that it provides cognitive organization to complex emotional experiences. Art psychotherapists use the mandala as a basic tool for self-awareness, self-expression, conflict resolution, and healing (Siegelis, 1987). Within the realm of art therapy, the mandala generally refers to any art form that is executed within a circular context. Although most research into the healing aspects of mandala drawing has been limited to case studies argue [sic] for using mandalas therapeutically within numerous populations and settings, including schizophrenia and psychotic disorders, dissociative disorders (Cox & Cohen, 2000), attention-deficit/hyperactivity disorder (Smitherman-Brown & Church, 1996), and dementia patients (Couch, 1997). Cox and Cohen note that, particularly for individuals regarding abuse, illustrative coding of traumatic events in drawings allows clients the ability to maintain secrecy (both from their therapists and from themselves), while at the same time symbolically communicating and resolving material (Cohen & Cox, 1989, 1995).

To date, empirical research on the use of mandalas as a therapeutic tool is limited. In one of the first attempts undertaken to examine scientifically Jung's theory that mandala creation promotes psychological health Siegelis (1987) found that those who drew inside a circle experienced more positive affect than those who drew within a square. Although the results of the Siegelis study lend support to the argument that mandalas have calming and healing properties, the experimental design and data were limited and inhibit the inferences that can be drawn from the results.

A recent study by Curry and Kasser (2005) evaluated the effectiveness of mandala drawing in the reduction of anxiety. Anxiety levels were measured before and after an anxiety induction exercise, and after one of the three coloring conditions (free-form, mandala-drawing, or plaid-form). Decreases in anxiety were experienced for those in the mandala and plaid-form conditions.

Although these results show potential, the design of the research used predrawn mandala forms and predrawn plaid patterns, so the results could be interpreted in various ways, such as the calming effects of art therapy in general versus the effects of actually creating a mandala.

Our study sought to test in a controlled manner, the psychological and physical health benefits of mandala drawing within a trauma population. In choosing a research design and methodology that would adequately achieve this goal, we drew upon the techniques and methodology used in a body of research by James Pennebaker and colleagues that examines the physical and psychological health benefits of disclosure of traumatic events through writing (Pennebaker, 1997a, 1997b; Pennebaker & Seagal, 1999; Pennebaker & Susman, 1988). Our study design is modeled closely after the recent study conducted by Sloan and Marx (2004a). It applies a creative variation of the disclosure paradigm and this sort of creative extension has been encouraged. (King, 2004, pp. 148–149)

The first questions to address are whether the researchers provided an adequate rationale for conducting the study and whether there are gaps clearly identified in the literature. Henderson and colleagues (2007) introduced research that supports the view that writing about trauma reduces stress and is beneficial. The answer to this first question is that the researchers do present an adequate rationale and cite relevant research. The citation of Pennebaker's work on using writing to reduce stress provides support for their view. Specifically, they suggested that writing allows for cognitive integration of the experience. They then introduced the idea of using art to improve psychological functioning and reduce stress and argued that it is similar to writing in expressing connections to the traumatic experience. Next, they introduced the idea of using art and specifically mandalas to achieve similar results to writing, that is, reduced stress and better physical and mental health. The authors noted the limitations of the research to support improving psychological functioning. However, they noted that there is preliminary research to support the use of art in reducing stress and anxiety. Their ultimate argument is that there is not enough research, or there are gaps, on using art to reduce the effects of PTSD, and more research needs to be conducted, the rationale for conducting their study.

The next questions to address are these: So what? What difference does conducting the study make to the field? The researchers do not explicitly state the effect of the study results on the field, but they provide an adequate rationale and a method for meeting the needs of the community. Counselors and therapists can use art therapy, specifically the drawing of mandalas, to promote psychological functioning and well-being. So, the authors are proposing a technique to use in counseling to assist those individuals with PTSD to improve their quality of life, reduce stress, and improve mental health functioning.

In regard to the third question, whether the literature review is thorough and comprehensive, it appears that the researchers do accomplish this goal. They cite research supporting their proposition that writing about PTSD affects stress levels and improves mental health functioning. Additionally, they provide research support for their proposal that art may be similar to writing about PTSD experiences and therefore is worthy of additional research coverage. Specifically, they cite research and theoretical views presented by Pennebaker to give a thorough review of the appropriate and relevant literature. Citations are generally 10 years old or newer, with the majority being published after 2000.

The fourth question about evaluating the research literature section of an article is this: Do the researchers present any potential biases in the literature review? The researchers do provide several different theoretical views on the use of writing and art in treating those with PTSD. Also, the researchers cite research that shows the limitations of using writing to treat those with PTSD; for example, it is not effective with those with schizophrenia, mental retardation, and other disorders. It appears that the researchers do not show any significant bias in presenting the literature review.

The next question that is important to address is this: Are all important concepts clearly defined by the researchers? PTSD is not defined, nor is traumatic event. It would be helpful for the reader to know explicitly how the researchers define these terms. Also, written disclosures are not well defined or clearly identified. Finally, mandalas are not clearly identified or defined. The study focuses on the use of mandalas as the treatment to be evaluated, but the researchers do not adequately define and identify the concept.

The final question to address is this: Do the researchers clearly describe previous methods that are relevant to understanding the purpose for conducting this study? The researchers do not describe in much detail any previous methods. They do cite previous researchers who have used mandalas (by naming Siegelis, [1987]), but they do not go into any detail about the methods used.

In summary, the researchers Henderson and colleagues (2007) do give an adequate rationale for conducting the study and how the study potentially can have important implications in the treatment of those with PTSD. Also, the literature review appears to be thorough and does not present any particular bias. Several important concepts are not clearly defined, and no description of previous methods is provided.

Metuki, Sela, and Lavidor (2012) conducted a study focused on the use of transcranial direct current stimulation (tDCS) and its effect on the left dorsolateral prefrontal cortex (DLPFC) for addressing verbal insight problems. TDCS involves placing electrodes over specified regions of the brain associated with specific brain functions, in this case, over the left DLPFC. Low-current brain stimulation, tDCS, uses a positive electrode (anode) and a negative electrode (cathode). Researchers have found that the anode increases neuronal potentiation (long-term potentiation), which influences neuronal plasticity and readiness for neurons to fire and function optimally (Stagg & Nitsche, 2011). The researchers, Metucki and colleagues (2012), describe the literature as:

Language processing and comprehension encompasses linguistic processes as well as non-linguistic processes. For instance, solving verbal insight problems requires one to perform multiple complex cognitive operations that involve language comprehension, semantic processing and problem solving (1). Previous studies have investigated the semantic aspects of this ability, demonstrating extensive involvement of a temporal bilateral network, with a right hemisphere (RH) prevalence when solving verbal problems with insight (2–4).

However, the role of executive functions associated with the problem solving aspects of this ability has received less research attention.

Cerruti and Schlaug (5) were able to enhance performance of verbal problem solving with the use of non-invasive stimulation of the left DLPFC (Broadmann's Area 9/46), a brain area associated with executive and cognitive control, and provided vital evidence for the importance of this region in supporting the processing of verbal insight problems.

However, the nature of the neuro-cognitive processes underlying the DLPFC support in solving verbal insight problems remained unclear. The main aim of the current study was to further explore the role of the DLPFC in solving verbal insight problems and in particular, to advance our understanding regarding the cognitive control components mediating the stimulation effect and the conditions in which cognitive control operations are required in order to promote solving these problems.

Accumulated findings from behavioural and imaging studies employing different methodological variations of this paradigm have shown converging evidence for a dominant involvement of the RH (2, 3). These consistent findings are in line with the predictions of the BAIS model for semantic processing (8), namely that temporal sites in the RH will have unique involvement when distant meanings are activated and integrated. In addition to the cortical activity attributed to the RH involvement in semantic processing, solving the CRA (Compound Remote Associations) items also invokes activity that has been attributed to processes related to general problem solving (3). The hypothesis that executive functions are likely to be involved in solving these complex verbal problems, beyond their semantic aspects, is further supported by two studies demonstrating cognitive control modulation of the semantic processes involved in this task (5, 9). Few studies of semantic processing have described cognitive control contribution to language processing, mediated by the PFC, using other semantic tasks. For instance neuroimaging studies have attributed the activation of regions within the left PFC (prefrontal cortex) during semantic processing to the recruitment of semantic memory systems (17, 18). Further evidence for the crucial role that the left DLPFC plays in executive control over semantic processing converges in various idiom damaged patients. In particular the DLPFC has been found to be involved in meaning retrieval from semantic memory, selection between alternative meanings and suppression of irrelevant information (19, 20). Cerruti and Schtaug (5) recently provided evidence for the DLPFC involvement in processing verbal insight problems, but the underlying processes of facilitating this involvement have not yet been described. The authors demonstrated that stimulation of the left DLPFC with transcranial direct current stimulation (tDCS) enhanced performance in solving Compound Remote Associate problems. In particular, they found that when given 30 subjects to solve Compound Remote Associate problems, subjects solved more problems after anodal tDCS to the left DLPFC stimulation compared to the sham condition. Taken together, these results indicate that stimulating the left DLPFC not only led to increased fluency in solutions generation, but also to performance in a simple verbal fluency task. The authors argued that the enhancement in the more complex Compound Remote Associate task was facilitated by neural networks associated with executive function (5). These findings prompt interesting questions regarding the role of cognitive control and the left DLPFC in solving verbal insight problems. Aiming to better describe the underlying neuro-cognitive processes that modulate verbal problem solving enhancement, we created a stimulation study with few methodological modifications compared to the procedure used by Cerruti and Schlaug (5). (pp. 110–111)

The first questions to address in evaluating this article and the literature review are these: Do the researchers present an adequate rationale for conducting the study, and are gaps in the literature clearly identified? The researchers provide information about research designed to improve performance in verbal problem solving; that is, "solving verbal insight problems requires one to perform multiple complex cognitive operations that involve language comprehension, semantic processing and problem solving" (Metuki et al., p. 110). They systematically review research that cites how solving verbal insight problems has been done in previous research. They cited a reason for conducting such a study and proposed that there needs to be more understanding of how a low-current brain stimulation of the left DLPFC impacts solving verbal insight problems. A second question is this: So what? Or, what difference will the study make to the fields of counseling or education? The researchers hint at what impact this study may have, which is to understand cognitive control processes, such as an ability to solve verbal insight problems, but they do not explicitly describe and identify how it will be beneficial. One can make inferences about the benefits of promoting cognitive functioning in performing multiple complex tasks, but this is not clearly stated. The third question to address in evaluating the literature review is whether the literature review is thorough and comprehensive. The researchers appear to have provided a thorough and comprehensive literature review. They discussed the Compound Remote Associate theory, which is focused on verbal insight problem solving. Also, the researchers discuss previous research on executive brain functions (although minimal) on brain stimulation. One criticism may be an introduction to the actual chemical processes of the effects of low-current brain stimulation. Another question to address in evaluating the literature review is this: Do the researchers demonstrate any potential biases in the literature review? The researchers provide 38 references and do not cite any of their own work. They do not provide any alternative explanations or ways of impacting or changing the ability to solve verbal insight problems. The next question is whether all important concepts are defined clearly by the researchers. The last question is this: Do the researchers clearly describe previous methods that are relevant to understanding the purpose for conducting this study? The researchers discuss previous methods and state, "A procedure used by Bowden & Jung Beeman (6,7), participants were presented with the problem words for a shorter duration of time and then presented with a target word. Participants were requested to solve the problem while the prime words were presented" (Metuki et al., p. 111). These researchers do provide important information on how previous methods of understanding verbal insight problems have been done.

Qualitative Research

The questions to address with qualitative research in evaluating the literature review are similar to those asked with quantitative research. So, the same questions will be used in the following example of a qualitative study.

Fry (2007) investigated first-year teachers' experiences in entering schools and their induction support, or support for entrance into the teaching profession. She used a qualitative method; specifically, she employed a case study method. The literature review is described below.

Many new teachers adopt traditional teaching methods during their student teaching and early in-service years instead of utilizing the innovative ones they were exposed to in teacher preparation (Feiman-Nemser, 2001; Veenman, 1984). This tendency can result from interactions with experienced colleagues who deride innovative research-supported teaching methods (Clark, 1999). Survival plays a role as well; faced with seemingly insurmountable classroom management issues, beginners often adopt traditional teaching methods that keep the students working quietly in their seats, and thus are easier to control (Veenman, 1984). These factors led Feiman-Nemser to conclude, "sink or swim" induction encourages novices to stick to whatever practices enable them to survive whether or not they represent "best" practice in that situation" (p. 1014).

In contrast, well-designed induction programs can provide beginning teachers with support that helps them survive the classroom management challenges, seemingly endless curriculum and instruction questions, and feelings of isolation that contribute to retained high percentages of beginning teachers. For example, studies of induction programs at Santa Clara, California; Walla Walla, Washington; and southern Illinois.

Reported retention rates that were greater than 90% over 6, 5, and 3 year time periods, respectively (Boss, 2001; Chubbuck, Clift, Allard, & Quinlan, 2001; Linik, 2001). Although these studies reported the successes of individual induction programs, the collective impact of induction programs may not be as significant. Smith and Ingersoll (2004) reported that nearly 80% of 1st-year teachers nationwide participated in some form of induction an increase of approximately 40% from 10 years earlier. This increase in induction program participation does not seem to have correlated in reduction of attrition rates, which remain near 29% for the first 3 years of teaching (Ingersoll, 2001, 2002).

Attrition rates may have remained stable despite increased participation in induction programs because of variability in the type of support offered. Smith and Ingersoll (2004) analyzed the impact different forms and combinations of induction had on attrition using results from the 1999–2000 Schools and Staffing Survey (SASS), a national study that includes data from approximately 52,000 elementary and secondary teachers. After controlling for differences in teacher and school characteristics, Smith and Ingersoll found that predicted attrition rate for beginning teachers receiving no form of induction support; mentoring, supportive communication from an administrator or department chair, common planning time with other teachers in the grade or content area, or seminars for beginning teachers. Receiving only one of these forms of induction support did not have a significant impact on the predicted attrition rate. A combination of mentoring and supportive communication from an administrator, which Smith and Ingersoll refer to as "basic induction," produced a predicted attrition rate of 39%. The predicted attrition was reduced to 27% when beginning teachers had basic induction plus common planning time with other teachers in the grade or content area, and participated in seminars for beginning teachers. The lowest predicted attrition rate was 18%; this was achieved when beginners received the combinations described above plus one of the following: a teacher's aide, reduced number of preparations, or participation in an external network of teachers. Smith and Ingersoll's analysis suggests that the mere presence of induction programs is not enough to reduce attrition rates among beginning teachers; the form and quality of induction that schools provide is important.

Smith and Ingersoll's (2004) research was based on a quantitative data set (SASS) that determines whether or not beginning teachers received specific forms of induction. SASS does not measure how useful teachers found their induction experiences. Since the presence of induction may not be enough to reduce attrition rates, research needs to move beyond determining the prevalence of induction and begin to assess form and quality. Interviewing beginning teachers about their experiences and the support they receive is a valuable way to assess the form and quality of induction in the schools. Interviews provide evaluative data immediately so schools do not need to wait until the 3-year induction period is over to see whether or not beginning teachers become attrition statistics. (pp. 216–217)

The same questions that were used to evaluate quantitative research can be used to evaluate the study by Fry (2007), which is a qualitative study. The first question is whether the researcher presents an adequate rationale for conducting the study. Fry notes the problems with school systems not providing adequate teacher induction programs and the use of traditional methods by new teachers that keep students docile and sitting in their seats. Fry describes these efforts as "survival" practices by the new teachers. Another major problem with not having helpful teacher induction programs is that there is a high attrition rate; new teachers leave shortly after beginning their careers in education. The author noted that a significant issue may not be simply the attrition rates of new teachers leaving the job but the quality of any induction methods used by school districts to keep and support new teachers. The rationale provided is clear and is based upon previous research, and the problem of attrition is a good rationale for conducting a study in this area. Also, finding specific factors that contribute to quality teacher induction appears to be reasonable.

The next questions to ask are these: So what? What difference will the study results make for those in counseling and education? The benefit of understanding the quality of teacher induction is noted, with the author stating, "Interviewing beginning teachers about their experiences and the support they receive is a valuable way to assess the form and quality of induction in schools. Interviews provide evaluative data immediately so schools do not need to wait until the 3-year induction period is over" (Fry, 2007, p. 218). The point here is that schools can benefit from the study information and can potentially provide improved quality of teacher induction methods.

The third question concerns whether the literature review is thorough and comprehensive. Fry (2007) discusses various induction programs for new teachers and cites numerous studies and writings on the topic. She cites seven different studies and describes two different programs that have used new teacher induction methods. The citations ranged from 1984 to 2004, with most citations being recent, within the previous 7 years. A related question is whether the author presents any potential biases in the literature review. The author does not cite her own research. However, she does not note any limitations or problems with other studies or research. She does cite research that found lower levels of successful induction procedures (Smith & Ingersoll, [2004]). It is not clear whether she demonstrates much bias in her literature review. It would have been helpful to see research outcomes showing a potential difference from the positive research she cites on new teacher induction.

The next question to address in evaluating the literature review is whether the author has defined important terms. The most important term in Fry's study is induction (new teacher induction). Fry (2007) does not define induction for the reader, so it is difficult to know exactly what she means by this term. She does describe induction support as referring to supportive communication from an administrator, common planning time with other teachers, and other efforts. Despite these descriptions, it is difficult to know what induction or induction support actually is.

The last question is whether the researchers describe previous methods. Fry (2007) does cite two other new-teacher induction programs in Washington and California but does not describe the methods used. More detail about the actual induction procedures would have been helpful to the reader.

Single-Subject Research

A study by Norell-Clarke, Nyander, and Jansson-Frojmark (2011) is an example of a single-subject study. These researchers studied sleep problems in adolescents and used cognitive therapy as a treatment. Consistent with a single-subject design, they studied three adolescents. The adolescents ranged in age from 16 to 18. They found that the insomnia the adolescents experienced was reduced by cognitive therapy. Norell-Clarke and colleagues described the literature review and stated,

Many adolescents of today sleep poorly. The most common sleep disorder, insomnia, means difficulties in falling asleep, staying asleep, or not feeling rested in the morning for a least one month combined with daytime symptoms. Between 5 and 16% of adolescents fulfil criteria of insomnia, with up to 25% reporting at least one symptom of insomnia (e.g. Roberts, Roberts & Duong, 2008). Adolescents who do not get enough sleep are more likely to develop problems with their somatic or psychological health (Roberts, et al., 2008) and they run a higher risk of developing depression (Breslau, Roth, Rosenthal and Andreski, 1996). Yet there have been few attempts to treat adolescents with poor sleep by using psychological methods there is need for more research on adolescents. Cognitive therapy is an evidence-based treatment for adult insomnia (Morin, et al., 2006), but adolescent sleep is affected by specific developmental and lifestyle factors so it cannot be concluded that treatments tested on adults would also be effective for adolescents. When psychological methods have been tested on youth with sleep problems, the study has either been school interventions aimed at participants without a sleep disorder diagnosis (Moseley & Gradisar, 2009; Sousa, Araujo & Stevens, 2005), or treatment for insomnia comorbid with drug addiction (Bootzin & Stevens, 2005). Treatments for adolescents with primary insomnia have yet to be studied. Recent research has emphasized the role of cognitive processes in insomnia. Five cognitive processes are theorized to maintain chronic insomnia by being present during both day and night and by reinforcing each other: worry; selective attention and monitoring; misperception; unhelpful beliefs about sleep and consequences of bad sleep; and safety behaviors. For a more detailed description see Harvey, 2005. A newly development treatment, Cognitive Therapy for Insomnia (CT-I) targets these maintaining processes and was efficient in an open trial with adult participants (Harvey, Sharpley, Ree, Stinson, and Clark, 2007). (pp. 367–368)

An analysis of the literature starts with this question: Do the researchers present an adequate rationale for conducting the study? The rational presented in the literature focuses on previous research showing that a significant proportion of adolescents suffer from sleep insomnia. The researchers further noted that minimal research has been conducted into the treatment of sleep insomnia for adolescents, but there has been considerable research on treatment of adults. The second question is this: So what? Or, what difference will the study make to the fields of counseling or education? The researchers suggest that developing a treatment for adolescent with insomnia may address negative outcomes such as worry, selective attention and monitoring, and consequences of bad sleep. A difference in finding a treatment for adolescent sleep insomnia appears to be important. The third question is this: Is the literature review thorough and comprehensive? The literature is somewhat brief, but the researchers provide previous research evidence that adolescent sleep insomnia is a problem. They also discuss relevant research addressing treatment of sleep insomnia. However, the researchers do not address any other treatment options of methods such as pharmacological interventions. The fourth question is this: Do the researchers demonstrate any potential biases in the literature review? One potential bias is that no other treatment interventions were discussed other than cognitive behavior for insomnia. Certainly, there are other treatments such as pharmacological treatment. Another question is this: Are all important concepts clearly defined by the researchers? Sleep insomnia was well defined in the literature review; the researchers defined sleep insomnia as difficulty "falling asleep, staying asleep, or not feeling rested in the morning for a least one month combined with daytime symptoms" (Norell-Clarke et al., 2011, p. 367). Finally, the last question is this: Do the researchers clearly describe previous methods that are relevant to understanding the purpose for conducting this study? The researchers do not discuss any previous research methods in the literature review but appropriately note where one can find a clear description of such methods, for example, Harvey, Sharpley, Ree, Stinson, and Clark (2007).

SUMMARY

The literature review is the initial introduction to the reader and consumer, outlining the argument or rationale for conducting a particular study. Generally, there should be a strong and clear argument developed by the researchers for conducting the study based on previous research, theory, or personal experience. Several criteria have been proposed for evaluation of the literature review. One of the most important guidelines or questions, for me, is the answer to the so-what question. Why is it important to conduct this study? What difference will it make to counseling and education? If this question cannot be adequately addressed, I do not see the need to continue reading or using a particular article or study. Both quantitative and qualitative research studies can be evaluated using the same set of questions.

Exercise

Directions: Locate an article in the professional literature addressing a topic you are interested in exploring. Evaluate the literature review based on the questions addressed in this chapter. Try to explain and justify your answers based on specific examples from the article.

1. Do the researchers present an adequate rationale for conducting the study, and are gaps in the literature clearly identified?

2. So what? What difference will the study make to the fields of counseling and education?

3. Is the literature review thorough and comprehensive?

4. Do the researchers demonstrate any potential biases in the literature review?

5. Are all important concepts clearly defined by the researchers?

6. Do the researchers clearly describe previous methods that are relevant to understanding the purpose for conducting this study?

12

EVALUATING THE PURPOSE STATEMENT AND HYPOTHESES

The purpose statement or aim of a study is an attempt by the researchers to identify, in a sentence or two, the intent of the study. Sometimes, the purpose is thought of as a research problem (McMillan, 2004). The purpose statement is generally devoid of technical terms and should be based on the argument developed in the literature review. Moore (1983) proposed that the purpose statement may be expressed in either a declarative statement or in the form of a question or questions. The purpose is typically found in the literature review section of an article, toward the end of the review, and most frequently in the last paragraph before the methods section. Many, but not all, researchers do not provide a purpose statement in the study but instead only use a hypothesis.

The purpose statement or research questions provide important information to the reader. First, the purpose statement should identify whether the study is a comparison among the groups of interest, an attempt to determine relationships between variables, an attempt to determine changes over time, or an attempt to clarify phenomena through descriptive or qualitative research. Identifying whether a study involves a comparison or a relationship directs the researchers in choosing a statistical method. It also gives the reader information about what type of study was conducted.

A comparison study may be identified when the researcher, in the purpose statement, affirms that there will be an attempt to determine differences between two or more groups. Kessler, Turkeltaub, Benson, and Hamilton (2012) provide an example of a study using a comparison. They stated, "In the current study, we aimed to compare the intensity of perceived sensations and other adverse effects between sham and active stimulation in subjects undergoing transcranial direct current stimulation during studies of cognition" (p. 156).

Researchers using the type of study that focuses on a relationship are interested in determining how two or more specific variables correlate. Baldwin, Wampold, and Imel (2007) conducted a study that focused on using correlational methods. They described their purpose as follows: "The primary aim of the present study was to explore the relative importance of patient and therapist variability in the alliance as they relate to outcomes. In addition, our analyses also have implications for the hypothesis that the alliance is a consequence of early symptom change" (p. 843). Essentially, they were interested in the correlation or relationship between therapist and client variables involving the therapeutic alliance between them and the outcomes of the treatment.

In single-subject research, many times, the intent is to determine the impact of an intervention over time. The comparison is actually within the subject and how he or she changes as a consequence of an intervention. Norelle-Clarke and colleagues (2011) described their purpose statement as follows: "The purpose of this study was to test a cognitive insomnia treatment on adolescents aged (15–18) by replicating a previous study with cognitive therapy for insomnia" (p. 368). The use of the term *test* suggests that the researchers are trying to determine if an intervention produced a change. They do not specify a change over time; one needs to review the methods section to determine they are using a single-subject design that is assessing the impact of the intervention over time.

In addition to comparisons and relationships, investigators may be interested in clarifying phenomena or events. This may be achieved, as discussed, through descriptive or some qualitative research methods. Therefore, the purpose statement will be expressed as an attempt to clarify or describe identified phenomena, characteristics, or events. Isaksson and colleagues (2007) conducted a qualitative study with the following purpose statement: "The aim of the current study was to describe how women with spinal cord injuries perceive the importance of social support for participation in occupation" (p. 24). The key term in this purpose statement is *describe,* which denotes an attempt to identify phenomena, events, or experiences.

Moore (1983) stated that the purpose statement should include delineation of the variables studied. Generally, in quantitative research methods involving the use of true experimental and quasi-experimental designs, the researcher identifies independent and dependent variables. An independent variable is defined as an event, condition, or measured attribute or characteristic that the researcher, for the most part, controls. (There is no manipulation or control of an independent variable that is measured, such as levels of IQ.) Additionally, an independent variable must have at least two levels or groups to compare. The dependent variable is defined in terms of changes in the subject as a consequence of the independent variable. For example, Taylor and Rowe (2012) described the independent and dependent variables in a study on the impact of music on math performance (the Mozart Effect): "The purpose of this study was to determine if a 'Mozart Effect' improves student performance on outcome assessments in mathematics" (p. 51). The independent variable was the music, and the outcome or dependent variable was math assessments.

Another example is provided by Hatinen, Kinnunen, Pekkonen, and Kalimo (2007), who described the independent and dependent variables in their purpose statement this way:

> The primary purpose of the present study was to test a new strategy for treating burnout and to compare it to the traditional strategy normally used in rehabilitation for burnout in Finland. We analyzed the short-term and long-term effects of both interventions on the outcome variables (burnout symptoms and perceived job conditions) over an intervention lasting one year. (p. 229)

The dependent variables were burnout symptoms and perceived job conditions, and the independent variable was the type of burnout intervention program, that is, new intervention versus traditional. The independent and dependent variables should be clearly and concisely identified in the purpose statement when the researchers decide to use quantitative methods.

Moore (1983) suggested that the identification of these two variables, independent and dependent, in the purpose statement should not be too detailed; specific, detailed descriptions should be provided in the methods section. In qualitative research and in quantitative descriptive studies, researchers typically do not have independent and dependent variables, but there are variables of interest that should be clearly and concisely identified.

A third component that should be included in a purpose statement is the identification of the population studied. Citation of the population should be clear but not too specific. When interpreting a study, readers of research articles need to know what specific population the results may be applied to. If the researchers identify the population too specifically, it may violate the subjects' confidentiality. The study (qualitative) by Isaksson and colleagues (2007) provides an example of identifying the population without being too specific. They stated that "the current study was to describe how women with spinal cord injuries . . ." (p. 24). The identification of the population is women with spinal cord injuries, and no specific information is provided that would identify them or give too specific information. Greenwell and Zygouris-Coe (2012) provide another example of identification of the population in the purpose statement. The researchers described the purpose as follows: "The purpose of this small qualitative case study was to explore the teaching practices of two reading endorsed secondary English language arts teachers at a central Florida high school" (p. 22). The population of interest is English language arts teachers. Despite noting these were teachers in central Florida, the researchers do not provide too much detail in identifying the population, for example, the specific school.

Another issue to address in understanding and evaluating the purpose statement is ensuring that the purpose and the problem are researchable (Moore, 1983). A study may be considered researchable if the independent variables, dependent variables, or variables of interest can be operationalized (i.e., converted into measurable and, preferably, objective operations). Examples of problems that are not researchable might include whether there are angels or whether there are unidentified flying objects (UFOs). With advances in science and technology, some "unresearchable" problems may become researchable, but we are concerned only with whether the study was researchable at the time it was done, given the available methods. King, Burton, Hicks, and Drigotas (2007) studied positive affect and superstitious beliefs such as whether there are ghosts. They were able to collect data on participants' moods and perceptions, which can be converted to measurable variables. The difference here is the opportunity to operationalize the dependent variable, so it can be measured.

GUIDELINES AND QUESTIONS FOR EVALUATING THE PURPOSE STATEMENT

I suggest using the following five topics and guidelines to evaluate the purpose statement:

1. Is the purpose statement clearly based on the argument developed in the literature review? Is there a clear connection?

2. Can the type of study that was conducted be identified based on the purpose statement? Does the researcher use words such as *comparisons, relationships, illuminate, change over time,* or *describe?*

3. Are the variables of interest clearly identified in the purpose statement? If the study is a true experimental design, do the researchers clearly identify the independent and dependent variables? What are they? In qualitative or descriptive studies, is there at least one variable of interest that is clearly identified? What is it?

4. Is the population of interest clearly identified in the purpose statement?

5. Do the study and the purpose statement focus on problems that are researchable?

EVALUATION OF EXAMPLES
FROM THE RESEARCH LITERATURE

Quantitative Research

Henderson and colleagues (2007) use the following purpose statement in their study focusing on the healing effects of mandalas:

The primary purpose of our study was to examine the healing aspects of drawing mandalas. Specifically, the psychological and physical health benefits of mandala drawing were viewed as a creative means of traumatic disclosure that would symbolically organize and integrate emotions and experiences, while serving the same function as writing a narrative. (p. 149)

The first question in our evaluation is whether the purpose statement is clearly based on the argument developed in the literature review. Is there a clear connection? We can refer back to Chapter 11 to determine whether the literature review provides a good argument for this purpose statement. The authors cite research that illustrates the benefits of using written expression in coping with traumatic events. They suggest that exposure to reviewing the experience through writing and other methods leads to reduction in psychological and physical problems. They attempt to bridge the connection between written forms of expression and other forms like art to achieve the benefits of reducing psychological and physical health problems. Other research that is cited, which is limited, focuses on the use of art therapy but with limited results in improving health benefits and psychological functioning. The argument then for using mandalas, which is presented as similar to art therapy, is less clear. However, the authors do cite some research into the effects of using art and mandalas in reducing anxiety.

The second question or guideline to address is this: Can the type of study conducted be identified based on the purpose statement? The researchers use the term *examine* in the purpose statement, which does not give the reader a clear understanding of what type of study was conducted. *Examine* could refer to a descriptive or comparative study. The researchers did not provide information in the purpose statement that they were comparing a control and experimental group.

The third question concerns the identification of variables of interest and whether they are clearly identified in the purpose statement. The researchers do identify the variables of interest, that is, the independent variable of drawing mandalas and the dependent variables of psychological and physical health.

A fourth question to address in evaluating the purpose statement concerns whether the population of interest is clearly identified in the purpose statement.

The researchers do not give any information on the population of interest in the purpose statement. It is clear in the methods and participants section that the population of interest are those with traumatic stress experiences and who experience posttraumatic stress: The researchers state, "Participants were prescreened for both the experience of trauma and trauma severity" (p. 149).

The final guideline or question I want to address is whether the purpose statement identifies a purpose that is clearly researchable. The researchers identify the purpose as examining the healing aspects of drawing mandalas and the outcome or effects being psychological and physical health as the dependent variables. Psychological and physical health both provide a researcher with variables that are researchable. One can measure psychological and physical health. There are numerous instruments for measuring psychological health and perceptions of psychological health.

In summary, the article by Henderson and colleagues (2007) provides a clear link between the literature review and the purpose statement. They stated that the study would focus on the psychological and physical well-being of those with traumatic stress. The type of study presented in the article does not give the reader a good idea of the purpose of the study. The researchers do not use any particular words or statements that identify the type of study being conducted, nor is the population of interest identified. The dependent variables of physical and psychological health are quantifiable and can be measured.

Qualitative Research

Fry (2007), in a study focusing on first-year teacher induction support, describes her purpose as follows:

The current investigation contributes to the induction literature by using qualitative research methods to determine how four 1st-year teachers were supported during induction and how they responded to this support. (p. 218)

This study is a qualitative study, but the same questions can be used to evaluate such methods. The first question is whether the purpose is based on the literature review. The researcher systematically discusses several specific examples of teacher induction programs like those in Santa Cruz, California, and Walla Walla, Washington. The researcher cites teacher attrition rate problems and states that these can be addressed with induction programs, but the author notes the lack of research that supports the use of induction methods.

Our second question concerns whether the purpose statement identifies the type of research methods employed in the study. The researcher states, "The current investigation contributes to the induction literature by using qualitative research methods" (p. 218). It is clear from the purpose statement that this is a qualitative study.

A third question to address is whether the variables of interest are clearly defined. The variables of interest in a qualitative study are not always as clearly defined as those in a quantitative study. The researcher identifies teacher induction or induction support as one variable of interest in the study. It is clear from the purpose statement that the target population is first-year teachers. Finally, we are interested in whether this study is clearly researchable. The study appears to be researchable because one can identify and observe induction procedures for first-year teachers.

In summary, the study conducted by Fry (2007) shows the purpose statement as partly connected and clear from the literature review. At times, the citations used are not consistent with the purpose of the study; for example, attrition rates are stable despite increases in the use of induction methods. The type of study conducted is clearly identified in the purpose statement. The variable of interest in the study is teacher induction methods, and this is clearly identified in the purpose statement. Also, the population of interest is clearly identified as first-year teachers. Finally, the study and the variable of interest, teacher induction procedures, are researchable and can be operationalized.

Single-Subject Research

Dionne and Martini (2011) conducted single-subject research study focused on the use of floor play time with a child with autism. They described their purpose as follows: "The purpose of this study was to determine the effectiveness of floor time play intervention with a child with autism" (p. 199). The first question is whether the purpose statement is clearly based on the argument developed in the literature review. Is there a clear connection? The researchers in this study described how there is strong agreement that early intervention with children with autism is important. However, they noted that agreement on the intervention is not so clear. They proposed that the purpose of many interventions with children with autism is the promotion or encouragement of appropriate behaviors. The researchers provided a detailed description of the use of floor play time with these children. Additionally, the researchers provide a clear description of the developmental activities of play associated with various ages and levels of development. It does appear the researchers do provide a clear connection to the literature review. They discussed various interventions used with children with autism and outlined how floor play time may be used with this population.

A second question is this: Can the type of study that was conducted be identified based on the purpose statement? Does the researcher use words such as *comparisons, relationships, illuminate,* or *describe?* The researchers use the term *effectiveness* in the purpose statement. There is no statement of a comparison or relationship. However, the use of effectiveness with a single-subject design suggests there is an attempt to identify changes over time. One needs to confirm the use of single-subject design to determine if change, in this case, effectiveness, is being studied.

The third question is whether the variables of interest are clearly identified in the purpose statement. If the study is a true experimental design, do the researchers clearly identify the independent and dependent variables? What are they? In qualitative or descriptive studies, is there at least one variable of interest that is clearly identified? What is it? One variable is the independent variable of floor play time. The researchers do hint at the dependent variable and suggest there will be an impact from floor play time. However, they do not identify exactly what the outcome or dependent variable is in the purpose statement.

The fourth question is this: Is the population of interest clearly identified in the purpose statement? The researchers do identify the population of interest very clearly, children with autism. The only limitation may be that they do not clarify the age of the population. Are they studying young children or adolescents with autism?

The last question is this: Do the study and the purpose statement focus on problems that are researchable? One can provide an opportunity for the children with autism to participate in floor play time. This can be observed and evaluated for the quality of the play. However, the researchers do not identify the dependent variable as has been noted earlier. Consequently, it is difficult to evaluate whether the dependent variable is researchable. With a glance at the methods section under instruments, one finds that the major dependent variable was measurement of reciprocal communication. A researcher can measure reciprocal communication and code the frequency and quality of such communication.

In summary, the researchers provide a clear connection between the purpose statement and the literature review. They also use the word *effectiveness* in the purpose statement, suggesting an effort to bring about a change over time. The independent variable is clearly identified in the purpose, but the dependent variable is not. The population of interest is identified but could be more clearly stated if the general age of the population was noted. Finally, the independent variable is one that can be operationalized, floor play time, but the dependent variable is not expressly stated the purpose. Reciprocal communication can be operationalized, which was found to be the dependent variable.

SUMMARY

The purpose statement should provide the reader with a clear description of the intent of the study. It may be presented as a declarative statement or in the form of one or more questions. Even though the purpose statement may be only a sentence or two, it can provide the reader with significant information and clues about the type of study conducted, the population of interest, and the variables of interest. I want to reiterate the intent of careful evaluation of different sections of a journal article, which is to provide a guide for consumers and users of research to systematically determine which components of a study are valid and which need to be accepted with caution. In evaluating the purpose, a poorly written intent or goal of a study is a problem because the reader may not know whether the researchers have accomplished an identified purpose.

Exercise

Directions: Locate an article in the professional literature addressing a topic that you are interested in exploring. Evaluate the purpose statement based on the questions addressed in this chapter. Try to explain and justify your answers by using specific examples from the article.

1. Is the purpose statement clearly based on the argument developed in the literature review? Is there a clear connection? Explain your response.

2. Can you identify the type of study conducted based on the purpose statement? Does the researcher use words such as *comparisons, relationships, illuminate, change over time,* or *describe?* Explain.

3. Are the variables of interest clearly identified in the purpose statement? If the study is a true experimental design, does the researcher clearly identify the independent and dependent variables? In qualitative or descriptive studies, is there at least one variable of interest that is clearly identified? Explain.

4. Is the population of interest clearly identified in the purpose statement? Explain.

5. Do the study and the purpose statement focus on problems that are clearly researchable? Explain.

QUANTITATIVE RESEARCH HYPOTHESES

A hypothesis is a formally stated expectation of outcomes; the researchers develop it based on theory, previous research, or personal experience. We make predictions and educated guesses about outcomes on a regular basis in our everyday lives. George Kelly (1955), a personality theorist, suggested that we are all scientists and that we all engage in hypothesis testing on a regular basis. What is the difference between this type of thinking and the scientific approach to hypothesis testing? The difference lies in the degree to which a formal argument is developed for the hypothesis in the literature review. As stated, the hypothesis may be based on theory, previous research, or personal experience. In our everyday lives, we generally do not make predictions based on theory or previous research results. Most of our hypothesizing in everyday life is based on personal experiences. A research hypothesis is developed from a clear argument based on the literature review. Obviously, in everyday life, we do not develop or formulate a formal written hypothesis about our expectations. A hypothesis may be used in research methods of true experimental, quasi-experimental, and descriptive comparative designs. Another approach to hypothesis testing is a Bayesian model (Matthews, 2011) for hypothesis testing. In this approach, the process is consideration of competing hypotheses. Considering competing hypotheses is followed by a review of outcomes and data supporting one over the other. Both approaches to hypotheses testing begin with an objective perspective and systematic gathering of data. Hypotheses are not typically used in most descriptive and qualitative designs. A different approach to hypothesis testing that can be used in qualitative methods will be described later in this chapter.

INDIRECT PROOF: AN ORIENTATION TO THE SCIENTIFIC APPROACH

To further understand the scientific approach to developing and evaluating a research hypothesis, I want to discuss the idea behind indirect proof. Moore (1983) stated that researchers should initially assume that there is no effect from the variables of interest to any outcome. Additionally, he stated that we can never prove a hypothesis. This is based on the notion that we conduct research on samples of the population, and they represent possible responses, but this is only a representation and not a fact. Instead of proving hypotheses, researchers gather evidence to support their hypotheses. Leary (2001) proposed the following: "Theories cannot be proved because obtaining empirical support for a hypothesis does not necessarily mean that the theory from which the hypothesis was derived is true" (p. 19). What it means is that there can be evidence that supports a theory, but it does not prove the theory. In fact, there can be research support from competing theories, but this does not prove that one theory is better than another (Leary, 2001). Leary (2001) further stated that the "merit of theories is judged, not on the basis of a single research study, but on the accumulated evidence from several studies" (p. 20). In essence, support for a particular theory or hypothesis is accomplished through a number of research studies, and the quality of these studies impacts the support provided. I frequently have heard researchers and doctoral students talk about proving their hypotheses. The previous discussion is meant to caution against such a perception or conclusion; science is conducted on samples (not the total population and not everyone's responses) with instruments that may or may not accurately measure outcomes, so we must maintain a view of indirect proof and we gather evidence to support a hypothesis and not prove it.

TYPES OF HYPOTHESES

Three different types of hypotheses have been identified: null, alternative nondirectional, and alternative directional (Bluman, 2012; Minium & King, 2003). The null hypothesis is where an investigator starts in the research process. I say this because the initial assumption the researcher should make is that there is no relationship or cause-and-effect outcome between the variables of interest. An assumption that there is no relationship or difference between groups is the key foundation of the scientific method, that is, maintaining an objective view. Leary (2001) described the null hypothesis as follows: "The independent variable did not have an effect on the dependent variable" (p. 246). Researchers have developed a method to represent the null hypothesis with symbols (Bluman, 2012): $H_0 \, \mu_1 \neq \mu_2$.

H_0 denotes the null hypothesis. The Greek letter *mu* (μ) indicates the population average or mean. And, μ_1 and μ_2 refer to two different groups of interest. Essentially, this may be interpreted as the means for population Group 1 being no different from the means for population Group 2, determined by the variables of interest (the dependent variables). The null hypothesis is grounded in statistical methods, and essentially, the researcher begins his or her investigation with the notion that there is no significant statistical difference between two or more groups of interests, based on comparison of results on the means of the dependent variable or variables. It is not typical that researchers state the null hypothesis. However, there is a journal, the *Journal of Articles in Support of the Null Hypothesis,* that publishes articles that do not find significant differences. However, in most published research, the reader is meant to infer that every researcher has started with the null hypothesis, even though this is not stated.

Researchers typically identify alternative types of research hypotheses in the literature when there is enough evidence to predict a difference or a given direction. One type of research hypothesis, the alternative nondirectional hypothesis, implies that the researcher has enough evidence from previous research to suggest that there is likely to be a difference in groups, but there is not enough evidence to predict the exact direction. Essentially, the researcher is stating that a significant difference is based on the variables of interests (in this case, the independent variable). An alternative nondirectional hypothesis is based on the statistical premise that the results will be that one group mean is significantly higher or lower than another or others but does not predict which direction. The researcher cannot predict the direction but is hypothesizing a difference. An alternative nondirectional hypothesis is symbolically denoted as $H_A\ \mu_1 \neq \mu_2$. H_A refers to the alternative nondirectional hypothesis. And μ_1 and μ_2 denotes the population means for the two groups.

The third type of hypothesis, the alternative directional hypothesis, is used when the researcher has enough evidence from previous research to support the prediction of a direction of outcome. This means that, if a researcher is comparing two groups using an independent variable, one group is expected to score higher on the dependent variable, as predicted by the researcher. Statistically, the researcher is indicating that the outcome of the research data will be either significantly above or below the mean and predicts the direction. The alternative directional hypothesis is denoted symbolically as $H_A\ \mu_1 > \mu_2$.

H_A indicates an alternative hypothesis, and μ_1 and μ_2 represent the population means for the two groups of interest. There can be more than two group comparisons, for example, three, four, and so on.

A hypothesis should be based on the argument developed in the literature review. In addition, the hypothesis should extend from the purpose statement. The purpose statement and hypothesis serve the researcher and consumer of research differently. First, the purpose statement provides the general intent of the study, whereas hypotheses are designed to provide insight into the researcher's anticipation and expectations about outcomes based on critical thinking: specifically, as presented as a foundation or argument in the literature review. This means that, in the literature review, the researcher should provide an argument for why he or she chose a particular alternative hypothesis (i.e., alternative directional or alternative nondirectional).

Researchers have proposed that hypotheses should be testable and falsifiable (Heiman, 1995). The issue of whether a hypothesis is testable is similar to the question used when evaluating the purpose statement: Is the purpose statement researchable? Heiman stated that, under this criterion, the researcher must be able to develop a method of testing and implementing a hypothesis. Gliner and Morgan (2000) described a hypothesis that should be "testable, by empirical methods; it should not be just a statement of your moral, ethical, or political position" (p. 47). An example of a hypothesis that is not testable is the statement that there is life in other solar systems. Currently, this is not testable because we do not have the technology to send spacecraft to the distances necessary to test this hypothesis. This may change over time because of technology advances, and at such a point, we would change this analysis and conclude that one can test whether there is life on other planets.

A hypothesis must also be falsifiable, which means that one can gather evidence to show that it is incorrect. An example of a hypothesis that is not falsifiable may involve, for example, supernatural phenomena, such as those said to occur in the Bermuda Triangle. We can establish methods for testing a hypothesis about unusual events happening in a particular region—we can go to Bermuda to collect information—but we do not have the instruments to measure supernatural events, such as unexplained reasons for loss of power in boat or airplane engines. Therefore, we cannot gather evidence that such a hypothesis is incorrect based on all reported incidences.

Another important issue to consider when evaluating a hypothesis is whether it is rational and parsimonious (Heiman, 1995). Heiman (1995) stated that a hypothesis should be rational, and this refers to whether it is even possible for the hypothesis to be true. For example, is it rational to hypothesize that IQ is related to bumps on someone's head? There is certainly no evidence that this is true, and there is no rationale that might support this view.

Parsimony concerns how well a hypothesis fits into current views of a particular theory or field of study. Parsimony, then, is concerned about whether the hypothesis is consistent with current theories (Heiman, 1995). An example of a violation of this issue might be a hypothesis in behavioral theory addressing intrapsychic processes such as dreaming. Studying dreams creates a basic conflict with this approach: In behavioral theory, phenomena must be observable and measurable, not intrapsychic.

Moore (1983) proposed that brevity and clarity also be considered important when evaluating the efficacy of a hypothesis. Brevity involves stating the hypothesis as concisely as possible. A hypothesis should not be several paragraphs long unless the researcher is proposing numerous hypotheses. Clarity refers to how easy it is for others to understand the hypothesis. As Heiman (1995) pointed out, the hypothesis should not be overly complex just for the sake of complexity. This creates something of a dilemma for researchers because they must identify the relevant variables of interest but not be too specific; at the same time, they must be clear enough, so the reader understands the hypothesis. A related perspective is broad versus narrow focus of the research hypothesis (Gliner & Morgan, 2000). They noted that science advances in small steps, and thus, one needs to limit studies that are too broad and cannot be conducted because of their complexity. Moore (1983) noted that it is not necessary to restate the population in the hypothesis once it is indicated in the purpose statement.

A hypothesis provides a guide for the researcher to use when determining which statistical tests are best suited to his or her research. The tests chosen will then be reported in the results section. There should be consistency between the hypothesis identified and the type of statistics employed. More specifically, if a researcher states that he or she expects one group to score higher than another group on a measure of stress, there should be a statistical test reported in the results section that addresses this hypothesis. Again, we are looking for consistency throughout a study. We will come back to answering this question in the results section: Does the researcher employ statistical methods reported in the results section that address each hypothesis identified?

GUIDELINES AND QUESTIONS FOR EVALUATING HYPOTHESES

The following questions may be used to evaluate the hypothesis proposed in a journal research article:

1. What type of hypothesis is presented? Is it an alternative nondirectional, an alternative directional, or a null hypothesis?

2. Do the investigators provide a clear rationale for the direction of their hypothesis based on the literature review?

3. Is the hypothesis testable and falsifiable?

4. Is the hypothesis rational, or is it reasonable to expect that it could be true based on theory or previous research?

5. Is the hypothesis parsimonious with current theories or research?

6. Is the hypothesis stated with brevity and clarity?

EVALUATION OF EXAMPLES FROM THE RESEARCH LITERATURE

Quantitative Research

Henderson and colleagues (2007) conducted a study focusing on the healing aspects of the use of mandalas. Mandalas are considered to be graphic or artistic representations, most often of the universe. The researchers stated,

It was hypothesized that individuals assigned to a mandala-drawing condition would show a significant increase in psychological and physical health relative to control group participants both immediately after the intervention and at a 1-month follow up. Improvements in psychological health would be evidenced by decreases in self-reported depression, anxiety, post traumatic stress disorder (PTSD) symptom severity, and an increase in spiritual meaning. Improvements in physical health were determined through decreases in the self-reported frequency of occurrence of physical health problems. (p. 149)

The researchers have chosen an alternative directional hypothesis for this study. They have clearly identified the direction of the hypothesis: "Those assigned to a mandala-drawing condition would show significant increase in psychological and physical health" compared to a control group. The researchers do present a clear argument for the direction of their hypothesis when they cite studies supporting the effectiveness of mandala drawing; they cited Curry and Kasser (2005). (See the Chapter 11 citation of the literature review.) The study by Slegelis (1987) also provided support, but as the authors noted, the research design was not necessarily strong.

The next question concerns whether the hypothesis is testable and falsifiable. Both physical and psychological health can be measured and tested, so the researchers do meet the requirement for the study being testable. In regard to whether the study is falsifiable, the researchers can have participants construct mandalas and collect data on the effects of the mandalas on their psychological and physical health. Consequently, the researchers can refute a hypothesis that the construction of mandalas has an impact on psychological or physical health.

The fourth issue in addressing the hypothesis focuses on whether it is rational or reasonable to expect that the hypothesis could be true based on theory or previous research. The researchers present an argument based on written disclosure paradigm and theory. For example, the theory states that "repeated exposure to aversive conditioned stimuli leads to the extinguishment of negative emotions . . ." (p. 148). A second theory included as part of the researcher's rationale is cognitive change theory. The hypothesis does present a rational link to the theories presented.

Related to whether the hypothesis is rational is whether it is parsimonious with current theories or research. The researchers state in the literature review, discussing cognitive change theory, that "cognitive restructuring serves to resolve the traumatic experience, as well as bring a sense of meaning to the event as insights are gained through the process of writing" (p. 148). This description of the theory is parsimonious with the hypothesis that proposes to increase psychological and physical health.

Finally, we want to know if the hypothesis is stated with brevity and clarity. Henderson and colleagues (2007) present a hypothesis that is relatively brief and gives clarity to the expectations of the researcher. The variables of interest are clear, and they are concisely stated.

In summary, the hypothesis presented by Henderson and colleagues (2007) gives a clear alternative directional hypothesis. They provide a rationale based on the literature for the direction of their hypothesis; they cite studies that have found positive effects of mandalas and the use of art with anxiety disorders. The study is testable and falsifiable because the researchers can collect information about psychological and physical functioning, and the use of mandalas can be implemented. Previous research provides a rationale for conducting the study because there have not been significant amounts of research into this area. The hypothesis is consistent with two theories, written disclosure theory and cognitive change theory. Finally, the hypothesis is stated with brevity and clarity, with the variables of interest identified and concisely stated.

EVALUATING A HYPOTHESIS IN QUALITATIVE RESEARCH METHODS

A formally stated hypothesis is generally not made in qualitative research. Qualitative research has been descried as theory building (Brannen, 1992) and involves formulating an area of interest and collecting information to develop, support, or refute a theory. Brannen (1992) suggested that qualitative, ethnographic methods may be defined in terms of a working hypothesis: a hypothetical explanation of phenomena in which information is gathered to determine whether the facts fit the working hypothesis or explanation. Typically, researchers present a working hypothesis in qualitative research in terms of theories to be tested rather than as formal hypotheses such as directional and nondirectional hypotheses, which would be found in quantitative research methods. Fry (2007) conducted a study that focused on induction support for new teachers. She used qualitative methods in her study. As has been mentioned earlier, qualitative studies typically do not involve the use of formal hypotheses. However, the researcher does provide insight into how she predicts expected results. For example, she stated, "Since the presence of induction may not be enough to reduce attrition rates, research needs to move beyond determining the prevalence of induction and begin to assess form and quality" (p. 218).

Different questions are relevant in determining the quality of the working hypothesis. One question is this: Do the researchers identify a working hypothesis or a theory they are testing? When evaluating qualitative research, not all qualitative studies identify a working hypothesis, in part because so little is known about a particular topic and also because of the nature of qualitative research, that is, an intent to explore the topic or issue without an expected outcome. The literature will typically provide some insight into whether enough information is available to generate working hypotheses. A second question to consider with qualitative research and a hypothesis is the following: Is the hypothesis parsimonious with current theories or research? As with quantitative research, qualitative research does consider theoretical perspectives (Best & Kahn, 1998).

Admi (1996) completed a descriptive exploratory study focusing on growing up with a chronic health condition, cystic fibrosis. Admi stated,

A different theoretical perspective, which challenges some of Goffman's (1963) assertions, is offered by current social-psychological view on disability and chronic health conditions (e.g., Fine & Asch, 1988; Frank 1988; Gliedman & Roth, 1980; Hahn, 1988; Mest, 1988; Schneider & Conrad, 1980). These theories are based on the minority group model, in which the problems of people with disabilities are assumed to stem primarily from society's discriminating attitudes and restricting physical environment. . . . The minority group model shifts the focus from the individual with the disability to the physical and attitudinal environment. (p. 167)

No working hypothesis is identified by Admi. In this statement, the researcher (Admi, 1996) makes clear that she is testing a theory, the minority group model. In answer to our second question (about parsimony), the researcher notes that there is disagreement in the literature on the processes of growing up with a disability. However, she provides support for her working hypothesis when she cites research and writings from the minority group model.

Single-Subject Research

Single-subject research more frequently uses questions rather than hypotheses. However, I want to use one example of a single-subject study that may serve as an example of a hypothesis. Simpson and Keen (2010) focused on the use of graphic symbols embedded with an interactive song to improve receptive labeling involving academic tasks of those with autism. Specifically, the researchers attempted to teach correct labeling of animal symbols while being presented with a PowerPoint and a song associated with touching a symbol. The researchers state the purpose as follows: "The aim of this study was to investigate whether children with autism could learn to receptively label animal symbols incorporated within an interactive song using a Powerpoint presentation and Interactive Whiteboard (IWB) and to generalise the learning to other non-music contexts" (p. 167). The closest example of a hypothesis is the following statement: "Given that some children with autism have shown a preference for computer instruction over typical teaching instruction (Moore and Calvert, 2000), the use of a computer-based presentation provided an opportunity to avoid researcher bias while possibly enhancing the engagement of participants" (p. 167). The first question is this: What type of hypothesis is presented? Is it an alternative nondirectional, an alternative directional, or a null hypothesis? The hypothesis appears to be an alternative directional hypothesis. The researcher proposed or hypothesized that the intervention will enhance the engagement of participants.

The second question is this: Do the investigators provide a clear rationale for the direction of their hypothesis based on the literature review? The researchers cited previous research that shows a mixed outcome between the use of music and attention or successfully completing academic tasks. One example of supporting the use of music and improved academic performance was a study by Stephens, and the researchers described the researcher supporting the use of music and academic performance. They stated, "Music has also been found to increase joint attention and engagement when compared to a play context for children with autism" (p. 166). Another study they cited is described as not showing a positive outcome and the use of music: "Kim et al (2008, 2009) compared the effects of improvisational music therapy or play sessions on joint attention during music therapy session compared with play sessions. However, little change was observed in either condition for initiating joint attention behaviors" (p. 166). It is typical that researchers will provide a review of research that shows inconsistency in outcomes, and as has been noted in the literature chapter, Chapter 11, it shows or demonstrates objectivity. However, the researchers only infer that, because there is such inconsistency, further research is needed.

The third question is whether the hypothesis is testable and falsifiable. A researcher can gather information about individual responses to learning and specifically learning identification and labeling of animals. Also, researchers can work with individuals with autism to test the hypothesis. The diagnosis of autism can be accomplished, and there are guidelines for doing so. The fourth question is whether the hypothesis is rational, or is it reasonable to expect that it could be true based on theory or previous research? The previous research cited shows a positive impact of music on learning labeling of animals. The hypothesis is parsimonious with current theories or research. Despite there being inconsistent outcomes of using music to improve successful labeling of animals, the researchers provided an objective view of previous research. They also provided adequate examples of successful use of music with those with autism in labeling animals. The last question is whether the hypothesis is stated with brevity and clarity. The suggested hypothesis is stated briefly. However, the variables of interest are not clearly identified, and the direction of the hypothesis is somewhat vague.

SUMMARY

In quantitative research methods, a hypothesis is a guess about expected outcomes. Different types of hypotheses have been identified: null, directional, and nondirectional. As with the purpose statement, we are interested in a clear explanation of how the hypothesis was developed (from the literature review), consistency, and clarity for the reader. It is important to remember that not all quantitative research will involve a hypothesis. Descriptive research generally does not present a hypothesis because the intent is to clarify the characteristics of phenomena. Traditional methods of presenting a hypothesis also are not employed in qualitative research. In qualitative research, there may be statements that describe efforts at theory building or working hypotheses. The use of a hypothesis is not as frequently used in single-subject research, and research questions are more likely to be used. Frequently, a reader can anticipate a hypothesis based on the purpose and literature review.

Exercises

Directions: Locate an article in the professional literature addressing a topic you are interested in exploring. Evaluate the literature review based on the questions addressed in this chapter. Try to explain and justify your answers based on specific examples from the article you choose.

Quantitative Research and Single-Subject Research

1. What type of hypothesis is presented (alternative nondirectional, alternative directional, or null hypothesis)?

2. Do the investigators provide a clear rationale for the direction of their hypothesis based on the literature review?

3. Is the hypothesis testable and falsifiable?

4. Is the hypothesis rational, or is it reasonable to expect that it could be true based on theory or previous research?

5. Is the hypothesis parsimonious with current theories or research?

6. Is the hypothesis stated with brevity and clarity?

Qualitative Research

1. Do the researchers identify a working hypothesis or a theory they are testing?

2. Is the hypothesis parsimonious with current theories or research?

13

EVALUATING THE METHODS SECTION
Sampling Methods

The methods section, which will be the focus for Chapters 13, 14, and 15, consists of the sample, the procedures, and the instrumentation. These three chapters include detailed descriptions of how the study was conducted. There are several reasons the scientific community requires researchers to provide detailed descriptions of their methods in a journal article. The first reason is to allow those reading the results to determine the efficacy of the study. The second reason concerns the potential for replication of the study; detailed information is needed if a researcher were interested in reproducing the results. As consumers of research, we are most concerned with the first reason: How effective are the methods used in the study in achieving reliable results? In this chapter, I will first review the basic principles of selecting a sample or subjects for a study. Second, I will present information on sample selection procedures. The next section will address sampling bias and sampling errors. Fourth, I will provide a series of questions or guides for evaluating the sample parts of the methods section. Finally, I will provide examples from the professional literature and evaluate several methods sections, focusing on the sample, to illustrate this approach to evaluation.

To understand what a sample is, we must start with concepts defining the population. Researchers are ultimately interested in understanding how research results apply in the natural environment and with a specific groups of individuals, that is, the population. Several definitions of a population have been proposed (Ary et al., 2014; Best & Kahn, 1998; Charles, 1995; Gall et al., 2002). Gall and colleagues (2002) differentiated the population and the sample: "Quantitative researchers attempt to discover something about a large group of individuals by studying a smaller group. The larger group that they wish to learn about is called a population, and the smaller group they actually study is called a sample" (p. 167). Ary and colleagues (2014) described a population as "all members of any well-defined class of people, events, or objects" (p. 161). Creswell (2012) defined a population as "a group of individuals who have the same characteristics" (p. 142). For our purposes, I want to define population as the group to which the researcher intends to apply his or her results and that is identified by clearly defined characteristics of interest. If a researcher is interested in understanding how a new counseling intervention works, the population of interest may be all those individuals with PTSD. The researcher may define the sample by stating that it is composed only of those with certain characteristics, such as those with PTSD as defined in the *DSM-5 (Diagnostic and Statistical Manual of Mental Disorders, 5th ed.),* only adults, and so on.

Two different types of populations have been identified (Ary et al., 2014): the target population and the accessible population. The target population is defined as all individuals or objects the researcher is interested in and to which the study results are applied. However, a researcher is generally not able to access the entire target population, particularly if it is a large population, so for practical reasons, an accessible population must be identified. If we return to our example of those with PTSD, we can see that a researcher cannot realistically access all those with PTSD throughout the world. Therefore, he or she is left with identifying the accessible population, for instance, those from the northeastern United States.

Most research involves populations that are quite large, which makes inclusion of all members of a population in a study practically impossible. First, the cost of including all individuals in a population would be prohibitive; for example, contacting them via mail, e-mail, or phone is expensive. Second, the time required to conduct such a study would be tremendous. Consequently, researchers have developed methods of selecting representatives of the accessible population (a sample). Ary and colleagues (2014) defined a sample as "a portion of a population" (p. 161). Creswell defined a sample as "a subgroup of the target population that the researcher plans to study for generalizing about the target population" (p. 142). For our purposes, I want to define a sample as a subset of individuals who are of interest to the researcher and who represent identified characteristics of the target population.

The first step in selecting a sample is to determine the characteristics of interest. As I noted previously, a researcher may want to study soldiers returning from a war zone and specifically study PTSD. Consequently, the researcher needs to decide how to identify those who fit the category he or she wants to study. For example, a researcher may want to study those with PTSD who have experienced direct combat versus those who might be flying jets and experience combat at a distance. A second major step in constructing a sample from the accessible population is the identification of relevant demographic characteristics. Examples of demographic characteristics include socioeconomic status (SES), gender, ethnicity, occupation, level of education, and religious affiliation. The researcher must determine relevant characteristics based on the population of interest. For example, a researcher would not identify occupation in a school-age population. Another example may be religious affiliation; if a characteristic does not concern the population of interest and the purpose of the study, then it would not be considered in constructing the sample and population. Key in deciding which demographic characteristics to identify are (1) the purpose of the study (e.g., understanding the impact of experiencing combat on PTSD) and (2) whether any relevant demographic characteristics potentially influence the outcome or the dependent variable.

Once a researcher identifies the population of interest, the next step is selecting a sample that is representative of the larger population. Researchers have raised the issue of whether it is truly possible to select a sample that mirrors the population of interest (Heppner et al., 1992). Gall and colleagues (2002) defined population validity as "the extent to which the results of an experiment can be generalized from the sample that participated in it to a larger group of individuals, that is, a population" (p. 164). There are sampling methods that improve the chance of obtaining a fairly representative sample. The extent to which a sample represents a population is critical in determining how easily and validly the researcher can generalize the results back to the entire target population; this is called population validity. Consequently, researchers have proposed several different methods of selecting a sample. These methods vary in their effectiveness in creating a sample that is most representative of the larger accessible population.

SAMPLING METHODS USED IN QUANTITATIVE RESEARCH

More common approaches to sampling in quantitative research include simple random sampling, systematic random sampling, stratified sampling, cluster sampling, and convenience sampling (see Table 13.1).

Simple random sampling generally involves selecting a subset of individuals from the accessible population so that every single individual has an equal chance of being chosen, and each selection is independent of any other selection (see Table 13.1). Several methods may be used to obtain a simple random sample. A random numbers table is one method of ensuring that every individual in the population has an equal chance of being selected for a study. A random numbers table typically consists of rows and columns of computer-generated random numbers. First, each person is assigned a number, and a researcher randomly selects where to start on the random numbers table. The researcher selects down the random numbers table until an adequate number of participants are selected. Another method of selecting a sample through random sampling is by simply assigning a number to all possible individuals from a population. Next, the researcher places the numbered slips of paper representing each person in the population in a container and then randomly draws out numbers and names. Those numbers drawn indicate who has been selected for the study. Numbered slips continue to be chosen until an adequate sample has been achieved. This approach is not often used because large populations make the procedure unwieldy.

A similar approach to simple sampling is systematic random sampling. This kind of sampling is more convenient and systematic than simple random sampling (see Table 13.1). The researcher can ensure that all in the population will be

Table 13.1   Types of Sampling: Quantitative Methods

Type of Sampling	Description	Advantages	Limitations
Simple random sampling	Every single individual in the population has an equal chance of being chosen.	If completed adequately, the results can be generalized readily back to the population.	It is difficult to ensure that every individual in the population has an equal chance of being chosen.
Systematic random sampling	A finite list of those in the population where every nth person is selected.	An easy, simple method to use.	Difficult to identify everyone in a population.
Stratified sampling (proportional and nonproportional)	Selection of individuals from the population who represent subgroups.	Ensures adequate representation on relevant variables (e.g., ethnicity).	May focus on a variable that is not as important as the others.
Cluster sampling	Random selection of intact groups (e.g., whole classrooms).	Allows the researcher to conduct studies with naturally intact groups.	The researcher cannot study differences between individuals in intact groups.
Convenience sampling	Section of a population that is convenient and accessible to the researcher.	Convenient; reduces costs and amount of effort in conducting a study.	Severely limits potential for generalizing the results back to the population; affects population validity.

considered as part of the sample based on the concrete list of the population. This method of sampling is implemented by the researcher, who assigns each person in a population a number and subsequently chooses the nth number, depending on the total number projected in the sample. More specifically, if there are 10,000 individuals in a population (it is assumed that the researcher has a list of all those belonging to a particular group) and the researcher has determined that a sample of 100 is adequate, then the researcher chooses every 100th person. He or she may start by choosing a number randomly from a random numbers table, and this will be the first person taken for the sample. Every 100th person after that will be selected for the sample.

A third type of sampling, stratified sampling, consists of selecting individuals from the population who represent subgroups (see Table 13.1). Choosing the subgroups is done in such a way as to ensure that there is adequate representation of the subgroups. Two strategies have been employed in stratified sampling. In proportional stratified sampling, the subgroup participants are chosen based on the same proportions found in the accessible population. For example, if a researcher is interested in studying reading achievement and he or she wants to ensure that various socioeconomic groups are represented, he or she would select participants based on the proportion of those in various socioeconomic groups in the population. So, if 20 percent of the population was from upper middle class, 20 percent of the sample would be selected from the upper middle class. Furthermore, if 25 percent were from the lowest SES, then, again, 25 percent would be chosen to represent the population from this subgroup.

A nonproportional, or equal-size, approach to stratified sampling involves equal numbers from each subgroup being chosen. For example, if the researcher is interested in obtaining a total of 100 participants and there are five subgroups, then 20 would be chosen from each subgroup, regardless of the proportion in the population. In this method of sampling, the researcher focuses on ensuring that there are equal sample sizes across the comparison groups.

The next approach to sampling, cluster sampling, is used when groups of the target population may not be separated (see Table 13.1). For example, if a researcher wanted to investigate the effects of a specific teaching approach to math, he or she would not necessarily be able to separate or assign high school students to a certain algebra class. Thus, if the researcher had access to a population of 30 algebra classes, he or she might randomly select 10 classes for the study, a cluster. As with simple random selection, the researcher might use random methods to choose the clusters, such as the use of a random numbers table.

Convenience sampling is the common approach used by researchers because many of the methods previously identified are more difficult to implement (see Table 13.1). Creswell (2012) stated, "In convenience sampling the researcher selects participants because they are willing and available to be studied" (p. 145). Gall and colleagues (2002) noted that researchers will frequently select a sample because it is easy for the researchers to access, such as a sample from an undergraduate college class (typically a psychology class). Another reason a researcher may choose a particular sample is that an administrator of an agency or school is associated with the researcher, and that administrator gives the researcher permission to use and access to a particular sample. The issue for the researcher and those reading and using the information in this study and article is to determine whether the results can be reasonably generalized to the population of interest when the sample is one of convenience and possibly not adequate to represent the intended population.

An important issue for researchers, regardless of the type of selection method used, is the use of volunteers or those agreeing to participate (Gall et al., 2002). Researchers must respect the right of those they have identified as desirable participants in a study to refuse participation. If a large number of those chosen refuse to participate, the researcher may lose the benefit of having selected participants randomly and objectively and obtain a sample that is not necessarily representative of the larger population of interest. To address the issue of volunteers, researchers sometimes attempt to determine whether those not choosing to participate in a study are significantly different in relevant variables from those participating. This is accomplished by contacting those not participating and asking them to provide relevant demographic characteristics and rule out any significant differences between those who choose to participate and those who choose not to participate.

Almost all current researchers use volunteers in their research because of federal guidelines protecting human subjects; for example, participation in research must be voluntary. The exception might be research not requiring institutional review, such as public observations that have no potential harm for the individual (recording hand washing in a restroom where individuals are not identified). One criterion used to determine whether this volunteer status affects the ability to generalize back to population is the return, or participation rate, of all requested to participate. Babbie (2006) stated that an acceptable response rate for survey research is at least 50 percent. The same criterion could be used to determine the appropriateness of requests to participate in an experimental study or manipulation.

SAMPLE SIZE

Another relevant issue that researchers consider when constructing a sample is sample size. Several factors influence the sample size used by a researcher. One factor is the design of the study and whether qualitative or quantitative methods are used. Different formulas have been suggested for different quantitative study designs, although it has been noted that the largest sample size feasible is a good rule to follow (Gall et al., 2002). For example, if researchers planned to use a true experimental design (e.g., a pretest–posttest design) and wanted to compare the effects of two counseling interventions and a control group, they would need a certain number of subjects. More subjects would be needed if they were comparing three treatment groups and a control group. Typically, researchers propose 15 subjects per group in a research design (Gall et al., 2002; Moore, 1983). Based on this formula, the first study would need at least 45 subjects, and the second study would require 60 subjects. Survey researchers should typically use a minimum of 100 subjects per major subgroup. A minimum of 30 subjects per variable is suggested for correlational research (Gall et al., 2002).

Researchers have developed a more sophisticated method of determining sample size when certain information is available and when they are using quantitative research methods. It is called statistical power analysis. Gall and colleagues (2002) defined statistical power analysis as "the probability that a particular test of statistical significance will lead to rejection of a false null hypothesis" (p. 141). A formula for determining the number of subjects needed to reject the null hypothesis is used. Four factors are considered in calculating statistical power: sample size (the larger the sample, the more likely there will be a rejection of the null hypothesis), level of significance, directionality, and effect size (Gall et al., 2002). Levels of significance involve the probability of an error's being made in statistical calculations. (Levels of significance have been defined in more detail in Chapter 3.) The stricter the level of significance (the less likely the chance of error), the more statistical power the researcher loses.

A third factor relevant to calculating statistical power analysis is directionality. Directionality involves statistics and concerns prediction by the researchers about the direction of outcomes, such as in a directional hypothesis. If a researcher is not sure whether one particular intervention is better than another and cannot predict the direction of the outcome, he or she loses statistical power.

The fourth factor in determining statistical power analysis is effect size. Effect size concerns researchers' expectations of or predictions about the strength of outcomes; this is typically based upon previous research results. Gall and colleagues (2002) noted that tables have been developed for calculating statistical power that consider these four factors and provide researchers with a systematic method of determining sample size. Also, there are statistical programs that provide the researcher with recommendations for determining sample size through calculation of statistical power based on effect size. Two common statistical programs are G*power and IBM SPSS Sample Power 3.

SAMPLING METHODS USED IN QUALITATIVE RESEARCH

Sampling methods in qualitative research share some similarities to those used in quantitative research, and there are some differences. Berg (2004) suggested that the use of simple random sampling, systematic random sampling, stratified random sampling, and convenience sampling may be used in qualitative research. We have discussed the procedures for obtaining a sample with these methods. Other methods of sampling in qualitative research include purposive sampling, maximal variation sampling, typical sampling, snowball sampling, and quota sampling (Creswell, 2012). No specific number of subjects or participants has been suggested for conducting qualitative research. In fact, single subjects may be used in qualitative research. Berg (2004) described purposive sampling as researchers using "their special knowledge or expertise about some group to select subjects who represent this population" (p. 36). A potential example of purposive sampling can be found with Abraham Maslow's (1976) study of self-actualization. Maslow stated, "The people I selected for my investigation were older people, people who had lived much of their lives out and were visibly successful" (p. 41). He further stated, "When you select out for careful study very fine and healthy people, strong people, creative people, saintly people, sagacious people—in fact, exactly the kind of people I picked out—then you get a different view of mankind" (p. 41).

Maximal variation sampling concerns selecting participants that provide a range of views or differences based on the focus of the study. Creswell noted that maximal variation is a form of purposive sampling. Creswell (2012) described maximal variation sampling as when "a researcher samples cases or individuals that differ on some characteristic or trait" (p. 208). A researcher may want to understand different sects of Amish and their family life. For example, a number of different Amish sects, based on level of conservatism, are older order Amish, Beachy Amish, or New Amish. Selecting different members of each sect fits with attempting to achieve maximal variation. Hoekstra, Korthagen, Brekelmans, Beijaard, and Imants (2009) described the use of maximal variation sampling this way:

We used a sample of 32 teachers who were voluntary subjects in a 14 month study on their learning. A smaller subsample of four teachers was studied in more depth. To achieve a representative subsample, six teachers who were not involved in formal teacher education were selected from a group of eight teachers who volunteered for the in-depth study. We further strived for variety in gender and subject. (p. 282)

Typical sampling involves choosing participants with the intention of using those who represent what one may expect to be "normal" (Creswell, 2012). Creswell noted that typical case sampling also may be understood as a variation of purposive sampling. An example of using typical case sampling in qualitative research may be third-grade students who earn Bs and Cs in math. A researcher may be interested in interviewing these "typical" students and use focus groups to discuss their attitudes and feelings about math. Pissanos (1995) provides an example of the use of typical case sampling in qualitative research. She described the selection of participants as follows: "Four experienced elementary school physical education teachers were selected as participants using the typical case purposeful sampling technique" (p. 215).

Snowball sampling is another approach used in qualitative research. Berg (2004) described the technique of snowball sampling: "The basic strategy of snowballing involves first identifying several people with relevant characteristics and interviewing them or having them answer a questionnaire. These subjects are then asked for the names of other people who possess the same attributes as they do" (p. 36). The intention is to find subjects with similar characteristics; this is particularly helpful with unique populations. Curry, Sporer, and Pugach (2007) investigated tobacco cessation programs for youth. They described their participant sampling techniques as follows:

Our goal was to identify contacts at the local level who were knowledgeable about tobacco cessation programs for youths in their communities or who could lead us to such persons. Snowball sampling progressed through 2 tiers and ended with the identification of a program informant who administered a tobacco cessation program for youths in the community. (p. 173)

Another approach to sampling in qualitative methods is the use of quota samples (Berg, 2004). This sampling method involves establishing characteristics of interest and then determining how many participants the researcher needs in each characteristic, or cell. Multiple cells or characteristics may be identified (Berg, 2004). Barton, Sulaiman, Clarke, and Abramson (2005) provide an example of using quota sampling in qualitative research. They studied the experiences of Australian parents in caring for their children with asthma. The researchers describe their sampling methods as a combination of random sampling, purposeful sampling, and quota sampling, which they say "was used to select a manageable number of care-givers for a home visit" (p. 304). They describe the specific approach to quota sampling this way: "Quota sampling was then used to obtain a minimum of ten participants each from the intervention and control" (p. 304).

SAMPLING ERRORS AND SAMPLING BIAS

Sampling error refers to the researchers not obtaining an accurate sample of the population. Wiersma and Jurs (2005) defined sampling error as "variation due to fluctuation when random samples are used to represent populations" (p. 301). Sampling errors occur by accident or chance when those selected do not represent the population. For example, smaller sample sizes may result in more frequent sampling errors because there is a greater chance of not obtaining a representative sample of the population when the sample size is too small. Conversely, larger sample sizes decrease the chance for sampling error.

Sampling bias is different from sampling error in that the former is under the control of the researcher. As with sampling error, the sample is not representative of the population but for different reasons. Wiersma and Jurs (2005) defined sampling bias as "a distortion caused by the way the sample was selected or formed, so that the sample is no longer representative of the population" (p. 301). In sampling bias, the researcher has actively chosen to select individuals in such a way that bias occurs in the sample. For example, samples of convenience typically contain sampling bias. An example of sampling bias is a researcher who wants to study different methods of teaching reading and has a friend in an elementary school who will let the researcher into the school to conduct the study. This is a sample of convenience and does not necessarily represent the larger population. The school may be in an affluent suburb. A great deal of psychological research has been conducted with undergraduate psychology students. This sample is one of convenience but is not necessarily representative of the larger population. Generalization of results from a sample of convenience to a larger population creates the potential for sampling bias and affects the validity of generalizing to the target population.

There are several methods a researcher can use to reduce sampling bias. The best solution to the problem of sampling bias is the use of random selection from the accessible population. A second way to reduce sampling bias that is not as reliable is for researchers to compare significant demographic characteristics of their sample to those in the population to ensure similarity.

GUIDELINES AND QUESTIONS FOR EVALUATING THE METHODS SECTION SAMPLE

The following questions may be used to evaluate the methods section sample proposed in a journal research article:

1. Are relevant demographic characteristics of the sample clearly identified?

2. Do the methods of sample selection used by the researchers provide a good representative sample based on the population?

3. Are there any apparent biases in selection of the sample?

4. Is the sample size large enough for the study proposed?

5. Does the researcher use the appropriate sampling technique for the purpose and type of research design employed?

6. Are volunteers used? If so, what is the response rate? If the response rate is low, has the researcher attempted to determine if those who volunteer are significantly different from those who do not participate?

EVALUATING EXAMPLES FROM THE RESEARCH LITERATURE

Quantitative Research

As in preceding chapters, I want to provide examples by evaluating two studies published in the professional literature using the questions and guidelines proposed here (Fry, 2007; Henderson et al., 2007). I want to start, as in other chapters, with the quantitative study. Henderson and colleagues (2007) described the participants as follows:

> Participants were prescreened for both the experience of trauma and trauma symptom severity using the Posttraumatic Stress Disorder Scale (PDS; Foa, 1995). Those who reported experiencing one or more traumatic stressors (determined by responses drawn from a checklist contained in the PDS) and who showed at least moderate levels of PTSD symptom severity (i.e. greater than 10 on the PDS) were regarded as potential participants for the study. Potential participants were excluded from the study if they reported being currently in psychotherapy or currently taking psychotropic medication. This exclusion criterion was included to ensure that changes in outcome measures were due to experimental manipulation and not the effects of therapy or medication. These criteria were modeled after the Sloan and Marx study on written disclosure (see Sloan & Marx, 2004a). (pp. 148–149)

The first question concerns whether the researchers have clearly identified relevant demographic characteristics of the sample. In this study, several major demographic characteristics are described: gender (37 females, 11 males), occupation (students at a public university), age (18 to 21 years), and years in college. In addition, the sample was identified to have experienced significant parental nurturance deprivation during childhood. It appears that several major demographic characteristics were well documented. One major demographic characteristic was missing from the description: the ethnicity of the sample. Additionally, it might have been helpful to know the status of intimate relationships of the sample. One could argue that individuals who have intimate relationships may have nurturing needs met.

Our second question in evaluating the sample given in the methods section is whether the sample is a good representation of the target population. Recall that, in this study, the target population was older adolescents who had been determined by the researchers to have experienced significant nurturance deprivation during childhood. It does not appear that a sample of college students from a public university is a good representation of the target population. Fewer than half of the citizens of the United States attend college, and consequently, the researchers were ignoring a large portion of their target group.

The third question is whether the researchers showed any biases in the selection of their subjects or sample. This appears to be a sample of convenience, one that is available to the researchers (it is likely that the sample was taken from students where the researchers were employed). Also, the sample was composed of volunteers. There appears to be sampling bias present in this study, basically because it was a sample of convenience and not necessarily representative of the larger target population. If the researchers had intended the target group to be college students, for whatever reason, then this might have been a better representation of the population.

The researchers used a true experimental design for the study and randomly assigned subjects to either an experimental or control group. The experimental group received the forgiveness education program and training focusing on forgiving their parents for not providing adequate nurturing and love. The control group did not receive any training. According to the basic formula presented earlier for determining sample size, the researchers needed at minimum 30 subjects, 15 for each group. Thus, the sample size for this study appears to be adequate, as 48 participated.

The next questions are these: What are the sampling techniques used? Are they appropriate for the research design used? It appears from the description that simple random sampling from a larger pool of individuals was used. Initially, 78 students who had been identified as meeting the desired criteria (scoring significantly on a parental love-deprivation scale) were used as the pool for selecting subjects randomly. However, this was not truly random sampling because each person in the larger accessible population did not have an equal chance to be selected to participate in the study. The researchers might more effectively have used stratified sampling and selected individuals from other groups of older adolescents, such as those attending a community college or technical school.

The final questions are whether volunteers were used and what the participation rate was. Based on the information provided, the researchers did use volunteers. No participants were reported to have refused participation from the larger group identified as possible subjects, that is, the 78 individuals identified as having experienced nurturance deprivation as children. However, if the researchers had used a more representative sample of the population, it might not have resulted in such a high response rate (it appears to have been 100 percent). College students are typically agreeable to research participation.

In summary, most relevant demographic characteristics were adequately identified, with the major exception of ethnicity. It does not appear that this sample was a good representation of the target or the accessible population. The sample was taken solely from a 4-year college population that did not include individuals from other settings where there are young adults. There appears to be sampling bias present in this study, basically, because the researchers used a sample of convenience that did not necessarily represent the larger target or accessible population. The sample size used appeared to be adequate based on the research design. Simple random sampling was used, but this was not truly random sampling because each person in the larger accessible population did not have an equal chance to be selected to participate in the study. Based on the information provided, the researchers did use volunteers, and no participants from the larger group identified as possible subjects were reported as having refused to participate. The selection methods used in this study were inadequate, and any attempt at generalizing the results back to the larger population should be made with caution.

Balk, Walker, and Baker (2010) provide an example of stratified random sampling. These researchers were interested in studying the prevalence and severity of undergraduate college students' experience with bereavement. The researchers described the acquisition of their sample as such:

The sampling frame included a list provided by the university registrar of all undergraduate students between the ages of 18 and 23. Drawn randomly, the sample was stratified by student's year in school, 433 students were contacted, and 118 agreed to participate, resulting in about a 27% response rate. Of the students, 41% were men and 59% were women. The sample consisted of 69% White Non-Hispanic, 12% African-Americans, 3% Native Indians, 4% Puerto Rican/Hispanics and 9% Other. (p. 462)

Additionally, they described the selection of the sample like this: "After drawing stratified random samples using a table of random numbers, the researchers contacted students via telephone and email message" (p. 463). Finally, they described the demographics that were collected: "Students provided information about their age, gender, racial/ethnic identity, religious affiliation and types of losses including deaths" (p. 462). Essentially, the stratification occurred based upon year in school.

The first question is this: Are relevant demographic characteristics of the sample clearly identified? The researchers clearly provide information about the demographics collected, for example, gender, age, religious affiliation, all relevant information for understanding bereavement. A second question follows: Do the methods of sample selection used by the researchers provide a good representative sample based on the population? The intended population is undergraduate college students. The use of a stratified sampling approach to include participants across undergraduate classes (e.g., freshmen, sophomores, etc.) does provide an opportunity to collect data that is representative of college students. However, the use of one university and no Asian Americans hinders the acquisition of a good representative sample of the population. The next question is whether there are any apparent biases in the selection of the sample. The biases are primarily related to using one secondary institution, one university. The use of stratified sampling does help with ensuring representation across classes.

The fourth question is next: Is the sample size large enough for the study proposed? The researchers attempted to provide simple descriptive statistics on undergraduates who report experiences with bereavement, for example, percentages that experienced bereavement issues. There is no statistical program that would provide estimates of sample size when analyzing data based on percentages. There is no comparison of groups or attempts at correlation among variables, and the researchers are not attempting to infer the results back to the population based on inferential statistics (inferential statistics are explained further in Chapter 16).

The next question is this: Does the researcher use the appropriate sampling technique for the purpose and type of research design employed? The researchers did use an appropriate sampling technique in an effort to understand bereavement across undergraduate classes. The researchers noted in the literature review that their intention was to avoid having a biased sample or a sample of convenience, which had been used in the past with previous research. The last questions to address are these: Are volunteers used? If so, what is the response rate? If the response rate is low, has the researcher attempted to determine if those who volunteer are significantly different from those who do not participate? The researchers clearly noted that they used volunteers, and the response rate was found to be 27%. The researchers did not attempt to follow up and determine if those not responding were different on demographic variables.

In summary, the researchers use an appropriate sampling technique, stratified random sampling. This sampling technique is significantly better than using a sample of convenience. However, the researchers do have a bias in not including Asian

Americans. The sample size appears to be adequate simply because the researchers are not using inferential statistics, which have more stringent guidelines for determining sample size. Finally, the researchers used volunteers but did not adequately determine if the sample was different from non-volunteers.

Qualitative Research

Fry (2007) provides an example of a qualitative study and describes her participants in the following way:

> Four 1st-year teachers participated in this study: Stella, Shari, Becca, and Laura (pseudonyms). The participants, all women, graduated with elementary education degrees from the same land-grant university located in the Rocky Mountain West. The university has approximately 10,000 undergraduate and graduate students, and approximately 120 elementary education majors graduate from the teacher preparation program each year. The participants were part of the same student teaching cohort, and were between 22 and 24 years old at the time of the study. Stella spent her first in-service year teaching 5th grade in a town of approximately 7,000 people that was located less than 20 miles away from a large city. Shari taught 3rd grade in a community of fewer than 1,200 people, located approximately 2½ hours away from the nearest major city. Becca and Laura taught kindergarden and 1st grade respectively. Becca's school was in a suburban area of a large city. Laura taught in a town of fewer than 30,000 people, located 90 minutes from the nearest city (All population data was obtained from the U.S. Census, 2000). (p. 218)

Participant involvement was requested based on involvement in an earlier, related study about the impact of an induction network they used during their student teaching experiences (Fry, 2007). Purposive sampling, a procedure that involves choosing participants with the qualities the researcher wants to investigate (Bogdan & Biklan, 2003), was used to identify appropriate participants for the original study. During the original study, Stella, Becca, Shari, and Laura demonstrated writing and speaking strengths as well as strong reflective abilities that may have developed as a result of their teacher preparation program's emphasis on educators being reflective practitioners. Each was able to clearly explain the rationale for her teaching decisions, thoughtfully ask questions to help improve her practice, and explain her students' behavior and learning in detail. Because these skills contribute to rich qualitative data, Stella, Becca, Shari, and Laura were invited to participate in the present study. No monetary or tangible incentive was offered for participation.

The first question is whether relevant demographic characteristics of the sample are clearly identified. The researcher does provide information about the ages and geographic locations of the participants. Also, information about the experience of the teachers is provided. No information is provided about race or SES of the participants. However, one might conclude that SES is middle class, given that the participants are teachers.

A second question concerns whether the methods of sample selection used by the researchers provide a good representative sample based on the population. The researcher stated she used purposive sampling. The purposive approach to sampling is consistent with a desire to identify those with special knowledge or expertise, for example, experience with teacher induction during the first few years of entering the teaching profession. As was noted above, the use of such sampling methods as purposive sampling does not necessarily provide a good representative sample of the population. It does not mean that the sample is not representative but simply that it may not be representative.

A third question is whether there are any apparent biases in the selection of the sample. The researcher noted that all participants graduated from the same university and also the same cohort of students. This suggests not only a sample of convenience but a potential bias in sample selection as well.

The next question is whether the sample size large is enough for the study proposed. The sample size in qualitative research is not based on a specific number but on other factors, such as the representation of the variables of interest in the study. The researcher focused on induction efforts for beginning teachers, and the participants met these criteria.

A fifth question is whether the researcher used appropriate sampling techniques for the purpose and type of research design employed. The researcher used purposive sampling, which is consistent with a qualitative study design. The question is whether the purposive sampling methods used in this study were truly designed to find those who were good representatives of this population, beginning teachers participating in induction methods.

The last question is whether volunteers were used and whether there was an adequate response rate. Qualitative research does not use large numbers of participants, so response rate is not a big issue. However, the research does not indicate whether any other individuals were asked to participate in the study.

In summary, Fry (2007) identified several important demographic characteristics of the participants. However, she left off important ones, including race. The use of the purposive approach to sampling is appropriate with the research design, a qualitative design. There does appear to be some bias in the selection of the sample based on the report that the participants came from the same cohort of students. There is no minimum in the sample size for a qualitative study, so the sample size is adequate. The use of purposive sampling is appropriate for the qualitative design employed, and volunteers were used; no information was provided as to whether anyone declined to participate.

In another example, Wadey, Evans, Hanton, and Neil (2012) conducted a qualitative study focused on hardiness throughout the sport injury process. The researchers employed a maximum variation approach in their sample selection. The researchers described the selection of their sample:

A four-step procedure was used to select a purposeful sample of participants from Wadey et al's (2012) original study that would provide a broader sense of context and a deeper and more meaningful understanding of the previous findings. First, previous participants high and low in hardiness were identified using theory-based sampling by reviewing their previous hardiness scores on the Dispositional Resilience Scale (DRS, Bartone, Ursano, Wright, & Ingaham, 1989). Consistent with the qualitative procedure outlined by Khoshaba and Maddi (1999) and recommendations from Funk (1992), those who scored above the 75th percentile for the hardiness composite and subscales (commitment, control, and challenge) were classified as high in hardiness whereas those who scored below the 25th percentile were considered as low in hardiness. Second, maximum-variation sampling was used within the low- and high-hardiness groups to account for several predetermined characteristics that would help to further contextualize the findings: sex, sport type, competitive level, and severity of injury. This resulted in each group consisting of males and females, team and individual sports, different standards and competition (e.g. club, regional, and national, and international), and injuries that varied in their severity. Third, those who at the time of this study had returned to competitive sport for more than 6 months were excluded. (pp. 873–874)

The researchers further described the demographics of the participants:

Ten athletes who had recovered from a sport-related injury and were either high (n-5) or low (n-5) in hardiness participated in this study (see Table 1). Six were males and four were females, ranging from 20 to 23 years of age. They represented a number of team (i.e. cricket, lacrosse, soccer, and rugby union) and individual (i.e. athletics and trampolining) sports and ranged from club to international levels of performance. Injury severity ranged from 5 weeks to 9 months. (p. 874)

An analysis of the sample in this study starts with this question: Are relevant demographic characteristics of the sample clearly identified? The researchers provide information about the gender of participants, age, and the type of sports injury. They do not provide any information about race or ethnicity or the geographic region where the study took place. The next question is this: Do the methods of sample selection used by the researchers provide a good representative sample based on the population? Wadley et al. state that participants were selected from a university from the mountain West. They also note that participants were involved in a previous study, and purposive sampling was used (the participants met selected criteria of the researchers). It is not clear what the criteria were. The researchers do not identify how others may have been excluded from those in the previous study. The researchers do note that the participants were selected based on their writing and reflective skills; however, no method of evaluation is noted. Next is the third question: Are there any apparent biases in the selection of the sample? There do not seem to be any apparent biases in the sample selection. The researchers intentionally focus on high and low hardiness levels (maximum variation), which is consistent with the purpose of the study. The fourth question concerns this issue: Is the sample size large enough for the study proposed? There are no specific numbers of participants needed for a qualitative study. The purpose of studying extremes or high and low scores on hardiness is addressed with the sample size and a distribution of the extreme scores.

The next question to address in analyzing a sample in a study is the following: Does the researcher use the appropriate sampling technique for the purpose and type of research design employed? The sampling technique appears to be appropriate for the purpose of the study and the type of research design utilized. Purposeful sampling combined with a specific use of maximum variation provided the researchers with a sample that addresses the intent of discovering how high and low levels of hardiness impact recovery from sports-related injuries. The last set of questions is this: Are volunteers used? If so, what is the response rate? If the response rate is low, has the researcher attempted to determine if those who volunteer are significantly different from those who do not participate? Volunteers were used in this study. No response rate was reported, and there was no effort to determine any reasons for those who did not choose to participate. No follow-up contact with those who did not choose to participate was reported.

In summary, the study by Wadey and colleagues (2012) used maximum variation in their sample selection. This approach, maximum variation, was consistent with the purpose of the study because it allowed them to understand high and low levels of hardiness. The researchers did not provide extensive demographic information such as race or ethnicity of the participants. Finally, the sample size seems to be adequate for the purpose of the study. Volunteers were used, but no effort was made to determine if there were any differences between those who participated and those who did not participate.

SUMMARY

The description of the sample used in a research study provides the reader with important pieces of information. It enables those reading the results to determine the efficacy of the study, and it provides necessary details to other researchers interested in replicating the study. We as consumers of research are particularly interested in determining the efficacy of a study. The adequate selection of a sample is important. First, it provides the reader with information about how valid the results may be in applying them to an identified population; second, as practitioners, we are concerned with appropriately applying the results. The methods a researcher may use in selecting a sample include simple random sampling, stratified sampling, cluster sampling, systematic random sampling, and convenience sampling. Convenience sampling provides the least valid approach to selecting a sample.

Sampling error and sampling bias affect the validity of sample selection. Sampling error refers to the researchers' not having obtained an accurate sample of the population; sampling bias concerns a sample that is not representative of the population because the researchers have actively chosen to select individuals in such a way that bias occurs in the sample. For example, samples of convenience typically contain sampling bias.

Sampling methods in qualitative research do not require the same kind of rigor as quantitative research methods. No specific number of subjects has been suggested for conducting qualitative research. Patton (1990) proposed several different sampling methods that can be used in qualitative research. The more commonly used methods include extreme case sampling, typical case sampling, maximum variation sampling, homogeneous sampling, and snowball or chain sampling.

Evaluating the selection or adequacy of a sample includes determining whether the methods of sample selection used by the researchers provide a good representative sample based on the population and whether there are any apparent biases in selection of the sample. Also, we are interested in whether the sample size is large enough for the study proposed and whether the researchers used the appropriate sampling technique for the purpose and type of research design employed.

Exercise

Directions: Locate an article in a professional journal that includes a methods section and describes the sample used in the study. Carefully read the sample description, and critique the study based on the questions and guidelines discussed in this chapter.

1. Are relevant demographic characteristics of the sample clearly identified?

2. Do the methods of sample selection used by the researchers provide a good representative sample based on the population?

(Continued)

(Continued)

3. Are there any apparent biases in selection of the sample?

4. Is the sample size large enough for the study proposed?

5. Does the researcher use the appropriate sampling technique for the purpose and type of research design employed?

6. Are volunteers used? If so, what is the response rate? Also, if the response rate is low, does the researcher attempt to determine if those who volunteer are significantly different from those who do not participate?

14

Evaluating the Methods Section
Procedures

The procedures section in a research article is intended to be a step-by-step description of how the study was conducted. This includes a discussion of the research design and methods used in the study. Recall that the scientific method requires that researchers submit their studies to public scrutiny, that is, the scientific or professional community. The procedures section provides the reader with information about determining the efficacy of the study. Second, the procedures section gives information to practitioners about how to implement the treatments in the target population. The ability to implement the treatment in the population is one of the more important purposes in conducting research in counseling and education.

In this chapter, I discuss how researchers present study variables, particularly the independent variables, if there are any, in the procedures section. Second, I describe the importance of random assignment to groups in true experimental and quasi-experimental designs. Third, I discuss internal validity and external validity and their importance in understanding and using results published in professional journals. In this discussion, I demonstrate how researchers may reduce threats to internal and external validity. Also, there is discussion of evaluating threats to internal and external validity for single-subject research. Next, I propose guidelines and questions for evaluating the procedures section. Finally, I demonstrate how to evaluate several research studies presented in the professional literature using the guidelines presented.

DESCRIPTION OF STUDY VARIABLES

An important consideration for researchers in the procedures section is to systematically and clearly describe the independent variable (if there is an

197

IV = manipulated
DV = stable

independent variable). Recall that the independent variable is defined in terms of the researcher's manipulating an event or phenomenon to study its effect on another variable, the dependent variable. Also, there are measurement types of variables that can be considered as independent variables (e.g., IQ). Whatever the independent variable is, the researcher should systematically describe it for the reader. This means that, if a particular treatment is used, a step-by-step description is provided in the procedures section. For example, if a researcher is testing the effectiveness of a counseling approach such as cognitive behavioral therapy with those who have been diagnosed with PTSD, the specific methods used must be described in the procedures section. This includes a discussion of the training received by those providing the counseling or the manipulation. In education, the researcher should describe the teaching method used in detail. Typically, researchers have developed specific training manuals for the interventions that are being tested.

The researcher should also detail how the control group was treated, if there is a control group used. The control group may experience no intervention at all, or it may experience something that is not connected to the independent variables (so there is no possible impact on the dependent variable) but that gives the control group a feeling that it received special attention like the experimental group.

Remember from evaluating the hypothesis and purpose statements that certain words can give the reader insight into the type of study conducted. The research design and description of all variables should be consistent with the purpose and the hypotheses presented in the introduction. Consistency can be judged by determining whether the procedures are congruent with the particular words used in the purpose or hypothesis—words like *comparison*, *relationship*, and *illuminate*. A comparison should involve the use of a research design that allows for the comparison of two or more groups, whereas a correlation-focused study may have multiple dependent variables to correlate with one group. It is important to keep in mind that some studies use several hypotheses and combine comparison, correlational, or descriptive approaches.

RANDOM ASSIGNMENT

Ong-Dean, Hofstetter, and Strick (2011) noted the importance of using random assignment of participants in educational research. Random assignment is defined as randomly assigning participants to groups (both experimental and control groups). As with random selection, random assignment means that all those selected from the population to participate in a study have an equal chance of being assigned to a particular group. Random assignment to groups is a separate procedure from random selection from the population. Random assignment is accomplished once the researcher has selected participants for the study. Once participants are selected, the researcher can randomly assign each one to a group, including experimental, control, traditional method, and so on. Ong-Dean and colleagues described the benefits and concerns about random assignment in educational research (and the benefits and criticisms apply to counseling as we share similarities in professional practice, e.g., issues of controlling the environment where studies are conducted). One major benefit of using a random assignment is that it improves internal validity (how well the treatments are implemented and how well a researcher can conclude that the impact of the independent variable affects the dependent variable). Essentially, the use of randomization, that is, assigning participants randomly to experimental and control groups, reduces the number of threats to validity of the study. One of the criticisms of random assignment is that there can be ethical concerns about assigning participants randomly and not giving them an opportunity to choose to participate in a particular group or experience. There is greater discussion of these threats to validity later in this chapter.

Not all research methods use random assignment. Descriptive research and qualitative methods do not. However, random assignment to groups does reduce the effects of some threats to validity. The definition of a true experimental study requires that a manipulation occur and that there be random assignment to groups. Random assignment protects against problems with internal and external validity. The intent with random assignment is to ensure that your groups are similar in relevant variables that may affect the outcome or dependent variables. Random assignment is not easily achieved, particularly in the natural environment. For example, if a teacher wishes to test a particular teaching strategy, he or she generally cannot ethically divide the class into an experimental and control group, with one receiving the experimental treatment and the other the control or nothing.

When evaluating the efficacy of the procedure employed in a study, two of the most important considerations are the internal and external validity of the methods. Stangor (2006) defined internal validity as "the extent to which changes in the dependent variable can confidently be attributed to the effect of the independent variable, rather than to the potential effects of confounding variables" (p. 226). More specifically, internal validity refers to how well the study was conducted with the sample and the extent to which extraneous variables were controlled for within the research design. The intent is to reduce all or as many variables as possible (other than the treatment or independent variable) that can influence the outcome or the dependent variable. Clearly, the purpose here is to be able to then state that the independent variable, and not some other extraneous variable, caused the outcome.

Creswell (2012) noted that external validity refers to "the validity of the cause and effect relationship being generalizable to other persons, settings, treatment variables and measures" (p. 303). Essentially, external validity refers to the extent to which the researchers can replicate the actual events occurring in the natural environment and thus can generalize the results back to the population. Key here is the efficacy of controlling for those factors that influence the researcher's ability to generalize and apply the results to the population from which the sample was drawn.

Information about the internal and external validity of a study can be found in the procedures section. Ary and colleagues (2014) noted the balance between internal and external validity. They stated, "Internal validity has long been considered the sine quo non of experimentation. As an experiment becomes more rigorously controlled (internal validity) it artificially tends to increase, and it becomes less generalizable and less externally valid" (p. 318). Theoretically, the more control the researchers have over the experimental condition, the higher the internal validity. This means that the researchers have considerable control over the implementation of the study and, potentially, can reduce the effects of extraneous variables by eliminating them through methods such as random assignment, the particular research method, and laboratory control over factors that may influence the natural environment.

Conversely, the lower the control the researchers impose through the use of the natural environment, the higher the external validity may be, although this is not always the case. The researchers clearly have less control over extraneous variables in the natural setting, where random assignment and fewer opportunities for controlling extraneous variables occur. However, it can be argued that observations and research conducted in the natural environment increase the ability to generalize to the population. The reality is that there needs to be a balance between the natural environment and the amount of control exercised by the researchers. As previously noted, too much control reduces the ability to generalize to the population because a fabricated situation is constructed by the researcher. However, the researcher does not want to concede too much control and reduce the internal validity of the study, which would also hinder the ability of the study to be generalized to the population. If too many variables can be determined to have influenced the outcomes, the researchers are basically left with no new useful information. Parsons and Brown (2002) noted that good internal validity is absolutely necessary to the researcher, even before one can consider external validity (generalizing the results to the population). Consequently, researchers must balance the amount of control exercised to ensure adequate internal and external validity. The procedures section provides the reader with the information to judge whether the study meets a reasonable level of balance, ensuring that both internal validity and external validity are adequate.

It is important to note here again that all research has some flaws in regard to problems with internal or external validity. Your job as a reader and user of the research literature is to determine whether the researchers have provided adequate protection of internal and external validity. Researchers have identified potential threats to validity that can provide criteria for determining whether a study has good internal and external validity (Bracht & Glass, 1968; Campbell & Stanley, 1966; Cook & Campbell, 1979). Campbell and Stanley (1966) noted that threats to validity were associated with specific research designs. It may be helpful to quickly review Chapter 4 and the discussion of quantitative research designs before reading the next section. Keep in mind, as the various threats to validity are discussed, that they are typically associated with specific designs. Most threats to validity are associated with research designs; however, a few external threats to validity are a result of how the sample was selected (selection bias or error; see Table 14.1).

Table 14.1   Summary of Threats to Internal and External Validity With Preexperimental Design

	Type of Threat	
Design	*Internal*	*External*
1. One-shot case study	history, maturation, selection, and mortality	Hawthorne Effect, novelty to disruption (possible), experimenter effect (possible), measurement of dependent variable (possible), interaction between time and measurement and treatment effects (possible)
2. One-group pretest–posttest	history, maturation, testing, instrumentation, interaction of selection, and other factors, such as maturation	Hawthorne Effect, novelty or disruption (possible), experimenter effects (possible), pretest and posttest sensitization, measurement of dependent variable (possible), interaction between time and measurement and treatment effects (possible)
3. Static group comparison	history (possible, if the experience studied takes place over an extended time period), maturation (possible), selection, mortality, and interaction of selection with other factors	measurement of dependent variable (possible), interaction between time of measurement and treatment effects (possible)

THREATS TO INTERNAL VALIDITY

Threats to internal validity have been identified (Ary et al., 2014; Campbell & Stanley, 1966; Creswell, 2012; Gall et al., 1996; Parsons & Brown, 2002), and these include history, maturation, testing, instrumentation, statistical regression, differential selection, mortality or attrition, selection-maturation interaction, and subject effects. These threats, as has been noted, may be reduced or eliminated by using certain research designs or through the use of certain participant selection methods.

The threat of history is defined as events occurring during the time of the study that are unrelated to the treatment or independent variables (Campbell & Stanley, 1966; Creswell, 2012; Gall et al., 1996; Parsons & Brown, 2002). Whenever studies are conducted over a period of time and there is no random assignment to groups, history can be a threat. Random assignment reduces or eliminates the effect of history because, theoretically, those randomly assigned to groups will experience similar events or histories. For example, if you have a community that experiences a tornado during an intervention in the schools with different treatment for different classrooms and schools (the classrooms having been randomly assigned with the use of cluster sampling), then the effects of the tornado should theoretically be systematically distributed (some parts of the community would be more or less affected). History is more of a problem for research methods such as descriptive or qualitative approaches. A qualitative approach using case study methods may provide detailed information to the researcher but at the same time be vulnerable to the threat to validity of history (see Table 14.2). For example, a researcher could study the interaction between second-grade students and their teacher using a case study approach. Events could occur that might affect the interaction between the teacher and the students. The teacher might experience personal problems at home that affect his or her teaching, and the same could be true for the children.

Table 14.2 Summary of Threats to Internal and External Validity With Quasi-Experimental Designs

Design	Type of Threat	
	Internal	*External*
1. Time series	history, instrumentation (possible)	pretest sensitization, posttest sensitization, Hawthorne Effect (possible), novelty or disruption (possible), experimenter effects (possible), measurement of dependent variable (possible), interaction between time and measurement and treatment effects (possible)

Table 14.2   (Continued)

	Type of Threat	
Design	*Internal*	*External*
2. Nonequivalent control group	history (possible if intervention takes place over time), interaction between selection and other factors, subject effect	Hawthorne Effect (possible), novelty or disruption (possible), experimenter effects (possible), John Henry Effect, pretest and posttest sensitization, measurement of dependent variable (possible), interaction between measurement and treatment effects (possible)
3. Multiple time series	interaction between selection and other factors (possible)	multiple treatment interference, experiment effects (possible), pretest and posttest sensitization, measurement of dependent variable (possible), interaction between time of measurement and treatment effects (possible)

Table 14.3   Summary of Threats to Internal and External Validity With True Experimental Designs

	Type of Threat	
Design	*Internal*	*External*
1. Pretest–posttest	subject effect	pretest sensitization and posttest sensitization, Hawthorne Effect (possible), novelty or disruption (possible), resentful demoralization, John Henry Effect, experimenter effects (possible), measurement of dependent variable (possible), interaction between time and measurement and treatment effects (possible)
2. Posttest only	subject effect	posttest sensitization, Hawthorne Effect (possible), novelty or disruption (possible), John Henry Effect, experimenter effects (possible), measurement of dependent variable (possible), resentful demoralization, interaction between time and measurement and treatment effects (possible)
3. Solomon Four-Group	subject effect	Hawthorne Effect (possible), novelty or disruption (possible), experimenter effects (possible), measurement of dependent variable (possible), resentful demoralization, interaction between time and measurement and treatment effects (possible)

A second type of threat to internal validity is maturation (Campbell & Stanley, 1966; Creswell, 2012; Gall et al., 1996). Maturation concerns possible physical or psychological changes that occur in the participants over the period of the study. This is particularly important for children and adolescents, who have the potential to experience significant changes over a relatively short period of time (e.g., 6 months). Participants, as a consequence of their development during the study period time, may do better because of maturational changes (Creswell, 2012). The shorter the period of time during which the study is conducted, the less likelihood that maturation will affect the participants. Additionally, the use of random assignment to treatment groups eliminates the threat of maturation. When participants are randomly assigned to groups, all members of the various groups (treatment and control) should, theoretically, experience similar changes in growth. Also, the threat of maturation may be present when the researcher is comparing groups progressing through distinctly different developmental stages. To address this particular issue, researchers generally avoid comparing such groups.

A third threat to internal validity is testing (Campbell & Stanley, 1966; Creswell, 2012; Gall et al., 1996). The threat of testing occurs when participants become sensitized to the intent of the study or the desired responses the researchers are seeking from pretest to posttest. Consequently, the participants perform better on the posttest not due to the treatment but because they have become aware of the desired responses, which they detected from taking the pretest. This threat is most problematic when multiple testing occurs due to the research design employed. For example, several quasi-experimental designs use multiple testing and occur over a period of time (e.g., the time series design). A way to reduce this threat is to reduce the number of test administrations or use a posttest only design.

A fourth threat to validity that is related to testing is instrumentation (Campbell & Stanley, 1966; Gall et al., 1996). Instrumentation concerns the quality of the instrument or the consistency of the instrument. An instrument that has low reliability results in an increased threat to internal validity. Scores may vary dramatically from pretest to posttest not as a consequence of the treatment but because of the low reliability of the instrument. Researchers (Creswell, 2012; Gall et al., 1996) have noted the problem with observational measures and internal validity. Creswell (2012) noted that, with observational measures, the observers may become more proficient with experience, and consequently, you may have differences in scores based on improvement in the skill of the observers. A solution is to develop standard procedures for the observers and train the observers prior to data collection.

Another threat to internal validity is statistical regression (Ary et al., 2014; Campbell & Stanley, 1966; Creswell, 2012). Regression toward the mean is primarily associated with the selection of participants who represent extreme scores on the dependent variable. The extreme scores are present when the researcher uses a pretest and posttest design, and changes in scores are likely to regress or move toward the mean. For example, if a teacher has a class of exceptionally bright children and gives a math exam and they all score perfectly, the second time the children take the exam, there is an increased likelihood that scores will regress toward the mean. This happens when lower or higher scores are achieved with participants or respondents selected for their extremities. Theoretically, an individual's score on a math exam is based on ability and chance (Gall et al., 1996). A low score would be a function of bad luck and ability. When the child takes a subsequent math exam on the same material, there is an increased likelihood that his or her scores will be higher. This occurs because, although a person's scores on responses based on ability will be retained, responses due to chance will result in overall scores regressing toward the mean.

Differential selection is a sixth contributor to threats to internal validity (Campbell & Stanley, 1966; Creswell, 2012; Gall et al., 1996). This threat occurs when the experimental and control groups are selected based on different criteria or when participants are assigned to groups differentially and not by random assignment. Most often, this threat is a result of using samples of convenience. Random assignment to groups eliminates this threat because all groups will have had equal opportunity to be assigned to control and experimental groups. If participants are not randomly assigned to groups, members of the control and experimental groups may differ significantly on relevant variables, which could influence the outcome or responses to the dependent variable.

A seventh threat to internal validity is attrition, or experimental mortality (Campbell & Stanley, 1966; Creswell, 2012). This involves participants dropping out of the study. Participants may drop out of a study for various reasons, and these might be based on the subject's participation in a particular experimental group, which clearly could have an impact on the results. Reasons could include dropping out of a control group because nothing is happening that the participant feels is worthwhile or moving away from the area where the study is being conducted. Also, the experimental group participants may drop out if the study procedures are too demanding or imposing. Gall and colleagues (1996) noted that reducing the effects of experimental mortality may be achieved, again, through random assignment to groups (theoretically, the researcher will have distributed dropouts equally among the groups) and ensuring that rewards for participants are equal for all groups. Researchers additionally may follow up on those who dropped out to determine if, based on relevant variables, they are significantly different from those who continued. Researchers may collect additional information about those dropping out, such as demographic data to be used to compare with those remaining in the study. Experimental mortality is more likely the longer a study is conducted. People move away or experience other significant events that prevent them from continued participation in a research study.

Another threat to internal validity is selection-maturation interaction (Ary et al., 2014; Campbell & Stanley, 1966; Gall et al., 1996). In this threat, the issue is that participants are selected based on certain developmental characteristics, which results in groups not being equal at the start of the study. The developmental or maturation characteristics further complicate interpretation of the results: Did the results occur as a consequence of the intervention or changes in maturation? For example, a researcher wants to know the effects of a particular science instruction approach and selects students in fifth and sixth grades. She has the intention of comparing fifth graders' progress (the control group) with sixth graders who are to receive the experimental method. Many of the sixth graders may have begun to enter into formal thinking stages and thus may make more progress in learning science than the fifth graders. Ary and colleagues (2014) noted that participants may start at the same place at pretest, but because of that selection of participants, that does not control for maturation. One group may mature during the research study faster than a comparison group, affecting the posttest results.

A last threat is subject effect (Ary et al., 2014). There are several different types of subject effects (see Table 14.3): resentful demoralization and the John Henry Effect, for example. Resentful demoralization is a threat that refers to circumstances where the control group is aware of not receiving the intervention, which is perceived to be of value (Creswell, 2012). Creswell (2012) suggested that a solution to this threat is to provide the control group the intervention at a later time, so they feel they are not excluded from the benefits of the treatment. Another solution is to provide the control group members an equally attractive experience but not focused on the outcome or dependent variable. The John Henry Effect refers to when the control group is aware they are in a study and make efforts to do better and outperform the experimental group. In essence, there is a competition between the control group participants and the experimental group participants, primarily based on the perceptions of the control group. A solution to reduce this threat is to provide the control group with an interesting experience that does not impact the dependent variable. Some studies do not give the control group any experience other than completion of the dependent variables.

Threats to Validity With Single-Subject Studies

Threats to internal validity for single-subject study research have been identified (Christ, 2007). In regards to single-subject research designs and measurement, Christ (2007) suggested that measurement (the threat of instrumentation) across the multiple measurements required should be similar. It is easy for a researcher to mistakenly alter the multiple measurements conducted over a time series single-subject design study. Also, Christ suggested that sufficient data should be collected so that adequate information is available. For example, a few measurements may have variability in them (due to changing conditions or experimenter diligence), and multiple measurements tend to smooth out any such changing conditions.

Mortality is another issue for single-subject research (Christ, 2007). According to Christ, this can be a consequence of a researcher selectively taking out participants who are not making changes based on beginning baseline data. Christ proposed that one solution is to extend the baseline until the participant achieves the desired beginning level and consequently includes more participants rather than losing them to mortality or dropping out of the study. Second, researchers should report any participants that are excluded in any publications, so those reading the results can correctly interpret and understand the impact of the threat of mortality to the study results.

The threat of history has been noted to be the most significant issue for single-subject research designs (Barlow & Hersen, 1984; Christ, 2007). The threat of history is particularly an issue when a single-subject design is conducted over a period of time. There are many events that may impact the participant, and there is no or minimal opportunity for random assignment, which potentially reduces the impact of history. Christ (2007) suggests one solution is to conduct studies that are short in duration, consequently reducing the possibility of history (outside events) impacting the results. A second solution is for the researcher to carefully collect data and evaluate whether any significant historical events (outside events) impacted the study participants (Christ, 2007).

Single-subject research designs do not allow for random assignment to groups, which is an effective approach to reducing many threats to validity. Researchers using single-subject research designs can still attend to threats to internal validity (Christ, 2007).

THREATS TO EXTERNAL VALIDITY

Twelve threats to external validity have been identified (see Table 14.4; Ary et al., 2014; Bracht & Glass, 1968; Creswell, 2012; Gall et al., 2006). These 12 threats are categorized into two major groups: population validity and ecological validity (Bracht, & Glass, 1968; Gall et al., 2006). Two threats to population validity have been proposed: (1) comparison of the accessible population and the target population and (2) interaction between personological variables (personal characteristics) and treatment effects. The 10 threats to ecological validity are explicit description of the independent variable, multiple treatment interference, the Hawthorne Effect, novelty and disruption effects, experimenter effect, pretest sensitization, posttest sensitization, interaction between history and treatment effects, measurement of the dependent variable, and interaction of time of measurement and treatment effects.

Table 14.4   Summary of Threats to External Validity

Type of Threat

Population validity

     1. Comparison of accessible population to target population

     2. Interaction of personological variables and treatment

Ecological validity

     3. Explicit description of the independent variable

     4. Multiple treatment interference

     5. Hawthorne Effect

     6. Novelty and disruption effects

     7. Experimenter effect

     8. Pretest sensitization

     9. Posttest sensitization

    10. Interaction of history and treatment effects

    11. Measurement of the dependent variable

    12. Interaction of time of measurement and treatment effects

Population validity is focused on generalization back to the population and whether the population would behave the same as the sample chosen (Ary et al., 2014; Bracht & Glass, 1968; Gall et al., 2006). The first threat to population validity, comparison of accessible population to target population, concerns the extent to which the researchers use an accessible population that is actually representative of the target population (Bracht & Glass, 1968; Gall et al., 2006). The researcher may be interested in a target population that is representative of certain groups residing in the United States, but he or she does not have access to the total population for geographic and economic reasons. For example, a researcher may be interested in studying the effects of a particular therapy approach in combination with medication for those who are diagnosed with major depression. The researcher could not feasibly set up this study in all geographic regions in the country, even though the intended target population is all those with a diagnosis of major depression. Consequently, the researcher may use only those from the Southeast. He or she could randomly select from a list of those from that geographic area who have been diagnosed with the condition. The threat to external validity in this example is whether this particular geographic area has individuals with major depression who are similar to those in other parts of the country. We could speculate about why they may be different: (1) Certain ethnic groups migrated to the area, and their genetics or physiology may be unique; (2) the weather is different from that in other parts of the country (e.g., it may be more dreary and thus lead participants to feel more depressed); and (3) social service agencies are quite active and provide more services in this area than they do in other parts of the country. These are only a few reasons that the accessible population may not be representative of the target population; many others could be identified. One example is where the researcher randomly selects individuals from other parts of the country to survey and determine if the accessible population is significantly different on relevant variables, such as ethnicity. The reality is that a significant number of studies suffer from this threat to external validity for the reasons cited earlier. Consequently, interpreting the results should be accomplished with care when applying them to a group you are working with in a community potentially different from the accessible population.

A second threat to population validity, interaction between personological variables and treatment (sample characteristics), concerns how specific personal characteristics of participants may interact with treatment and influence the outcome in a way not representative of how the population may respond (Ary et al., 2014; Bracht & Glass, 1968). An example may be a study focusing on the language development of grade-school children in which the accessible population is only those from affluent suburban communities. These communities may have children who come from families whose parents are well educated and highly verbal. Consequently, these children may perform differently in the experimental interventions than those from urban or rural communities. One method of reducing this threat is to build relevant personological variables into the study design (Gall et al., 2006). In this example, the researchers would include children and schools from suburban, urban, and rural communities to reduce any effects of personalogical variables that influence treatment, for example, reduce the unique benefits that those in affluent suburban communities may have with additional resources that give them an advantage in language development.

Ecological validity is associated with representing the environment as close as possible to the natural environment, for example, addressing the relevant variables that provide the best representation. One threat to ecological external validity, explicit description of the independent variable, concerns how clearly the researchers describe the independent variable, making it possible for others to replicate the intervention with others in the population (Ary et al., 2014; Bracht & Glass, 1968). Others' ability to replicate the independent variable with those from the target population is basically dependent on how well the researchers operationalized the intervention. As mentioned earlier, it is typical to develop an instructional and procedural manual with an intervention. Researchers who use standard approaches to an intervention address this threat to validity. For example, comparing different therapy approaches, such as person-centered and psychodynamic approaches, may involve a description of the intervention adequate to allow others to replicate it. If no formal manual or approach is available, researchers should provide a detailed description in the procedures section of the intervention.

Multiple treatment interference can potentially occur when the researchers introduce two or more treatments consecutively to the same participants (Ary et al., 2014; Bracht & Glass, 1968). The researchers cannot determine which intervention affected the outcome or if it was both. The problem occurs when others (practitioners) try to implement the intervention with individuals in the population and use only one of the interventions studied. As a consequence, the outcomes may be different because of the interaction between the two interventions. The solution to reducing this threat is to use only one treatment or compare both interventions separately with the combined treatments. Another solution is to implement only the multiple treatments together, thus replicating the research conducted.

The Hawthorne Effect is a third threat to ecological external validity. The Hawthorne Effect was first noted from studies at Western Electric Company in the 1920s and 1930s. Jones (1992) described the Hawthorne Effect: "Behaviour during the course of an experiment can be altered by a subject's awareness of participating in the experiment" (p. 451). If a participant is aware of his or her involvement in a research study, his or her responses to the dependent variables may consequently be altered from the way they would normally be (Ary et al., 2014; Bracht & Glass, 1968). Responses may be based on the participants' personality characteristics, whether they typically comply and are cooperative or prefer to act defiantly and resist providing accurate information, even though they agreed to participate. There are times when participants want to see a particular intervention not succeed and may exaggerate their responses. Control group members may attempt to compete with the experimental group to outperform them on dependent variables. The solution to this threat is to use a placebo or an intervention that is designed to have no effect on the dependent variable. In a study comparing stress-management training techniques, in which there are two different methods or the researcher is interested in comparing two different stress-management training techniques, a third group could be a placebo group. The placebo group might be asked to engage in a neutral activity, such as writing a letter. A fourth group could be a control group, which would experience no activity and would provide a comparison for determining Hawthorne Effects. Another solution is to use unobtrusive measures so the participants are not aware they are being observed or measured on the dependent variable.

Novelty or disruption effects is a fourth threat to external ecological validity (Ary et al., 2014; Bracht & Glass, 1968). Any dependent measure gains are a consequence of being exposed to something that is novel (the independent variable) rather than the actual effects of the treatment. This threat is particularly relevant when the treatment is short term and the novelty does not have a chance to wear off. Theoretically, the novelty will wear off after a period of time; responses to the dependent variables will then be more accurate. When disruption effects occur, they may actually lower responses to the dependent variables. The introduction of a new approach may be so different from previous approaches that it will take time to adjust to the new methods. The solution to this problem is, again, to have a longer intervention time before measuring the dependent variables. A researcher who introduced a new technique or intervention should acknowledge the possibility of a novelty effect and how it was addressed in the study.

The Hawthorne Effect and novelty and disruption effects are somewhat similar, but they have their differences. The Hawthorne Effect concerns the participants' active efforts to change the outcome because they are aware of their participation. Novelty and disruption effects are more like experiencing a new toy. It is quite possible that both threats to validity operate in a study and impact the outcome.

A fifth threat to external ecological validity, experimenter effects, involves the experimenter communicating to the participants in a way that influences responses. One example is where the researcher communicates what outcomes he or she would like to achieve (Ary et al., 2014; Bracht & Glass, 1968). The researchers may be interested in seeing a particular intervention be successful and may communicate this desire in some way to participants. Also, the researchers may be biased in their scoring of the dependent variables, particularly where the dependent measure requires a judgment on the part of the scorer. For example, classroom observations may be used and be open to interpretation. An approach to avoiding this problem is to reduce the actual influence the researcher has on the implementation of the study by having another implement the study and score any subjective dependent measures. A sophisticated method is to use a double-blind approach, in which those implementing the study are unaware of its intent. In regard to scoring, the researchers can use scorers who are unaware of the intent of the study but are instructed in how to score the dependent variables.

Pretest sensitization is another threat to ecological external validity and involves the participants becoming aware of the desired response to the dependent variable (Ary et al., 2014). In situations where the dependent variable is a self-report, it is possible for pretest sensitization to occur, which impacts their responses on the posttest (e.g., it informs them how to respond). With self-report measures, it is possible for participants to actually foster learning and subsequently alter their responses (Moore, 1983). The solution to resolving this problem is to use either a posttest-only design or a Solomon Four-Group Design (a combination of a pretest–posttest design and a posttest-only design). With the Solomon-Four Group Design, the researcher can determine the effects of pretesting on responses.

Another threat to external ecological validity is interaction between history and treatment effects (Bracht & Glass, 1968; Creswell, 2012). This threat refers to how events occurring at the time of the intervention or treatment affect the outcome. For example, if a community had just experienced an economic downturn, this could affect even responses that are unrelated to the treatment. Another example is a community experiencing a natural disaster like a tornado or hurricane. This threat is a difficult one to evaluate because researchers typically do not address such events in the description of their study. Moore (1983) suggested that extending the study beyond the anticipated impact of the uncontrolled event is a way for the researcher to address this threat. For those of us evaluating the study, it is necessary to rely on the news media to determine if any major events might have affected the study. Creswell (2012) suggested that replication of the study at another time may reduce the threat before attempting to generalize the results.

Measurement of the dependent variable concerns how effectively the researcher operationalized the dependent variables (Bracht & Glass, 1968). The instrument chosen by the researchers may have been poorly constructed, for example, with low reliability or validity. (Validity in regard to an instrument refers to how well the instrument measures the concept that it was intended to measure.) The best solution for reducing this threat is for researchers to choose instruments that have good reliability and validity and report them, so the reader can evaluate them.

The last threat to ecological external validity is interaction between time of measurement and treatment effects. The threat of interaction between time of measurement and treatment effects involves the impact of treatment being greatest just after the intervention is implemented. Consequently, the actual long-term effects are unclear (Ary et al., 2014; Bracht & Glass, 1968). Typically, researchers administer posttests just after the intervention when, theoretically, the impact of the intervention is greatest; the problem is that such effects may be short term. To avoid this threat, researchers administer a follow-up assessment of the dependent variables several months after the intervention to determine the long-term impact.

Five questions are suggested as a guide for evaluating the methods section (procedures) of a research article:

1. What type of research design was used in the study?

2. Is the research design consistent with the purpose and hypothesis presented in the introduction?

3. Are the independent variables clearly defined? Are the independent variables so clearly defined that they can be replicated using the information provided in the procedures section?

4. Identify any threats to internal validity. How are they threats?

5. Identify any threats to external validity. How are they threats?

EVALUATION OF EXAMPLES FROM THE LITERATURE

Quantitative Research

Henderson and colleagues (2007) described the procedures section as follows:

The process of approval for human subjects research by the University's institutional review board was followed and approval was obtained. The conditions of each session were assigned randomly, and the participants did not know which group they would be attending. Participants in the experimental ($n = 19$) and control conditions ($n = 17$) were tested separately in small groups of five to ten individuals. Using the example of various Pennebaker, et al. written disclosure studies (Pennebaker, 1997a, 1997b; Pennebaker & Seagal, 1999; Pennebaker & Susman, 1988), the drawing sessions took place across 3 consecutive days, with all participants drawing for a total of 20 minutes each session.

At the beginning of the first session for each condition, the lead investigator briefly explained the purpose of the study and written informed consent was obtained. This included informing participants of the sensitive nature of the study and providing them with a list of individuals or psychological service providers to contact if they felt distressed at any time during or after the experiment.

All participants completed the time one measures for PDS, BDI-II STAI, SMS, PILL, and a demographic questionnaire immediately before drawing at the first session. With the exception of the demographic questionnaire, the same measures were completed immediately after the last drawing session (time two) and at a 1-month follow-up (time three). When participants in both conditions finished the self-report measures, they were given a large envelope containing one blank sheet of paper and an instruction sheet specific to their condition. For simplicity and standardization, a box of crayons and a pencil were also provided. A trained research assistant instructed them to open their envelopes and follow along as the specific instructions provided within their envelope were read aloud by the assistant.

The participants in the mandala condition were asked to draw a large circle on their paper and then fill the circle with representations of feelings or emotions to their trauma using symbols, patterns, designs, and colors (but no words) that felt right to them. In the control condition, participants were instructed to draw an object over the next 3 days. Each day they were given a different drawing assignment (cup, bottle, or pens) and told to make their drawing as detailed as possible. The research assistant instructed the participants to draw for 20 minutes. Their drawing and the instruction set were put in the envelope before leaving. Participants were thanked for their participation and reminded to return the following day.

At the end of the third session, a trained research assistant debriefed participants after they completed the second set of dependent variable measures (i.e., the PDS, BDI-II, STAI, and SMS) and the drawing. However, this debriefing did not involve telling participants the true nature of the study for fear of biasing the results at the follow-up session. Therefore, this was an abbreviated debriefing that focused more on how they were doing and ascertaining whether there were any problems they have experienced. A full debriefing as to the nature of the study and the expected results was provided to the participants after the completion of the third set of dependent variable measures at the 1-month follow-up. The researchers waited a month to ask about the symbolic meaning of the mandala drawings because having the participants put their feelings in words could have confounded results. This information was used for a brief examination of the qualitative features and symbolic meaning of the mandalas. (p. 150)

The first question to address in evaluating the methods section (procedures) is to identify the type of research design used in the study. The researchers described the use of assigning participants randomly to either the control or experimental group. Also, the researchers described in detail the intervention used with the experimental group. The researchers used a pretest–posttest research design. The research design is consistent with the hypotheses presented. For example, it was hypothesized that those randomly assigned to a mandala-drawing condition would experience significantly better psychological and physical health compared to those in the control group, who did not experience the intervention. The independent variable, the mandala condition, is described in relatively good detail. The description of what the participants in the experimental group were asked to do is stated concisely; for example, they were asked to "draw a large circle" (p. 151). Specific instructions to participants were not provided, and this would have been helpful to understand the exact presentation made to the participants in the experimental condition. The experimental condition would be somewhat difficult to replicate without the exact instructions given to the participants.

Many threats to internal validity are addressed with a true experimental design involving the use of random assignment to groups. The instruments, Beck Depression Inventory, the State-Trait Anxiety Inventory, and others, were given pretest–posttest, and consequently, the participants may have developed hypotheses about what the investigator was attempting to assess. Participants could have altered their responses based on this information from taking the pretest to taking the posttest. The only control for this threat is the use of posttest-only designs or Solomon Four-Group Designs. No information is provided on how the participants were recruited, and there were only 36 total participants in both the experimental and control groups. This appears to be a sample of convenience and potentially results in a threat to external validity—population validity—an experimentally accessible population versus the target population. The target population appears to be those with PTSD. There may be several other threats to external validity, that is, ecological validity: novelty and disruption effects and pretest sensitization. Novelty and disruption effects may be a consequence of simply being exposed to a new program and a novel experience, in this case, drawing mandalas. The researcher uses a pretest–posttest design, and there potentially is pretest sensitization.

The questions to address when evaluating the methods and procedures section of a qualitative research study are similar to those posed in evaluating a quantitative study, but there are still some differences. It is important to identify the type of research design used and the consistency of the design with the purpose of the study. There is no independent variable, so a question about the independent variable is not necessary. However, there should be a clear description of the procedures used to collect the data and information, for example, phenomenological methods. The potential threats to validity of qualitative research are significant, and typically, a researcher does not address such issues because the intent is to focus more on external validity and what happens in the natural environment. Bogdan and Biklen (2007) concluded that the use of generalizability in qualitative research is different from what is termed to be generalizability in quantitative research. They concluded that qualitative researchers are interested in obtaining universal conclusions of social processes specifically related to human functioning. A question to address with qualitative research is whether the researcher can obtain data or information that can result in universal conclusions based upon his or her methods. Qualitative research can involve immersion into the environment that is being studied to obtain an in-depth understanding. A criticism of such efforts is that a researcher can inject his or her own biases into the study (Bogdan & Biklen, 2007). Another question is whether the researcher has impacted the outcome with his or her own biases.

Qualitative Research

Research questions to address when evaluating a qualitative study and its methods and procedures follow:

1. What type of research design was used in the study?

2. Is the research design consistent with the purpose presented in the introduction?

3. Does the researcher attempt to identify universal processes, which can result in broader generalization?

4. Did the researcher introduce any bias into his or her procedures based on the procedures used?

An example of a description of qualitative research and the methods and procedures section is provided by Fry (2007), who described her procedures in the following way:

The researcher plays an integral role in qualitative research, serving as the "principal instrument" (Merriam, 1998, p. 20) for data collection and analysis. This role allows a qualitative researcher to "obtain the intricate details about phenomena such as feelings, thought processes, and emotions" (Strauss & Corbin, 1998, p. 11). Toma (2000) explained that another benefit of qualitative research occurs when the researcher is subjective rather than objective as traditionally called for in research with human subjects. Subjectivity allows "researchers and subjects to collaborate to determine meaning, generate findings, and reach conclusions" (p. 177). Toma suggested such research partnerships generate good qualitative data because when researchers "care deeply about what and who they are studying" (p. 177), they are more likely to become "insiders" (p. 183) who get to know and negotiate meaning about their research topic.

At the start of this study I already cared about the four participants. In addition to working with them during the earlier investigation of student teaching induction (Fry, 2006), when the participants were pre-service teachers, I was their professor and field supervisor. Through the experiences we shared, I developed personal relationships with each. I hoped they would be successful beginning teachers and cared about their personal well-being. In addition to undertaking new research about a timely topic, this investigation allowed me to continue to be supportive of these four young teachers long after the time when a university professor's involvement in a beginning teacher's career typically ends. My attachment to this research topic was not just limited to an interest in the research participants. I spent my 1st year teaching in a district that provided an effective induction program. I was far more successful teaching in the district where I received induction support. Thus, I am predisposed to see induction as useful because of my own experiences.

Influenced by Toma's (2000) guidelines, I designed this investigation as a person who was "genuinely interested in the subject—both in terms of the overall phenomenon and the people who can set light on it" (p. 180). I have shared the nature of my interest, which is also a source of potential bias in this study. Accordingly, I also used a systematic research protocol for data collection and analysis to enhance the credibility, dependability, and confirmability of the findings (Lincoln & Guba, 1985). This protocol, along with the relationship I had with the participants (Toma, 2000) was designed to reduce the impact of my bias on the investigation. Ultimately, as Bogdan and Biklen (1998) aptly explained, "data . . . provide a much more detailed rendering of events than even the most creatively prejudiced mind might have imagined prior to the study" (p. 34).

A case study research design was selected for this investigation. According to Yin (1994), case study is the proper research design when a phenomenon's variables cannot be separated from its context. In the case of this study's participants, there was no way to separate their response to their induction support from the context of their teaching positions, relationships with their colleagues, and other variables unique to each teacher. Because of the numerous independent variables that influence beginning teachers' responses to induction, an experiment that isolated the impact of induction was not possible. A case study approach, however, provided insight into beginning teachers' responses to their induction support. This approach was also selected based on Merriam's (1998) definition of a case as "a phenomenon that is inherently bounded, with a finite amount of time for data collection or a limited number of people who could be interviewed or observed" (p. 27).

Phone interviews, emails, teacher journals, and exit interviews were used to answer the research questions. The principal data for this investigation were collected through monthly interviews with each participant. The interviews were semi-structured, and four questions provided the initial framework.

1. How is teaching going so far this year/since the last time we talked?
2. How did your student teaching experiences prepare you for your 1st year of teaching?
3. What additional experiences (in student teaching) might have been helpful?
4. Is there anything you would like to bring up that I haven't asked about?

Depending on how detailed the response was, I would ask follow-up questions. After the first three interviews, it became clear that the second and third questions provided less meaningful information than I anticipated when I designed the investigation. Instead of investigating beginning teachers' induction experiences and retroactive evaluation of their student teaching experiences, which was my initial objective when I began, my emphasis switched to induction based on the themes that emerged in the data.

Since the participants' induction experiences provided such intriguing data, I replaced the second and third questions. The new questions follow-up on aspects of each participant's induction experience based on information they shared in previous interviews. I implemented this new questioning technique for the fourth set of interviews. The questions were different for each participant and each subsequent interview. (p. 220)

Fry (2007) provided an example of how questions were altered as a consequence of earlier responses. She goes on to describe her methods and procedures:

Participant-initiated emails and participants' teaching journals provided additional data. These additional data were collected because they helped me understand the interviews more fully. Participant-initiated emails and journal entries often addressed topics that were discussed in interviews.

For example, a week after our April interview, Shari sent me an email with the subject, "I need some help!!" In the text of the message she explained that she had been invited to apply for a job in another school district and asked for my opinion about how she should proceed. Her email provided additional details about her contract-renewal—something we discussed in an earlier interview. The additional information helped to clarify questions I had after reviewing my interview notes. The email contact was beneficial because it kept me informed about Shari's induction experiences in the time between our monthly interviews. Exit interviews served as the final data point, providing a sense of closure for the investigation. (p. 221)

The first question concerns what type of research design was used in the study. Fry (2007) noted that she used a case study approach, a qualitative method. The use of a case study design is consistent with the purpose of discovering the quality of induction methods for beginning teachers. The researcher stated that she wanted to understand the quality of induction for beginning students, and a qualitative method can give detailed information about the process. The researcher acknowledges that she was very familiar with the cases (participants) and attempted to develop an argument for using them in her study, for example, citing literature that supports this approach, but it is not a clear argument. She cited one author, Toma, who suggested that such research can be accomplished best when the researcher is subjective because he or she can enter the world of the participant. Interest in a topic and entering the world of the participant are components of a qualitative design, but this researcher acknowledged more than simple interest and stated she wanted the participants to be successful (almost like functioning in a parental role versus a research role). An important question is whether she addresses this bias in the discussion section and notes the limitations of the methods. She concluded in the section of limitations of the study that "I hesitate to declare my close relationship with the participants a limitation of the study because it was an intentional part of the research design" (p. 234). It appears she did express a bias with her methods.

Single-Subject Research

Wendt and Miller (2012) proposed additional questions to consider when evaluating the quality of single-subject research designs. Wendt and Miller discussed a detailed analysis of various elements of single-subject research and noted the importance of strong baseline data. The one area that is different and unique to single-subject research is the use of a baseline. Recall one of the major limitations of single-subject research is the lack of between-group comparison, for example, the opportunity to compare any impact of an independent variable on two or more independent groups of individuals. One question concerns whether the baseline provides for repeated measurement of the dependent variable. The use of multiple measurements at baseline provides a comparison within subjects. A second question proposed by Wendt and Miller states whether the baseline provides information about a pattern of performance so that one can determine the impact of the independent variable. If there is no pattern at baseline, it is difficult to make conclusions about the effect of the independent variable when it is introduced. Two additional questions are suggested when evaluating a single-subject study:

1. Does the baseline phase provide a repeated measurement of the dependent variable, generally a minimum of five measurements?

2. Does the baseline show a pattern that is stable and provides consistent data that can be compared to outcomes after introduction of the independent variable?

Fry, Botterill, and Pring (2009) conducted a study aimed at investigating the therapeutic effect of an intensive group therapy program for those who stutter. The researchers described their procedures and sample:

The criteria for selection to take part in this single-subject study were that the participants were aged between 16 and 19 years, had been diagnosed as stuttering by two specialist speech and language therapists, had obtained a severity of stuttering score on the Stuttering Severity Instrument-3. (p. 13)

The researchers (Fry et al., 2009) further described the participant: "TM was a male, mono-lingual English speaker of African ethnic background, aged 18 at the beginning of the study. He had no history of identified speech, language, communication, or other difficulties. There was a family history of persistent stuttering" (p. 13).

Fry and colleagues (2009) described the intervention in the following way:

The program consists of 10 days which take place over a 2-week period, with 5 hours of therapy each day. This is followed by a 5-week consolidation period where skills are practiced and therapy is self-managed. Four follow-up days, each consisting of 5 hours of therapy are scheduled for the group as a whole. The first take place at the end of the consolidation period, 5 weeks after the end of the 2-week course. The next follow-up days are held 3 months, 6 months and 10 months after the course. The group consists of a maximum of 10 clients and is facilitated by two specialist therapists from the Michael Palin Centre who are typically assisted by four student speech and language therapists, giving a specialist/client ratio of 1:5 and a specialist/student/client ratio of 1:1:6. (p. 14)

The research design was described by Fry and colleagues (2007) as follows:

The study had four phases. Phase A consisted of a 5-week baseline during which TM received no therapy. Phase B consisted of a 2-week intensive treatment phase, while Phase C consisted of a 5-week consolidation phase during which treatment was self-managed and which ended with the first follow-up meeting. Phase D consisted of a 1-month maintenance phase which included three additional follow-up meetings. (p. 14)

The researchers described how the dependent variable was assessed and stated (Fry et al., 2009):

Two dimensions of overt stuttering behaviours were analysed quantitatively. The frequency of stuttering was measured by calculating the percentage of structured syllables (%SS), while the average duration of stuttered syllables was measured by calculating the mean of the three longer stuttered syllables in each sample as timed with a stopwatch. Speech samples were taken from five-minute video recordings that TM made at home while talking to either a family member or friend. . . . The study involved making recordings twice a week in phase A, each day in phase B, twice a week in phase C, and once a month in phase D. (pp. 14–15)

The first question to address concerns an identification of what type of study design was used. It is clear that Fry and colleagues (2009) used a single-subject research design. One participant or subject was used in the study. The researchers also stated "the criteria for selection to take part in this single-subject study" (p. 13), which clearly notes the use of a single-subject research design. My personal bias is that every study should clearly identify the type of study rather than the reader trying to identify it. The next question states: Is the research design consistent with the purpose presented in the introduction? The literature review provides a rationale for studying an intervention with stuttering. The researchers systematically review the various interventions that have been effectively used in the treatment of stuttering, for example, cognitive behavioral therapy. Also, the researchers provided an explanation for using intensive group therapy in the treatment of stuttering.

The third set of questions to address in evaluating the procedures is this: Are the independent variables clearly defined? Are the independent variables so clearly defined that they can be replicated using the information provided in the procedures section? The researchers carefully described in detail the intervention and how the therapy program was implemented; for example, "The program consists of 10 days." The researchers provided much more detail in the article about the therapy program and intervention. Based on the detail provided by the researchers, it is possible to replicate the study and the interventions used in this study. Fry and colleagues (2009) provide a much more detailed description of the procedures than most researchers, and this is a strength of this study.

Another question focuses on threats to internal validity: Identify any threats to internal validity. How are they threats? There are several potential threats to internal validity with this study. One internal threat to validity is history. Recall that single-subject research is particularly vulnerable to the threat of history. The study takes place over several weeks and includes a follow-up at 10 months. There are potentially many opportunities to impact and affect the single subject used in this study that are not controlled by the researchers. We do not know if anything unusual happened to the single subject, but there certainly is the potential. A second threat is maturation. The participant was 18, and over a 10-month period, he may have had developmental changes that influenced his maturation and speech and stuttering. A third possible threat to internal validity was testing. Collection of data for the dependent variables was completed over a number of assessments. As was stated earlier, the use of multiple assessments can result in errors and accuracy. This can be particularly an issue for multiple assessments over time, 10 months from beginning to the end of the study. Raters can forget how scoring was to be done with such a wide range of time between assessments.

The next question to address when evaluating the procedures is this: Identify any threats to external validity. How are they threats? There are a several threats to external validity that can be addressed. One is the possible threat to external ecological validity, this is, interaction between history and treatment effects. Similar to internal validity, the potential for a threat to external validity with history and treatment effects is relevant here. As has been noted, history can be a particular problem with single-subject research designs. The study took place over 10 months, and this allows for many outside events impacting the single participant in the study. The researcher does not know what events may have impacted the subject and altered his responses on the dependent measures. A second external threat, interaction between time of measurement and treatment effects, is probably addressed well in this study. The primary reason is that the researchers conducted several post-intervention assessments to minimize the effects of measurement just after treatment and focused on determining any long-term effects.

One of the additional questions specific to single-subject research is this: Does the baseline phase provide a repeated measurement of the dependent variable, generally a minimum of five measurements? There were four phases reported by the researchers and four assessments. Phase A was the initial baseline. Phases B, C, and D involved introduction and altering the independent variable. There does not seem to be repeated measurement of the dependent variable with baseline. The second additional question is next: Does the baseline show a pattern that is stable and provides consistent data that can be compared to outcomes after introduction of the independent variable? Because there was only one baseline measurement, it is difficult to achieve a pattern of performance that provides a basis for comparison with the introduction of the independent variable.

In summary, there are several strengths to the procedures employed in this single-subject research study. One, the researchers clearly described the independent variable. Second, the researchers explicitly identified the type of research study. Third, the researchers reduced the threat of external validity, specifically, interaction between time and measurement of the dependent variable. A potential limitation of this study is focused on internal validity. There is a potential threat to internal validity of history and testing. The lack of multiple comparisons with baseline is another limitation of the study. There are both strengths and weaknesses of this single-subject study, and additional research using a similar focus could address these limitations.

SUMMARY

The procedures section of the methods is a step-by-step, detailed description of what the researcher did to complete the study. It is the research methods used. One purpose of the procedures section is to clearly identify the variables of interest (dependent and independent). A second purpose is to provide information to the reader about the research design used, so an assessment can be made as to the rigor of the study and the potential for any threats to internal and external validity.

Exercises

Directions: Choose an article, and review the procedures section. Your review should address the following questions relevant to quantitative research:

1. What type of research design was used in the study?

2. Is the research design consistent with the purpose and hypothesis presented in the introduction?

3. Is the independent variable clearly defined? Is the independent variable so clearly defined that it can be replicated using the information provided in the procedures section?

4. Identify any threats to internal validity. How are they threats?

5. Identify any threats to external validity. How are they threats?

Here are questions for review of a qualitative research study:

1. What type of research design was used in the study?

2. Is the research design consistent with the purpose presented in the introduction?

3. Does the researcher attempt to identify any universal processes that can result in broader generalization?

(Continued)

4. Did the researcher introduce any bias in his or her procedures based on the procedures used?

Directions: Select a single-subject research study, and answer the following additional questions (in addition to the eight questions under quantitative research):

1. Does the baseline phase provide a repeated measurement of the dependent variable, generally a minimum of five measurements?

2. Does the baseline show a pattern that is stable and provides consistent data that can be compared to outcomes after introduction of the independent variable?

15

Evaluating the Methods Section

Instruments

survey?

Instrumentation is that area of the methods section where the researchers systematically describe the dependent measures used in the study. There are a number of different ways to measure the dependent variable, and the type of research design and the purpose of the study influence what measures are used. As with the procedures section, the instrumentation section must spell out clearly which instruments were used and how they were administered so that others who wish to replicate the study or want to use similar methods in actual practice can do so. Also, a clear description of the instruments allows those reading the study to determine the quality of the measures used and whether they are appropriate to the intent of the study. Researchers have noted the importance of achieving objectivity and obtaining reliable and accurate measures in the tests they use (Gall et al., 2002; Salkind, 2006; Thorndike & Thorndike-Christ, 2010). There are several relevant issues I want to review when evaluating the instrumentation section. One issue concerns the standardization of the instrument, and a second concerns how culture, diversity, and gender influence administration of the instruments and dependent variables. Additionally, the researcher should address the reliability and validity of the dependent variables. Last, there is a discussion of how to measure the dependent variable and the strengths and weaknesses of each approach.

STANDARDIZATION OF INSTRUMENTS

An important consideration in assessing the objectivity and quality of a dependent measure is the extent to which the procedures and scoring methods are standardized (Gall et al., 2002; Thorndike & Thorndike-Christ, 2010). Standardization in administering the dependent measure theoretically provides more objective data. A manual for administering the dependent variable is a major method of establishing standardization. Manuals may include what is told to those taking the test or measure, time allotted for responses, follow-up questions if certain answers are given, and so on.

Another consideration in standardizing the dependent variable is consistent, systematic scoring methods (Thorndike & Thorndike-Christ, 2010). The test developers generally include standardized scoring methods in the manual for a standardized instrument. There are generally two types of approaches to scoring in a formal measure: criterion referenced and norm referenced. Criterion-referenced scores are based on a predetermined level of performance, or a criterion. An example from education might be an elementary school-age child demonstrating the ability to multiply single digits, with a criterion of 100 percent success.

A second type of score using a standardization for the dependent variable, as mentioned, is the norm-referenced approach. In this approach, scores are interpreted based on the comparison of one group's performance with other groups', all of whom represent a clearly defined population. An example might be a national achievement test such as the Stanford Achievement Test. The test is described as measuring a student's progress toward academic standards (retrieved June 12, 2013, from http://www.pearsonassessments.com/HAITWEB/cultures/en-us/productdetail.htm?pid=SAT10C).

CULTURE, GENDER, AND DIVERSITY BIAS

Researchers and practitioners have noted the importance of using measures of the dependent variable that are culturally, gender-issue, and diversity-issue appropriate (Drummond, 2000; O'Bryant & McCaffrey, 2006; Thorndike & Thorndike-Christ, 2010). Anastasi and Urbina (1997) stated, "No single test can be universally applicable or equally 'fair' to all cultures" (p. 342). Use of an inappropriate test or dependent measure can result in test bias and problems with interpreting outcomes. Several potential problems in testing have been identified when researchers use samples from populations such as those from minority backgrounds, individuals with disabilities, and other populations who are characterized by different worldviews (diversity) than that for which the instrument was originally intended and developed (Drummond, 2000; Thorndike & Thorndike-Christ, 2010). Thorndike and Thorndike-Christ (2010) noted that many tests and measures are designed to "reflect the values and experiences of typical middle-class" (p. 16). Possible sources of problems include the establishment of equivalents across diverse groups; lack of appropriate norms among diverse groups; differences in language and meanings of test items in different cultures, genders, and so on; and varying attitudes among diverse groups toward test taking. Drummond (2000) noted the importance of using culturally and racially sensitive instruments. He also noted the APA Standards for Educational and Psychological Tests, which acknowledge the relevance of using instruments that are sensitive to diversity. Also, the ACA (2005) Code of Ethics states the following in regards to using tests and diversity: "E.5.b Culture sensitivity. Counselors recognize that culture reflects the manner in which clients' problems are defined. Clients' socioeconomic and cultural experiences are considered when diagnosing disorders." The National Education Association (NEA) addresses the importance of considering diversity in working with children but does not specifically address assessment or testing. The NEA Code of Ethics (1975), Principle 1, Item 6 states, "Shall not on the basis of race, color, creed, sex, national origin, marital status, political or religious beliefs, family social or cultural background or sexual orientation unfairly: a) exclude any student from participating in any program and b) deny benefits to any student."

The important point for all professional codes is use of culturally fair tests, whether administered for counseling diagnosis or assessment of learning outcomes. Counselors and educators should review the professional literature for research and knowledge that addresses how testing is impacted by culture and diversity and ensure that assessments are appropriate for those with whom they are working. For the consumer of research, evaluating the use of a particular dependent measure in a study is important, particularly if you plan to use it in your professional practice and if you have a diverse group with whom you are working.

RELIABILITY OF INSTRUMENTS

Researchers have noted that one of the most important considerations in determining the quality of the dependent measures is the reliability of the instruments and dependent variables (Drummond, 2000; Gregory, 2007; Heiman, 1995; Urbina, 2004). Thorndike and Thorndike-Christ (2010) described reliability and stated, "Reliability refers to the accuracy or precision of a measurement procedure. Indices of reliability give an indication of the extent to which the scores produced by a particular measurement procedure are consistent and reproducible" (p. 118). Gregory (2007) proposed that reliability "refers to the attribute of consistency in measurement" (p. 96). He further noted that there are not many psychological tests that are totally consistent but that they can vary quite readily. He further described this variability in the following way: "The concept of reliability is best viewed as a continuum ranging from minimal consistency of measurement (e.g. simple reaction time) to near perfect repeatability of results" (p. 96). Both these definitions propose that reliability involves consistency in the scores. A particular test score contains both a true score and error. Error refers to all the potential effects that alter the true score, such as the limitations of the test (if the items being presented are unclear, considerable interpretation may be needed by the responder), time of day in responding to the measure (responses to tests given late at night may be affected by respondents' fatigue), lack of consistent administration procedures, human errors in scoring, and so on. Several methods have been proposed to determine the degree of reliability and, conversely, the amount of error, and these include test-retest reliability, alternate-form reliability, scorer reliability, and internal consistency. These various forms of determining reliability measure different types of error. Reliability is reported as a correlation expressed as the degree of the relationship between two sets of scores. Possible scores in these correlations can range from −1.0 to +1.0. A higher positive correlation indicates a strong relationship between the two sets of scores, whereas a negative correlation denotes an inverse relationship between scores. Generally, scores of .80 and higher are considered strong indicators of reliability in a particular test or measure (Thorndike & Thorndike-Christ, 2010; Urbina, 2004).

There are several different ways to determine reliability. These include test-retest, alternate form, inter-rater, and internal consistency. All are important contributors to test reliability and determine different types of test reliability. Test-retest is one approach to determining reliability; it involves the measurement of the consistency of the scores over a period of time. The researchers administer the dependent measure at one point and then again at another time. The distance between administrations should not be too close (e.g., an hour apart). The respondents may remember the question and their answers. Nor should the retest be too long after the initial test; if, for instance, the retest is a year after the test, the concept measured may change and not be a consequence of lowered reliability of the instrument. For example, if I measure stress, the concept of stress is variable from day to day, and on any given day, stress may be high or low. Consequently, the reliability of measuring stress may be lower because of the actual variability of the construct. The test-retest method of determining reliability addresses problems such as consistency in administering the measure.

Alternate-form reliability concerns the consistency of a measure based on content, for instance, when two forms of the measure are administered to a sample, and reliability coefficients are obtained between them (Drummond, 2000; Urbina, 2004). The intent is to have alternate forms of a test that consistently measure the same concept. Alternate forms allow a researcher to measure something at different times and control for the effects of testing (testing occurs when a test taker recalls items on a test and his or her performance is possibly influenced by pretest). One major benefit of establishing alternative-form reliability involves circumstances where a user wants to avoid the respondent remembering the questions from a previous administration but retain assessing the construct.

Scorer reliability, or inter-rater reliability, means that objective observational data are collected and, therefore, requires several scorers to interpret responses. To avoid subjective bias with only one scorer, researchers will use several scorers to ensure adequate reliability. Inter-rater reliability is the extent to which a scoring key is developed and used with consistency. Correlation scores are obtained between raters scoring the same target variables. Low correlations between scorers indicate low reliability and consistency. This also concerns any other type of scoring procedure, such as machine scoring, in which errors can occur with the reading of smudged responses on a computer-generated scoring sheet. Another method of determining inter-rater reliability is the calculation of Kappa. Thorndike and Thorndike-Christ (2010) described calculation of Kappa as the "proportion agreements, corrected for the probability of agreement by chance" (p. 329).

The last type of reliability is internal consistency, which is the most frequently reported type of reliability. It involves the extent to which the items in a measure correlate or are related to each other or to their homogeneity. More specifically, this type of reliability refers to how consistent the responses are within a measure of a particular construct or concept. Thorndike and Thorndike-Christ (2010) described internal consistency: "The procedure for estimating the reliability of a test from a single administration of a single form depends on the consistency of each individual's performance from item to item and is based on the variance of the test scores and the variances of the separate items" (p. 127).

VALIDITY OF INSTRUMENTS

Gregory (2007) described the importance of validity and stated, "Psychometricians have long acknowledged that validity is the most fundamental and important characteristic of a test" (p. 120). Validity is defined as the degree to which a test measures what it is designed to measure. A clear definition of validity is provided in the Standards for Educational and Psychological Testing, which states, "Validity refers to the degree to which evidence and theory support the interpretations of test scores entailed by proposed uses of tests" (American Educational Research Association, American Psychological Association, and National Council on Measurement in Education, 1999, p. 9). For example, if a test is designed to measure intelligence, then the items are evaluated by the extent to which they measure this dependent variable. Thorndike and Thorndike-Christ (2010) proposed that a test with good reliability is important but is not enough if the validity of the instrument is poor, for example, having an instrument that does not measure what it purports to measure. Using a scale to measure weight may have good validity if one wants to know one's weight but does not have good validity to measure height.

One specific value of validity is difficult to obtain and report (Gregory, 2007; Urbina, 2004). Generally, establishment of validity is obtained through comparisons with test results and actual behavior or outcomes. Gregory (2007) further noted that the accumulation of evidence for the validity of a test may be determined to be weak, acceptable, or strong. Three types of validity have been identified as important in developing an argument for the strength of test validity: construct validity, content validity, and criterion-related validity (Gall et al., 2002; Gregory, 2007; Thorndike & Thorndike-Christ, 2010; Urbina, 2004).

The most general type of validity is construct validity because it supposedly concerns the degree to which a test measures an intended theoretical concept or construct. Thorndike and Thorndike-Christ (2010) proposed that construct validity may be thought of as a measure to best describe or identify a construct of interest. For example, if one wants to determine and evaluate intelligence, what measure best helps one make this conclusion? Can the measure identify those with high and low measures of intelligence? Urbina (2004) has identified three components of construct validity, which include the following sources of evidence: content-related sources, convergence and divergence sources, and criterion-related sources. Content-related sources include determining the relevance and representativeness of the items on the test. There are a number of different sources for convergence and divergence evidence, which include factor analysis, structural equation modeling techniques, correlations among tests, and differentiation in scores based upon certain variables such as age, where differences in scores would be expected. The last source, criterion related, is composed of obtaining evidence of prediction of a particular construct or accuracy in identifying a construct in practice. As mentioned earlier, validity is the degree to which a test measures the intended concept or construct. It has been noted that there is no single source for determining construct validity, but it is more often a consequence of gathering evidence from other types of validity (Urbina, 2004).

Content validity is a basic type of validity that concerns the extent to which responses on test items represent a particular content. For example, if a counselor wants to measure aggression in a client, the content validity is the degree to which the items represent client aggressive behaviors, such as yelling, hitting, and so on. Content validity is generally determined by having experts in a particular content area rate the degree to which the items represent the content or concept intended (Gregory, 2007). One method is to have experts rate whether items should be included in a particular test. Correlations among the experts provide a numerical value that illustrates the degree of content validity. The higher the positive correlation (closer to +1.0), the better the content validity.

A third type of validity is criterion-related validity, which involves how well a test predicts outcomes based on a particular behavior or skill. This type of validity is established by determining a set of criteria that predicts future outcomes. Thorndike and Thorndike-Christ (2010) described the qualities of developing criterion measurements. They stated that a "criterion measure to be relevant to the extent that standing on the criterion measure corresponds to, exemplifies, level of status on the trait we are trying to predict"(p. 169). Essentially, a good criterion measure should provide evidence of the identified trait through associated behaviors. Correlations may be used to establish criterion-related validity. Correlations with scores on the test are made with actual outcomes of the set criterion. Concurrent validity is another type of criterion-related validity, defined as the extent to which a particular test relates or correlates with an accepted standard test that has an intended similar construct or concept. This approach is used when developing a new test while correlating scores to an accepted standard test.

APPROACHES TO MEASURING THE DEPENDENT VARIABLE

A number of different methods and approaches to measuring the dependent variable in quantitative research methods have been suggested. They include direct observation and behavioral measures, self-report and inventories, ratings of others' behavior, physiological approaches, and interviews (Eid & Diener, 2006; Gall et al., 2006; Heiman, 1995; McMillan, 2004; Merrell, 1999). Qualitative researchers typically employ a few of the methods used in quantitative research, such as direct observation, interview, together with triangulation methods to increase the reliability and validity of their observations and data collection (Berg, 2004; Creswell, 2012; Taylor & Bogdan, 1984). Other methods of obtaining data in qualitative research are documents and audiovisual materials (Creswell, 2012).

Direct observation and behavioral measures involve a focus on observable behavior (Bakeman & Quera, 2012). Merrell (1999) stated as follows: "Direct observation of behavior is one of the cornerstone tools for the assessment of behavior, social, and emotional problems" (p. 48). Trained observers or scorers are used to record or evaluate behavior of the target sample and target behavior (the dependent variable). Bakeman and Quera (2012) described observational sessions and stated, "An observational session is a sequence of coded events for which continuity generally can be assumed" (p. 207). In essence, observations are units of measurement and can be divided into various segments that match the intent of the research; for example, observations can be segmented in time or actions and behaviors. This approach to measuring the dependent variable may be used in both quantitative and qualitative research methods. Bakeman and Quera proposed that there are three types of circumstances where observations are most appropriate: measuring nonverbal behavior, observing naturally occurring behavior, and a focus on process and not just outcomes of a situation. Measuring nonverbal behavior may be best utilized in situations such as studying infants and children, for example, observing infants' nonverbal communication with parents (facial movements and eye gaze). There are many circumstances where measurement in a natural environment may be best accomplished through observations, for example, observing and measuring classroom behaviors such as aggression or helpful behaviors. Observations may provide information about the process or interaction that occurs in various settings such as counseling sessions, intimate relationship interactions, and classroom interactions, that is, the sequence of events occurring within such settings. The actual use of observations requires training and careful analysis of observer agreement. Heppner and colleagues (1992) noted that there are several advantages to using direct observational methods rather than approaches like self-reports, for example, if the measurement is of direct behavior and not inferred or projected outcomes. Consequently, the measurement (theoretically) is more objective. There are limitations with direct measures. Even though direct measures are considered more objective, there remains the possibility of bias among the observers or raters. This may be particularly true in cases where there is only one rater rather than several raters. Also, Heppner and colleagues stated that individual views or idiosyncrasies of the raters may influence what is observed and thus influence the reliability of the measure.

Self-report and inventories are one of the most frequently used method of measuring the dependent variable in psychology, counseling, and education. This approach to measuring the dependent variable is more frequently used in quantitative than qualitative research. In self-report approaches to measuring the dependent variable, respondents or study participants are generally asked to rate the extent to which an identified behavior, attitude, or feeling is present. There are hundreds of inventories and self-report measures from which a researcher can choose to measure the dependent variable (Conoley & Impara, 1995; Eid & Diener, 2006). There are self-report measures of stress, coping strategies, career interests, a host of attitude measures, self-esteem, and so on. Items on these scales may involve the use of simple yes-or-no responses, Likert-type gradations (rating the extent of agreement with statements based on choices like *agree* or *disagree*), rank order, forced choice (choosing one of two items), or open-ended responses. The following is an example of a Likert-type scale.

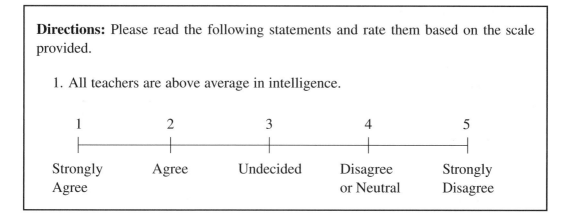

Directions: Please read the following statements and rate them based on the scale provided.

1. All teachers are above average in intelligence.

1	2	3	4	5
Strongly Agree	Agree	Undecided	Disagree or Neutral	Strongly Disagree

An example of an instrument requiring ranking of responses is demonstrated in the following example of a possible scale designed to measure work ethic.

Directions: Read each set of statements (a through f) and **rank** the statements in terms of how well each statement represents your values or how you feel. Rank in order of 1 to 6, with **1 being most representative** of your values and **6 being least representative** of your values.

a. People should spend more time in leisure activities.

b. I believe one should not do a sloppy job.

c. If one works hard enough, one is likely to make a good life for oneself.

d. It is important for one to show respect for one's supervisor.

e. I think it is important to be on time for work.

f. One should not work overtime because it cuts into family time.

Rasinski, Lee, and Krishnamurty (2012) noted the importance of careful consideration of the order of questions or the effect of question order. Issues such as the context of where and when questions are answered may impact the understanding or interpretation of question order. Asking questions about political affiliation during a presidential election may have a different impact on response than asking the same question during an off-presidential election year. Consider research has been published on the impact of question order effect (Rasinksi et al., 2012).

Heppner and colleagues (1992) have noted the advantages and disadvantages of self-report and inventories. One of the most important advantages to researchers in using self-report and inventories is the ease and time of administering them (see Table 15.1). Self-report approaches generally do not require extensive training to administer and for the most part are brief. A second advantage is that the researcher can assess non-observable events such as cognitions and feelings that generally cannot be measured through direct observation.

Heppner and colleagues (1992) suggested that the most serious problem with self-report measures is the possibility of distortion or bias by the responder (see Table 15.1). Respondents may deny or repress feelings or cognitions that are troublesome or incongruent with how they see themselves. Another reason respondents may show bias in their responses may be because they wish to give socially desirable responses, to present themselves in a more positive way, or to attempt to respond the way they perceive the researcher wants them to on the self-report. A second problem with self-report measures is that respondents may not be aware of certain feelings, attitudes, or behaviors they possess and thus cannot accurately indicate what occurs in actual practice (Heppner et al., 1992). For example, a researcher interested in how Alzheimer's disease affects behavior may find that it is difficult for the person with Alzheimer's to report because of the effects of the condition on self-awareness. Consequently, a different approach to measuring dependent variables with this population may be more appropriate.

Rating of others' behavior is a third method of measuring a dependent variable. This method of assessment is used in both quantitative and qualitative research approaches. This approach basically involves the use of some standardized method of scoring the behavior of others in some systematic way. An example is a music teacher evaluating the singing ability of a student. The standardized method here is the student's attempt to replicate specific musical notes. In counseling, an example is the assessment of a client's psychological functioning (e.g., the Global Assessment System [GAS]). Heppner and colleagues (1992) noted that the use of experts in the ratings of others increases the effectiveness of the rating method. One advantage then is that the use of experts increases the accuracy of the measurement. A second advantage of this approach is that it is generally not very time-consuming and is simple to administer (see Table 15.1). A possible problem with ratings of others is that raters may interject their own biases into the process (see Table 15.1). For example, if a counselor rates a client's progress and is seeking a particular outcome, the ratings may be biased. One method of reducing individual rater bias is to use multiple raters and determine inter-rater reliability.

A fourth approach to measuring the dependent variable is through the use of physiological methods (Harmon-Jones & Amodio, 2012; Tassinary, Hess, &

Carcoba, 2012). Advances in technology have significantly increased the potential and use of physiological measures in counseling and education research. Physiological measurement may involve the use of responses such as heart rate, electrical activity of the heart (electrocardiogram [ECG]), blood pressure, galvanic skin response (GSR), brain waves (EEG), and immune system response. An important contribution of using physiological measures is that one can obtain a fairly accurate baseline reading of the identified measure to be assessed. Obtaining a good baseline measure of the dependent variable provides a good comparison to determine impact of the independent variable and changes that may occur. A major advantage is that such measurement is generally considered objective and accurate (see Table 15.1). One problem with this method of measuring the dependent variable is that it is generally time-consuming (see Table 15.1). A second problem is that the equipment for measuring the variable of interest is expensive. Third, measurement generally must take place in a very controlled environment, typically in a clinic.

Another approach to measuring the dependent variable is through the use of interviews; this is the most popular method of collecting social science data (Madill, 2012). A key to using interviews is the skill of the interviewer in developing an appropriate relationship, so the interview can be effectively completed. The most common format for interviews is the semi-structured approach, which involves establishing a set of general questions and format. A semi-structured interview allows the researcher to deviate from the interview questions as determined by the interviewer and explore an issue further, given certain responses. Interviewing is a skill and may involve the use of open- and closed-ended questions (Madill, 2012). Interviewers ask respondents a set of questions; this may involve relating brief or detailed responses. Interviews are used frequently in qualitative methods and less frequently in quantitative research studies because they do not allow for easy quantification of the responses. Heppner and colleagues (1992) stated that one advantage of the interview method is the flexibility of how information and data are collected (see Table 15.1). Researchers can alter the questions asked based on the responses given and adjust to the flow of the interview. Another advantage of the interview method is that in-depth information may be gathered, as opposed to the superficial information available from structured self-report measures.

Problems with the interview method are that it is time-consuming and costly (Heppner et al., 1992). The interviewer must take the time to develop a relationship with the interviewee before there is a focus on the topic of interest (see Table 15.1). The interviewer generally receives in-depth training, which is expensive to complete. Another problem with the interview method is a difficulty in achieving a standard approach to scoring responses in a systematic way.

Table 15.1 Approaches to Measuring Dependent Variables

Approach	Description	Strength	Limitation
Direct observation	Trained observers or scorers are used to evaluate behavior.	The measurement is more objective.	Possibility of bias among the observers or raters.
Self-report inventories	Rate the extent to which an identified behavior, attitude, or feeling is present.	Ease and time of administration, do not require extensive training, and achieve access to non-observable events.	Possibility of distortion bias by the responder attempting to achieve socially desirable responses; responder may not be aware of certain feelings, attitudes, or behaviors.
Ratings	Use of some standardized method of scoring behavior of others.	Measurement is not time-consuming, increases the accuracy of the measurement.	Rater may interject own biases into the process.
Physiological methods	Assessment of responses such as heart rate, ECG, blood pressure, GSR, EEG, and immune system response.	Measurement is objective and accurate.	Method is generally time-consuming; measuring the variable of interest is expensive.
Interviews	Interviewers ask respondents a set of questions that may involve brief or detailed responses.	There is flexibility in the way information and data are collected; in-depth information may be collected.	The method is time-consuming and costly; it is difficult to achieve a standard approach to scoring responses.

GUIDELINES AND QUESTIONS FOR EVALUATING THE INSTRUMENTS: QUANTITATIVE RESEARCH

1. Is there a clear and adequate description of the instrument?

2. What types of measures were used in the study (direct observation and behavioral measures, self-report and inventories, ratings of others' behavior,

physiological approaches, or interview)? Identify any problems or limitations with the types of measures used.

3. To what extent are the instruments standardized, and what types of standardized scoring were used (criterion referenced or norm referenced)?

4. Does the instrument appear to be appropriate for the sample (e.g., are there any cross-cultural, gender, or diversity biases)? Explain.

5. Is the reliability of the instruments reported? What type of reliability is reported?

6. Is the reliability reported for the instruments adequate? Explain.

7. What types of validity are reported for the instruments used?

8. Is the validity of the instruments adequate? Explain.

EVALUATING EXAMPLES FROM THE RESEARCH LITERATURE: QUANTITATIVE RESEARCH

We can go back to the study used in previous chapters, Henderson and colleagues (2007), which focused on the use of mandalas for healing those with posttraumatic stress disorder. The researchers used five measures in this study; however, only two are used to illustrate how to evaluate the instruments. Henderson and colleagues (2007) described their instruments in the following way:

> The PDS (Foa, 1995) is a 49-item self-report measure to aid in the detection and diagnosis of PTSD. Participants report on PTSD symptoms that they have experienced within the last month. This measure not only yields PTSD diagnostic information but also provides an index of PTSD symptom severity. Items are rated with regard to presence (i.e. yes, or no) and with regard to symptom severity. Symptom severity scores are rated from below 10 (mild), 10–20 (moderate), 21–35 (moderate-to-severe), to above 35 (severe) (Foa, 1995).
>
> PDS symptom severity scores were used as the primary means of indicating changes in the severity of participants' traumatic symptoms from baseline (Time 1) to completion of the intervention (Time 2) to 1-month follow-up (Time 3). The coefficient alpha for the PTSD symptom severity scores was .87 in the current study. (p. 149)

The first question is whether there is a clear and adequate description of the instrument. It is noted to be a self-report measure, the Posttraumatic Stress Disorder Scale (PDS), and it was designed to identify the levels of severity of posttraumatic stress. However, no items are presented to illustrate the scale, nor is there any information about how the different levels of severity are differentiated. As has been noted above, some of the advantages in using self-report and inventories are the ease and time of administering them and that it can assess nonobservable events, such as cognitions and feelings, that generally cannot be measured through direct observation. The most significant problem with self-report measures is the potential for distortion or bias by the respondent.

The next question to address is the extent to which the instruments are standardized and what types of standardized scoring were used (criterion referenced or norm referenced). No information is provided about the standardization of the PDS, nor is there any information about whether the scores are based on and compared with criterion-referenced or norm-referenced scores.

Another question is whether the instrument is appropriate for the sample (e.g., are there any cross-cultural, gender, or diversity biases). Participants in the study were prescreened for posttraumatic experiences or stressors. However, no information is provided about whether the instrument is appropriate or sensitive based on culture or gender differences. Also, the reader of the article has not seen examples of the items, and this gives the reader minimal information about the appropriateness of the instrument for diverse groups.

The next two questions concern reliability. One question is whether the reliability of the instruments is reported. Little information is provided on the reliability of the instrument. The researchers do report the coefficient alpha for the instrument to be .87 in the current study. Coefficient alpha concerns the internal consistency of the instrument, and .87 is an adequate level of internal consistency. A problem is that no other reliability from previous studies is reported, nor is any other reliability reported, such as test-retest. The last questions concern the validity of the instrument. Again, no information is provided on the validity of the instrument, as with the information provided on the reliability. Both of these issues are significant problems in the use of this instrument in the study. The reader cannot judge whether this instrument is reliable and valid, so the results are easily identified as questionable.

Another scale or instrument used in this study was the State-Trait Anxiety Inventory (STAI). Henderson and colleagues (2007) described the instrument as follows:

The State-Trait Anxiety Inventory (STAI; Speilberger, 1983) is a 40-item, self-report measure that assesses levels of transitory feelings of anxiety, worry, and fear (state), and the more stable (trait) tendencies to feel worried and react anxiously. The STAI was included in this study to assess changes in both state and trait anxiety levels from baseline to follow-up at Times 2 and 3. Coefficient alphas of .90 and .92 were found in the current study for state and trait anxiety. (p. 149)

Again, the first question is whether there is there a clear and adequate description of the instrument. The researchers describe the instrument as assessing different levels of anxiety, worry, and fear (which they defined as state anxiety) and more stable reactions of feeling worried and anxious, which they termed a trait. This description provides some information on the intent of the instrument but does not provide information about actual items that illustrate the content. Again, this is a self-report measure, and one advantage is the ease and time of administering them. Also, because the focus is on non-observable events (anxiety and cognitions), it can still be assessed through self-report. The problem is the potential for bias or distortion by the respondent.

The second question concerns whether the instrument is standardized. There is no mention of whether the STAI is standardized, and there is no information about comparing scores to criterion- or norm-referenced data. No information is provided on the appropriateness of the instrument with diverse groups. Again, the coefficients alpha are reported (the internal consistency of the instrument), which were found to be .90 and .92, respectively, for state and trait anxiety. Finally, no validity is reported for the instrument. Based on the information provided to the reader, it is difficult to conclude that either instrument evaluated (the PDS or the STAI) gives the researcher a strong basis for making decisions about the findings with such limitations in the reported quality of the instruments.

GUIDELINES AND QUESTIONS FOR EVALUATING THE INSTRUMENTS: QUALITATIVE RESEARCH

The questions for evaluating qualitative research are similar for three questions. They do not cover issues like standardization of the instruments or reliability or validity because these involve the use of numerical values. Fry (2007) described the use of the following instrument in her qualitative study:

Phone interviews, emails, teacher journals, and exit interviews were used to answer the research questions. The principal data for this investigation were collected through monthly interviews with each participant. The interviews were semi-structured, and four questions provided the initial framework.

1. How is teaching going so far this year/since the last time we talked?

2. How did your student teaching experiences prepare you for your 1st year of teaching?

3. What additional experiences (in student teaching) might have been helpful?

4. Is there anything you would like to bring up that I haven't asked you about?

Depending on how detailed the response was, I would ask follow-up questions. After the first three interviews, it became clear that the second and third questions provided less meaningful information than I anticipated when I designed the investigation. Instead of investigating beginning teachers' induction experiences and retroactive evaluation of their student teaching experiences, which was my initial objective when I began, my emphasis switched to induction based upon the themes that emerged in the data.

Since the participants' induction experiences provided such intriguing data, I replaced the second and third questions. The new questions follow-up on aspects of each participant's induction experience based on information they shared in previous interviews. I implemented this new questioning technique for the fourth set of interviews. The questions were different for each participant and each subsequent interview. Participant-initiated emails and participants' teaching journals provided additional data. These additional data were collected because they helped me understand the interviews more fully. Participant-initiated emails and journal entries often addressed topics that were discussed in interviews. (pp. 220–221)

The following are questions to address in evaluating qualitative research:

1. Is there a clear and adequate description of the instrument?

2. What types of measures were used in the study (direct observation and behavioral measures or interviews)? Identify any problems or limitations with the types of measures used.

3. Does the instrument appear to be appropriate for the sample (e.g., are there any cross-cultural, gender, or diversity biases)?

The first question is whether there is an adequate description of the instruments. The instruments used in this qualitative study included interviews, journals, and e-mail messages. The journals and e-mail messages may be categorized as self-report. The researchers provided considerable information about the interviews and how they were conducted, including the questions that were asked. Minimal information was provided about the participant-initiated e-mails and journals. No detail is given about how the e-mails or journals were solicited or formatted, for example, their content or focus.

Interviews, e-mails, and journals were used in data collection. As noted, interviews are used frequently in qualitative methods, and one advantage of the interview method is the flexibility regarding how information and data are collected. The researchers can alter the questions asked based on the responses given, and therefore, they can adjust the flow of the interview to the responses. There are several problems and limitations with the interview method. Interviews can be time-consuming and costly. Also, they may involve considerable time to train the interviewers to obtain quality data. A limitation of interviews is that it is difficult to standardize responses, and this hinders objective interpretation to some degree.

The next question is whether the instruments were appropriate for the participants. There is little information about the demographic characteristics of the participants, except that they were all women, there were four participants, and they received their degrees from a university in the western United States. It is difficult to determine adequately if the instruments were appropriate, given this sparse information.

SINGLE-SUBJECT EXAMPLE

Silva, Correia, Lima, Magalhaes, and de Sousa (2011) conducted a single-case study focused on using dogs with children with Autism Spectrum Disorder to improve therapy outcomes. A single participant, a 12-year-old boy, was the focus. He was diagnosed using *DSM-IV* criteria for Autism Spectrum Disorder. The dog used was a Labrador retriever who was certified as a therapy dog. A therapist trained as a psychologist and who was certified as an assistance dog handler conducted the intervention. The research design used was a single-case design with baseline and experimental conditions. Implementation of the design is described as follows: "Each week the participant was exposed to 'T (therapist alone, which was the baseline condition)' and 'Tdog (therapist and dog together or the experimental condition)' sessions for 45 minutes on different and non-consecutive days. All sessions were video-recorded for data-coding purposes and were held at the participant's usual treatment place" (p. 656). The therapy sessions, both alone with therapist and with the dog and therapist followed a structured format and were described as such: "This structured protocol included structured one-to-one activities previously defined to promote prosocial behaviors in the participant (e.g. playing ball with the participant, questioning the participant about specific events)" (p. 656). Silva and colleagues (2011) described the method of measuring the dependent variable and prosocial and aggressive behaviors and stated,

Fifteen (15) minutes of each session, including 5-minute periods (randomly selected by an independent researcher) of the initial, middle and last parts of the video recordings, were analysed and the following variables were coded: (1) negative behaviors of the participant, including physical aggressive behaviour, verbal aggressive behaviour, repetitive smelling, obsessive staring, grabbing behaviour, as well as self-absorption; and (2) positive behaviors of the participant, including affectionate behaviour, play, visual contact, as well as smiling. . . . Coding was performed using the Observer XT Software version 7.0 which allows an automatic reading of duration and frequency of behavioural events. Interobserver reliability using Pearson's r correlation was assessed between two coders who independently scored all video recordings. (p. 656)

The first question to address in evaluating the instrument in this single-case study is whether there is a clear and adequate description of the instrument. Silva and colleagues (2011) provide a clear description of the instrument, specifically, direct observation. The researchers describe how they recorded sessions and how raters identified both prosocial and aggressive behaviors of the study participant. They identify what were defined as prosocial behaviors (e.g., affectionate behavior, visual contact) and aggressive behaviors (e.g., grabbing behavior, obsessive staring). The researchers provide general categories for both types of behaviors, but do not give specific examples, which would be helpful in understanding the measurement.

The researchers use direct observation and behavioral measures. A major advantage of using direct observation is that, typically, they are more objective than many other types of measures, such as self-reports. A potential limitation concerns how well the observers agree on the targeted behaviors being assessed. There needs to be good training of observers, so there is agreement among their evaluations. The next question concerns to what extent the instruments are standardized and what types of standardized scoring were used (criterion referenced or norm referenced). Coding was performed by using the Observer XT Software version 7.0 (Noldus Information Technology, Wagerningen, the Netherlands). However, no information is provided in regards to how the coding may have been standardized. Also, little information was provided about how interobserver ratings were achieved, for example, training of the observers. The fourth question is this: Does the instrument appear to be appropriate for the sample (e.g., are there any cross-cultural, gender, or diversity biases)? No information is provided about the sample that was used to develop the coding system, that is, Observer XT Software version 7.0. It is difficult to determine whether diverse groups were considered in establishing the coding system.

The next question to address is whether the reliability of the instruments is reported and what type. Reliability of the raters reported that they used a Pearson r correlation to determine the interobserver reliability. There are problems with using a Pearson r in determining interobserver reliability, and a better measure would have been to calculate a Kappa. Hunt (1986) noted the problems with using Pearson's correlation with inter-rater agreement and stated, "Caution must be used in the interpretation of Pearson's correlation because it is unaffected by the presence of any systematic biases" (p. 128). The sixth question to address in evaluating the quality of the dependent variable is whether the reliability reported for the instruments adequate. It is noteworthy that the researchers state that interobserver reliability was calculated and reported to be .9, which is adequate (generally reliability above .80 is considered adequate). Again, however, it would have been more appropriate to use a Kappa to calculate interobserver reliability. The seventh question is to determine what types of validity are reported for the instruments used and if the validity is adequate. The researchers do not report any information about the validity of the instrument or measure used. Researchers not reporting the validity of the instrument is fairly common; it is much more difficult to establish validity than reliability. One would want to accept with caution the application of this measure in interpreting these results given that no validity of the instrument is reported.

In summary, the researchers do provide a clear description of the instrument, and they use direct observation for the dependent variable. The instrument appears to have been developed based on standard coding used with specific software, that is, Observer XT Software version 7.0. No information is provided as to whether the coding is based on diverse populations. The reliability of the instrument is adequate, but no information is provided about the validity of the instrument.

SUMMARY

The instrumentation section is where the researchers describe how they operationalized the dependent variables. The information presented here can provide the reader and consumer of research with important information about the efficacy of the study. Inadequate or inappropriate measures can affect the results obtained and, consequently, the validity of the study. Several questions and guides are useful in determining whether a study is valid. We typically are concerned with whether the researchers have provided a clear description of the instruments used and what types of measures were employed. Also, it is important to know whether an instrument is standardized and if any potential diversity biases exist. Most important, the researchers should report the reliability and validity of the instruments used. Without information on the reliability and validity of the instruments used in a quantitative study, it is difficult to conclude whether the study results obtained are accurate.

The questions for evaluating the instruments in qualitative research include several questions similar to those that are used in quantitative research.

Exercises
Select a quantitative research article, and answer the following questions:

  1. Is there a clear and adequate description of the instrument?

  2. What types of measures were used in the study (direct observation and behavioral measures, self-report and inventories, ratings of others' behavior,

(Continued)

(Continued)

physiological approaches, or interviews)? Identify any problems or limitations with the types of measures used.

3. To what extent are the instruments standardized, and what types of standardized scoring were used (criterion referenced or norm referenced)?

4. Does the instrument appear to be appropriate for the sample (e.g., are there any cross-cultural, gender, or diversity biases)? Explain.

5. Is the reliability of the instruments reported? What type of reliability is reported?

6. Is the reliability reported for the instruments adequate? Explain.

7. What types of validity are reported for the instruments used?

8. Is the validity of the instruments adequate? Explain.

Select a qualitative study and answer the following questions:

1. Is there a clear and adequate description of the instrument?

2. What types of measures were used in the study (direct observation and behavioral measures or interviews)? Identify any problems or limitations with the types of measures used.

3. Does the instrument appear to be appropriate for the sample (e.g., are there any cross-cultural, gender, or diversity biases)?

16

Evaluating the Results Section

Reading and understanding the results section is probably the most daunting part of evaluating a research article for those who are somewhat intimidated by research and the use of math and statistics. Students have frequently commented to me that they skip over the results section with all its statistical procedures and numbers. They are intimidated by statistics and prefer to read the discussion section, which summarizes the results with words rather than numbers. I encourage and challenge you to become more comfortable reading the results sections of journal articles.

Those who are conducting and writing these sophisticated research articles typically have extensive backgrounds in statistics or employ a consultant who has considerable expertise with statistics. There are entire, separate graduate-level courses in statistical procedures such as analyses of variance, regression, structural equation modeling, nonparametric statistics, and so on. Therefore, it would not be reasonable to assume that one chapter on reading statistics and results would conclude with the reader's having gained considerable expertise in statistical methods. However, the intent of this chapter, in keeping with the purpose of this book, is to prepare you to feel more comfortable in identifying and understanding basic statistical concepts and procedures in your efforts to evaluate the efficacy of a particular research report.

This chapter is separated into two major parts. The first part addresses the understanding and evaluation of quantitative research, and the second focuses on interpreting and evaluating qualitative research results. I also propose guidelines for evaluating the results section, followed by an evaluation of examples from the research literature using these guidelines.

PART I. QUANTITATIVE RESEARCH RESULTS

Results obtained through quantitative research methods are presented mathematically. Recall from Chapter 3 that there are two major categories of statistical methods employed in quantitative research: descriptive and inferential statistics. Descriptive statistics are used to report results based on the sample, whereas inferential statistics are designed to make it possible to infer, from the results of a study (and the sample of the population), back to the larger population, and generalize back to the target population.

DESCRIPTIVE STATISTICS

Descriptive statistics have been described as efforts by researchers to systematically summarize the data collected (Urdan, 2005). The idea is for the researchers to present data descriptively in a way that is easy to understand and that conceptualizes general characteristics of the sample's responses. Descriptive statistics address the sample only and are in no way connected to understanding or generalizing back to the population. Generally, descriptive statistics are presented first in the results section of an article, followed by inferential statistics. The important issue for the researcher is which methods to use in presenting descriptive statistics. Most commonly presented methods are mean and standard deviation. It is rare to use mode and median. Tables and graphs can be used to visually illustrate descriptive statistics.

INFERENTIAL STATISTICS

The ultimate purpose of conducting a quantitative study is to test hypotheses, and this involves using statistical methods that allow the researchers to infer, from data gleaned from the sample, information that can be applied to the larger population. Inferential statistics are methods that allow the researchers to do this. Numerous inferential statistical methods are used; see Chapter 3 for a review.

An important question to address when reading the results section is whether any violations of assumptions were made. This gives the reader information about whether the researcher used appropriate statistics, that is, either parametric or non-parametric. Recall from a review of Chapter 3 the potential violation of assumptions. The four possible violations of assumptions are normality, homogeneity of variance, independence, and linearity. Normality refers to data that are normally distributed (distributed based on a normal curse). Homogeneity of variance concerns similarity of variance, that is, how scores are similar or different between the comparison groups. The third assumption involves independence of scores; for example, the same individual is not compared from a pretest and posttest. The last assumption refers to relationships between variables. Specifically, the assumption of linearity involves a relationship that is linear between variables as compared to nonlinear (e.g., curvilinear). Recall that no specific number of violations of assumptions has been associated with the decision to use particular statistical methods.

Inferential statistics, as stated earlier, are used to make decisions or reach conclusions about whether results obtained from a sample can be applied to the target population. All the methods discussed as inferential statistics are associated with quantitative research methods. The majority of the methods used in inferential statistical procedures involve making comparisons between groups. The intent of using inferential statistics is to answer hypotheses or research questions as they relate to the population of interest, and the decision for the reader of quantitative research is whether the researcher addressed what was intended with the statistics used.

SUMMARY

Understanding and evaluating a research article that employs and reports quantitative research may appear to be a daunting task, but there are several important points to focus on that may reduce the confusion and difficulty in reading and using such research information. Much of the research you will read in counseling and education will be based on data collected that fit a normal curve. Data that are based on the normal curve allow researchers to analyze outcomes with sensitive and more powerful statistical methods as opposed to data that violate the assumption of normality, therefore requiring that nonparametric statistical methods be employed.

Descriptive statistical methods are used by researchers to summarize the data collected based on the sample in a particular research study. This includes calculating measures of central tendency (mean, median, and mode) and measures of variability (standard deviation, etc.). Inferential statistical methods are used by researchers to generalize results back to the population of interest. These types of statistical methods are used to support or refute stated hypotheses. There are two major types of inferential statistical methods: parametric and nonparametric. Parametric statistical methods require adherence to certain assumptions about the data collected (e.g., normality, independence). When these assumptions are violated, the researcher must employ nonparametric statistical methods. The choice of statistical methods is also influenced by the purpose of the study, specifically, whether it is a comparison or descriptive study.

GUIDELINES FOR EVALUATING THE RESULTS SECTION: QUANTITATIVE RESEARCH

As stated earlier, the presentation of information in the results section of an article is probably where the differences between quantitative and qualitative methods are most noticeable. Consequently, I have suggested several guidelines for evaluating quantitative research in Part I. Listed below are the guidelines and questions for evaluating the results section in an article based on quantitative research.

1. What descriptive statistics were used? Do they adequately describe the sample?

2. Were any violations of assumptions present, considering the types of data collected?

3. What types of inferential statistics were used? Are the inferential statistics used adequate to answer the research hypotheses or questions?

EVALUATING EXAMPLES FROM THE RESEARCH LITERATURE: QUANTITATIVE RESEARCH

Quantitative Study Example

A review of the study by Henderson and colleagues (2007) shows that they completed an ANCOVA. The researchers used ANCOVA to control for differences between the two groups at three different observation times. They described their statistical calculations as follows:

A series of one-way analyses of covariance (ANCOVA) comparing the experimental and control groups were conducted for all outcome measures at Time 2 and at 1-month follow-up. Because the two randomly assigned groups had different initial levels of trauma symptom severity, depression, anxiety, and health symptom severity at Time 1, the use of ANCOVA as opposed to analysis of variance was warranted. Using ANCOVA permitted the researcher's to detect mean differences between treatment groups at Times 2 and 3, while controlling for differences at baseline. Although baseline differences between groups were not statistically significant, they were large enough to warrant the use of ANCOVA. As indicated by Table 1, all variables were correlated with themselves over time, and this also spoke to the importance of using ANCOVA to control for baseline levels of the outcome variables.

The covariate for each ANCOVA was the value for the respective outcome variable at the beginning of the study, before the mandala-drawing manipulation (or control drawing manipulation). Controlling for baseline levels of traumatic symptoms as measured by the PDS, participants in the mandala condition were experiencing fewer symptoms of trauma than those in the control condition at 1-month follow-up ($F(1, 35) = 6.615$, $p < .015$).

Whereas there were differences between the two groups with respect to PTSD symptoms, there were no significant differences on the other measures (i.e., the BDI-II, State-Trait Anxiety Inventory, SMS, or PILL), suggesting that the mandala-drawing exercise was specific to symptoms of traumatic stress (see Table 3). (p. 151)

The first question to address is what descriptive statistics were used and if they adequately describe the sample. The researchers write in the last paragraph: "Whereas there were differences . . ." and note that means and standard deviations were described in Table 3. Means and standard deviations for the control and experimental groups were provided on the various assessment instruments, such as the Beck Depression Inventory (BDI), STAI, Spiritual Meaning Scale (SMS), and the Pennebaker Inventory of Limbic Languidness (PILL).

The second question concerns whether there were any violations of assumptions present, considering the types of data collected. All the measures used were based upon interval types of data, so the issue of normality was not violated (although no chi-square goodness-of-fit was calculated). Linearity was not violated as no regression analysis was calculated. Independence of scores also was not violated because comparisons were made between groups at different times and not within groups. Finally, homogeneity of variance was not violated because the standard deviations between control and experimental groups were not noticeably different (more than three times different). However, no calculations of the F Maximum test for homogeneity of variance were included.

The last question to address is the evaluation of the types of inferential statistics that were used and whether the inferential statistics used were adequate to answer the research hypotheses. The researchers used an ANCOVA to compare differences. The Henderson and colleagues (2007) hypothesis was stated as follows: "It was hypothesized that individuals assigned to a mandala-drawing condition would show a significant increase in psychological and physical health relative to control group participants both immediately after the intervention and at a 1-month follow-up" (p. 151). The use of the ANCOVA allowed for comparisons at different times and controlled for an extraneous variable (differences in symptoms at onset) between the experimental and control group.

The researchers provided information through descriptive statistics about the sample through reporting means and standard deviations. There were no clearly noted violations of assumptions, and the researchers, Henderson and colleagues (2007) used inferential statistics, that is, ANCOVA, to adequately answer the hypothesis.

Single-Subject Study Example

Ross, Register-Mihalik, Mihalik, et al. (2011) conducted a study focused on comparing single-task and dual-task performance on cognition and balance. The researchers used a pretest-posttest research design, and 30 participants were involved. They described their results as:

Differences in balance performance on the SOT (Sensory Organization Test) during a dual task compared with the single task were analyzed using a single 2-way Task (single or dual) × Test Session (1 or 2) within-subject ANOVA. In addition, differences in balance performance on the BESS (Balance Error Scoring System) between the 2 task conditions were also analyzed using a single, 2-way Task (single or dual) × Test Session (1 or 2) within-subject ANOVA. Furthermore, differences in PRT (Procedural Reaction Task) and PAT (Procedural Auditory Task) performance between the dual-task and single-task conditions were analyzed using 3 separate (PRT eyes open SOT, PAT eyes closed SOT, and PAT BESS) 2-way Task (single or dual) and test session (1 or 2) within-subject ANOVAs. No direct comparisons were made between the SOT and BESS or the PRT scores. Task (single or dual) and test session (1 or 2) were used as the 2 within-subject independent variables. Paired-samples t tests were employed on the average accuracy scores on each test battery to determine whether there were statistical differences between PAT performances only on the eyes-closed conditions on the SOT and the BESS. (p. 303)

Ross and colleagues (2011) described their statistical analyses:

We examined the difference in balance performance on the SOT and on the BESS during a dual task compared to a single task (Table 1). Results from the SOT revealed no significant test-by-task interaction ($F_{1,29} = 0.340$, $p = .564$). There was a significant main effect for test session ($F_{1,29} = 35.695$, $p < .0005$) and task ($F_{1,29} = 9.604$, $p = .004$), with the first and in the dual task compared with the single task. Results from the BESS revealed no significant test-by-task interaction ($F_{1,29} = .004$, $p = .953$) or task ($F_{1,29} = 1.961$, $p = .172$). (pp. 303–304)

Table 1 showed the means and standard deviations of the single and dual tasks on the outcome variables (SOT, BESS, PRT score, etc.). Additional descriptions of analyses stated,

Means and standard deviations for task and test time concerning PRT and PAT are presented in Table 2. Results for the PRT test battery during the eyes-open conditions of the SOT revealed no significant test-by-task interaction ($F_{1,29} = .082$, $p = .777$) but there was a significant main effect for test session ($F_{1,29} = 57.252$, $p = < .001$) and task ($F_{1,29} = 7.673$, $p = .01$), with significant improvement in the second test session compared with the first and the dual task compared with the single task. . . . PAT tests on the BESS also revealed no significant test-by-task interaction ($F_{1,29} = .342$, $p = .563$), main effect for test session ($F_{1,29} = 3.678$, $p = .65$), or main effect for task ($F_{1,29} + 2.225$, $p = .147$). There was no significant difference found between these 2 measures of balance ($t_{29} = 1.239$, $p = .185$). (p. 304)

The first question to answer in evaluating the results is this: What descriptive statistics were used? Do they adequately describe the sample? Means and standard deviations were listed for each type of task. These results described the sample in regards to the dependent variables (SOT, BESS, PRT scores, etc.).

The next question is whether there are any violations of assumptions present, considering the types of data collected. Interval data were collected on dependent variables such as balance performance, for example, ratings on balance tasks. Use of interval data suggests normality of the data, although it is not guaranteed. The researchers did not conduct any tests of normality such as a chi-square goodness-of-fit test and Kolmogorov-Smirnov goodness-of-fit test. Such tests determine how well the data from a variable fit a normal distribution. In this study, no such test was reported, so we do not know if this violation of assumption occurred. The next question is whether the respondents are independent of each other. There was a violation of independence; participants were measured over time on the dependent variables; the comparison was not between subjects but within subjects. The researchers then used statistical procedures that addressed violation of independence, for example, paired *t*-tests and within-subject ANOVA (repeated-measures ANOVA).

The third question concerns the following: What types of inferential statistics were used? Are the inferential statistics used adequate to answer the research hypotheses or questions? The researchers used several inferential statistical methods. These included paired *t*-tests and repeated-measures ANOVAs. They conducted five ANOVAs with repeated measures. The researchers compared: changes in SOT, changes from a single to a dual task, changes on a PRT, changes on BESS, and changes on a PAT. The researchers conducted their research to determine the effects of single and dual tasks on cognition and balance. The comparisons they made, ANOVAs, answered these questions. A paired *t*-test also was used to answer one question, that is, differences between measures of balance. All of their inferential statistics were used to make comparisons, which fits with the intent of the study. Also, because these analyses involved dependent samples, or comparisons within subjects, they used appropriate inferential statistics, for example, repeated-measures ANOVAs and paired *t*-tests.

PART II. EVALUATING THE RESULTS SECTION: QUALITATIVE RESEARCH

The results sections in qualitative research studies will look quite different from those in quantitative studies. The results section is probably where you will find the biggest differences from quantitative research in the presentation and the kinds of results. Whereas in quantitative research, numbers and statistical procedures are cited, qualitative research is characterized by descriptions. It has been noted that qualitative research methods are based on language to communicate research results (Gall et al., 2002). Consequently, analysis and reporting of data in qualitative research are communicated through linguistic methods, or language.

GUIDELINES FOR EVALUATING THE RESULTS SECTION: QUALITATIVE RESEARCH

Listed below are the guidelines and questions for evaluating the results section in an article based on qualitative research.

1. What units of analysis are used, and are they clearly identified? (See Chapter 5 for a review.)

2. What tactics or strategies for coding and interpreting the data are made (e.g., identifying themes, clustering, or creating metaphors)? Are they clearly described?

3. Are concrete examples of the data clearly linked to identified themes, concept, or theories? Are these examples adequate?

EVALUATING EXAMPLES FROM RESULTS SECTIONS: QUALITATIVE RESEARCH

In her study of first-year teachers and induction processes, Fry (2007) reported using descriptive and interpretative categories in her data analysis. The first question to address is whether units of analysis are reported and if they are clearly defined. Fry does not clearly identify the units of analysis. One might hypothesize the unit of analysis is relationships. A second question to use in evaluating the results section of a qualitative study is what tactics or coding methods are used. It appears Fry uses themes as the major method of coding data. One major theme or category identified was time and collegiality, and the following example was provided:

"Everyone keeps telling me the 1st year is the hardest, and it better be because otherwise I don't want to do this." (Stella, September 14, 2004). Stella, Shari, Becca, and Laura faced challenges common to beginning teachers. All four began the school year working long hours; 10–12 hour days during the week plus 10 or more hours on the weekend were common. Stella reported being so exhausted that she went to bed as early as 7:45 p.m. during the first month of school. Each participant experimented with different strategies to make their schedules more manageable. By late October, they had found more balanced approaches. (p. 224)

Negotiating a balance between work and collegial relationships proved problematic for Stella as well. Stella taught in a school where two veteran teachers were assigned as mentors for all of the new teachers in her building. . . . Stella and her assigned mentor did not form a strong connection, but Stella did find an authentic mentor in one of her building administrators. They connected on a personal as well as professional level, and their relationship provided Stella with comfort and support. (p. 225)

A second theme that was reported was "the transition from student teacher to teacher." Fry (2007) provided the following examples from the results section:

For Stella, the biggest challenge stemmed from teaching 5th grade after student teaching in a 2nd grade class. The students had higher skill levels and abilities, and initially, Stella struggled with planning and teaching. In our first interview she said: "I was ready to quit the Tuesday after we started. . . . Everything was overwhelming. I know I student taught the first day (of school) but it's different when it's all on you. I need to get my feet under me, but they're just not there yet." (September 14, 2004). (p. 226)

A third theme identified by Fry (2007) was mentoring and administrative support. She provided several examples of this theme:

If I had it all to do over again, I would ask for a mentor who has been around for longer and has things figured out." (Laura, October 26, 2004). Stella, Shari, and Laura were each assigned a mentor teacher. Shari and Laura's mentors were teachers at the same grade level, while Stella was assigned one of two teachers who served as mentors for every new teacher in her school. Becca's school district had no mentoring program. As Laura's quote at the beginning of this section suggests, her mentor was new to the grade level at which they both taught. The mentor also was in her 4th year of teaching, which is just one year beyond the induction years. (pp. 227–228)

Fry (2007) presented her data conclusions with several different themes and systematically used concrete examples from her collection methods. She clearly explained the connection to the themes and provided good examples.

Binder, Moltu, Sagen, Hummelsund, and Holgersen (2013) provided another example of using qualitative research, and this study can be used to analyze presentation of results. The purpose of the study is stated as: "We explored how adolescents experience assessment and diagnostic evaluation in psychotherapy, and the types and qualities of interaction associated with these activities" (p. 1). The researchers used a qualitative research method to address their research interests. They described the data analysis as follows:

> By comparing the individual accounts, we wanted to identify both patterns of commonalities and differences in how adolescent clients experienced the assessment processes in psychotherapy and formulate these themes. . . . In analyzing the adolescents' experiences with going through the process of assessment and diagnosis in psychotherapy, we found a tension between two themes that represent a polarity to each other (Figure 1). The first is the participants' experiences of standardized assessment as potentially *obscuring contact with the unique personhood of the client,* and the second *is providing hope through trust in the therapist's competence in understanding* the problems they face. These two themes were represented across most of the accounts and often they were present within the same account; that is, one participant could both experience formal assessment as alienating and providing safety and hope with the same therapeutic process. We found a third theme related to how the tension between the polarities of the first two was resolved: the *degree of perceived relational authenticity* allowing for collaboration during professional procedures. A further important theme in the analyses was the participants' experiences of *how pressure from systems outside the dyad* influenced the interaction around assessment issues. (p. 4)

The researchers (Binder et al., 2013) further described examples of themes identified:

> A theme in our analysis was the fear the participants experienced that assessment and diagnosis could stand in the way of the therapist seeing that which is unique and healthy about them. . . . The following quote serves to illustrate this experience of not being met in a way that builds trust: If you talk about a buddy in a café, then you just talk. But the therapist just sits there and writes! I do not know what, a letter to his girlfriend? (laughs) And you just don't feel met. Not at all. It is the same, with family, friends and in therapy—when persons don't have eye-contact with you, then you don't feel met. And what I don't like with therapy is that they write down everything. To remember it! But you do not have to remember every word, but to remember the essential things. It can't be that difficult to remember. (p. 5)

Another example that illustrated a second theme was providing hope by developing trust in the therapist's competence. The example stated was as follows:

> Perhaps it made me see that this is something that has happened before, with others. In reality this was something that I already knew. But the fact that it has happened so many times that it fits into some kind of structure . . . is quite comforting, because, it there is a system, then perhaps there is a solution too. (p. 7)

The researchers explained the assessment as how the therapist provided insight for the client into how the assessment was to be used and how it was important to complete. Further, the researchers explained how such a statement provided hope for a solution, and the client did not feel he or she was so unique that he or she could not be helped.

A third theme concerned the perceived authenticity of the counseling relationship. Binder and colleagues (2013) again provided an example of this theme. They stated,

We did this MINI examination. And actually I think that none of us is a huge fan of this, really. Those questionnaire things. But it is something that has to be done. I guess that it is good in many ways. But I feel very skeptical toward this, to those questionnaire things. But he managed to fool me into it, and make me do it anyway. (p. 8)

The researchers pointed out that this quote illustrates how the therapist was able to use his relationship with the client to engage him in the completion of questionnaires even though he does not like them.

The first questions to use in evaluating the results of a qualitative study are thee: What units of analysis are used, and are they clearly identified? The researchers did not specifically state what the unit of analysis is. However, one can hypothesize the unit of analysis is relationship, for example, the relationship between the therapist and the adolescent client. The second question to address in evaluating the results is this: What tactics or strategies for coding and interpreting the data are made? Are they clearly described? Binder and colleagues (2013) appear to use themes in the analysis of their data. Four themes are identified, and there is no attempt to layer the themes. A third set of question to address in evaluating the results section of a qualitative study is this: Are concrete examples of the data clearly linked to identified themes, concept, or theories? Are these examples adequate? The researchers provide clear and concrete examples of the themes identified. They also explain the examples as they relate to the themes.

SUMMARY

Analysis and reporting of results in qualitative research are based on linguistic structures and communicating results through language. There are three important steps and components that should be included in the results section of a qualitative research study: data reduction, data display, and drawing conclusions. This last step is important in reading qualitative research and gives the reader information about the conclusions reached. Such conclusions are reported in terms of tactics used for analyzing data. There are a number of different tactics for analyzing qualitative research data, and these include counting, noting patterns or themes, determining plausibility, clustering, creating metaphors, differentiation or splitting, noting relationships between variables, and making conceptual theoretical coherence. Finally, the researchers should illustrate the themes, concepts, or phenomena with concrete examples from the data.

Exercises

Directions: Select a study from the research literature that uses a quantitative design, and evaluate the results section based on the questions below.

1. What descriptive statistics were used? Do the researchers adequately describe the sample?

2. Were any violations of assumptions present considering the types of data collected?

3. What types of inferential statistics were used? Are the inferential statistics used adequate to answer the research hypotheses or questions?

Select a study from the research literature that uses a qualitative design, and evaluate the results section based on the questions below.

1. Are units of analysis reported, and if so, what are the units reported?

2. What tactics or strategies for coding and interpreting the data are made? Are they clearly described?

3. Are concrete examples of the data clearly linked to identified themes, concepts, or theories? Are these examples adequate?

17

EVALUATING THE DISCUSSION SECTION

The discussion section is designed to summarize the intent of the research project and present implications for actual practice. We are particularly interested in this section because, as practitioners, we want to know what works and how it may be applied. The discussion section should address the practical significance of the results (Heiman, 1995; LaFountain & Bartos, 2002). In a sense, the researchers must go beyond the numbers and statistics reported in the results section and interpret the findings so that they may be of practical application.

In this chapter, I address the important components that should be included in a discussion section: restatement of the purpose; presentation of the implications of the findings and how they relate to theories, others' findings, and actual practice; alternative explanations; citation of the potential limitations of the study and the results; and discussion of possible directions for future research (LaFountain & Bartos, 2002; Vierra & Pollock, 1988). Next, I present guidelines or questions to be used in evaluating the efficacy of a discussion section. Finally, there are examples provided using the guidelines and questions presented here.

Ideally, the researchers will restate the purpose of the study at the beginning of the discussion section. This is done to remind the reader of the purpose and link it with the results. This approach theoretically ensures that the purpose and the hypotheses or research questions are answered. Second, the researchers should summarize the results, without using any numbers or statistics, and relate them to previous research, theories, and practice. In summarizing the results, the researchers need to be succinct and note the significant points of the findings. It is important that the researchers address how the research questions or hypotheses relate to the findings. Additionally, the researchers need to relate the results to theory or practice in a clear and understandable manner. Finally, the researchers will want to relate the results to previous research that either supports or refutes prior findings.

The researchers may need to propose alternative explanations when the results do not meet expected outcomes or are not consistent with the theories addressed. It is important that the researchers systematically address any results in which there are some discrepancies from what was expected based on other research or based on the hypotheses presented. In addition, this analysis should include speculation regarding why such alternative findings were obtained.

A fourth issue to be addressed in the discussion section is a review of the potential limitations of the study. The researchers specifically review the research methods employed and the method of selecting participants, which may have resulted in limitations or threats to internal and external validity. In evaluating this section of the discussion, it is necessary to review the potential threats to validity based on the research design used and the methods of selecting participants. Almost every study has limitations, and the researchers' acknowledgment of possible limitations demonstrates an understanding of the cautions that should be taken in interpreting the results.

Generally, the last point for the researchers to address in the discussion section is to suggest further issues to study. This section is of interest to other researchers who may want to investigate the topic of research. However, as consumers of research, we are also interested because a discussion of future areas of investigation allows insight into what else needs to be accomplished and provides further information about the limits of what is known about the topic of interest.

GUIDELINES FOR EVALUATING THE DISCUSSION SECTION

1. Do the researchers clearly restate the purpose and research hypotheses or questions?

2. Do the researchers clearly discuss the implications of the findings and how they relate to theories, others' findings, and actual practice?

3. If relevant, do the researchers provide alternative explanations of the results obtained when there is discrepancy with other sources or expected outcomes?

4. Do the researchers identify potential limitations of the study and the results?

5. Do the researchers identify possible directions for future research?

EVALUATING EXAMPLES FROM THE RESEARCH LITERATURE

Quantitative Research

The comparison by Henderson and colleagues (2007) of an intervention for posttraumatic stress provides an example for analysis. They stated, in the discussion section, the following:

In our study, we examined the benefits that individuals suffering from clinical levels of traumatic distress could gain from processing their trauma through the creation of mandalas. Although it was hypothesized that there would be significant improvements in numerous health outcomes, the only outcome for which there was significant relative improvement was PTSD symptom severity. Such results are only partially consistent with studies relying on verbal processing tasks (Sloan & Marx, 2004a, 2004b), because gains in the current study were specific to trauma symptom severity, whereas gains in verbal processing tasks appear to be more broadly ranging. Results of the current investigation are nevertheless noteworthy, because the condition of interest in the current study was PTSD and participants were selected who had elevated levels of traumatic distress, although not necessarily elevated levels of depression, anxiety, or physical symptoms, or decreased levels of meaning in life. Therefore, the mandala-drawing exercise seemed effective in ameliorating symptoms of the clinical condition for which participants were specifically chosen. The current mandala-drawing exercise and similar ones should be investigated as ways of supplementing or substituting for verbal processing treatments for trauma victims, particularly those who, because of personality features or cognitive factors, are unable or unwilling to process traumatic experiences through verbal means. (pp. 152–153)

Two obvious weaknesses of this study are the small sample size and the differences in the numbers of males and females. The Henderson and colleagues (2007) project was a small initial study to test the feasibility of this line of research, and similar studies with greater sample size and more balanced gender distribution need to be conducted. Furthermore, although the participants were undergraduate college students with PTSD, it would be beneficial to have a sample from a larger population of individuals suffering from more severe levels of trauma. Another shortcoming was the lack of direct comparison of a mandala-drawing task with other control groups, such as a pre-drawn mandala coloring condition, another art therapy condition, and a writing condition. Another condition might be desirable in which individuals would be asked to reflect on their trauma but not allowed to symbolically depict or write about that trauma. Ideally, all or some of these conditions could be examined in future studies, and the different health benefits for different manipulations might be uncovered.

Extending this line of research with children and adolescents who are victims of abuse would be an area of great interest. Some children, depending on age and educational opportunities, lack the ability to adequately and effectively express traumatic experiences through written or verbal language. Furthermore, children are often shamed into secrecy by their abusers and are fearful to disclose incidences of abuse. Mandalas drawn by such children could serve the need of expression of traumatic experiences in a simpler and less threatening way than writing or talking about the events. The current findings suggest that research in such areas would prove fruitful.

Scientific research into Jungian theory is uncommon. Jung's theories are often criticized as being too vague or complex and difficult to understand and, therefore, better left to the realms of art or religion (Slegelis, 1987). It seems as though Jungian theory has been unable to gain respect among more scientific schools of thought because of this lack of scientific research.

Similarly, the field of art psychotherapy has lacked the credibility and respect of more scientific fields due to a lack of empirical research. Future research ought to be conducted that might bridge the worlds of the artistic and the scientific in an effort to increase awareness of healing techniques derived from Jungian theory and art psychotherapy.

The researchers do restate the purpose by starting with the discussion with "we examined the benefits" and a summary of the hypothesis: "It was hypothesized that there would be significant improvements" (Henderson et al., p. 153). The second question concerns whether the researchers connect the findings to other research findings and theory. The researchers do make connections to previous research: "Such results are only partially consistent with studies relying on verbal processing tasks (Sloan & Marx, 2004a, 2004b)" (p. 151). The researchers do attempt to connect the results to alternative explanations or concepts by stating: "The current mandala exercise and similar ones should be investigated as ways of supplementing or substituting for verbal processing treatments for trauma victims, particularly those who, because of personality features or cognitive factors, are unable or unwilling to process traumatic experiences through verbal means" (p. 154). They attempted to suggest that their findings may be best used with those who do not process experiences through verbal means but still recognize the relevance of this approach.

The researchers have a separate section addressing the strengths and weaknesses of the study. They noted that one weakness was the small sample size and the fact that there were so many more females than males. They also acknowledged that they used college students, who may not be representative of the larger population. Finally, they suggested that the use of a more similar control group experience would have provided clearer results.

The researchers also have a separate section for directions for additional research. They suggested expanding the population studied to include children and adolescents with PTSD. They note that the use of art with children may be particularly useful because children like this type of medium of expression.

Qualitative Research

Fry (2007) cited in her discussion section the findings of her study on first-year teacher induction. She stated,

---

This study examined the induction experiences of four 1st-year teachers and how they responded to available induction support. The findings indicated that these 4 beginning teachers had different support needs. The participants also received variable forms of support. The one common experience seemed to be the inadequate nature of the induction support each participant received.

Smith and Ingersoll's (2004) research on induction appears to be the most comprehensive in the literature, yet the quantitative data set they used did not ask questions about whether or not the forms of induction were meaningful. In the current investigation, the participant who received the best induction combination (best meaning the combination that has the greatest likelihood of reducing attrition) was dissatisfied with her induction experience. Therefore, Table 1 highlights the support each teacher received using the forms of induction Smith and Ingersoll analyzed in order to provide a framework for discussing the present investigator's results. As discussed in the literature review, basic induction (mentoring and supportive communication from an administrator) has no statistically significant impact on reducing the predicted level of attrition (with no induction support, predicted attrition was 40%; with basic induction predicted attrition was 39%). When basic induction was combined with Level II, the predicted level of attrition was reduced to 27%, and when combined with II and III, the rate was reduced to 18%.

Comparing this summary of the participants' induction experiences to Smith and Ingersoll's (2004) levels of induction support presents an interesting synthesis. Based on the number of support components, it appears that Stella received the "best" induction. However, she only found two of the components worthwhile: administrator communication and common planning time. Laura received three induction components, but mentoring was problematic because her assigned mentor was new to teaching at her grade level and only a 4th year teacher. Although she found the communication from her administrator supportive, the frequency, form and duration were inadequate. Shari's mentoring and common planning time were somewhat helpful, but she found the communication from administrator too supportive.

Instead, she would have preferred critical feedback in addition to praise. Becca shared the latter concern, and her common planning time was rarely spent with the other teachers at her grade level because of their unsuccessful team dynamics. In conclusion, for the four 1st-year teachers in this study, the amount of induction support received did not correspond to satisfaction in terms of their perceptions of the effectiveness of their induction support. Nevertheless, all four continued teaching after their 1st year.

There has been a growing trend in professional development to avoid "one size fits all" approaches where veteran teachers and beginners all receive the same forms of training. This trend recognizes teachers' developmental spectrum and endeavors to provide salient professional development (Marzano, 2003).

This same approach may be appropriate for induction. The participants in this study indicated a range of competencies and self-perceived deficit areas. For example, Stella, who was comfortable with her approach to classroom management, would have benefited more from induction meetings about implementing guided reading groups instead of classroom management sessions. Meanwhile, Laura would have liked further opportunities to learn about classroom management as well as guided reading. Just as teachers are encouraged to differentiate their diverse students in K–12 classrooms, school districts should differentiate professional learning opportunities for beginning teachers (p. 232).

In summary, I present the following list of suggestions for how Stella, Shari, Becca, and Laura's induction experiences could have been strengthened. In regard to mentoring: assign new teachers caring, eager, and capable mentors who have a common planning period and teach at the same (or close) grade level/content area. The mentors should be veteran teachers with at least one year experience at the grade level they are currently teaching (p. 233).

Practical Support

Encourage a school climate where beginning and veteran teachers comfortably ask colleagues and administrators for help so beginning teachers are confident asking for help.

Researcher Reflections

When I designed this study, I intentionally adapted a research design that allowed me to be subjective, care about my participants, become an insider, and make meaning of the study's data with participants (Toma, 2000). What I did not anticipate was that I would essentially become part of the phenomenon I was investigating: the participants' induction experience.

Limitations of the Study and Suggestions for Future Study

Because of limitations to this study, the results may not be generalizable to a larger population. Stella, Shari, Becca, and Laura were all graduates of the same elementary education teacher preparation.

Program

The participants were also all female, between 22–24 years of age, and taught in a rural or suburban school districts. The limitations created by the small, heterogeneous sample in this investigation suggest a need for future investigations about 1st-year teacher responses to induction experiences using more diverse participants. Qualitative and quantitative methods can be used to investigate how beginners value their induction experiences.

Such research has the potential to help school districts refine their induction efforts to better meet beginning teachers' needs.

I hesitate to declare my close relationship with the participants a limitation of the study because it was an intentional part of the research design. (p. 228)

The five questions to address in evaluating the discussion start with whether the researcher clearly restated the purpose and research hypotheses or questions. Fry (2007) started the discussion with the statement: "This study examined the induction . . ." (p. 226). A second question concerns whether the researcher discussed the implications of the findings. The researcher provided a summary of the findings and suggested specific approaches to improve teacher induction procedures. The researcher did not provide any alternative explanation of the results and noted the similarity to other study outcomes only. The researcher suggested that the results may not be generalizable because of the small sample size and specific characteristics of the sample. However, she went on to state that her close relationship with the participants was a limitation of the study. Despite noting the limitation, the researcher retracted this caution by stating it was her intention to develop a close relationship with the participants. Finally, the researcher did identify potential areas for future research that include a combination of qualitative and quantitative methods to further understand teacher induction procedures.

Single-Subject Research

Storlie (2012) studied presleep self-suggestion and dream recall using a single-subject research design. The hypothesis was that presleep self-suggestion impacted dream content. The dependent variable was dream recall, and the independent variable was self-suggestion prior to sleep. The researcher described his discussion as follows:

In this experiment, I used a single-subject A/B design to test the hypothesis that dream recall would be enhanced using pre-sleep self-suggestion. Results of phase A were given a numerical value of 26. Results of phase B were given a numerical value of 25. As the numerical ratings across phases were nearly identical, the hypothesis that pre-sleep suggestion would enhance dream recall was tentatively rejected. Although the amount of dream material consciously recalled was slightly greater during the intervention phase, the total number of dreams consciously recalled during intervention was less than baseline. There are numerous variables that might impact conscious dream recall. The research process I used can be easily duplicated to explore other possible variables. For example, if the mental states conducive to recalling dreams are similar to being asleep, as suggested by Stross and Shevrin (1967), then it would seem reasonable that lying still after first awakening could contribute to dream recall—but for how long? This is one variable that could be tested in future research. Other testable variables include participant gender and age, presence or absence of a sleeping partner; level of reported sleep comfort, e.g. fit of blankets, pillow, mattress, temperature of the sleeping area, presence of ventilation such as an open window or not; presence of sleep apnea, pain or other medical conditions; presence of inside or outside noises; current weather conditions; time of going to sleep/time of awakening and number of hours slept; number of nocturnal awakenings; use of medications and supplements; elapsed time since last meal was eaten prior to sleep, presleep activity, e.g. visiting, watching television, sexual activity, whether participant awakens via alarm clock or naturally; means of recording remembered dreams; interest in dreams throughout the day; mental rehearsal of dream recall during waking hours and wording of pre-sleep suggestion. Sigmund Freud believed dreams were clinically significant (Kaplan & Sadock, 1998). I agree. The chief limitation of this design is a lack of external validity. Other shortcomings are its vulnerability to threats of internal validity and the use of participant self-report for data collection. Self-report is highly vulnerable to bias. Yet, in order for clinicians to utilize a client's dream material in therapeutic sessions, the client must first be able to recall his or her dreams. More research needs to be done before this question can be answered with any degree of confidence. (p. 149)

The first question is this: Do the researchers clearly restate the purpose and research hypotheses or questions? The researcher does not restate the purpose of the study in the discussion section. The researcher could have restated the purpose of the study to determine if presleep suggestion would impact the number of dreams remembered. The second question concerns whether the researchers clearly discuss the implications of the findings and how they relate to theories, others' findings, and actual practice. The researcher does provide a brief explanation of how the results may be applied in practice. He stated that clients need to recall dreams if they are to be used in therapy and that methods to increase such recall are important.

The researcher does provide some alternative explanations of the results obtained, including those different from the hypothesis. He suggested there could be a number of other variables that influence dream recall such as lying still after awakening. The next question to address in evaluating the discussion section is this: Do the researchers identify potential limitations of the study and the results? The researcher does identify limitations, that is, the use of self-report, which is noted as potentially resulting in bias. The last question is whether the researchers identify possible directions for future research. The researcher outlines a number of other variables that could be studied in the future and that potentially could impact dream recall. These included variables such as gender and age, presence or absence of a sleeping partner, level of reported sleep comfort, and so on.

SUMMARY

The discussion section is where the researchers attempt to summarize and make sense of the results. First, the researchers should restate the purpose of the study and summarize the findings. Next, the researchers should link the findings to theories or previous research and discuss any alternative explanations for the results that are not consistent with their own conclusions. It is important for any limitations to be noted and for future research areas to be identified.

Exercise

Directions: Locate an article in the professional literature addressing a topic you are interested in exploring. Evaluate the discussion section based on the questions addressed in this chapter. Try to explain and justify your answers based on specific examples from the article you have chosen.

(Continued)

1. Do the researchers clearly restate the purpose and research hypotheses or questions?

2. Do the researchers clearly discuss the implications of the findings and how they relate to theories, others' findings, and actual practice?

3. If relevant, do the researchers provide alternative explanations of the results obtained when there is discrepancy with other sources or expected outcomes?

4. Do the researchers identify potential limitations of the study and the results?

5. Do the researchers identify possible directions for future research?

SECTION III

APPLICATION OF RESEARCH
AND EVALUATION

18

DEVELOPING A RESEARCH PROPOSAL AND CONDUCTING RESEARCH IN PRACTICE

There has been considerable debate in the counseling and educational literature over the extent to which research should be emphasized in the training and actual practice of counselors and educators (Border, Bloss, Cashwell, & Rainey, 1994; Heppner et al., 1992; Love et al., 2007; Merlo, Collins, & Bernstein, 2008; Overholser, 2012; Sexton & Whiston, 1996; Townend & Grant, 2006). Despite this debate, there has been a recent emphasis on the importance of research in practice, or evidence-based practice (see Chapter 9). The importance of accountability in practice is pressuring professionals to care about research and link research to practice. There is a distinct conflict between the training that educators (those training practitioners) have and the training that those practitioners would prefer to receive. Educators assume that training their students to be scientist–practitioners is appropriate, whereas practitioners would rather focus on becoming practitioner–scientists. Graduate-level training for counselors has, for the most part, focused on the scientist–practitioner model (Hoshmand & Polkinghorne, 1992; Kanfer, 1990; Townend & Grant, 2006).

Three problems have been noted with the scientist–practitioner training approach (Heppner et al., 1992; Hoshmand & Polkinghorne, 1992; Szymanski, Ozegovic, Phillips, & Briggs-Phillips, 2007). One problem has been identified as the possible lack of effective training in research and scientific methods, which results in minimal scholarship activity by practitioners (Szymanski et al., 2007). A second problem that has been identified is the question of how useful and applicable research reported in the literature may be to actual practice (Hoshmand & Polkinghorne, 1992). A third problem that has been suggested as one that limits the use of research in practice is the appropriateness of research designs and whether they represent sterile, controlled research laboratories or the natural environment (Whiston, 1996).

Szymanski and colleagues (2007) suggested a novel approach to fostering the development of research skills for those primarily interested in practice. They proposed the importance of an academic research training environment (RTE). The components of an RTE are faculty modeling of research activity, reinforcement of student interests, practical application of statistical methods, and opportunities to link research knowledge to practice (Szymanski et al., 2007). The last component is particularly important to fostering student research self-efficacy. This means requiring and promoting research activities during field experiences. Such efforts foster student understanding and comfort level with conducting research in a practice setting.

At this point in our discussion (and at this point in the text), I hope that the importance of using research and the scientific approach in practice is clear, but I want to cite several additional views that have emphasized the importance of practitioners using a scientific approach to practice. Increasingly, counselors and educators are being required to demonstrate the effectiveness of their work, such as with student performance or client outcomes (Odom et al., 2005; Sexton, 1996; Sexton & Whiston, 1996). Funding sources (taxpayers and insurance companies), government organizations, and consumers themselves (parents of students and clients in counseling) are demanding demonstrations of effectiveness. Those interested in demonstrations of effectiveness want solid, objective evidence and not simply professional opinion (e.g., "We believe our interventions to be effective"). Other research has suggested, and I have noted in earlier chapters, that the research process is valued in our society as one of the most important sources of knowledge in decision making (Kettlewell, 2004; Sexton, 1996; Sexton & Whiston, 1996). The dilemma for counselors and educators is not necessarily whether research methods should be used, but how they can be most efficiently and effectively used to inform the work we do and provide documentation that what we do is effective.

A second reason the research process is important to our professions is simply that professions are in part defined by having an organized body of knowledge (Brown & Srebalus, 1996; Merlo et al., 2008). Developing an organized body of knowledge is best achieved through the mutual interaction of research and practice. In essence, science informs practice and practice informs science, creating evidence-based practice.

A third reason for the practitioners to conduct research is to maintain enthusiasm for the work. There has been considerable writing and research on professional burnout for educators and counselors. I personally believe that one method of reducing burnout is to develop and participate in research. One reason for burnout is a feeling of ineffectiveness and monotony. Developing and conducting research provide the hope of finding alternative methods to practice and the possibility of changing the issues and problems confronting the professional. Additionally, conducting research and finding effective methods of practice may lead to professional advancement opportunities—it demonstrates initiative.

Overholser (2010) suggested 10 criteria to consider with regard to research as a practitioner. The criteria are focused on clinical psychologists, but several of them can clearly be applied to practitioners in education and counseling. A basic premise is that practitioners make a commitment to research and participation in research. The first criterion is for the practitioner to remain active in scholarship (Overholser, 2010). Overholser (2010) noted that involvement in research may take many forms and is not limited to publications in professional journals. One can participate in research that results in sharing information among other professionals both formally and informally. Formal distribution may be accomplished through presentations at professional conferences, both local and national. Also, many states have professional organizations and opportunities to publish research results in newsletters or state chapter journals (state chapters of national organizations such as the ACA and the Council on Exceptional Children).

The second criterion according to Overholser (2010) that one should consider when participating in research as a practitioner is to make contributions at the national level or the international level. Certainly, as a practitioner, there can be a real benefit both professionally and personally. Recognition through such presentations is not achieved often and can be important to the field and to your organization (school, agency, or hospital). However, the rigor required for submission and acceptance of national and international presentations is generally great. As a practitioner, you may not have the time or knowledge to conduct such research. If you do, it can be very rewarding. It would be unfortunate for practitioners not to conduct or be involved in research if the sole goal was to present at national and international conferences because, as noted, success is somewhat limited.

A third criterion is to participate in teaching (Overholser, 2010) or sharing research through supervision. Overholser (2010) suggested that teaching may not have a significant impact on the field, that is, education and counseling, but I contend that teaching about the research process can have a significant impact. Also, using supervision to impart knowledge that was gathered through research can be valuable and effective because the supervisee is seeing and hearing about research in practice and likely may place more credence on the findings because of the respect and practical application that can be demonstrated by a supervisor or someone conducting research.

The next criterion is that the practitioner uses evidence-based research in practice (Overholser, 2010). A practitioner who conducts and participates in research is probably better prepared to evaluate evidence-based research and how it can be applied in practice. There is a dynamic interaction between the practitioner conducting and participating in research and the skills needed to effectively evaluate and apply research published or presented professionally.

Overholser (2010) proposed another criterion to consider based on a scientist–practitioner model is that the focus of any research conducted by the practitioner is on central issues in the profession. For example, in education one might focus on science, technology, engineering, and mathematics (STEM) research, which currently is an important issue in education. An example in counseling might be research focused on matching treatments to diagnoses or symptoms. It may be interesting to conduct research on a particular topic in one's discipline that is not mainstream or commonly identified problem, but the results may not have a significant impact on the field.

The last criterion that Overholser (2010) identified as important for practitioners in counseling and education is selection of good, reliable, and valid measures when collecting research data. As I have discussed in Chapter 15, the quality of instruments used are important in evaluating the efficacy of research. The same holds true in choosing measures to assess a research study outcome or measure the dependent variable.

PRACTITIONER–RESEARCHERS

It is hoped, at this point in your understanding and reading of this text, that other courses you have taken and personal experience have led to an appreciation of the important link between research and practice. In this chapter, I describe the process of developing, participating in, and conducting research, mainly from a practitioner's perspective, the practitioner–scientist approach. Consequently, I will describe how to develop and conduct a research project. This will be based on a step-by-step process. Second, I describe how practitioners in counseling and education can implement research in a practical way and still meet the daily demands of the employment setting.

DEVELOPING A RESEARCH PROPOSAL

There are slightly more steps in developing a research proposal than are found in an article published in a professional journal. Keep in mind that a research proposal is essentially your map (a detailed and readable map) for conducting the study. Consequently, the more detail you have in your steps, the better. (See Table 18.1.)

The first step is identifying a problem or an issue to address. As mentioned earlier, the practitioner–scientist approach should be a mutual exchange between research and practice, and this is also quite true in identifying a problem or issue. Wiersma and Jurs (2005) noted the importance of identifying a good research problem. There are several different methods of developing a research problem. These include a review of theories that have the potential to explain a phenomenon, discussions with colleagues, observing issues confronted in practice, and a review of current professional literature and current issues. Heath and Tynan (2010) provided suggestions for identifying research problems and stated, "Researchers can find ideas for research topics from various sources, such as talking with experts in the field, including potential supervisors; searching in the 'recommendations for further research' sections of books and academic papers; consulting with published theses, dissertations, conference proceedings, practitioner journals and other reports; discussing with colleagues; or listening to the media" (p. 148). Charles (1995) suggested several helpful considerations when identifying research topics. These include (1) personal interest in the topic, meaning a topic that will be rewarding and motivating to see through to completion; (2) an important topic, meaning one that will answer the so-what question we ask in evaluating others' research; (3) the amount of time required to complete the project—will it be possible to conduct the study, given your current day-to-day job demands; and (4) potential costs of conducting the study (in particular, will it require considerable amounts of money). Wiersma and Jurs (2005) cautioned against choosing a research problem that is more philosophical or abstract, which makes it difficult to research. An example of a research problem that is more philosophical or abstract that may be difficult to research is whether there are aliens visiting Earth. One can investigate people's attitudes toward whether aliens are visiting Earth, but studying the physical evidence of aliens is a much more abstract idea.

Table 18.1 Steps in Developing a Research Plan

Step 1. Identify a problem or issue to address.

Step 2. Identify current status of the problem from other research.

Step 3. Operationalize the problem or issue.

Step 4. Develop purpose statement or hypotheses.

Step 5. Select research design and procedures.

Step 6. Operationalize dependent variable and select measures.

Step 7. Identify population and sample, and determine sample selection procedures.

Step 8. Conduct the study, and collect data.

Step 9. Analyze the data.

Step 10. Report the data.

Once you have identified a problem or issue you wish to investigate, your next step is to determine what currently exists in this area in the research literature. Has any research been conducted on the topic? Ary and colleagues (2014) concluded that a review of the literature is not an exploration in discovering new research but uncovering what has been already done and what is currently known in a particular area of research. Were the findings what you would have hypothesized? (Review Chapter 2 for searching the literature.) In determining the status of current research on the topic, you will gain information that will help you make a decision to pursue a research project or not. In your review, you will want to use your recently acquired skills in evaluating journal articles and determine whether the studies are of relatively solid quality and whether they address the issues you are interested in studying. If you determine that you wish to pursue a study, the literature review will provide you with a basis for developing other sections of your proposal, such as operationalizing the problem, hypotheses, and so on. Another benefit in becoming informed about a particular research topic is that you will become more knowledgeable and be able to share this information with others.

A third step in developing your proposal is operationalizing the problem or issue so the study may be conducted. This step may also be defined in terms of developing the purpose statement. This step is not an easy one; it requires a clear identification of the problem, so the research variables may be developed from the target problem. If the purpose statement is poorly constructed, it will be difficult to successfully complete the other steps. For example, if you saw a problem with children learning science, you could focus on developing a teaching method or on how the children learn or on both. The perspective you choose to use to define the problem will influence your efforts in developing and refining the proposal. To operationalize the problem, you must develop a concrete expression of it so that it may be observed and measured. Many problems can be discussed in the abstract, but to be studied, they must be conceptualized concretely. You will need to determine the population of interest and complete a clear statement of the intent of your study (the purpose statement). This includes identifying the type of study (e.g., comparison, descriptive, or relationship). Heath and Tynan (2010) noted that developing a realistic, practical purpose is important. Many times, young researchers suggest a purpose that is too broad and too ambitious. Review Chapter 12 for information about constructing a good purpose statement. Also, you will need to identify clearly the variables of interest (dependent and independent) if it is a true experimental or quasi-experimental design.

An example of an abstract statement of the problem of the initial research idea for a study of children learning science might be as follows "There is a need for innovative curriculum for teaching science to elementary school children." A concrete statement of the problem might be stated as such: The purpose of this study is to determine whether an authentic curriculum method will increase elementary students' understanding of science better than traditional methods of instruction (see Table 18.2 for additional examples of good and abstract statements of a problem).

The next step is to develop your hypotheses. In stating the hypotheses, you will want to think about the types of hypotheses based on previous research literature, a theory, or personal clinical experience. Examples of linking theory to a hypothesis can be found in writing about conceptual change, integration of cognitive and sociocultural developmental views, and approaches to learning (Mason, 2007; Vosniadou, 2007). Vosniadou (2007) described how children begin to learn from birth:

> Cognitive developmental research has shown that the knowledge-acquisition process starts soon after birth and that infants organize the multiplicity of their sensory experiences under the influence of everyday culture and language into narrow but relatively coherent frameworks that allow distinct types of explanations and predictions and embody causal notions and epistemological commitments know, as "naïve theories." (p. 58)

Vosniadou (2007) noted that the teaching of science is typically restricted to the school environment. Such an approach is not consistent with how humans learn, that is, developing hypotheses from experience, known as authentic learning.

Table 18.2   Examples of Abstract Versus Concrete Problem Statement

Abstract Examples	*Concrete Examples (Good Examples)*
We sought to determine whether good parents compared to custody samples were different on personality tests (adapted from Resendes & Lecci, 2012).	We sought to determine whether a parent competence group compared to a child custody group differed on personality tests and MMPI-2 profiles (adapted from Resendes & Lecci, 2012).
The purpose of this study was to determine how nutrition information is presented in the classroom (adapted from Watts, Pinero, Alter, & Lancaster, 2012).	The purpose of this study was to explore how nutrition information is taught in an elementary classroom (adapted from Watts et al., 2012).
The aim of this investigation was to study how therapy and using certain eating habits helped achieve weight loss (adapted from Masheb, Grilo, & Rolls, 2011).	The aim of this study was to investigate whether cognitive behavior therapy and lowering energy density could achieve weight loss in obese patients with binge eating disorders (adapted from Masheb et al., 2011).

A possible hypothesis of such a study might be as follows: Elementary school children receiving science instruction based upon a conceptual change, authentic learning approach will have higher standardized test scores on science than those receiving a traditional science instruction method.

As with the evaluation of a research article and the hypotheses developed by researchers, you will want to ensure that your hypotheses are testable. This will be addressed partly in the development and operationalizing of your purpose statement. The study must be able to be conducted and operationalized in such a way as to measure the dependent variables. If you are conducting the study alone, you may want to discuss your hypotheses with others, either peers or individuals who regularly conduct research. Even though the hypotheses may make sense to you, they may not be clear to others, and having others read your hypothesis will provide you with feedback about the clarity and conciseness of your hypotheses.

Finally, you want to consider what type of hypothesis you wish to make. Recall from Chapter 12 that there are essentially three different types of hypotheses: null hypothesis, nondirectional hypothesis, and alternative directional hypothesis. The null hypothesis states there is no effect or no differences in comparisons made or in relationships between variables. The nondirectional hypothesis states there is an effect but no direction or prediction is made as to the direction. An alternative directional hypothesis does provide a direction or prediction of a direction of the effect (see Table 18.3 for examples of three different types of hypotheses).

Table 18.3   Examples of Types of Hypotheses

Null Hypotheses	*Nondirectional Hypotheses*	*Alternative Hypotheses*
We predicted a null effect with respect to the popularity of individual versus team written top Billboard songs (Pettijohn, & Ahmed, 2010, p. 3).	We hypothesized that the effect of tDCS (transcranial direct current stimulation) on learning should be sensitive to current strength and electrode location (Clark, Coffman, Mayer, et al., 2012, p. 121).	We hypothesized that among disaster victims, victimization would be a significant predictor of mental health (Becker-Blease, Turner, & Finkelhor, 2010, p. 1042).
Work role was predicted to be nonsignificant in relation to midlife mothers' life satisfaction (adapted from Kasimatis & Guastello, 2012, p. 52).	It was hypothesized that there would be differences in test scores due to an arousal effect created by the perceptions of the stimuli as compared to the less organized conditions of traffic noise and silence (Roth & Smith, 2008, p. 398).	Differences in the choice of a word from a list would be found after the target word has been presented subliminally within a piece of music (Edwards, Valero-Cabre, Rotenberg, et al., 2006, p. 34).

The next step is the development of your research methods, procedures, and design. This is a most important step in your study: How you establish the methods will determine to a considerable degree the efficacy of your study (Gall et al., 2006). Designing a research study has been noted to be a problem-solving process (Heiman, 1995) because you are attempting to come up with an effective method for testing out hypotheses. Gall and colleagues (2006) noted that "no research design is perfect. Each is susceptible to different flaws" (p. 20). Choosing the best design with the fewest flaws requires careful review and matching the design to the purpose, research questions, and hypotheses. Heiman (1995) suggested four considerations in designing a study: the intent or nature of the hypotheses, the focus or nature of the behavior to be studied, concerns over validity, and ethical and practical considerations.

The first consideration in determining a research design is to think about the purpose and hypotheses of your study. As stated earlier, we want consistency between the purpose or hypotheses and the research design. Thus, if you are conducting a study to identify and clarify an event or phenomenon, you will probably choose a descriptive or qualitative research design. To determine relationships between variables and issues, you will be collecting data that focus on two or more variables and conducting correlational analyses. For studies in which you wish to compare outcomes from those receiving services with outcomes from those not receiving services, you will want to decide between using a true experimental design and using a quasi-experimental design. To decide which designs make sense for you to use based on your purpose, it may be helpful to refer back to Chapters 4 and 5. There are a number of other texts that can also provide a detailed, step-by-step discussion on the procedures for conducting research and choosing particular research designs (Ary et al., 2014; Cooper, 2012; Creswell, 2012; Gall et al., 2006; Heiman, 1995). Many of these texts are designed primarily to teach methods of conducting research.

According to Heiman (1995), a second consideration in selecting a procedure is the characteristics of the variables you are studying. For example, if you are studying the effects of gender on learning math, you cannot randomly assign subjects or participants to groups—you cannot randomly assign someone to a particular gender. Therefore, you must choose a design that takes into consideration this restriction, for example, a quasi-experimental design or a descriptive-causal comparative design.

Heiman (1995) noted that issues of validity are a third consideration in determining your research design. Recall the discussion in Chapter 14 of internal and external validity and how the use of a particular research design influences the validity of a study. Typically, we will want to balance the threats to internal and external validity. For example, if there is a high internal validity and a large amount of control by the researcher, there should be less control and a more natural measurement of the variables of interest (external validity). Heppner and colleagues (1992) stated, "A study that exerts a high amount of experimental control will most likely depart from a naturalistic setting, and a study that examines variables in a highly naturalistic setting can have only limited experimental control" (p. 68). A researcher, particularly in applied professions like counseling and education, must balance the amount of control employed to achieve as high a level of validity, both internal and external, as possible.

A fourth consideration is that of ethics and practice (Heiman, 1995). Our professional ethics state that we should do no harm, so we want to plan studies that do not harm those whom we serve, clients (counseling) or students (education). Procedures have been developed to protect the rights of subjects in research studies (Office of Protection From Research Risks, 1993). Also, most important for the practitioner are practical considerations. The research design must not take up considerable amounts of time, particularly if it interferes with performing day-to-day duties and job requirements. A second ethical consideration is the impact of potential results on the population (Gostin, 1991). Gostin described ethical considerations involved in making decisions about the impact of particular research on populations. He concluded that "ethical principles applied to larger groups of people or populations are designed to protect the human dignity, integrity, self-determination, confidentiality, rights, and health of populations and the people comprising them" (p. 191). Researchers frequently forget about how potential results may impact the population when results are published.

To summarize, I would suggest a research design for the practitioner that is straightforward, not complex, not time-consuming, and probably most important, fits well into the day-to-day practice of his or her profession. The use of qualitative research designs and quasi-experimental designs is probably most appropriate for practitioners in counseling and education and is also less intrusive (Townend & Grant, 2006). There are several reasons why these designs may be more appropriate for practitioners to use in counseling and education. One reason is that the sample size need not be as high as is typically required in quantitative methods. For example, case study research, which may be used in both qualitative and quasi-experimental methods, may involve only one participant. A second reason is that random assignment is not necessary or is frequently not used with these designs; this is desirable because random assignment is not possible in the natural environment.

The next step in developing a research proposal is the selection of instruments or the operationalization of the dependent variable. The type of instrument or operationalization of the dependent variable will depend to some degree on the research design used, quantitative or qualitative. For quantitative research methods, in which numbers of quantification are important, you will want to consider the following issues: objectivity; standard conditions of administering the test; and the use of normative comparisons, reliability, and validity (Gall et al., 2006). Objectivity refers to the use of self-report, observations, the use of others for scoring, and so on. Self-report measures have the potential for respondent bias but offer ease in administration. Standard conditions for administering the test reduce test error. Normative comparisons allow for, theoretically, more valid interpretations of results. Reliability addresses how consistent the measure is. Validity addresses the degree to which you are actually measuring what you want or intend to measure. There are several important sources to consult when attempting to identify an appropriate test. These include *The Sixteenth Mental Measurements Yearbook* (Plake & Spies, 2005) and *Tests in Print* VIII (Murphy, Geisinger, Carlson, & Spies, 2011). Typically, you will be able to find these books in the references section of your library. They provide descriptions of the tests and information about test properties such as reliability and validity.

There are several important considerations in selecting a test. One is to ensure that the test measures the dependent variable of interest. A second is that the test must be appropriate for use with the population or sample you are using. One approach to finding a measure that best fits the dependent variable is to review the literature for other studies investigating a similar dependent variable. It is helpful if there is a measure that is commonly accepted as measuring the dependent variable of interest. For example, to measure depression, a frequently used measurement tool is the BDI-II (Seignourel, Green, & Schmitz, 2008).

In qualitative research, observational, recording, and interview methods are typical. There is no attempt to quantify the responses; instead, the object is to develop categories of response or themes. Use of observational methods requires that the researcher has a focus (e.g., groups and their interaction in a specific context or dyads in a work setting, such as supervisor–supervisee). Recall from Chapter 5 that a common approach to understanding and interpreting qualitative research is to determine your unit of analysis or data collection: social practice, episodes, encounters, roles, relationships, and so on (Lofland et al., 2006). You should determine your unit of analysis prior to data collection so you can focus on the variable of interest.

A key approach to data collection and operationalization of the dependent variable in qualitative research is triangulation. This involves the use of multiple sources of data collection to identify the themes or constructs of interests. This means that you might possibly have several observers reviewing the same phenomena or coding audio- or videotaped sessions.

Another step in developing and planning a research study is to systematically select your sample from your identified population. If you are teaching third-grade students and wish to study how an innovative science program might compare to a more traditional method, your population may be all third-grade students in the United States. Once you have determined the population, your next consideration is how to effectively select a sample that is manageable and accessible. As a practitioner, you will not typically have unlimited time to contact multiple sites to obtain permission to recruit subjects or participants for a study. If you use a qualitative or quasi-experimental design with your own class, your study will be much more manageable, but as we discussed in Chapter 14, this will result in several limitations to the study and threats to external validity. Even so, it may still be important to conduct such a study to determine the effectiveness of a new approach and bring about the potential for change in how subjects are taught.

Another approach is to collaborate with colleagues in other schools in your district or other parts of your state or throughout the United States and have them attempt to implement a similar research design using basically the same methods. Consequently, you would have a larger sample than simply your own classroom with which to test your technique. Also, expanding the study to other schools allows for greater generalization and addresses some of the threats to external validity.

A third approach is to switch teaching the subject of the study with another teacher in your school and provide the intervention with that classroom. This may be accomplished through a mutual exchange: The other teacher teaches your class, and you teach his or hers. This reduces the bias of other factors influencing the outcome of the study in cases when the only access you have to the sample is your work with them regarding the intervention. In actual practice, it is not unusual for teachers to team teach or switch classes, so (theoretically) it should not be too disruptive.

In counseling and education, practical approaches to conducting research would include the use of case study methods when using both qualitative and quasi-experimental designs and the use of single-subject research designs. You may work with a client or a student and find that a new, innovative approach is warranted, and you want to test it out systematically. A case study approach may be the most sensible approach. You could certainly implement the new technique with several clients. Generally, it is not feasible to switch with other counselors and take on their clients, as teachers can do with their classes. Clients become attached to counselors and are not easily traded to other counselors.

An important consideration in any study conducted with clients or students is consent to participate. Your ethical responsibilities as a researcher are to ensure that anyone you ask to participate in a research study has freely given informed consent. Those working with children (minors) must obtain informed consent from a parent and assent from the child. An important step in ensuring ethical research is processing any request through an institutional human subjects committee.

PRACTICAL CONSIDERATIONS IN CONDUCTING RESEARCH

There are several practical considerations that must be addressed when conducting research as a practitioner–scientist. One issue concerns the devotion of time to the project. It is critical that you set aside time to conduct the study. It may not involve significant amounts of time if you have incorporated the study carefully into your practice, but it will require attention on a consistent basis. A second consideration is the support from your administration and your colleagues. Conducting research without consulting your supervisor or administration could create problems for you (e.g., they may wonder how you are spending your time). A third consideration is the development of a well-thought-out, written plan for your study. The plan should clearly outline your steps, and it may be helpful to develop a timeline for implementation of those steps. A fourth issue is how you will code and analyze the data. If you are using a qualitative study, you may want to consult with a faculty member at a local university who is familiar with coding qualitative information or is familiar with some of the computer programs for coding qualitative data, such as Nonnumerical, Unstructured Data—Indexing, Searching and Theorizing (QSR NUD*IST; QSR International, 1997). For studies conducted with quantitative methods, again, you may want to consult with a faculty member at a local university who can assist in data analysis if you want to complete more complex calculations such as ANOVAs. There are several computer programs that can be used in the analysis of quantitative data, including the Statistical Package for the Social Sciences (SPSS) and the Statistical Analysis System (SAS).

SUMMARY

In summary, it may not be as difficult as you might think to conduct research during the daily practice of your profession in counseling or education. Your key considerations are the devotion of time to the project and plans to systematically evaluate the data collected. It is important to construct a plan of action for conducting your study. I have found that having a detailed plan alerts me to gaps in my design or potential problems. One of the most important issues is to select a topic that is interesting and potentially exciting to you. It will maintain your interest and provide increased satisfaction to you in your daily activities.

19

Development and Application of Program Evaluation Research

Our society, including political and social institutions, has increasingly required more accountability in social service and educational programs (Chouilnard, 2013). One example of the relevance of accountability was passage of the Government Performance and Results Modernization Act of 2010. Chouilnard (2013) described the act and stated that it was introduced by the Barack Obama administration with a "focus on performance information, results, and cost efficiency to manage federal programs" (p. 239). A related philosophical view of accountability is the New Public Management (NPM) model (Chouilnard, 2013). According to Chouilnard, this philosophy, NPM, is an attempt to bring accountability into the private sector and nonprofit and for-profit organizations. Accountability is based on the use of evaluation tactics and strategies to determine whether a program achieves or reaches desired results.

Stufflebeam and Shinkfield (2007) noted the importance of evaluation and stated, "Evaluation arguably is society's most fundamental discipline. It is oriented to assessing and helping improve all aspects of society" (p. 4). Gall and colleagues (2006) discussed the importance of evaluation and stated, "The main reason is that public administrators have come to view evaluation as an important tool in policy analysis and program management" (p. 542). I would suggest that we as professionals should be interested in the quality and outcomes of the services and professional activities we provide as well as in the importance of providing funding sources with information about the effectiveness of education and counseling programs. Program evaluation is a systematic approach to gathering information about our professional practices and gives us a tool for improving our programs. It also is different in intent from traditional research, although one might use similar methods at different points in the process. Gall and colleagues (2006) noted the similarities between research and evaluation and also outlined differences. First, they cited the similarities by stating,

"In practice, evaluators make substantial use of the research designs, measurement tools, and data analysis techniques that constitute the methodology of educational research" (p. 543). Despite the use of many methods in educational research, there are differences. Gall and colleagues (2006) outlined three differences between research and evaluation. One difference is that the actual impetus for the evaluation is initiated by someone other than the researcher, and the use of the outcome information is to make decisions about policies, programs, or management activities (Gall et al., 2006). A program evaluator is frequently hired or requested to complete an evaluation by an organization, an administrator, or a governmental body to assist in making specific decisions. Conversely, a research study is conducted to uncover information about a particular phenomenon or issue. Research is much more broadly based in focus, and the focus is on the researcher's interests. A second difference, according to Gall and colleagues (2006), is the degree to which the results are generalized. Evaluation is designed to answer a specific set of questions for a particular group, organization, or agency. Research, on the other hand, is intended to generate outcomes that provide results on a much broader scale to generalize back to a large target population. The third difference between evaluation and research concerns the emphasis on value judgments (Gall et al., 2006). Evaluation is engaged in making conclusions that may involve judgment about the worth of a program, whereas research is intended to uncover evidence that is more in the nature of discovery.

DEFINITIONS OF PROGRAM EVALUATION RESEARCH

Several definitions of program evaluation research have been offered, but they share common components (Gall et al., 2006; Rossi & Freeman, 1993; Stufflebeam & Shinkfield, 2007). For example, Rossi and Freeman (1993) defined program evaluation as "a systematic application of social science research procedures in assessing the conceptualization and design, implementation, and utility of social intervention programs" (p. 19). More specifically, they suggested that program evaluation involved efforts to improve through planning and through monitoring the effectiveness of health, education, and human service programs. Gall and colleagues (2006) defined educational evaluation as "the process of making judgments about the merit, value or worth of educational programs" (p. 542). The Joint Committee on Standards for Educational Evaluation (1994) proposed a definition stating that "evaluation is the systematic assessment of the worth or merit of an object" (p. 3). Stufflebeam and Shinkfield (2007) suggested that evaluation is "the systematic assessment of an object's merit, worth, probity, feasibility, safety, significance, and/or equity" (p. 13). The commonality of these definitions is an assessment of the worth and merit of an object or program. (See Table 19.1.)

Table 19.1 Similarities and Differences Between Research and Evaluation

	Research	*Evaluation*
Purpose	Test theories, and develop practices and procedures	Decision making and information for social programs
Audience	Professional and scientific community	Specific group or communities such as funding sources or governmental agencies
Method	True experimental, quasi-experimental, nonexperimental (descriptive) qualitative, and so on	True experimental, quasi-experimental, nonexperimental (descriptive) qualitative, and so on

PROFESSIONAL STANDARDS AND GUIDELINES FOR PROGRAM EVALUATION

Several different standards and principles for conducting program evaluation have been proposed (American Evaluation Association, 2004; Joint Committee on Standards for Educational Evaluation, 1994). The standards from the Joint Committee on Standards for Educational Evaluation were first developed in the early 1980s. There are 30 standards that fall into four general categories: utility, feasibility, propriety, and accuracy. These standards were established to guide the evaluator in setting up high-quality, professional evaluations. The standards for utility, according to Stufflebeam and Shinkfield (2007), concern whether the information gained from an evaluation addresses the needs of the identified audience. Feasibility standards address whether the evaluation is realistic to conduct (Stufflebeam & Shinkfield, 2007). Feasibility also includes the cost of conducting the evaluation—is the cost too high or inflated? The third general category of standards is propriety, which concerns the extent to which an evaluation and its results are legally and ethically conducted with regard for those affected by the results (Stufflebeam & Shinkfield, 2007). Finally, accuracy, according to Stufflebeam and Shinkfield (2007), is the extent to which the information and data collected accurately reflect the program being assessed or evaluated.

The Guiding Principles of Evaluators (American Evaluation Association, 2004) focus on five basic principles: systematic inquiry, competence, integrity and honesty, respect for people, and responsibilities for general and public welfare. Systematic inquiry concerns the use of appropriate evaluation methods and clearly communicating the results to the appropriate stakeholders. Competence refers to ensuring that the evaluation team has the appropriate credentials and skills to conduct the evaluation and that they have awareness of cultural issues that may impact an evaluation. Competence also includes ensuring that evaluation teams practice within their areas of competence and that they seek to improve their skills. A third principle refers to integrity and honesty in the application of the evaluation (American Evaluation Association, 2004). Implementation of integrity and honesty in evaluation involves clearly disclosing and conflicting relationships in roles regarding the evaluation and clearly stating the procedures used in the evaluation. A fourth principle is respect for people, which includes communicating the importance of program participants and stakeholders in the evaluation process. This principle also involves adhering to professional ethics in the practice of evaluation. The last principle, responsibilities for general and public welfare, concerns the ultimate purpose of evaluation, which is to provide accountability to the public. Specifically, this principle involves ensuring a balance between a quality evaluation, sharing results with program stakeholders, and communicating the results to the general public as is appropriate.

TYPES OF EVALUATIONS

Three major different types of evaluation have been identified: need, formative, and summative (Gall et al., 2006; Stufflebeam & Shinkfield, 2007). Assessments of needs are designed to identify the discrepancy between actual conditions and what is sought or desired (Gall et al., 2006). A focus on needs may include assessment of particular types of education programs or counseling services such as crisis services or special school services like after-school programs. Rossi and Freeman (1993) defined needs assessment as the "systematic appraisal of type, depth, and scope of problems perceived by study targets or their advocates" (p. 90). Typically, a needs assessment is conducted prior to designing more comprehensive programs. One would not want to develop a program, even if it were a great program, if the need was not there. This is particularly true today, given social and political oversight of programs and the scrutiny over expenditure of public funds.

A second type of evaluation, process or formative evaluation, concerns whether a program is implemented as designed, for example, how well the program was implemented. Focusing on evaluation of effort or process does not generally address whether a program is effective, but it does answer important questions about the amount and quality of effort needed to implement a program.

A third type of evaluation is evaluation of outcome, also referred to as a summative evaluation. Evaluation of outcome concerns how successful a program is in achieving designated goals. Typically, summative evaluation results are provided to policy makers such as politicians (Stufflebeam & Shinkfield, 2007), whereas formative evaluation results are generally given to those who are implementing the program.

EVALUATION MODELS

A number of different models of conducting evaluations have been proposed (Stufflebeam & Shinkfield, 2007). These designs may utilize both quantitative and qualitative methods of data collection. One model of evaluation that has been developed is the case study model (Stake, 1994; Stufflebeam & Shinkfield, 2007). Stufflebeam and Shinkfield (2007) described case study evaluation this way: "A case study evaluation's signature feature is an in-depth examination of the case and issuance of a captivating, illuminative report" (p. 309). Case study research typically involves the use of qualitative methods most frequently and a much deeper investigation into the processes of a program. However, as Stufflebeam and Shinkfield (2007) noted, the case study evaluation method generates considerable data and information, and the evaluator must organize and present the information to help the decision makers use the findings.

Another evaluation model is the consumer-oriented approach (Scriven, 1991; Stufflebeam & Shinkfield, 2007). Stufflebeam and Shinkfield (2007) describe this model as being consumer oriented, and the importance of the outcome data is interpreted in terms of how those who are receiving the services or program are affected. So, the evaluation is focused on determining the worth or value of a program. The use of checklists in evaluating programs is a key component of this model (Stufflebeam, 2004).

Another evaluation model is the context, input, process, and product evaluation (CIPP) model (Stufflebeam, 2003). Stufflebeam and Shinkfield (2007) describe the CIPP model as focused on both formative and summative evaluation. Questions are asked about the object of evaluation, such as: "What needs to be done? How should it be done? Is it being done? And is it succeeding?" (p. 327). Stufflebeam and Shinkfield (2007) described the CIPP model this way: "The model's intent is to supply evaluation users—such as policy boards, administrators, and project staffs—with timely, valid information of use in identifying an appropriate area for development; formulating sound goals, activity plans, and budgets" (p. 327). It is a broad approach to evaluation that focuses on improvement of programs and accountability. It originally was developed to evaluate schools and has since been expanded to be used in various arenas (Stufflebeam & Shinkfield, 2007).

There are several other evaluation models, and I want to give you a brief introduction to some of these, but the purpose of this book and this chapter is essentially an introduction to evaluation. There are a number of different resources that address these models and others in much greater detail (Chen, 2005; Davidson, 2005; Stufflebeam & Shinkfield, 2007).

STEPS IN AN EVALUATION

There are systematic steps in conducting program evaluation, just as there are with scientific research (Gall et al., 2006; Stufflebeam & Shinkfield, 2007). Steps in conducting a program evaluation include forming the evaluation team, identifying relevant stakeholders, determining the focus of the evaluation, identifying the evaluation questions to be answered, selecting the evaluation methods and designs, selecting the measures for the evaluation, collecting the data, organizing and analyzing the data, and reporting the results to relevant stakeholders. (See Table 19.2.)

The first step in the evaluation process is the formation of an evaluation team. Stufflebeam and Shinkfield (2007) discussed potential roles for evaluation team members, such as measurement and evaluation specialist, subject matter specialist, evaluation manager, and so on. It is desirable to have an evaluation team rather than a sole individual conducting an evaluation, particularly when the organization being evaluated is a large one or when there is a large amount of evaluation material to be collected. There are several reasons for using an evaluation team: The use of an evaluation team provides a more varied perspective and, theoretically, more objectivity, and a team may be needed to share the volume of work and activities involved. Some have suggested that relevant stakeholders should be included in an evaluation team (Houser, Anderson, & Wang, 1995; Whyte, 1990).

The Joint Committee on Standards for Educational Evaluation (1988) proposed standards for personnel who conducted evaluations. Twenty-one standards were proposed that focus on four general categories, as do the general standards: utility, feasibility, propriety, and accuracy. Further, the Joint Committee stated that "evaluations (must) be conducted legally, ethically, and with due regard for the welfare of evaluatees and clients of the evaluations" (p. 269).

An important question is whether those conducting the evaluation are insiders or outsiders. An insider, someone who works for the organization, may have a good understanding of the issues confronting an organization. Also, an insider may obtain cooperation from others quite readily because of his or her relationships with members of the organization. A problem may be the objectivity of an insider, who may have a vested interest in finding certain outcomes. An outsider typically brings a more objective view but may need more time understanding the dynamics of the organization. Also, he or she may not be accepted or trusted by members of the organization and may therefore have difficulty obtaining the desired information. A solution to the limitations of insiders and outsiders is to form an evaluation team that includes both insiders and outsiders.

The second step in the evaluation process is the identification of relevant stakeholders. Stakeholders are all those who may potentially be affected by the results of an evaluation. For example, if a school system is evaluating the effectiveness of a particular curriculum in elementary grades, relevant stakeholders would include parents, teachers, aides, administrators, community members, and children. Stakeholders may be used in the development of the evaluation, in (obviously) conducting the evaluation, and in interpreting the results. It has been suggested that, if relevant stakeholders are not included in planning an evaluation, they may sabotage the process (Gall et al., 2002).

The third step is the determination of a focus for the evaluation. Gall and colleagues (2002) suggested that determining the focus of the program evaluation should involve identifying the relevant characteristics of the program that will be studied and evaluated. Relevant program characteristics may include the evaluation of quality of staff, the achievement of program goals, the use of resources, the effectiveness of management, and so on. Typically, an evaluation does not include all components of a program because they would be too time-consuming and costly to evaluate, so it is important to determine the exact focus of the evaluation, which is typically obtained from the source requesting the evaluation and from the relevant stakeholders.

A fourth step in an evaluation is the identification of the evaluation questions to be answered. Questions to be answered may be predetermined by the source

---

Table 19.2   Steps in Program Evaluation

Step 1. Formation of the evaluation team

Step 2. Identification of relevant stakeholders

Step 3. Determination of a focus for the evaluation

Step 4. Identification of evaluation model and methods

Step 5. Selection of evaluation methods and designs

Step 6. Selection of measures for the evaluation

Step 7. Collection of the data

Step 8. Analysis of the data

Step 9. Reporting of the results to relevant stakeholders

---

requesting the evaluation (e.g., a governmental organization or administration). Even when the evaluation questions are predetermined, an evaluator or the evaluation team will want to discuss the questions with those requesting the evaluation to ensure that there is an understanding of those questions.

The next step in the evaluation process is to select the evaluation models and designs. Several models of evaluation have been proposed: decision making (Stufflebeam, 2005), consumer driven (Scriven, 1987), needs assessment (Cook, 1989), and responsive evaluation (Stake, 1994). Each of these approaches uses specific methods in conducting the evaluation and data collection. For example, Stufflebeam's (2005) decision-making model uses surveys and interviews, and Stake's (1994) transaction model uses case studies and interviews. I will not go into extensive detail describing these models, but I will state that, when you decide to conduct an evaluation, you will want to identify a particular model that meets the needs of the intent of the evaluation. Stufflebeam and Shinkfield (2007) provide a systematic discussion of the various models and provide an analysis and classification of the models. They note that some evaluations are not valid or well founded, and they term these evaluations *pseudoevalautions.* The various proponents of these evaluation models have written extensively about their methodologies and procedures, and it is important to become familiar with the method you choose to use. It is not my intent in this chapter to provide detailed information about the different models; to comprehensively cover the models would require considerably more than just one chapter. Also, the models are described elsewhere in great detail (Guba & Lincoln, 1992; House, 1993; Rossi & Freeman, 1993; Stufflebeam & Shinkfield, 2007).

The sixth step, as in traditional research, is to select measures for the evaluation. As with traditional research, the program evaluators will want to choose instruments and measures that assess the intended variables. This is accomplished by operationalizing the outcome variables of interest, for instance, a reading program in which the children's reading scores on a particular test are used. The program evaluator may use many of the same types of measures as those used in traditional research, such as surveys, observations, and interviews. There are certain methods that are preferred, such as interviews, surveys, and observations, which are frequently used. It is not unusual for evaluators to develop an instrument that is specific to the program being evaluated—reliability and validity may therefore be compromised to some degree. However, there are methods to reduce problems with reliability and validity. Evaluators should field-test new measures and check reliability and validity before the measure is used in the actual evaluation. An evaluator may use qualitative methods, which have benefits to gathering and using the data. Gall and colleagues (2002) observed that qualitative methods do not always allow for in-depth understanding of stakeholders' perceptions.

The seventh and eighth steps are the collection and analysis of the data. Collection of data should be accomplished systematically with timelines identified to ensure completion of the required tasks. It is helpful in conducting an evaluation, whether accomplished through a team or by a sole evaluator, to develop a written plan and dictate who will take care of which components of the data collection.

Evaluators will analyze data based on methods similar to those used in traditional research. Both descriptive and inferential statistical methods may be used. For qualitative methods of evaluation, the researcher may also use methods of analysis similar to research approaches, such as using computer programs to analyze and search for common themes in interview transcripts. Key in choosing methods of analyzing data and information gathered is considering the questions to be answered during the evaluation. For example, if an evaluator is interested in determining if a particular science teaching method is best, he or she may choose to use a correlated *t*-test to compare differences pre- and posttest, comparing the same group at two different times.

The ninth and final step is reporting the results to relevant stakeholders. An evaluation report will usually look much different from a journal article. Generally, the report begins with a statement of the purpose of the evaluation. No citation of previous research is provided. The rationale presented in the report is simply that the evaluation was requested by a specific source with a particular purpose in mind. There may be several reports developed, one for each stakeholder group, as each may have different needs and interests in the findings. The questions to be addressed in the evaluation will be restated. Because they are visual, tables and graphs are particularly helpful in presenting program evaluation results. An important consideration in preparing evaluation results for different stakeholder groups is to write in language that is appropriate for the population reading it. Conclusions are arrived at regarding the initial questions asked, and recommendations are specific to the program being evaluated. This is different from the way conclusions and recommendations are made in professional research articles.

As with traditional research, the program evaluation report will include a clear description of the procedures used. Thus, the instruments will be described as well as the ways in which participants were contacted.

EVALUATION EXAMPLE

Cook, O'Donnell, Dinnen, et al. (2013) conducted a formative evaluation focused on evaluating Veterans Administration residential programs treating those with PTSD. The authors described the initiation of the study: "From July 2008 through March 2011, the VA's National Center for PTSD conducted a formative evaluation to identify favored services and facilitate interprogram exchanges in the residential PTSD treatments programs that have participated in a longstanding outcome monitoring initiative led by VA's Northeast Program and Evaluation Center" (p. 57). The evaluators further described the evaluation, which involved a 2-day site visit by a clinical psychologist who interviewed program directors and staff of the residential programs. The interviews focused on the use of prolonged exposure and cognitive processing therapy in the treatment of PTSD. They completed transcripts of the interviews and collected field notes. Additionally, two program evaluators collected information from providers on their use of prolonged exposure and cognitive processing therapy, and they converted this information into ratings. The evaluators found that some programs did not use prolonged exposure or cognitive processing therapy. They discovered the reason for not using these two treatments mostly was a result of characteristics of the residential programs, for example, not enough time for treatment or not enough staff for implementation. Additionally, the evaluators found that some staff did not follow the protocol for the intervention. The evaluators concluded that implementation and use of prolonged exposure and cognitive processing therapy is best implemented on an individual basis and an individual program basis. Finally, the evaluators disseminated the results of the evaluation to all qualified providers treating veterans with PTSD.

SUMMARY

Recently, there has been considerable pressure from governments and consumers for social and educational programs to demonstrate effectiveness, including the influence of evidence-based practice. A key approach to documenting effectiveness is through the use of program evaluation. The field of evaluation has progressed significantly over the past three decades because of the pressures for documenting effectiveness. Professional evaluators have suggested certain criteria for conducting evaluations (Joint Committee on Standards for Educational Evaluation, 1994).

Several types of program evaluation methods have been proposed: needs assessment, formative, and summative. As in traditional research, program evaluation research is based on systematic methods, and there are sequential steps to conducting an evaluation: formation of the evaluation team, identification of relevant stakeholders, determination of the focus of the evaluation, and so on. Counselors and educators likely will participate in or conduct program evaluation research on a regular basis in the completion of their job duties. Consequently, it is important for them as professionals to become familiar with the methods and approaches to program evaluation. A good way to become familiar with and knowledgeable about program evaluation is through participation as an evaluation team member. Having program evaluation skills will enhance your professional skills and future career opportunities.

20

THE USE OF TECHNOLOGY IN RESEARCH

Technology has been used in applying research for decades. Volti (2006) defined technology as "a system that uses knowledge and organization to produce objects and techniques for the attainment of specific goals" (p. 6). Behavioral science research has a long history of using technology, not always sophisticated technology like we might think of today. An early example was introduced during the 1700s by Benjamin Rush, who is considered the father of American psychiatry. Rush invented several technologies, such as the tranquilizing chair, developed to treat those with mental illness (invented in the mid-1700s). B. F. Skinner was well known for developing technology and techniques for conducting research in the 1950s. He was one of the first researchers to introduce a teaching approach using technology known as programmed instruction (his first teaching machine is in the National Museum of American History). Since the 1950s, the use of technology in research has grown significantly as with advances in technology throughout our society.

The use of technology in research is quite varied and may involve a wide range. For example, the use of EEGs in collecting data is an example of a technology that may be used in research. Another example, using the Internet to provide counseling, may be an interest in research, for example, text chats and Skype. Additional examples used to determine the effectiveness of various technologies in professional applications include bug in ear, use of the Internet, use of video, use of computers, iPhones, and iPads, virtual reality, tDCS (low-current brain stimulation), and neurofeedback devices. These are only a few examples, but I want to provide an introduction to how technology may be used in research and how it can be applied in counseling and education.

THE INTERNET AND RESEARCH

Jones and Stokes (2009) have stated that online counseling is new to the counseling profession, and it has been identified as starting around 1972. Rochlen, Zack, and Speyer (2004) defined *Internet therapy* as "any type of professional therapeutic interaction that makes use of the Internet to connect qualified mental health professionals and their clients" (p. 270). Online counseling has grown dramatically over the past decade (Chester & Glass, 2006; Maheu & Gordon, 2000; Rochlen, Beretvas, & Zack, 2004). Several different methods have been used with online counseling, and these include asynchronous e-mail, synchronous chat, and videoconferencing. Asynchronous generally involve e-mail formats; e-mail formats was one of the earlier approaches to online counseling. Mallen and Vogel (2005) defined the use of e-mail counseling as "online letter writing." The use of e-mail in counseling provides the client and the counselor with saved transcripts of communications.

Chester and Glass (2006) studied the use of online counseling. They found that, generally, experienced counselors engaged in online counseling, and they provided counseling primarily to female clients. Also, the interventions used were short-term interventions. In another study using the Internet in counseling, Rochlen, Zach, and Speyer (2004) investigated the development of an instrument to assess consumer and client attitudes toward Internet counseling. They found that consumers reported favorable attitudes toward online counseling. A related concept involving the use of technology and the Internet concerns psychological presence. Presence is defined as a sense of being there in a shared environment despite not experiencing a physical presence with others. There have been different types of technology tools that have been studied in understanding psychological presence (Flynn, van Schaik, Blackman, et al., 2003; Jerome & Jordon, 2007). For example, avatars have been studied in virtual environments and how they impact psychological presence (Schuemie, van der Straaten, Krijn, & van der Mast, 2001). Schuemie and colleagues (2001) discussed how virtual reality contributes to presence in the use of technology and therapy environments. Researchers and practitioners have used a virtual environment, for example, Second Life, an online virtual environment, to provide counseling through avatars (avatars are virtual representatives of an entity, a human, in an online environment). The opportunities for using technology and the Internet in research are wide-open. The rapid advances that have been made in developing technology that increases feelings of presence and being there with others will only continue. An example of how the Internet and the use of avatars can be used in counseling raises questions: Is there a difference between treatment outcomes for those experiencing counseling in a virtual world through an avatar versus those experiencing counseling in an office setting? There are numerous other examples of possible research with technology and the Internet.

TEACHING ONLINE

Searson, Jones, and Wold (2011) stated that "virtual education is quickly transforming K–12 education and current forecasts indicate that as many as half of all secondary school courses will be offered in virtual schools by end of the decade" (p. 363). The introduction of online teaching in schools is a significant change from the traditional face-to-face classrooms that have existed for centuries. Searson and colleagues (2011) noted that an important research area with virtual education is the training of teachers who have understanding of the technologies and how best to use them. Additionally, they noted that "there are many possibilities where virtual education could allow us to reimagine schools, and we must continue to explore emerging ideas such as incorporation of mobile devices, integration of informal learning models such as gaming, and incorporation of hybrid learning environments" (p. 367). Certainly, the potential for using technologies in education is in its infancy, and research is needed to promote these significant opportunities.

Ruble, McGrew, Toland, Dalrymple, and Jung (2013) also compared face-to-face teacher coaching and Web-based approaches. These researchers focused on those coaching those with autism through the different mediums, that is, technology versus face-to-face. The researchers used Web-based coaching as one independent variable. The Web-based format included teachers using video and Web cams to provide the coaching to students who have been diagnosed with autism. Those who received the Web-based instruction performed as well as those receiving traditional face-to-face coaching, supporting the hypothesis that technology-based coaching was equally effective.

INTERACTIVE VIDEO

Another technology that has been used in conducting research is interactive video (Baron & Hutchinson, 1984; Rees & Stone, 2005). Rees and Stone (2005) studied psychologists' reactions to observing a face-to-face counseling session versus a videoconference session. The researchers found that psychologists rated the face-to-face sessions superior to the videoconference sessions. In this case, the technology was rated as inferior to the face-to-face counseling sessions. Baron and Hutchinson (1984) discussed the use of interactive video in training counselors. They concluded that such interactive video could be used by counselors to learn various skills at their own pace.

BUG IN EAR

Bug in ear is a technology that was used in the 1960s in counseling, but it is not used much any longer. In counseling, computers have replaced bug in ear, a computer placed behind a client so the counselor can see any comments or feedback. Bug in ear has been introduced into education more recently and is an approach that allows for immediate feedback at a distance (Sheeler, Congdon, & Stansbery, 2010). Sheeler and colleagues (2010) used bug in ear to coach teachers in working with children with special needs. The researchers found that the use of this technology was effective, and the participants, teachers, generalized the feedback they received to other settings with success.

iPADS AND iPHONES

The use of iPads and iPhones has shown significant potential in education and counseling (Geist, 2011; Jabaley, Lutzker, Whitaker, & Self-Brown, 2011). Geist (2011) discussed the use of an iPad in higher education. He noted the need to rethink how teaching occurred in higher education, particularly the relevance of using technology to improve learning. He further stated, "The next generation of students will be vastly different from any before due to mobile devices and the ubiquitous availability of information and data. Pedagogy will need to evolve to meet the needs of these students" (p. 760). Geist studied the use of iPads in a teacher education program. He was interested in the benefits and uses of iPads by preservice teachers and the faculty member teaching the course. An example of one of the questions he addressed was "how the students would creatively use this technology in their teaching experiences" (p. 763). This is one example of how an iPad might be used in research.

Jabaley and colleagues (2011) studied the use of iPhones in promoting effective parenting and reducing childhood maltreatment. The iPhone in the study was used to video the home environment and provide feedback on how to reduce danger for the child. The iPhone was used in place of some home visits and increased the opportunity to provide feedback to the parents by the home visitor. The researchers concluded that future research could focus on additional interventions to promote child safety. Also, the iPhone can facilitate quality and more frequent interaction between parents and professionals. It is much easier to communicate through a mobile device like an iPhone than make a home visit, which takes time and costs more.

VIRTUAL REALITY

Another use of technology that has been particularly important in counseling is the use of virtual reality (Anderson, Price, Edwards, et al., 2013; Opris, Pintea,

Garcia-Palacios, et al., 2012). The use of virtual reality has been used in the treatment of various mental health disorders such as anxiety disorders. Anderson and colleagues (2013) focused on the use of virtual reality in the treatment of social anxiety. They used virtual reality exposure therapy, exposing the person to a social situation that created anxiety for them but using virtual reality for the exposure rather than a real-life situation. An example of the virtual reality situation is described by the researchers: "Virtual environments included a virtual conference room (about five audience members), a virtual classroom (35 audience members), and a virtual auditorium (100 + audience members). Therapists could manipulate audience reactions in a number of ways including making them appear interested, bored, supportive, hostile, distracted" (p. 4). One can see the benefit of using this type of technology where the circumstances can be controlled as well as designed to fit the needs of the client (e.g., in this circumstance, treating social anxiety).

One of the early uses of virtual reality in counseling has been with the treatment of combat veterans who have been diagnosed with PTSD (McLay, McBrien, Wiederhold, & Wiederhold, 2010; Ready, Gerardi, Backscheider, Mascaro, & Rothbaum, 2010; Rothbaum, Hodges, Alarcon, et al., 1999). Rothbaum and colleagues (1999) conducted one of the first studies using virtual reality in the treatment of PTSD. They focused their treatment on those who were combat veterans in Vietnam. They used virtual reality glasses (as the technology), and they provided two immersive environments, replicating experiences and environments in combat (experiencing riding in a combat helicopter). Also, the participant was able to use a joystick that allowed him to walk through the environment. Sounds of the environment were added that replicated gunfire, mine explosions, and verbal commands by colleagues. The virtual reality experience was introduced systematically along with interventions, that is, teaching a breathing relaxation method. Ready and colleagues (2010) conducted another study that used virtual reality in the treatment of PTSD with Vietnam veterans. In the Ready study, they compared the use of virtual reality to treatment using person-centered therapy. They again replicated the Vietnam combat environments with the virtual reality technology. They did not find any differences, but the technology allowed them to attempt to replicate the veterans' experiences and attempt an alternative treatment. The use of virtual reality with veterans has continued with more recent combat veterans (McLay et al., 2010). The treatment took place in a combat theater, Fallujah, Iraq. Through exposure therapy and the use of virtual reality, the researchers presented 3-D images of combat environments, which were viewed through a head-mounted display (technology). The researchers found that the use of virtual reality did reduce PTSD symptoms. Research using virtual reality with those experiencing combat and PTSD has shown significant promise, and future research continues with this technology.

Opris and colleagues (2012) completed a meta-analysis of the use of virtual reality exposure therapy and treatment of anxiety disorders. They cited 23 studies, and they found that the use of virtual reality therapy did have a better effect than those who did not receive treatment. They noted that future research may involve comparing virtual reality exposure therapy to other treatments, including technology-based treatments such as Internet counseling.

NEUROSCIENCE AND TECHNOLOGY

Technologies used in neuroscience that are applicable to counseling and education, educational neuroscience, and research have shown significant advances. Three examples of this type of technology are the use of EEG, tDCS, and neurofeedback. EEG is used primarily in assessment (Harmon-Jones & Amodio, 2012). EEG involves collecting electrical brain activity from the scalp (Harmon-Jones & Amodio, 2012). Harmon-Jones and Amodio (2012) described what occurs so that EEG may be collected and stated, "Electrical activity that is associated with neurons comes from action potentials and postsynaptic potentials. Action potentials are composed of a rapid series of electrochemical changes that run from the beginning of the axon at the cell body to the axon terminals where neurotransmitters are released" (p. 503). The Food and Drug Administration recently approved the use of EEG in the assessment of attention deficit hyperactivity disorder (ADHD; http://www.fda.gov/newsevents/newsroom/pressannouncements/ucm360811.htm). Autism spectrum disorder is another condition that has been diagnosed with EEG, quantitative electroencephalogram (qEEG; Linden & Gunkelman, 2013). QEEG is founded on comparing an individual to a normed reference group. Linden and Gunkelman (2013) noted that the use of qEEG can result in identification of abnormal amplitude, that is, high or low amplitude in certain brain waves.

The past 12 years have seen a dramatic increase in the use of tDCS in the treatment of a number of conditions in an effort to promote brain functioning (Jacobson, Koslowsky, & Lavidor, 2012; Marangolo, Marinelli, Bonifazi, et al., 2011; Schutter, 2012); there have been more than 200 studies reported in the professional literature. Researchers have studied many different brain functions using tDCS, and they include decision making (Hecht, Walsh, & Lavidor, 2010), language production (Wirth, Rahman, Kuenecke, et al., 2011, cognitive (Jacobson et al., 2012), and speech apraxia (Hecht et al., 2010). These studies suggest that the stimulation of specific brain regions through anodal stimulation (positive electrode) results in an increase of neuronal potentiation (Jacobson et al., 2012). In contrast, cathode stimulation (negative electrode) results in reduced functioning of the neurons and reduction in potentiation of the neurons

(Jacobson et al., 2012; Marshall, Molle, Siebner, & Born, 2005). Researchers also have found that repeated anodal stimulation (positive anode) produces longer-term effects (Boggio, Nunes, Rigonatti et al., 2007).

There have been a few studies using tDCS and applications to counseling (Mattai, Miller, Weisinger, et al., 2011). Mattai and colleagues (2011) investigated the use of tDCS with childhood-onset schizophrenia. They were initially interested in how well children could tolerate the administration of tDCS. They did find that these children were able to tolerate sessions of tDCS. Fregni, Boggio, Nitsche, Rigonatti, and Pascul-Leone (2006) discussed the use of tDCS in the treatment of depression. They applied the positive electrode, or anode, to the left dorsolateral prefrontal cortex. They did not impact the symptoms of depression, but they improved working memory through repeated administrations. The potential to use tDCS with mental health issues is significant, and there needs to be additional research.

Houser and colleagues (2013) conducted a study to determine if stimulation of the left intraparietal sulcus (IPS) improved statistical calculations, for example, educational neuroscience. A posttest-only research design with random assignment was used. There were three conditions, two experimental and one control. The control group was connected to the tDCS stimulator, and the sham condition was administered. The two experimental conditions received either a 1 or 2 mA stimulation for 20 minutes. The researchers found that those who received low-current, 1 mA, stimulation (anodal) over the left IPS performed significantly better than those receiving a 2 mA stimulation (anode placed over the left IPS and the cathode placed over or the left DLPFC). It appears that lower scores for the 2 mA group may be a result of the placement of the cathode, or negative electrode, which may have impacted selective attention and higher executive function, decreasing long-term potentiation (long-term depression).

The use of neurofeedback is another technology that has potential for both counseling and education. Neurofeedback is based upon an initial assessment of brain functioning through EEG. According to Gunkelman and Johnstone (2005), an EEG shows rhythmic waveforms, or brain waves. Waveforms have been categorized into alpha, beta, theta, delta, and gamma waves. Waves are a consequence of electrical oscillations due to neuronal activity (Nunez, 1974). Brain waves are categorized according to frequency bands, shapes, and amplitudes (Heinrich, Gevensleben, & Strehl, 2007; Myers & Young, 2012). Delta waves are associated with sleep and generally are less than 4 Hz. Theta waves occur when people are daydreaming or experience drowsiness and are associated with 4 to 8 Hz (Heinrich et al., 2007; Myers & Young, 2012). Alpha waves represent the brain and neurons in readiness for action but in a standby state (8 to 13 Hz). Also, alpha waves are associated with a relaxed state. Beta waves (13–30 Hz) are associated with thinking, focusing, and maintaining attention, whereas high beta waves (20–32 Hz) are associated with hyperactivity and anxiety (Myers & Young 2012). Finally, gamma waves in essence serve to bind the other waves and appear to be involved in connectivity between different brain regions (30–80 Hz). Colgin, Denninger, Fyhn, et al. (2009) described gamma waves as a binding mechanism for neurons, so they fire together. Gamma waves have been associated with cognitive functioning (Colgin et al., 2009). Vernon (2005) stated that the goal of neurofeedback training is "to teach the individual what specific states of cortical arousal feel like and how to activate such states voluntarily. For example, during neurofeedback training the EEG is recorded and the relevant components are extracted and fed back to the individual using an online feedback loop in the form of audio, visual or combined audio/visual information" (p. 348). Neurofeedback is based on operant conditioning and reinforcement of changes in the neuronal structure or brain waves.

There has been initial research into the use of neurofeedback attempting to change abnormal brave wave functioning for those with various conditions. Those with conditions such as ADHD and autism have been found to have differences in brain waves compared to those who do not have these conditions (Chan & Leung, 2006; Gunkelman & Johnstone, 2005). For example, those with ADHD have been found to have increased theta activity in the frontal regions (Barry, Clarke, Hajos, et al., 2010). Barry and colleagues (2010) also found reduced levels of gamma in children with ADHD. Neurofeedback has been used to increase performance in those that do not have significant impairments too (Heinrich et al., 2007). Egner and Gruzelier (2003) attempted to change the alpha-to-theta ratio for students with a goal of enhancing musical performance. Others have used neurofeedback to improve cognitive performance (Vernon, 2005). Use of neurofeedback in counseling and education is in its infancy, and the potential for future research is wide-open.

SUMMARY

Technology is having an increasing role in counseling and educational research. The use of technology in research is incredibly varied. Technologies that are being used in counseling and education include EEG, use of bug in the ear, use of the Internet, use of video, use of computers, iPhones and iPads, virtual reality, tDCS (low-current brain stimulation), and neurofeedback devices. There are other technologies that are being used in counseling and education, and I have only introduced a few examples. Such technologies have the potential to significantly change how counseling and education professionals engage in our practice. There is potential excitement with these advances because they can transform the professions and improve the quality and efficacy of our disciplines.

21

Current and Future Issues in Counseling and Educational Research

Counseling and education practitioners are confronted more and more with pressure to incorporate research into practice. Sociopolitical influences increasingly require demonstration of effectiveness in practice. At this point in the discussion, I hope that you have a broad appreciation of the importance of the study and application of research in the practice of your profession. In this chapter, I hope to solidify your (positive) attitudes toward a practitioner–scientist or a scientist–practitioner (if you prefer) model for your profession and alert you to current and future issues confronting counseling and educational research. Therefore, there is discussion of the following issues: the relevance of the practitioner–scientist view, the connection of the practitioner–scientist and scientist–practitioner view with evidence-based practice, and how to conduct and implement research from a cross-cultural and diversity perspective.

THE PRACTITIONER–SCIENTIST MODEL

There has been considerable debate over why the scientist–practitioner model has not worked for professionals practicing in the fields of counseling and education (Hoshmand & Polkinghorne, 1992; Kanfer, 1990; Love et al., 2007; Lowman, 2012; Overholser, 2010). This tension, as has been noted earlier, centers on training programs that expect practitioners to embrace research and share a worldview of research similar to that of those training the practitioners, that is, the university faculty members of the training institutions (Barnette, 2006). However, others have noted problems with this view and that practitioners cannot pragmatically share such a worldview concerning how much time and effort should be devoted to conducting research in a practice setting (Bernstein & Kerr, 1993; Heppner et al., 1992; Love et al., 2007). Another view is that those most of the research, or academics, have lost touch with practice (Overholser, 2010). A variation of the scientist–practitioner model is the practitioner–scientist model. In the practitioner–scientist approach, the emphasis is on practice but practice that is based on a perspective and foundation of science and evidence-based research.

Several researchers have offered helpful viewpoints in understanding and potentially implementing the practitioner–scientist model (Hoshmand & Polkinghorne, 1992; Kanfer, 1990; Love et al., 2007; Luebbe, Radcliffe, Callands, Green, & Thorn, 2007). Hoshmand and Polkinghorne (1992) stated that "the test for knowledge is whether it serves to guide human action to attain goals. . . . The test is pragmatic" (p. 58). As Gelso (2006) suggested, training in the scientist–practitioner model need not be rigidly implemented with equal emphasis on research and practice. In addition, Heppner and colleagues (1992) suggested that there can be much different configuration than a simple 50–50 split of time between practice and research—80 percent focus on practice and 20 percent on research, for instance. The issue, as I see it, for practitioners in counseling and education is to find the pragmatic and realistic proportion of emphasis on practice and research. Related to the issue of emphasis is a further clarification and definition of what it means to operate from a practitioner–scientist model, and this will need to come from practitioners who realistically use and conduct research in their practices.

Kanfer (1990) proposed steps to bridging science and practice based on a problem-solving approach. These steps include (1) identifying the problem; (2) operationalizing the problem; (3) identifying principles, theories, and research that are applicable to solving the problem; (4) identifying desired outcomes; (5) selecting a strategy; (6) implementing and monitoring the strategy; and (7) returning to (3) if the desired outcomes are not achieved. Basically, Kanfer (1990) suggested continuous, systematic hypothesis testing and experimentation to resolve practice issues. Key in this approach is the search for information, scientific research information that will form the basis of the intervention or strategy. You can use the newly developed skills acquired from the research published in the professional literature to identify relevant and potentially effective strategies to test.

Love and colleagues (2007) proposed a creative approach to integrating science and practice. They suggested early learning experiences with research during academic training. Faculty and student research teams can facilitate the development of research self-efficacy and provide support through the process. Also, they noted the importance of an academic environment that supports and encourages research activities. One aspect of such an environment is faculty modeling successful integration of research into practice. Another important aspect of the academic environment, according to Love and colleagues (2007) is working as a team on research projects. These researchers found that team effort on a research project resulted in higher research self-efficacy ratings.

Luebbe and colleagues (2007) provided an interesting view of differentiating more traditional science views and evidence-based practice views. The differentiation is focused on understanding the definitions and practical aspects of two different scholarly activities: empirically supported treatment and evidence-based practice. They defined empirically supported treatment as follows: "An empirically supported treatment is a product derived from randomized clinical trials" (p. 645). They differentiated the two views, science views and evidence-based practice views. They defined evidence-based practice this way:

> Evidence-based practice in psychology is a process that incorporates the retrieval and examination of scientific evidence. Further, EBP presents a method for finding and evaluating the best available research evidence, whether it means randomized clinical trials (the foundation of EST) or other forms of high quality evidence. (p. 645)

Essentially, empirically supported treatment is a subset of evidence-based practice in which clinical trials provide important evidence to facilitate in the decision making, whereas evidence-based practice is a broader process focused on discovering the best available research evidence, including evidence not found in empirically supported treatment. Evidence-based practice may include the best available evidence (research results from several research sources), not just clinical trials. The use of an evidence-based practice process for practitioners focuses the effort on collecting and evaluating scientific information, which fits well with a practitioner–scientist orientation.

As a practitioner, you cannot take time to search out scientific information for each individual you work with in a counseling or educational setting. However, several criteria may be helpful to employ when considering the use of the scientific approach: (1) Note whether progressively difficult situations arise that are resistant to change and in which repeated attempts with traditional methods are unsuccessful; (2) determine if there are multiple situations or persons who share similar issues and could benefit from a new approach or intervention; (3) if you are working with certain ethnic, racial, gender, or other variables, decide whether traditional strategies are applicable or whether less-traditional methods may be more appropriate; or (4) focus on a particular interest of your own that will be exciting and stimulating to explore.

In summary, the practitioner–scientist issue concerns a need to clarify the definition and characteristics of a practitioner–scientist model. Practitioners and academics (those training practitioners) also need to identify practical methods of implementing a practitioner–scientist model based in reality, one that is not an unachievable ideal. A question to consider for yourself as you enter your professional practice is how you will integrate research into your everyday work. Lowman (2012) offered three helpful suggestions on how to provide a link between science and practice: "1) Work with issues that are important; 2) measure outcomes that are important (at multiple levels of satisfaction); and 3) share knowledge effectively" (p. 152).

THE RELEVANCE OF RESEARCH TO PRACTICE

The issues presented here are not mutually exclusive; they are distinctly related. The second issue confronting counselors and educators, beyond an orientation of practitioner–scientist or scientist–practitioner, is the relevance of research to practice. The issue of making research relevant to practice has been a consistent debate over the past several decades (Berninger, Dunn, Shin-Ju, & Shimada, 2004; Pfeiffer, Burd, & Wright, 1992; Sexton, 1996; Sexton & Whiston, 1996). It has been noted that practitioners typically have negative attitudes toward research (Barnette, 2006). Several reasons may be cited for these negative attitudes, attitudes that contribute to the problem of connecting research to practice. One reason is the use of highly technical language typically presented in professional journals, as you most likely have experienced in reading articles for earlier chapters of this book. This has been a problem in a lot of the counseling and educational literature. Researchers typically are academics, and therefore, write research articles for other academics and not for practitioners. However, in applied fields such as counseling and education, the purpose (for the most part) of research published in professional journals is the application of the knowledge gained, and application is most likely to be accomplished by practitioners. Thus, those publishing professional journals will need to address this problem of making published research more readable (this does not mean less sophisticated or complex).

The second problem concerning the issue of relating research to practice is an attempt to find the best methods of research. Traditional scientific methods, which were developed from the natural sciences and use a laboratory model, have dominated the social sciences until recently. In applied fields like education and counseling, laboratory research results may not be as applicable as field-based research methods. There has been a significant increase in the use of qualitative methods, which typically involve efforts to study naturally occurring events. However, there has been a reluctance to accept field-based research to some degree because of the suspected limitations (e.g., threats to internal validity). The recent introduction of evidence-based practice processes is helping to change the efforts to link research to practice.

It has been noted that there has been a conflict surrounding the practitioner's view that research reported in the professional literature is based on laboratory research methods and not the natural environment. This conflict has led some researchers to propose alternative research designs. Hoshmand (1989) suggested that acceptance of any alternative research designs in the social sciences (and other disciplines) has been slow, but some progress has been made recently. The major argument concerns loss of control when one does not use traditional laboratory methods, which (theoretically) increases threats to internal validity. In reality, until recently, it has been difficult for researchers to get research published in professional journals when the research is not based on traditional scientific methods. There are concerns over loss of control, for instance, when a study is conducted in the natural environment, where the researcher typically has little control over extraneous variables.

Several researchers have proposed interesting ideas on how to address this issue of the use in the social sciences of traditional quantitative methods versus nontraditional or qualitative designs (De Anda, 2007; Ferguson & Bibby, 2004). De Anda (2007) proposed a model for conducting research that involves the use of quasi-experimental methods. She suggested using a single-group, pretest–posttest design and collecting data over several groups at different times to include in comparisons. The comparison would be a correlated test but with the use of several groups over a period of time. She noted that it is possible to use the interventions with different groups over a period of time, which would help in controlling for threats, such as history. For example, a researcher could study a particular teaching method with students in high school algebra and conduct a pretest–posttest analysis. An important additional step is to try the teaching method with additional algebra classes over a period of time.

I discussed ways for practitioners to systematically implement research and evaluation in actual practice situations in previous chapters. I also noted that certain methods are more feasible to implement than others (e.g., quasi-experimental designs and qualitative designs). However, it is important to be aware that this issue of whether traditional or alternative methods are better exists and that it may create problems in gaining acceptance of results obtained by alternative methods.

In summary, there are two problems with the issue of relating research to practice. First, the use of highly technical writing in professional journals that describes research and is designed to be read by academics creates problems when relating research to practice. Second, the fields of counseling and research need to develop methods of conducting research that are considered relevant and useful to the practitioner, methods that may not necessarily be based on traditional laboratory methods.

CONDUCTING RESEARCH: A CROSS-CULTURAL AND DIVERSITY PERSPECTIVE

We live in a world that is becoming more and more diverse, with fewer homogeneous groups, and we are confronted with the issue of how to provide counseling and educational services to a diverse target population (Adams, 2012; Sandford, 2010; Van Tassel-Baska, 2013). Van Tassel-Baska (2013) noted that future educational research addressing diversity should involve comparative studies across cultures and countries. The issues surrounding research from a cross-cultural and diversity perspective are based on concerns such as who should conduct cross-cultural research and how research results can be applied ethically to a diverse population (population research).

The first issue, who should conduct cross-cultural research, has received spirited debate (Fitzgerald, 2006; Ponterotto, 1993; Sue, 1993). Parham (1993) questioned whether those from white racial backgrounds could effectively conduct minority research. Fitzgerald (2006) cited several concerns in conducting cross-cultural research. First, there are issues in the use of measurements for two reasons. One is that the stimuli of the measurements may not be sensitive to different cultures; for example, the translation of the instrument may not be consistent. Second, the instrument may not be appropriate for the cultural population. Another issue centers on assumptions made in making comparisons; that is, a cultural group is relatively homogeneous. Fitzgerald (2006) pointed out that there can be more differences within cultures than between cultures. Ponterotto (1993) noted that white researchers may experience concerns over rejection and challenge in conducting research focusing on minorities. The question then becomes, should only those from minority backgrounds conduct minority and cross-cultural research? Sue (1993) noted increased tension among different racial and ethnic minority groups. Consequently, can researchers from one racial or ethnic group conduct research that addresses all groups? Several investigators have suggested that one group may not be "qualified" to conduct cross-cultural research, and it has been proposed that the best solution is for researchers from different racial backgrounds to collaborate in developing and conducting research (Atkinson, 1993; Mio & Iwamasa, 1993).

An issue that is sensitive for most professionals as they work with their populations is the role of spirituality and religion (Adams, 2012; Walker & Aten, 2012). Adams noted how slowly professionals have embraced the relevance of spirituality in practice. Additionally, she noted that most professionals are uncomfortable addressing these topics: spirituality and religion. However, survey research has found that more than three-fourths of the U.S. population believes in God or report that spirituality and religion are important to them. An additional issue beyond the view that most professionals are uncomfortable with addressing spirituality and religion in practice is the issue that training programs do not prepare professionals to address these topics. Future research needs to be conducted that explores how spirituality and religion are taught and how professionals may best utilize this natural connection to those with whom they work.

Another concern is whether research results can be ethically applied to diverse populations, which is particularly relevant to you as a practitioner. As has been noted previously in Chapter 10, Ethics and Research, the application of research results may cause harm to a population, particularly if the results portray a particular ethnic group negatively. Population research may be a problem when the interpretation of the results is based on a particular orientation, such as that of the dominant majority. It has been suggested that, to avoid interpreting and applying research results inappropriately, which could possibly harm a population, there should be training in and awareness of cross-cultural issues for practitioners (LaFromboise & Foster, 1992).

SUMMARY

Several issues confront counseling and educational research: the application of the practitioner–scientist view, the relevance of research to practice and how to use alternative research designs, and how to conduct and implement research from a cross-cultural and diversity perspective. There are not any easy solutions to these issues. However, as a practitioner, it is important for you to be aware of the issues when you go about the practice of your profession. It will be essential for you to continue reading and using the professional literature so that you can practice your profession ethically and effectively. At this point in your training, it is hoped that you have a certain amount of respect for the research process, tempered with a critical eye, so that you can systematically assess what will be potentially useful to you in the practice of your profession.

GLOSSARY

AB single-subject research design The most basic single-subject design is the AB design. This design starts with a baseline A, which is then followed by an intervention B.

ABA single-subject research design This design begins with a period of baseline A, followed by an intervention B, which is then followed by a return to baseline A. All assessment phases, baseline or intervention, in single-subject research involve multiple or continuous assessments.

ABAB single-subject research design The primary format for this design is the introduction of a clear baseline setting or environment followed by introduction of the intervention or independent variable, ABAB.

accessible population All individuals of the target population who can feasibly be accessed for participation in a study.

alpha level The level of (statistical) significance set by the researcher for rejecting the null hypothesis.

alternative hypothesis A statistical hypothesis based on a rejection of the null hypothesis.

analysis of covariance (ANCOVA) A statistical calculation comparing differences of means between two or more groups that statistically controls for one or more extraneous variables. The results are reported in adjusted means for the groups, based on the influence or effects of the extraneous variables.

analysis of variance (ANOVA) A parametric inferential statistical procedure designed to compare differences between the means of two or more groups.

baseline The natural level of performance as measured from the dependent variable of the sample prior to introduction of the independent variable or an intervention.

case study A detailed investigation of an individual, group, organization, or other assemblage.

chi-square A nonparametric inferential statistical procedure designed to determine whether collected data (nominal data) are significantly different from what was expected.

cluster sampling A sampling technique in which a sample is chosen of naturally occurring groups or intact units, and all individuals in the group are studied.

concurrent validity The degree to which responses on a new test correspond to responses on an established test. Also, the extent to which scores on a test correspond to the present behavior of an individual.

confounding variable A variable other than those being studied that could potentially affect the research outcome. Extraneous variable.

construct A concept that is proposed to explain commonalities among phenomena or theories.

construct validity The degree to which scores on a test measure an actual construct that they are intended to measure.

content validity The extent to which the test items represent the concepts that they intend to measure.

control group A group used in an experimental study that receives no treatment and that is compared to an experimental group based on dependent measures.

convenience sample A sampling technique that is based on availability of the sample (e.g., a sample that is easy to access).

correlation coefficient An expressed strength of relationship between two variables and the direction of the strength of the relationship.

correlational research A type of study that focuses on clarifying the extent of correlation between two variables.

criterion-related validity The degree to which scores obtained on a dependent measure correlate to an identified standard or observable behavior.

dependent variable The variable that is affected by the independent variable.

descriptive research Research that involves defining existing conditions or characteristics.

descriptive statistics Statistical methods used to summarize the results of a sample.

directional hypothesis A hypothesis that is based on previous research, theory, or personal experience and that involves predicting the direction of the outcome.

ecological validity The degree to which research results obtained in a certain situation can be generalized back to the natural environment.

effect size The degree to which an independent variable influences the dependent variable.

ethnographic research Qualitative research methods that focus on exploring and describing cultural or social phenomena.

evidence-based practice An organized process of systematically gathering research evidence to support the choice of a particular practice.

experimental group The group in an experiment that receives the intervention or manipulation (the group that receives the independent variable).

experimental mortality The degree to which study participants drop out during the course of the study.

external validity The degree to which results from an experiment can be generalized to other individuals beyond the study.

extraneous variable A variable in a study that has the potential to influence results but that is not the focus of the study.

face validity The extent to which a measure or technique appears to measure what it is designed to measure.

factor analysis A statistical procedure in which clusters of items are highly correlated and form factors that relate to a criterion.

formative evaluation Evaluation that involves assessing the effort and quality needed to implement a program. It does not concern the effectiveness of the program but how well the program is implemented.

Hawthorne Effect A change in the outcome or dependent variable as a consequence of receiving special attention (e.g., awareness of being in a research study might have an effect that would not be related to the independent variable).

historical research A research method that is designed to study past phenomena or events to understand current situations.

hypothesis A formally stated prediction of an outcome that is based on previous research, theory, or personal experience.

independent variable Generally, the variable that is manipulated and affects another variable, that is, the dependent variable. There are also measurement types of independent variables that are not manipulated but are hypothesized to affect another variable.

indirect proof Refers to seeking clarification about the validity of a theory through scientific methods but never obtaining direct proof supporting a theory or hypothesis.

inferential statistics Parametric statistical procedures that are used to make inferences about results from a sample to a population.

informed consent The research subject's agreement to participate in a study after a researcher has performed his or her ethical and legal duty to inform potential subjects about their freedom to choose to participate in the study and what that participation would entail.

internal consistency The extent to which items on a test correlate to each other. It refers to respondents to a test making consistent types of responses to items on a test.

internal validity The degree to which a researcher controls for and reduces the effects of extraneous variables that can affect study outcomes so that they represent true outcomes.

inter-rater reliability The degree to which raters agree in their scores of the same observable behavior.

interval scale A measurement scale that is expressed in equal units with no true zero. Most mathematical operations may be performed on interval data.

intervening variable A variable that influences the relationship between the independent and dependent variables. There would be a different outcome between the independent and dependent variables without the intervening variable's influence.

levels of significance The probability that results obtained from one sample (experimental) group will differ significantly from those obtained from another (control) group.

mean The arithmetic average of scores.

measurement scales Units of measurement defined in terms of nominal, ordinal, interval, and ratio data.

measures of central tendency A mathematical expression that summarizes scores and distribution of scores based on a sample.

measures of variability A mathematical expression of how scores in a distribution vary from one another.

median A score in a distribution of scores that is exactly at the 50th percentile.

meta-search engine A computer search engine that combines requests into several search engines, so the user can access results from several different sources without searching individual sources.

mode The most frequently occurring score in a distribution.

multiple analysis of variance (MANOVA) A statistical calculation used to compare differences between means of two or more groups and differences between two or more dependent variables (the dependent variables correlate in some way).

multiple baseline research design A single-subject design that involves the use of different baselines, for example, across individuals, different behaviors, or different settings.

multiple regression A statistical procedure in which the magnitude of the relationship between a predicted variable and two or more predictor variables is calculated.

multiple time series design A quasi-experimental design that involves several groups receiving treatment in which multiple assessments of the dependent variable occur.

nominal scale A scale in which data or scores identify categories, such as gender and ethnicity.

nondirectional hypothesis A prediction that there is a difference between research groups (e.g., the control and experimental groups), but no direction is indicated.

nonparametric statistics Inferential statistics that are based on data that are not necessarily normally distributed.

normal distribution A frequency distribution of scores, typically represented by a bell-shaped curve and symmetrically shaped around the mean.

null hypothesis A prediction that no differences or relationships exist between the dependent variables and the effects of any independent variables among groups studied.

ordinal scale The organization of data that are represented by rank order (e.g., military rank).

parameters Numbers that define certain characteristics of the population.

parametric statistics Inferential statistics used to analyze data that are normally distributed.

paradigm A pattern of defined scientific practices.

Pearson correlation coefficient A mathematical expression of the strength of the relationship between two or more variables. Scores may range from –1.0 to +1.0.

plagiarism Occurs when someone uses another's ideas or writings as his or her own. Plagiarism can be intentional or unintentional.

population The group of individuals that is identified as having certain characteristics of interest to the researcher. A sample with well-defined characteristics is drawn from a population.

population validity The degree of accuracy with which results from a particular study may be generalized to the population of interest.

post-hoc comparisons Mathematical procedures used with certain inferential statistical methods (ANOVAs) to determine whether significant differences exist between three or more groups.

predictive validity The degree to which one measurement or set of data predicts what actually, naturally occurs.

process evaluation The method of collecting information that will be used to evaluate how effectively a program is being implemented.

program evaluation The methods employed to evaluate the goals, objectives, and outcomes of social programs.

qualitative research Established approaches to studying social phenomena using language to define and describe the outcomes. No numbers or mathematical operations are employed in qualitative research approaches.

quantitative research Well-established research methods that employ numbers and mathematical procedures to express and explain research outcomes.

quasi-experimental research An experimental method in which there is a manipulation of the independent variable but no random assignment.

random assignment The method of assigning individuals from a sample to experimental or control groups. The basis of this method is that everyone chosen for a sample must have an equal chance of being in any of the groups.

random selection A collection of methods of selecting study participants (a sample) from a population. These methods include simple random sampling, systematic random sampling, stratified random sampling, and others.

range A measure of variability that is expressed in terms of the lowest and highest scores in a distribution of scores.

ratio scale Data or scores that include a true zero in which scores are equidistant. Ratio scales allow for computing with any mathematical calculations.

regression toward the mean A change in the extreme scores, with subsequent testing to more moderate scores as a result of chance influences not consistently expressed.

reliability The degree of consistency in data or scores, either within scores or over time.

sample A group or unit selected from a larger target population. The sample is intended to be representative of the larger population.

search engine A program designed to search the Internet (the World Wide Web) for information.

science The acquisition of knowledge, a systematic approach, and an objective analysis with opportunities for conclusions about how our world may function.

scientific misconduct Refers to data falsification or plagiarism.

single-subject experimental design The use of a single subject with a manipulation or experiment conducted over a period of time. In addition, there are multiple measurements of the dependent variable (e.g., behavioral observations of the dependent variable).

Spearman correlation A linear correlation between nonparametric data (pairs of ranks).

split-half reliability A type of test of reliability that involves the calculation of a correlation between two different parts of a test (e.g., calculating the correlation between all odd questions and all even questions).

standard deviation A standard measure of the degree to which scores vary from the mean.

stratified random sampling A method of selecting participants for a study in which certain characteristics are identified as relevant to control. Participants are then chosen randomly to reflect these characteristics of the population. Stratification may be proportional or nonproportional.

structural equation modeling A statistical technique that is used in theory testing.

systematic random sampling A method of selecting a sample in which every nth participant is chosen from an accessible population.

t-*test* A parametric statistical procedure that involves the comparison of two means.

test-retest reliability A measure of test reliability that involves the correlation or consistency between two different administrations of the same test at two different times.

time series design A research design that involves a manipulation with one experimental group and uses multiple measurements of the dependent variables over a period of time.

triangulation The convergence of data collection through several methods or procedures.

true experiment A study that includes two conditions: (1) random assignment to experimental groups and (2) a manipulation of the independent variable.

type I error A decision based on statistical calculations in which rejection of the null hypothesis is made when the hypothesis should not be rejected (e.g., when the null hypothesis is true).

type II error A decision based on statistical calculations in which the null hypothesis is accepted when it should be rejected.

validity The degree to which a method or procedure measures what it is intended to measure.

variable A construct or concept that can be measured or operationalized and that can be quantified.

variance The degree to which scores are dispersed about the mean. It is calculated by squaring the standard deviation.

Wilcoxon signed-rank test A nonparametric statistical procedure to determine the differences between two groups, based on an identified dependent variable.

References

Adams, J. (2012). Spiritual issues in counseling: What do students perceive they are being taught? *Counseling and Values, 57*, 66–79.

Admi, H. (1996). Growing up with a chronic health condition: A model of an ordinary lifestyle. *Qualitative Health Research, 6*(2), 163–183.

Alcoholics Anonymous. (1952). *Twelve steps and twelve traditions.* New York: Alcoholics Anonymous World Services.

Alise, M., & Teddlie, C. (2010). A continuation of the paradigm wars? Prevalence rates of methodological approaches across the social/behavioral sciences. *Journal of Mixed Methods Research, 4*(2), 103–126.

Aljughaiman, A., & Ayoub, A. (2012). The effect of an enrichment program on developing analytical creative, and practical abilities of elementary gifted students. *Journal for the Education of the Gifted, 35*(2), 153–174.

American Counseling Association. (1995). *Code of ethics and standards of practice.* Alexandria, VA: Author.

American Counseling Association. (2005). *ACA code of ethics.* Alexandria, VA: Author.

American Educational Research Association, American Psychological Association, & National Council on Measurement in Education. (1999). *Standards for educational and psychological testing.* http://www.apa.org/science/programs/testing/standards.aspx

American Evaluation Association. (2004). *Guiding principles for evaluators.* Retrieved July 24, 2013, from http://www.eval.org/p/cm/ld/fid=51

American Psychological Association. (2003). *Ethical principles of psychologists and code of conduct.* Washington, DC: Author.

American Psychological Association. (2006). Evidence-based practice in psychology. *American Psychologists, 61*(4), 271–285.

American Psychological Association. (2010). *Ethical principles of psychologists and code of conduct: Including 2010 amendments.* Washington, DC: Author.

American Psychological Association Presidential Task Force on Evidence-Based Practice. (2006). Evidence-based practice in psychology. *American Psychologist, 61*(4), 271–285.

Anastasi, A., & Urbina, S. (1997). *Psychological testing* (7th ed.). Upper Saddle River, NJ: Prentice Hall.

Anderson, P., Price, M., Edwards, S., Obasaju, M., Schmertz, S., Zimand, E., & Calamaras, M. (2013). Virtual reality exposure therapy for social anxiety disorder: A randomized controlled trial. *Journal of Consulting and Clinical Psychology, 81*(5), 751–760.

Apel, K. (2011). Science is an attitude: A response to Kamhi. *Language, Speech, and Hearing Services in Schools, 42,* 65–68.

Ary, D., Jacobs, L., & Razavieh, A. (2002). *An introduction to research in education*. Belmont, CA: Wadsworth.

Ary, D., Jacobs, L., & Sorensen, C. (2010). *Introduction to research in education* (8th ed.). Independence, MO: Cengage Learning.

Ary, D., Jacobs, L., Sorensen, C., & Walker, D. (2014). *Introduction to research in education*. Belmont, CA: Cengage Learning.

Atkinson, D. (1993). Who speaks for cross-cultural counseling research? *Counseling Psychologist, 21*(2), 218–224.

Baban, A., & Craciun, C. (2007). The nature and relevance of qualitative research in the era of evidence-based practice. *Cognition, Brain, Behavior, 11*(2), 223–228.

Babbie, E. (2006). *The practice of social research* (11th ed.). Belmont, CA: Wadsworth.

Babbie, E. (2011). *The basics of social research* (5th ed.). Belmont, CA: Wadsworth.

Bakeman, R., & Quera, V. (2012) Behavioral observation. In *APA handbook of research methods in psychology: Volume 1. Foundations, planning, measures, and psychometrics* (pp. 207–226) Washington, DC: American Psychological Association.

Baldwin, S., Wampold, B., & Imel, Z. (2007). Untangling the alliance–outcome correlation: Exploring the relative importance of therapist and patient variability in the alliance. *Journal of Consulting and Clinical Psychology, 75*(6), 842–852.

Balk, D., Walker, A., & Baker, A. (2010). Prevalence and severity of college student bereavement examined in a randomly selected sample. *Death Studies, 34*, 459–468.

Ballespi, S., Jane, M., & Riba, D. (2012). The Behavioral Inhibition Scale for children 3 to 3 (BIS 3–6): Validity based on its relation with observational measures. *Journal of Psychopathology Behavioral Assessment, 34*, 487–496.

Bandura, A. (1977). Self-efficacy: Toward a unifying theory of behavior change. *Psychological Review, 84*, 191–215.

Barclay-Goddard, R., Ripat, J., & Mayo, N. (2012). Developing a model of participation post-stroke: A mixed methods approach. *Qualitative Life Research, 21*, 417–426.

Barlow, D. & Hayes, S. (1979). Alternating treatments designs: One strategy for comparing effects of two treatments in a single subject. *Journal of Applied Behavior Analysis, 12*, 199–210.

Barlow, D. & Hersen, M. (1984). *Single case experimental designs: Strategies for studying behaviour change* (2nd ed.). New York: Pergamon Press.

Barlow, D., Nock, M., & Hersen, M. (2009). *Single case experimental designs: Strategies for studying behavior change* (3rd ed.). Boston: Pearson.

Barnette, V. (2006). A scholarly work commitment in practice. *Counselling Psychology Quarterly, 19*(3), 253–263.

Baron, A. & Hutchinson, J. (1984). Interactive video: A promising technology for counseling services. *Journal of Counseling & Development, 63*(4), 244–247.

Barry, R., Clarke, A., Hajos, M., McCarthy, R., Selikowitz, M., & Dupuy, F. (2010). Resting-state EEG gamma activity in children with attention-deficit/hyperactivity disorder. *Clinical Neurophysiology, 121*(11), 1871–1877.

Barton, C., Sulaiman, N., Clarke, D., & Abramson, M. (2005). Experiences of Australian parents caring for children with asthma: It gets easier. *Chronic Illness, 1*(4), 303–314.

Baumrind, D. (1964). Some thoughts on ethics of research: After reading Milgram's "Behavioral study of obedience." *American Psychologist, 19*, 421–423.

Beauchamp, T. & Childress, J. (2001). *Principles of biomedical ethics*. New York: Oxford University Press.

Beck, V., Boys, S., Rose, C., & Beck, E. (2012). Violence against women in video games: A prequel or sequel to rape myth acceptance? *Journal of Interpersonal Violence, 27*(5), 3016–3031.

Becker-Blease, K., Turner, H., & Finkelhor, D. (2010). Disasters, victimization, and children's mental health. *Child Development, 81*(4), 1040–1052.

Belter, R. & du Pre, A. (2009). A strategy to reduce plagiarism in an undergraduate course. *Teaching of Psychology, 36,* 257–261.

Berg, B. (2004). *Qualitative research methods for the social sciences* (5th ed.). Boston: Pearson.

Bernard, R., Cohen, L., & Moffett, K. (2009). A token economy for exercise adherence in pediatric cystic fibrosis: A single-subject analysis. *Journal of pediatric psychology, 34*(4), 354–365.

Berninger, V., Dunn, A., Shin-Ju, C., & Shimada, S. (2004). School evolution: Scientist–practitioner educators creating optimal learning environments for all students. *Journal of Learning Disabilities, 37*(6), 500–506.

Bernstein, B. & Kerr, B. (1993). Counseling psychology and the scientist-practitioner model: Implementation and implications. *Counseling Psychologist, 21*(1), 136–151.

Best, J. & Kahn, J. (1998). *Research in education* (8th ed.). Boston: Allyn & Bacon.

Best, J. & Kahn, J. (2003). *Research in education* (9th ed.). Boston: Allyn & Bacon.

Binder, P., Moltu, C., Sagen, S., Hummelsund, D., & Holgersen, H. (2013). *Journal of Psychotherapeutic Integration,* March, 1–13.

Bishop, D., Barry, J., & Hardiman, M. (2012). Delayed retention of new word-forms is better in children than adults regardless of language ability: A factorial two-way study. *Plos One, 7*(5), 1–7.

Blanton, D. & Dagenais, P. (2007). Comparison of language skills of adjudicated and nonadjudicated adolescent males and females. *Language, Speech, and Hearing Services in Schools, 38*(4), 309–314.

Bluman, A. (2012). *Elementary statistics: A step by step approach* (8th ed). New York: McGraw-Hill.

Boellstorff, T. (2010). A typology of ethnographic scales in virtual worlds. In *Online worlds: Convergence of real and the virtual* (pp. 123–133). London: Springer.

Bogdan, R. & Biklen, S. (2007). *Qualitative research for education: An introduction to theories and methods* (5th ed.). Boston: Allyn & Bacon.

Boggio, P., Nunes, A., Rigonatti, S., Nitsche, M., Pascual-Leone, A., & Fregni, F. (2007). Repeated sessions of noninvasive brain DC stimulation is associated with motor function improvement in stroke patients. *Restorative Neurology and Neuroscience, 25*(2), 123–129.

Bohon, L., Santos, S., Sanchez-Sosa, J., & Singer, R. (1994). The effects of a mental health video on the social skills knowledge and attitudes of Mexican immigrants. *Journal of Applied Social Psychology, 24,* 1794–1805.

Border, L., Bloss, K., Cashwell, C., & Rainey, L. (1994). Helping student apply the scientist–practitioner model: A teaching approach. *Counselor Education and Supervision, 34,* 172–179.

Bracht, G. & Glass, G. (1968). The external validity of experiments. *American Educational Research Journal, 5,* 437–474.

Brannen, J. (1992). *Mixing methods: Qualitative and quantitative research.* Brookfield, VT: Avebury.

Brayer, S., MacKinnon, D., & Page, M. (2003). *Levine's guide to SPSS analysis of variance* (2nd ed.). Florence, KY: Psychology Press.

Bredart, S., Lampinen, J., & Defeldre, A. (2003). Phenomenal characteristics of cryptomnesia. *Memory, 11*(1), 1–11.

Brooks, F., Lewinson, T., Aszman, J., & Wolk, J. (2012). Voucher users and revitalized public-housing residents 6 years after displacement. *Research on Social Work Practice, 22*(1), 10–19.

Brown, D. & Srebalus, D. (1996). *Introduction to the counseling profession* (2nd ed.). Boston: Allyn & Bacon.

Brown, E. (2006). Good mother, bad mother: Perceptions of mothering by rural African-American women who use cocaine. *Journal of Addictions Nursing, 17*(1), 21–31.

Brunelle, N., Cousineau, M., & Brochu, S. (2005). Juvenile drug use and delinquency: Youths' accounts of their trajectories. *Substance Use & Misuse, 40*(5), 721–734.

Brunoni, A., Nitsche, M., Bolognini, N., Bikson, M., Wagner, T., Merabet, L., et al. (2012). Clinical research with transcranial direct current Stimulation (tDCS): Challenges and future directions. *Brain Stimulation, 5*(3), 175–195.

Bryan, C., Stone, S., & Rudd, M. (2011). A practical, evidence-based approach for means-restriction counseling with suicidal patients. *Professional Psychology: Research and Practice, 42*(5), 339–346.

Campbell, D. T. & Stanley, J. C. (1966). *Experimental & quasi-experimental designs for research.* Chicago: Rand McNally.

Castro, F. & Coe, K. (2007). Traditions and alcohol use: A mixed methods analysis. *Cultural Diversity and Ethnic Minority Psychology, 13*(4), 269–284.

Chan, A. & Leung, W. (2006). Differentiating autistic children with quantitative encephalography: A 3-month longitudinal study. *Journal of Child Neurology, 21*(5), 391–399.

Charles, D. (1995). *Introduction to educational research* (2nd ed.). White Plains, NY: Longman.

Charmaz, K. (2006). Measuring pursuits, marking self: Meaning construction in chronic illness. *Journal of Qualitative Studies on Health and Well-Being, 1*(1), 27–37.

Chen, H. (2005). *Practical program evaluation: Assessing and improving planning, implementation, and effectiveness.* Thousand Oaks, CA: Sage.

Chester, A. & Glass, C. (2006). Online counselling: A descriptive analysis of therapy services on the Internet. *British Journal of Guidance & Counselling, 34*(2), 134–150.

Chouilnard, J. (2013). The case for participatory evaluation in an era of accountability. *American Journal of Evaluation, 34*(2), 237–253.

Christ, T. (2007). Experimental control and threats to internal validity of concurrent and nonconcurrent multiple baseline designs. *Psychology in the Schools, 44*(5), 451–459.

Clark, V., Coffman, B., Mayer, A., Weisend, M., Lane, T., Calhoun, V., et al. (2012). TDCS guided using fMRI significantly accelerates learning to identify concealed objects. *NeuroImage, 59,* 117–128.

Clark, V. & Creswell, J. (Eds.). (2008). *The mixed methods reader.* Thousand Oaks, CA: Sage.

Colgin, L., Denninger, T., Fyhn, M., Hafting, T., Bonnevie, T., Jensen, O., et al. (2009). Frequency of gamma oscillations routes of flow of information in the hippocampus. *Nature, 462*(19), 353–357.

Conoley, J. & Impara, J. (1995). *The twelfth mental measurement yearbook.* Lincoln: University of Nebraska Press.

Cook, D. (1989). Systematic need assessment: A primer. *Journal of Counseling and Development, 67,* 462–464.

Cook, J., O'Donnell, C., Dinnen, S., Bernardy, N., Rosenheck, R., & Hoff, R. (2013). A formative evaluation of two evidence-based psychotherapies for PTSD in VA residential treatment programs. *Journal of Traumatic Stress, 26,* 56–63.

Cook, T. & Campbell, D. T. (1979). *Quasi-experimentation: Design and analysis issues for field settings.* Chicago: Rand McNally.

Coolidge, F. (2006). *Statistics: A gentle introduction* (2nd ed.). Thousand Oaks, CA: Sage.

Coombes, K., Wang, J., & Baggerly, A. (2007). Microassays: Retracing steps. *Nature Medicine, 13*(11), 1276–1277.

Cooper, H. (2012). *APA handbook of research methods in psychology.* Washington, DC: American Psychological Association.

Cox, C. & Cohen, B. (2000). Mandala artwork by clients with DID: Clinical observations based on two theoretical models. *Art Therapy, 17*(3), 195–201.

Creswell, J. (2007). *Qualitative inquiry and research design: Choosing among five approaches* (2nd ed.). Thousand Oaks, CA: Sage.

Creswell, J. (2012). *Educational research: Planning, conducting, and evaluating quantitative and qualitative research* (4th ed.). Boston: Pearson.

Culatta, B., Reese, M., & Setzer, L. (2006). Early literacy instruction in a dual-language (Spanish–English) kindergarten. *Communication Disorders Quarterly, 27*(2), 67–82.

Curlette, W. (2006). A framework for research studies: Mixed methods through combining Bayesian statistics and qualitative research in individual psychology. *The Journal of Individual Psychology, 62*(3), 239–249.

Curry, N. & Kasser, T. (2005). Can coloring mandalas reduce anxiety? *Journal of the American Art Therapy Association, 22,* 81–85.

Curry, S., Sporer, A., & Pugach, O. (2007). Use of tobacco cessation treatment among young adult smokers: 2005 national health interview survey. *American Journal of Public Health, 97*(8), 1464–1469.

Daehler, M. & Bukatko, D. (1985). *Cognitive development.* New York: Knopf.

Davidson, E. (2005). *Evaluation methodology basics: The nuts and bolts of sound evaluation.* Thousand Oaks, CA: Sage.

Davison, G., & Lazarus, A. (2007). Clinical case studies are important in science and practice of psychotherapy. In S. Lillenfeld & W. O'Donohue, *The great ideas of clinical science: 17 principles that every mental health professional should understand.* New York: Routledge.

De Anda, D. (2007). Intervention research and program evaluation in the school setting: Issues and alternative research designs. *Children & Schools, 29,* 87–94.

Denzin, N. K., & Lincoln, Y. S. (Eds.). (2000). *Handbook of qualitative research* (2nd ed.). Thousand Oaks, CA: Sage.

Denzin N. K. & Lincoln, Y. S. (2011). *The Sage handbook of qualitative research.* Thousand Oaks, CA: Sage.

DeTienne, D. & Chandler, G. (2007). The role of gender in opportunity identification. *Entrepreneurship Theory & Practice, 31*(3), 365–387.

Dionne, M. & Martini, R. (2011). Floor time play with a child with autism: A single subject study. *Canadian Journal of Occupational Therapy, 78*(3), 196–203.

Driver, S., O'Connor, J., Lox, C., & Rees, K. (2004). Evaluation of an aquatics programme on fitness parameters of individuals with a brain injury. *Brain Injury, 18,* 847–859.

Drummond, R. (2000). *Appraisal procedures for counselors and helping.* St. Paul, MN: Merrill.

Eaves, R., Rabren, K., & Hall, G. (2012). The post-school outcomes transition survey: A tool for effective decision making? *Assessment for Effective Intervention, 38*(1), 30–39.

Edwards, D., Valero-Cabre, A., Rotenberg, A., Pascual-Leone, A., Ferrucci, R., Egermann, H., et al. (2006). Is there an effect of subliminal messages in music on choice behavior? *Journal of Articles in Support of the Null Hypothesis, 4*(2), 29–45.

Egner, T. & Gruzelier, J. (2003). Ecological validity of neurofeedback: modulation of slow wave EEG enhances musical performance. *Neuroreport, 14*(9) 1221–1224.

Eid, M. & Diener, E. (2006). *Handbook of multimethod measurement in psychology.* Washington, DC: American Psychological Association.

Ellis, L. & Chen, E. (2013). Negotiating identify development among undocumented immigrant college students: A grounded theory study. *Journal of Counseling Psychology, 60*(2), 251–264.

Erickson, K., Hatton, D., Roy, V., Fox, D., & Renne, D. (2007). Literacy in early intervention for children with visual impairments: Insights from individual cases. *Journal of Visual Impairment & Blindness, 10*(2), 80–95.

Ernst, J. & Monroe, M. (2006). The effects of environment-based education on students' critical thinking skills and dispositions toward critical thinking. *Environmental Education Research, 12(3–4),* 429–443.

Esterling, B., L'Abate, L., Murray, E., & Pennebaker, J. (1999). Empirical foundations for writing in prevention and psychotherapy: Mental and physical health outcomes. *Clinical Psychology Review, 19*(1), 79–96.

Farber, N. (2006). Conducting qualitative research: A practical guide for school counselors. *Professional School Counseling, 9*(5), 367–375.

Farynaiarz, J. & Lockwood, L. (1992). Effectiveness of microcomputer simulations in stimulating environmental problem solving by community college students. *Journal of Research in Science Teaching, 29,* 453–470.

Felce, D., de Kock, U., Mansell, J., & Jenkins, J. (1984). Providing systematic individual teaching for severely disturbed and profoundly mentally handicapped adults in residential care. *Behavior Research and Therapy, 22,* 299–309.

Ferguson, E. & Bibby, P. (2004). The design and analysis of quasi-experimental field research. In G. Breakwell (Ed.), *Doing social psychology research* (pp. 93–127). Leicester, UK: British Psychological Society.

Fitzgerald, H. (2006). Cross cultural research during infancy: Methodological considerations. *Infant Mental Health Journal, 27*(6), 612–617.

Flynn, D., van Schaik, P., Blackman, T., Femcott, C., Hobbs, B., & Calderon, C. (2003). Developing a virtual reality-based methodology for people with demetia: A feasibility study. *Cyberpsychology & Behavior, 6*(6), 591–611.

Forsyth, D. & Leary, M. (1997). Achieving the goals of the scientist-practitioner model: The seven interfaces of social and counseling psychology. *Counseling Psychologist, 25*(2), 180–200.

Fregni, F., Boggio, P., Nitsche, M., Rigonatti, S., & Pascual-Leone, A. (2006). Cognitive effects of repeated sessions of transcranial direct current stimulation in patents with depression. *Depression and Anxiety, 23,* 482–484.

Frein, S. (2011). Comparing in-class and out-of-class computer-based tests to traditional paper tests in introductory psychology courses. *Technology and Teaching, 38,* 282–287.

Fry, S. (2007). First-year teachers and induction support: Ups, downs, and in-betweens. *The Qualitative Researcher, 12*(2), 216–237.

Fry, J., Botterill, W., & Pring, T. (2009). The effect of an intensive group therapy program for young adults who stutter: A single subject study. *International Journal of Speech-Language Pathology, 11*(1), 12–19.

Frye, N. (1965). Varieties of literary utopias. In F. Manuel (Ed.), *Utopias and utopian thought* (pp. 25–49). Boston: Houghton Mifflin.

Gall, M., Borg, W., & Gall, J. (1996). *Educational research: An introduction* (6th ed.). White Plains, NY: Longman.

Gall, M., Gall, J., & Borg, W. (2002). *Educational research: An introduction* (7th ed.). White Plains, NY: Longman.

Gall, M., Gall, J., & Borg, W. (2006). *Educational research: An introduction* (8th ed.). Boston: Pearson Education.

Gallo, L., Bogart, L., Vranceanu, A., & Matthews, K. (2005). Socioeconomic status, resources, psychological experiences, and emotional responses: A test of the reserve capacity model. *Journal of Personality and Social Psychology, 88*(2), 386–399.

Gamble, V. N. (1993). A legacy of distrust: African Americans and medical research. *American Journal of Preventive Medicine, 9*(6), 3–38.

Gay, L., Mills, G., & Airasian, P. (2012). *Educational research: Competencies for analysis and applications* (10th ed.). Boston: Pearson.

Geist, E. (2011). The game changer: Using iPads in college teacher education classes. *College Student Journal, 45*(4), 758–768.

Gelso, C. (2006). On the making of a scientist–practitioner: A theory of research training in professional psychology. *Training and Education in Professional Psychology, 5,* 3–16.

Gergin, K. (1985). The social constructionist movement in modern psychology. *American Psychologist, 40,* 266–275.

Gliner, J. & Morgan, G. (2000). *Research methods in applied settings: An integrated approach to design and analysis.* Mahwah, NJ: Lawrence Erlbaum.

Goldfried, M. (1984). Training the clinician as scientist–professional. *Professional Psychology: Research and Practice, 15,* 477–481.

Gortmaker, V. & Brown, R. (2006). Out of the college closet: Differences in perceptions and experiences among out and closeted lesbian and gay students. *College Student Journal, 40*(3), 606–619.

Gostin, L. (1991). Ethical principles for the conduct of human subject research: Population-based research and ethics. *Law, Medicine, and Health Care, 19*(3–4), 191–201.

Goswami, U. (2006). Neuroscience and education: From research to practice. *Nature Reviews Neuroscience, 7,* 406–413.

Gowers, S. (2006). Evidence based research in CBT with adolescent eating disorders. *Child and Adolescent Mental Health, 11*(1), 9–12.

Gravetter, R. & Wallnau, L. (2008). *Essentials of statistics for the behavioral sciences* (6th ed.). Belmont, CA: Wadsworth.

Greenwell, S. & Zygouris-Coe, V. (2012). Exploring high school English language arts teachers' responses to professional development in reading instruction. *Journal of Reading Education, 37*(2), 21–26.

Gregory, R. (2007). *Psychological testing: History, principles, and applications.* Boston: Allyn & Bacon.

Guba, E. (1990). *The paradigm dialog.* Thousand Oaks, CA: Sage.

Guba, E. & Lincoln, Y. (1992). *Effective evaluation: Improving the usefulness of evaluation results through responsive and naturalistic approaches.* San Francisco: Jossey-Bass.

Gunkelman, J. & Johnstone, J. (2005). Neurofeedback and the brain. *Journal of Adult Development, 12*(2/3), 93–98.

Habermann, B., Broome, M., Pryor, E., & Ziner, K. (2010). Research coordinators' experiences with scientific misconduct and research integrity. *Nursing Research, 59*(1), 51–57.

Hall, E., Verheyden, G., & Ashburn, A. (2011). Effect of a yoga programme on an individual with Parkinson's disease. A single-subject design. *Disability and Rehabilitation, 33*(15–16), 1483–1489.

Hamilton, D. (1992). Traditions, preferences, and postures in applied qualitative research. In N. Denzin & Y. Lincoln (Eds.), *Handbook of qualitative research* (pp. 60–69). Thousand Oaks, CA: Sage.

Harmon-Jones, E. & Amodio, D. (2012). Electroencephalographic methods in psychology. In H. Cooper, P. Camic, D. Long, A. Panter, D. Rindskopt, & K. Sher. *APA handbook of research methods in psychology: Volume 1. Foundations, planning, measures and psychometrics.* Washington, DC: American Psychological Association.

Hatinen, M., Kinnunen, U., Pekkonen, M., & Kalimo, R. (2007). Comparing two burnout interventions: Perceived job control mediates decreases in burnout. *International Journal of Stress Management, 14*(3), 227–248.

Heath, M. & Tynan, C. (2010). Crafting a research proposal. *The Marketing Review, 10*(2), 147–168.

Hecht, D., Walsh, V., & Lavidor, M. (2010). Transcranial direct current stimulation facilitates decision making in probabilistic guessing task. *Journal of Neuroscience, 30*(12), 4241–4245.

Heiman, G. (1995). *Research methods in psychology.* Boston: Houghton Mifflin.

Heinrich, H., Gevensleben, H., & Strehl, U. (2007). Annotation: Neuro feedback-train brain to train behaviour. *Journal of Child Psychology and Psychiatry, 48*(1), 3–16.

Henderson, P., Rosen, D., & Mascaro, N. (2007). Empirical study on the healing nature of mandalas. *Psychology of Aesthetics, Creativity, and the Arts, 1*(3), 148–154.

Henry, R., Anshel, M., & Michael, T. (2006). Effects of aerobic and circuit training on fitness and body image among women. *Journal of Sport Behavior, 29*(4), 281–303.

Heppner, P., Kivlighan, D., & Wampold, B. (1992). *Research design in counseling.* Pacific Grove, CA: Brooks/Cole.

Hernandez, A. (2012). Review of program evaluation in practice. Core concepts and examples for discussion and analysis. *Journal of Psychoeducational Assessment, 30*(3), 309–311.

Hersch, G., Hutchinson, S., Davidson, H., Wilson, C., Maharaj, T., & Watson, K. (2004). Effect of an occupation-based culture heritage intervention in long-term geriatric care: A two-group control study. *The American Journal of Occupational Therapy, 66*(2), 224–232.

Hinkin, T., Holtom, B., & Klag, M. (2007). Collaborative research: Developing mutually beneficial relationships between researchers and organizations. *Organizational Dynamics, 36,* 105–118.

Hogan, J., Dolan, P., & Donnelly, P. (2009). *Approaches to qualitative research: Theory and its practical application.* Cork, Ireland: Oak Tree Press.

Hoekstra, A., Korthagen, F., Brekelmans, M., & Imants, J. (2009). Experienced teachers' informal workplace learning and perceptions of workplace conditions. *Journal of Workplace Learning, 21*(4), 276–298.

Hollowood, T., Salisbury, C., Rainforth, B., & Palobaro, M. (1994). Use of instructional time in classroom serving students with and without severe disabilities. *Exceptional Children, 61*(3), 242–253.

Horner, R., Carr, E., Halle, J., McGee, G., Odom, S., & Wolery, M. (2005). The use of single subject research to identify evidence-based practice in special education. *Exceptional Children, 71,* 165–179.

Horner, R. & Kratochwill, T. (2012). Synthesizing single-case research to identify evidence-based practices: Some brief reflections. *Journal of Behavioral Education, 21,* 266–272.

Hoshmand, L. (1989). Alternate research paradigms: A review and teaching proposal. *Counseling Psychologist, 17*(1), 3–79.

Hoshmand, L., & Polkinghorne, D. (1992). Redefining the science–practice relationship and professional training. *American Psychologist, 47*(1), 55–66.

House, E. (1993). *Professional evaluation: Social impact and political consequences.* Newbury Park, CA: Sage.

Houser, R., Anderson, D., & Wang, J. (1995). Participatory Action Needs Assessment: A unified approach to needs assessment within the state/federal VR system. *Journal of Applied Rehabilitation Counseling, 26,* 55–58.

Houser, R. & Thoma, S. (2012). *Ethics in counseling and therapy: Developing an ethical identity.* Thousand Oaks, CA: Sage.

Houser, R., Thoma, S., Stanton, M., O'Connor, E., Jiang, H., & Dong, Y. (2013). *The effect of transcranial direct current stimulation (tDCS) on learning and performing statistical calculations* (under review).

Houser, R., Wilczenski, F., & Ham, M. (2006). *Culturally relevant ethical decision-making in counseling.* Thousand Oaks, CA: Sage.

Hunsley, J. (2007). Addressing key challenges in evidence-based practice in psychology. *Professional Psychology, 38*(2), 113–121.

Hunt, R. (1986). Percent agreement, Pearson's correlation, and Kappa as measures of inter-examiner reliability. *Journal of Dental Research, 65*(2), 128-130.

Isaksson, G., Lexell, J., & Skar, L. (2007). Social support provides motivation and ability to participate in occupation. *Occupation, Participation and Health, 27*(1), 23–30.

Ivankova, N., Creswell, J., & Stick, S. (2006). Using mixed-methods sequential explanatory design: From theory to practice. *Field Methods, 18*(1), 3–20.

Iverson, G., Brooks, B., Collins, M., & Lovell, M. (2006). Tracking neuropsychological recovery following concussion in sport. *Brain Injury, 20*(3), 245–252.

Jabaley, J., Lutzker, J., Whitaker, D., & Self-Brown, S. (2011). Using iPhones to enhance and reduce face-to-face home safety sessions within safecare: An evidence-based child maltreatment prevention program. *Journal of Family Violence, 26,* 377–385.

Jacobson, L., Koslowsky, M., & Lavidor, M. (2012). TDCS polarity effects in motor and cognitive domains: A meta-analytic review. *Experimental Brain Research, 1,* 1–10.

Jerome, L. & Jordon, P. (2007). Psychophysiological perspectives on presence: The implications of mediated environments on relationships, behavioural health and social construction. *Psychological Services, 4*(2), 75–84.

Jick, T. (2008). Triangulation as the first mixed methods design. In V. Clark & J. Creswell (Eds.), *The mixed methods reader* (pp. 105–118). Thousand Oaks, CA: Sage.

Joint Committee on Standards for Educational Evaluation. (1988). *The personnel evaluation standards.* Newbury Park, CA: Sage.

Joint Committee on Standards for Educational Evaluation. (1994). *The program evaluation standards* (2nd ed.). Thousand Oaks, CA: Sage.

Jones, E. (2011). Why a black Baptist community uses Christian media: An ethnographic treatment of a working-class community where Christian media use is shaped by sacred tenets, social influences, and personal factors. *Journal of Media and Religion, 10,* 1–23.

Jones, G. & Stokes, A. (2009). *Online counseling: A handbook for practitioners.* New York: Macmillan.

Jones, J. (1981). *Bad blood: The Tuskegee syphilis experiment.* New York: Free Press.

Jones, S. (1992). Was there a Hawthorne effect? *American Journal of Sociology, 98*(3), 451–468.

Kaiser, A. (2007). Addressing challenging behavior: Systematic problems, systematic solutions. *Journal of Early Intervention, 29*(2), 114–118.

Kamhi, A. (2011). Balancing certainty and uncertainty in clinical practice. *Language, Speech, and Hearing Services in Schools, 42,* 59–64.

Kamps, D. & Abbott, M. (2007). Use of evidence-based small group reading instruction for English language learners in elementary grades: Secondary tier intervention. *Learning Disability Quarterly, 30*(3), 153–168.

Kanfer, F. (1990). The scientist–practitioner connection: A bridge in need of constant attention. *Professional Psychology: Research and Practice, 21*(4), 264–270.

Kang, T. & Oh, D. (2012). Treatment of hemispatial neglect in patients with post-hemiparesis: A single-subject experimental design using a whole-body tilt exercise plus mental practice. *Neurorehabilitation, 31,* 197–206.

Kartalova-O'Doherty, Y. & Doherty, D. (2008). Coping strategies and styles of family careers of persons with enduring mental illness: A mixed methods analysis. *Scandinavian Journal of Caring Sciences, 22*(11), 19–28.

Kasimatis, M. & Guastello, D. (2012). Parenting style trumps work role in life satisfaction of midlife women. *Journal of Articles in Support of the Null Hypothesis, 9*(1), 51–59.

Kazdin, A. (2011). *Single-case research design: Methods for clinical and applied settings* (2nd ed.). New York: Oxford University Press.

Kelly, G. (1955). *The psychology of personal constructs* (Vols. 1 and 2). New York: W. W. Norton.

Kelman, H. (1967). Human use of human subjects: The problem of deception in social psychological experiments. *Psychological Bulletin, 67*(1), 1–11.

Kessler, S., Turkeltaub, P., Benson, J., & Hamilton, R. (2012). Differences in the experience of active and sham transcranial direct current stimulation. *Brain Stimulation, 5,* 155–162.

Kettlewell, P. (2004). Development, dissemination, and implementation of evidence-based treatment: Commentary. *Clinical Psychology: Science and Practice, 11*(2), 190–195.

King, L., Burton, C., Hicks, J., & Drigotas, S. (2007). Ghosts, UFOs, and magic: Positive affect and the experiential system. *Journal of Personality and Social Psychology, 92*(5), 905–919.

Klomegah, R. (2007). Predictors of academic performance of university students: An application of the goal efficacy model. *College Student Journal, 41*(2), 407–415.

Koronyo-Hamaoui, M., Danziger, Y., Frisch, A., Stein, D., Leor, S., Laufer, N., et al. (2002). Association between anorexia nervosa and the hsKCa3 gene: A family-based and case control study. *Molecular Psychiatry, 7,* 82–85.

Kram, K., Wasserman, I., & Yip, J. (2012). Metaphors of identity and professional practice: Learning from the scholar-practitioner. *Journal of Applied Behavioral Science, 48*(30), 304–341.

LaFountain, R. & Bartos, R. (2002). *Research and statistics made meaningful in counseling and student affairs.* Pacific Grove, CA: Brooks/Cole.

LaFromboise, T. & Foster, S. (1992) Cross-cultural training: Scientist–practitioner model and methods. *Counseling Psychologist, 20*(3), 472–289.

Landau, J., Druen, P., & Arcuri, J. (2002). Methods for helping students avoid plagiarism. *Teaching of Psychology, 29*(2), 112–115.

Lane, D. & Corrie, S. (2006). *The modern scientist–practitioner: A guide to practice in psychology.* New York: Routledge.

Leary, M. (2001). *Introduction to behavioral research methods* (3rd ed.). Boston: Allyn & Bacon.

Leong, F. & Zachar, P. (1991). Development and validation of the scientist–practitioner inventory for psychology. *Journal of Counseling Psychology, 38*(3), 331–341.

Liang, L., Fulmer, G., Majerich, D., Clevenstine, R., & Howanski, R. (2012). The effects of a model-based physics curriculum program with a Physics First approach: A causal-comparative study. *Journal of Science Education and Technology, 21*(1), 114–124.

Lincoln, Y. & Guba, E. (1985). *Naturalistic inquiry.* Thousand Oaks, CA: Sage.

Linden, M. & Gunkelman, J. (2013). QEEG-D. QEEG-guided neurofeedback for autism: Clinical observations and outcomes. In M. Casanova, A. El-Baz, & J. Suri (Eds.), *Imaging the brain in autism* (pp. 45–60). New York: Springer.

Linder, F. & Bauer, D. (1983). Perception of values among male and female undergraduate students. *Perceptual and Motor Skills, 56,* 59–63.

Little, A. (2006). Life as we know it. *Atlantic Monthly, 298,* 54–55.

Locicero, J. (2002). A comparison of non-certified and certified grief counselors in regard to education, experience, credentials, and supervision. *OMEGA, 46*(1), 5–13.

Lofland, J., Snow, D., Anderson, L., & Lofland, L. (2006). *Analyzing social settings: A guide to qualitative observations and analysis* (4th ed.). Belmont, CA: Wadsworth.

Lomax, R. & Hahs-Vaughn, D. (2012). An introduction to statistical concepts (3rd ed.). Florence, KY: Routledge.

Love, K., Bahner, A., Jones, A., & Nilsson, J. (2007). An investigation of early research experience and research self-efficacy. *Professional Psychology, 38*(3), 314–320.

Lowman, R. (2012). *The scientist–practitioner consulting psychologist, 64*(3), 151–156.

Luebbe, A., Radcliffe, T., Callands, T., Green, D. & Thorn, B. (2007). Evidence-based practice in psychology: Perceptions of graduate students in scientist-practitioner programs. *Journal of Clinical Psychology, 63*(7), 643–655.

Luszcyznska, A. & Sobczyk, A. (2007). Planning to lose weight: Randomized controlled trial of an implementation intention prompt to enhance weight reduction among overweight and obese women. *Health Psychology, 26*(4), 507–512.

Lynch, D., Teplin, S., Willis, S., Pathman, D., Larsen, L., Steiner, B., et al. (2001). Interim evaluation of the rural health scholars program. *Teaching and Learning in Medicine, 13*(1), 36–42.

Maas, E., Butalla, C., & Farinella, K. (2012). Feedback frequency in treatment for childhood apraxia of speech. *American Journal of Speech-Language Pathology, 21,* 239–257.

Madill, A. (2012). Interviews and interviewing techniques. In H. Cooper, P. Camic, D. Long, A. Panter, D. Rindskopt, & K. Sher. *APA handbook of research methods in psychology: Volume 1. Foundations, planning, measures and psychometrics* (pp. 249–276). Washington, DC: American Psychological Association.

Maheu, M. & Gordon, B. (2000). Counseling and therapy on the internet. *Professional Psychology: Research and Practice, 31*(5), 484–489.

Mallen, M. & Vogel, D. (2005). Introduction to the major contribution: Counseling psychology and online counseling. *Counseling Psychologist, 33,* 761–774.

Manicas, P. & Secord, P. (1983). Implications for psychology of the new philosophy of science. *American Psychologist, 38,* 399–413.

Manning, C. & Cheers, B. (1995). Child abuse notification in a country town. *Child Abuse and Neglect, 19*(4), 387–413.

Marangolo, P., Marinelli, C., Bonifazi, S., Fiori, V., Ceravolo, M., Provinciali, L., et al. (2011). Electrical stimulation over the left inferior frontal gyrus (IFG) determines long-term effects in the recovery of speech apraxia in three chronic aphasics. *Behavioural Brain Research, 225*(2), 498–504.

Marsh, B. (2007). *Plagiarism: Alchemy and remedy in higher education.* Albany: State University of New York Press.

Marshall, L., Molle, M., Siebner, H., & Born, J. (2005). Bifrontal transcranial direct current stimulation slows reaction time in a working memory task. *BMC Neuroscience*, 6–23.

Marshall, C. & Rossman, G. (2006). *Designing qualitative research* (4th ed.). Thousand Oaks, CA: Sage.

Marshall, C. & Rossman, G. (2010). *Designing qualitative research* (5th ed.) Thousand Oaks, CA: Sage.

Masheb, R., Grilo, C., & Rolls, B. (2011). A randomized controlled trial for obesity and binge eating disorder: Low-energy-density dietary counseling and cognitive-behavioral therapy. *Behaviour Research and Therapy, 49*(12), 821-829.

Maslow, A. (1976). *The farther reaches of human nature.* New York: Penguin.

Mason, L. (2007). Introduction: Bridging the cognitive and sociocultural approaches in research on conceptual change: Is it feasible? *Educational Psychologist, 42*(1), 1–7.

Mastel-Smith, B., Binder, B., Malecha, A., Hersch, G., Symes, L., & McFarlane, J. (2006). Testing therapeutic life review offered by home care workers to decrease depression among home-dwelling older women. *Issues in Mental Health Nursing, 27,* 1037–1049.

Matheny, K. & Edwards, C. (1974). Academic improvement through an experimental classroom management system. *Journal of School Psychology, 12*(3), 222–232.

Mattai, M., Miller, R., Weisinger, B., Greenstern, D., Bakalar, J., Tossell, J., et al. (2011). Tolerable aspects of tDCS stimulation on childhood onset schizophrenia. *Brain Stimulation, 4,* 275–280.

Matthews, W. (2011). What might judgment and decision making research be like if we took of Bayesian approach to hypothesis testing? *Judgment and Decision Making, 6*(8), 843–856.

Maxwell, J. (2009). Designing a qualitative study. In L. Bickman and D. Rob (Eds.)., *Applied social research methods* (2nd ed.). Thousand Oaks, CA: Sage.

Mayer, D. (2004). *Essential evidence-based medicine.* New York: Cambridge University Press.

McLay, R., McBrien, C., Wiederhold, M., & Wiederhold, B. (2010). Exposure therapy with and without virtual reality to treat PTSD while in the combat theatre: A parallel case series. *Cyberpsychology, Behaviour, and Social Networking, 13*(1), 37–42.

McMillan, J. (2004). *Educational research: Fundamentals for the consumer* (4th ed.). Boston: Pearson.

McNaught, C., Lam, P., & Cheng, K. (2012). Investigating relationships between features of learning designs and student learning outcomes. *Education Technology, Research Development, 60,* 271–286.

McNaughten, D. & Gabbard, C. (1993). Physical exertion and immediate mental performance of sixth-grade children. *Perceptual and Motor Skills, 77,* 1155–1159.

Mendelsohn, E. & Nowotny, H. (Eds.). (1984). *Nineteen eighty-four: Science between utopia and dystopia.* Boston: Reidel.

Mendenhall, W. (1983). *Introduction to probability and statistics* (6th ed.). Boston: Duxbury.

Merlo, L., Collins, A., & Bernstein, J. (2008). CIDCP-affiliated clinical psychology: Student views of their science training. *Training and Education in Professional Psychology, 2*(1), 58–65.

Merrell, K. (1999). *Behavioral, social, and emotional assessment of children and adolescents.* Mahwah, NJ: Lawrence Erlbaum.

Messersmith, E., Garrett, J., Davis-Kean, P., Malanchuk, O., & Eccles, J. (2008). Career development from adolescence through emerging adulthood: Insights from information technology occupations. *Journal of Adolescent Research, 23*(2), 206–227.

Metfessel, B. & Greene, R. (2012). A nonparametric statistical method that improves physician cost of care analysis. *Health Services Research, 47,* 2398–2417.

Metuki, N., Sela, T., & Lavidor, M. (2012). Enhancing cognitive control components of insight problems solving by anodal tDCS of the left dorsolateral prefrontal cortex. *Brain Stimulation, 5,* 110–115.

Miles, M. & Huberman, M. (1994). *Qualitative data analysis: An expanded sourcebook* (2nd ed.). Thousand Oaks, CA: Sage.

Milgram, S. (1963). Behavioral study of obedience. *Journal of Abnormal and Social Psychology, 67*(4), 371–378.

Milgram, S. (1974). *Obedience to authority: An experimental view.* New York: Harper and Row.

Minium, E. & King, B. (2003). *Statistical reasoning in psychology and education* (4th ed.). Hoboken, NJ: Wiley & Sons.

Mio, J. & Iwamasa, G. (1993). To do or not to do: That is the question for white cross-cultural researchers. *Counseling Psychologist, 21*(2), 197–212.

Moore, G. (1983). *Developing and evaluating educational research.* Boston: Little Brown.

Moore, M., & Calvert, S. (2000). Vocabulary acquisition for children with autism: Teacher or computer instruction. *Journal of Autism and Developmental Disorders, 30(4),* 359–362.

Morawski, J. G. (1992). There is more to our history of giving: The place of introductory textbooks in American psychology. *American Psychologist, 47*(2), 161–169.

Mozdzierz, G., Peluso, P., & Lisiecki, J. (2011). Evidence-based psychological practices and therapist training: At the crossroads. *Journal of Humanistic Psychology, 51*(4), 439–464.

Murphy, L., Geisinger, K., Carlson, J., & Spies, R. (2011). *Tests in print VIII.* Lincoln, NE: Buros Institute of Mental Measurements.

Myers, J. & Young, S. (2012). Brain wave biofeedback: Benefits of integrating neurofeedback in counseling. *Journal of Counseling & Development, 90,* 20–28.

National Education Association. (1975). *Code of ethics.* Washington, DC: Author.

National Institutes of Health (NIH). (1994). *Outreach notebook for the NIH guidelines on inclusion of women and minorities as subjects in clinical research.* Bethesda, MD: Author.

Nelson, M. & Neufeldt, S. (1996). Building on an empirical foundation: Strategies to enhance good practice. *Journal of Counseling and Development, 74,* 609–615.

Nicholson, D., Knapp, P., & Gardner, P. (2011). Combining concurrent and sequential methods to examine the usability and readability of websites with information about medicines. *Journal of Mixed Methods Research, 5*(1), 25–51.

Nisbet, M. & Myers, T. (2007). The polls—trends: Twenty years of public opinion about global warming. *Public Opinion Quarterly, 71*(3), 444–470.

Norelle-Clarke, A., Nyander, E., & Jansson-Frojmark, M. (2011). Sleepless in Sweden: A single subject study of effects of cognitive therapy for insomnia on three adolescents. *Behavioural and Cognitive Psychotherapy, 39,* 367–374.

Nunez, P. (1974). The brain wave equation: A model for the EEG. *Mathematical Biosciences, 21*(3–4), 279–297.

Nystul, M. (1999). *Introduction to counseling: An art and science perspective.* Boston: Allyn & Bacon.

O'Bryant, S. & McCaffrey, R. (2006). Preliminary findings on the cross cultural test of face recognition. *Applied Neuropsychology, 13*(4), 223–229.

Odaci, H. & Kalkan, M. (2010). Problematic Internet use, loneliness and dating anxiety among young adult university students. *Computers & Education, 55,* 1091–1097.

Odom, S., Brantlinger, E., Gersten, R., Horner, R., Thompson, B., & Harris, K. (2005). Research in special education: Scientific methods and evidence-based practices. *Exceptional Children, 71*(2), 137–148.

Office of Protection From Research Risks. (1993). *Protecting human research subjects: Institutional Review Board guidebook.* Washington, DC: U.S. Government Printing Office.

Okasha, S. (2002). *Philosophy of science: A short introduction.* Oxford, UK: Oxford University Press.

Olvera, A., Stewart, S., Galindo, L., & Stephens, J. (2007). Diabetes, depression, and metabolic control in Latinas. *Cultural Diversity and Ethnic Minority Psychology, 13*(3), 225–231.

O'Neill, T., Yamagata, L, Yamagata, J., & Togioka, S. (2012). Teaching STEM means teacher learning. *Kappan, September,* 36–40.

Ong-Dean, C., Hofstetter, C., & Strick, B. (2011). Challenges and dilemmas in implementing random assignment in educational research. *American Journal of Evaluation, 32*(1), 29–49.

Onwuegbuzie, A. & Leech, N. (2005). On becoming a pragmatic researcher: The importance of combining quantitative and qualitative research methodologies. *International Journal of Social Research Methodology, 8*(5), 375–387.

Opris, D., Pintea, S., Garcia-Palacios, A., Botella, C., Szamoskozi, S., & David, D. (2012). Virtual reality exposure therapy in anxiety disorders: A quantitative meta-analysis. *Depression and Anxiety, 29,* 85–93.

Overholser, J. (2010). Ten criteria to qualify as a scientist–practitioner in clinical psychology: An immodest proposal for objective standards. *Journal of Contemporary Psychotherapy, 40,* 51–59.

Overholser, J. (2012). Ten criteria to qualify as a scientist–practitioner in clinical psychology: An immodest proposal for objective standards. *Journal of Contemporary Psychotherapy, 40,* 51–59.

Padgett, D. (2004). *The qualitative research experience.* Boston: Thomson Brooks/Cole.

Painter, K. (2012). Outcomes for youth with severe emotional disturbance: A repeated measures longitudinal study of a wraparound approach of service delivery in systems of care. *Child Youth Care Forum, 41,* 407–425.

Pandiani, J., Banks, S., & Schacht, L. (2001). Consumer satisfaction and incarceration after treatment. *Administration and Policy in Mental Health, 29*(2), 145–155.

Park, C. (2003). In other (people's) words: Plagiarism by university students—literature and lessons. *Assessment and Evaluation in Higher Education, 28*(5), 471–488.

Parham, T. (1993). White researchers conducting multicultural research: Can their efforts be "mo betta"? *Counseling Psychologist, 21*(2), 25–256.

Park, S., Chang, S., & Chung, C. (2005). Effects of a cognition–emotion focused program to increase public participation in papanicolaou smear screening. *Public Health Nursing, 22*(4), 289–298.

Parsons, R. & Brown, K. (2002). *Teacher as reflective practitioner and action researcher.* Belmont, CA: Wadsworth.

Patton, M. (1990). *Qualitative evaluation and research methods* (2nd ed.). Thousand Oaks, CA: Sage.

Patton, K. & Campbell, S. (2011). Introduction: educational neuroscience. *Educational Philosophy and Theory, 43,* 1–6

Pettijohn I. T. & Ahmed, S. (2010). Songwriting loafing or creative collaboration? A comparison of individual and team written *Billboard* hits in the USA. *Journal of Articles in Support of the Null Hypothesis, 7*(1), 1–6.

Pfeiffer, S., Burd, S., & Wright, A. (1992). Clinicians and research: Recurring obstacles and some possible solutions. *Journal of Clinical Psychology, 48*(1), 140–145.

Pissanos, B. (1995). Providers of continued professional education: Constructed perceptions of four elementary school physical education teachers. *Journal of Teaching in Physical Education, 14*(2), 215–230.

Pistrang, N. & Barker, C. (2012). Varieties of qualitative research: A pragmatic approach to selecting methods. In H. Cooper, P. Camic, D. Long, A. Panter, D. Rindskopt, & K. Sher. *APA handbook of research methods in psychology: Volume 2. Research designs: Quantitative, qualitative, neuropsychological and biological* (pp. 5–19). Washington, DC: American Psychological Association.

Plake, B. & Spies, R. (Eds.) (2005). *The sixteenth mental measurements yearbook.* Lincoln, NE: Buros Institute of Mental Measurements.

Ponterotto, J. (1993). White racial identity and the counseling professional. *Counseling Psychologist, 21*(2), 213–217.

Pottick, K., Kirk, S., & Hsieh, D. (2007). Judging mental disorders in youths: Effects of client, clinician, and contextual differences. *Journal of Consulting and Clinical Psychology, 75,* 1–8.

Preechawong, S., Zauszniewski, J., Heinzer, M., Musil, C., Keresmar, C., & Aswinanonh, R. (2007). Relationships of family functioning, self-esteem, and resourceful coping of Thai adolescents with asthma. *Issues in Mental Health Nursing, 28*(1), 21–36.

Pring, R. & Thomas, G. (2004). *Evidence-based practice in education: Conducting educational research.* New York: McGraw-Hill.

QSR International. (1997). *Nonnumerical, unstructured data-indexing, searching, and theorizing.* Victoria, Australia: Author.

Rasinski, K., Lee, L., & Krishnamurty, P. (2012). Question order effects. In *APA handbook of research methods in psychology: Volume 1. Foundations, planning, measures, and psychometrics* (pp. 229–248). Washington, DC: American Psychological Association.

Raykov, T. & Marcoulides, G. (2006). *A first course in structural equation modeling.* Mahwah, NJ: Lawrence Erlbaum.

Ready, D., Gerardi, R., Backscheider, A., Mascaro, N., & Rothbaum, B. (2010). Comparing virtual reality exposure therapy to present-centered therapy with 11 U.S. Vietnam veterans with PTSD. *Cyberpsychology, Behavior, and Social Networking, 13*(1), 49–54.

Redman, B. & Merz, J. (2008). Scientific misconduct: Do the punishments fit the crime? *Science, 321,* 775.

Rees, C. & Stone, S. (2005). Therapeutic alliance in face-to-face versus videoconferenced psychotherapy. *Professional Psychology: Research and Practice, 36*(6), 649–653.

Reid, P. & Finchilescu, G. (1995). The disempowering effects of media violence against women on college women. *Psychology of Women Quarterly, 19,* 397–411.

Resendes, J. & Lecci, L. (2012). Comparing the MMPI-2 scale scores of parents involved in parental competency and child custody assessments. *Psychological Assessment, 24*(4), 1054–1059.

Robinson-Zanartu, C., Pena, E., Cook-Morales, V., Pena, A., Afshani, R., & Nguyen, L. (2005). Academic crime and punishment: Faculty members' perceptions of and responses to plagiarism. *School Psychology Quarterly, 20*(3), 318–337.

Rochlen, A., Beretvas, S., & Zack, J. (2004). The online and face-to-face counseling attitudes scales: A validation study. *Measurement and Evaluation in Counseling and Development, 37*(2) 95.

Rochlen, A., Zack, J., & Speyer, C. (2004). Online therapy: Review of relevant definitions, debates, and current empirical support. *Journal of Clinical Psychology, 60*(3), 269–283.

Roig, M. (1997). Can undergraduate students determine whether text has been plagiarized? *The Psychological Record, 47*(1), 113–123.

Roig, M. & Caso, M. (2005). Lying and cheating: Fraudulent excuse making, cheating, and plagiarism. *The Journal of Psychology, 139*(6), 485–494.

Rosaldo, R. (1989). *Culture and truth: The remaking of social analysis.* Boston: Beacon.

Rosenhan, D. (1973). On being sane in insane places. *Science, 19,* 250–258.

Rosenthal, J. (2001). *Statistics and data interpretation for the helping professions.* Pacific Grove, CA: Brooks/Cole.

Ross, L., Register-Mihalik, J., Mihalik, J. McCulloch, K., Prentice, W., Shields, E., et al. (2011). Effects of a single-task versus a dual-task paradigm on cognition and balance of health subjects. *Journal of Sport Rehabilitation, 20,* 296–310.

Rossi, P. & Freeman, H. (1993). *Evaluation: A systematic approach* (5th ed.). Newbury Park, CA: Sage.

Roth, E. & Smith, K. (2008). The Mozart effect: Evidence for the arousal hypothesis. *Perceptual and Motor Skills, 107,* 396–402.

Rothbaum, B., Hodges, L., Alarcon, R., Ready, D., Shahar, F., Graap, K., et al. (1999). Virtual reality exposure therapy for PTSD veterans: A case study. *Journal of Traumatic Stress, 12*(2), 263–271.

Rousseau, D. & McCarthy, S. (2007). Educating managers from an evidence-based perspective. *Academy of Management Learning & Education, 6*(1), 84–101.

Ruble, L., McGrew, J., Toland, M., Dalrymple, N., & Jung, L. (2013). A randomized controlled trial of COMPASS web-based and face-to-face coaching in autism. *Journal of Consulting and Clinical Psychology, 81*(3), 566–572.

Sackett, D. L., Straus, S. E., Richardson, W. S., Rosenberg, W., & Haynes, R. B. (2000). *Evidence-based medicine: How to practice and teach EBM* (2nd ed.). London: Churchill Livingstone.

Salkind, N. (2006). *Exploring research* (6th ed.). Upper Saddle River, NJ: Pearson/Prentice Hall.

Salloum, A., Avery, L., & McClain, R. (2001). Group psychotherapy for adolescent survivors of homicide victims: A pilot study. *American Academy of Child and Adolescent Psychiatry, 40,* 1261–1267.

Sandage, S. (2012). The tragic-ironic self: A qualitative case study of suicide. *Psychoanalytic Psychology, 29*(1), 17–33,

Sanders, J. (1994). *The program evaluation standards: How to assess evaluations of educational programs.* Thousand Oaks, CA: Sage.

Sandford, K. (2010). The next 25 years?: Future scenarios and future directions for education and technology. *Journal of Computer Assisted Learning, 26,* 74–93.

Sawilowsky, S. & Markman, B. (1990). Another look at the power of meta-analysis in the Solomon Four-Group design. *Perceptual and Motor Skills, 71,* 177.

Schuemie, M., van der Straaten, P., Krihn, M., & van der Mast, C. (2001). Research on presence in virtual reality: A survey, *Cyberpsychology & Behavior, 4*(2), 183–202.

Schutter, D. (2012). Noninvasive stimulation of the cerebral cortex in social neuroscience. In H. Cooper, P. Camic, D. Rindskipf, & K Sher. *APA handbook of research methods in psychology: Volume 1. Foundations, planning, measures, and psychometrics* (pp. 601–618). Washington, DC: American Psychological Association.

Schwartz, C. & Revicki, D. (2012). Mixing methods and blending paradigm: Some considerations for future research. *An International Journal of Quality of Life Aspects of Treatment, Care & Rehabilitation, 21*(3), 375–376.

Scriven, M. (1987). New frontiers in evaluation. In D. S. Corday & M. W. Lipsay (Eds.), *Evaluation studies: Review annual* (Vol. 11, pp. 54–91). Newbury Park, CA: Sage.

Scriven, M. (1991). *Evaluation thesaurus* (4th ed.). Newbury Park, CA: Sage.

Searson, M., Jones, W., & Wold, K. (2011). Editorial: Reimaging schools: The potential of virtual education. *British Journal of Educational Technology, 42*(3), 363–371.

Seignourel, P., Green, C., & Schmitz, J. (2008). Factor structure and diagnostic efficiency of the BDI-II in treatment-seeking substance users. *Drug and Alcohol Dependence, 93*(3), 271–278.

Sellbom, M., Lee, T., Ben-Porath, Y., Arbisi, P., & Gervais, R. (2012). Differentiating PTSD symptomatology with the MMPI-2-RF (Restructured Form) in a forensic disability sample. *Psychiatric Research 197,* 172–179.

Sells, S., Smith, T., & Sprenkle, D. (1995). Integrating qualitative and quantitative research methods: A research model. *Family Process, 34,* 199–218.

Sexton, T. (1996). The relevance of counseling outcome research: Current trends and practical implications. *Journal of Counseling and Development, 74*(6), 590–600.

Sexton, T. & Whiston, S. (1996). Integrating counseling research and practice. *Journal of Counseling and Development, 74*(6), 588–589.

Sharpe, D., Adair, J., & Roese, N. (1992). Twenty years of deception research: A decline in subjects' trust. *Personality and Social Psychology Bulletin, 18*(5), 585–590.

Shearer, B. (2004). Multiple intelligences theory after 20 years. *Teachers College Record, 106,* 2–16.

Sheeler, M., Congdon, M., & Stansbery, S. (2010). Providing immediate feedback to co-teachers through bug-in-ear technology: An effective method of peer coaching in inclusion classrooms. *Teacher Education and Special Education, 33*(1), 83–96.

Shimahara, N. (1988). Anthroethnography: A methodological consideration. In R. Sherman & R. Webb (Eds.), *Qualitative research in education: Focus and methods* (pp. 76–89). New York: Falmer.

Shore, B. A., Lerman, D. C., Smith, R. G., Iwata, B. A., & DeLeon, I. G. (1995). Direct assessment of quality of care in a geriatric nursing home. *Journal of Applied Behavior Analysis, 28,* 435–338.

Silva, K., Correia, R., Lima, M., Magalhaes, A., & de Sousa, L. (2011). Can dogs prime autistic children for therapy? Evidence from a single case study. *Journal of Alternative and Complementary Medicine, 17*(7), 655–659.

Silverman, D. (2011). *Interpreting qualitative data* (4th ed.). Thousand Oaks, CA: Sage.

Simpson, K. & Keen, D. (2010). Teaching young children with autism graphic symbols embedded within an interactive song. *Journal of Developmental Physical Disabilities, 22,* 165–177.

Slegelis, M. (1987). A study of Jung's mandala and its relationship to art psychotherapy. *The Arts in Psychotherapy, 14,* 301–311.

Slocum, T., Spencer, T., & Detrich, R. (2012). Best available evidence: Three complementary approaches. *Education and Treatment of Children, 35*(2), 156–181.

Sorin-Peters, R. (2004). The evaluation of a learner-centred training programme for spouses of adults with chronic aphasia using *Qualitative Case Study Methodology, Aphasiology, 18*(10), 937–949.

Spencer, T., Detrich, R., & Slocum, T. (2012). Evidence-based practice: A framework for making effective decisions. *Education & Treatment of Children, 35*(2), 127–151.

Spooner, F., Knight, V., Browder, D., & Smith, B. (2012). Evidence-based practice for teaching academics to students with severe developmental disabilities. *Remedial and Special Education, 33*(6), 374–387.

Spurling, L. (Ed.). (1989). *Sigmund Freud: Critical assessments.* London: Routledge.

Stagg, C. & Nitsche, M. (2011). Physiological basis of transcranial direct current stimulation. *The Neuroscientist, 7*(1), 37–53.

Stake, R. (1994). Case studies. In N. Denzin & Y. Lincoln (Eds.), *Handbook of qualitative research* (pp. 236–247). Thousand Oaks, CA: Sage.

Stake, R. (2000). Case studies. In N. Denzin & Y. Lincoln (Eds.), *Handbook of qualitative research* (2nd ed., pp. 443–466). Thousand Oaks, CA: Sage.

Stangor, C. (2006). *Research methods for the behavioral sciences.* Boston: Houghton Mifflin.

Streubert, H. & Carpenter, D. (1995). *Qualitative research in nursing: Advancing the humanistic imperative.* Philadelphia: J.B. Lippincott.

Stenhoff, D. & Lignugaris-Kraft, B. (2007). A review of the effects of peer tutoring on students in secondary settings. *Exceptional Children, 74*(1), 8–30.

Stoltenberg, C., McNeil, B., & Elliot, T. (1995). Selected translations of social psychology to counseling. *Counseling Psychologist, 23,* 603–610.

Storlie, T. (2012). Presleep self-suggestion and dream recall: A single-subject study. *International Journal Dream Research, 5*(2), 148–150.

Strasser, F., Binswanger, J., Cerny, T., & Kesselring, A. (2007). Fighting a losing battle: Eating-related distress of men with advanced cancer and their female partners. A mixed-methods study. *Palliative Medicine, 21,* 129–137.

Strohmer, D., Pellerin, M., & Davidson, K. (1995). Rehabilitation counselor hypothesis testing: The role of negative information, client disability, and counselor experience. *Rehabilitation Counseling Bulletin, 39,* 82–93.

Stufflebeam, D. (2003). The CIPP model for evaluation. In T. Kellaghan & D. L. Stufflebeam (Eds.), *The international handbook of educational evaluation* (pp. 31–62). Dordrecht, Holland: Kluwer.

Stufflebeam, D. (2004). *Evaluation design checklist.* Kalamazoo, MI: Western Michigan University Evaluation Center. Retrieved September 30, 2013 from https://communities.usaidallnet.gov/fa/system/files/Evaluation+Design+Checklist.pdf

Stufflebeam, D., & Shinkfield, A. (2007). *Evaluation theory, models & applications.* San Francisco: John Wiley.

Sue, D. W. (1993). Confronting ourselves: The white and racial/ethnic minority researcher. *Counseling Psychologist, 21*(2), 244–249.

Szymanski, D., Ozegovic, J., Phillips, J., & Briggs-Phillips, M. (2007). Fostering scholarly productivity through academic and internship research training environments. *Training and Education in Professional Psychology, 1*(2), 135–146.

Tanenbaum, S. (2003). Evidence-based practice in mental health: Practical weaknesses meet political strengths. *Journal of Evaluation in Clinical Practice, 9,* 287–301.

Tashakkori, A. & Teddlie, C. (2008). The evolution of mixed methods research. In V. Clark and J. Creswell (Eds.), *The mixed methods reader* (pp. 5–26). Thousand Oaks, CA: Sage.

Tassinary, L., Hess, U., & Carcoba, L. (2012). Peripheral physiological measures of psychological constructs. In *APA Handbook of research methods in psychology: Volume 1. Foundations, planning, measures, and psychometrics* (pp. 461–488). Washington, DC: American Psychological Association.

Taylor, J. & Rowe, B. (2012). The "Mozart Effect" and the mathematical connection. *Journal of College Reading and Learning, 42*(2), 51–65.

Taylor, S. & Bogdan, R. (1984). *Introduction to qualitative research methods: The search for meaning* (2nd ed.). New York: John Wiley.

Tedlock, B. (2000). Ethnography and ethnographic representation. In N. Denzin & Y. Lincoln (Eds.), *Handbook of qualitative research* (2nd ed., pp. 455–482). Thousand Oaks, CA: Sage.

Thomas, S. & Quinn, S. (1991). The Tuskegee syphilis study, 1932 to 1972: Implications for HIV education and AIDS risk education programs in the black community. *American Journal of Public Health, 81*(11), 1498–1505.

Thorndike, R. & Thorndike-Christ, T. (2010). *Measurement and evaluation in psychology and education* (8th ed.). Boston: Pearson.

Thyer, B. (2005). *Program evaluation: An introduction.* Belmont, CA: Wadsworth.

Todd, Z., Nerlich, B., McKeown, S., & Clarke, D. (2004). *Mixing methods in psychology: The integration of qualitative and quantitative methods in theory and practice.* New York: Psychology Press.

Toothaker, L. & Miller, L. (1996). *Introductory statistics for the behavioral sciences* (2nd ed.). Pacific Grove, CA: Brooks/Cole.

Townend, M. & Grant, A. (2006). Integrating science, practice and reflexivity cognitive therapy with driving phobia. *Journal of Psychiatric and Mental Health Nursing, 13*(5), 554–561.

Urbina, S. (2004). *Essentials of psychological testing.* Hoboken, NJ: Wiley.

Urdan, T. (2005). *Statistics in plain English* (2nd ed.). Mahwah, NJ: Lawrence Erlbaum.

Van Tassel-Baska, J. (2013). The world of cross-cultural research: Insights for gifted education. *Journal for the Education of the Gifted, 36*(1), 6–18.

Vernon, D. (2005). Can neurofeedback training enhance performance? An evaluation of the evidence with implications for future research. *Applied Psychophysiology and Biofeedback, 30*(4), 347–364.

Vespia, K., Sauer, E., & Lyddon, W. (2006). Counselling psychologists as scientist–practitioners: Finding unity in diversity. *Counselling Psychology Quarterly, 19,* 223–227.

Vierra, A. & Pollock, J. (1988). *Reading educational research.* Scottsdale, AZ: Gorsuch Scarisbrick.

Volti, R. (2006). *Car and culture: The life story of a technology.* Westport, CT: Greenwood.

Vosniadou, S. (2007). The cognitive-situative divide and the problem of conceptual change. *Educational Psychologist, 42*(1), 55–66.

Wadey, R., Evans, L., Hanton, S., & Neil, R. (2012). An examination of hardiness throughout the sport-injury process: A qualitative follow-up study. *British Journal of Health Psychology, 17,* 872–893.

Walker, D. & Aten, J. (2012). Future directions for the study and application of religions and spirituality, and trauma research, *Journal of Psychology & Theology, 40*(4), 349–353.

Walker, W. (2005). The strength and weakness of research design involving qualitative approaches. *Journal of Research in Nursing, 10*(5), 571–582.

Wampold, B., Goodheart, D., & Levant, R. (2007). Clarification and elaboration on evidence-based practice in psychology, *American Psychologist, 62*(6), 616–618.

Watts, S., Pinero, D., Alter, M., & Lancaster, K. (2012). An assessment of nutrition education in selected counties in New York state elementary schools (Kindergarten through fifth grade). *Journal of Nutrition Education and Behavior, 44*(6), 474–481.

Weikel, W. & Palmo, A. (1996). *Foundations of mental health counseling* (2nd ed.). Springfield, IL: Charles C. Thomas.

Wendt, O. & Miller, B. (2012). Quality appraisal of single-subject experimental designs: An overview and comparison of different appraisal tools. *Education and Treatment of Children, 35*(2), 235–268.

Whaley, A. & David, K. (2007). Cultural competence and evidence-based practice in mental health services: A complementary perspective. *American Psychologist, 62*(6), 563–574.

What Works Clearinghouse. (2011). *What Works Clearinghouse: Procedures and standards handbook.* Washington, DC: U.S. Department of Education, Institute of Education Sciences. Retrieved July 2, 2013, from http://ies.ed.gov/ncee/wwc/pdf/reference_resources/wwc_procedures_v2_1_standards_handbook.pdf

Whiston, S. (1996). Accountability through action research: Research methods for practitioners. *Journal of Counseling and Development, 74*(6), 616–623.

Wholey, J., Hatry, H., & Newcomer, K. (2004). *Handbook of practical program evaluation.* San Francisco: Jossey-Bass.

Whyte, W. (1990). *Participatory action research.* Thousand Oaks, CA: Sage.

Wiersma, S. & Jurs, S. (2005). *Research methods in education: An introduction.* Boston: Pearson.

Willig, C. (2001). *Introducing qualitative research in psychology.* Philadelphia: Open University Press.

Wikles, J., Marcus, M., Bright, A., Dapelo, M., & Psychol, M. (2012). Emotion and eating disorder symptoms in patients with anorexia nervosa: An experimental study. *International Journal of Eating Disorders, 45*(7), 876–882.

Wirth, M., Rahman, R., Kuenecke, J., Koenig, T., Horn, H., Sommer, W., et al. (2011). Effects of transcranial direct current stimulation (tDCS) on behavior and electrophysiology of language production. *Neuropsychologia, 49*(14), 3989–3998.

Wolcott, H. (1994). *Transforming qualitative data: Description, analysis and interpretation.* Thousand Oaks, CA: Sage.

Worley, M., Tate, S., & Brown, S. (2012). Mediational relations between 12-step attendance, depression and substance use in patients with comorbid substance dependence and major depression. *Addiction, 107,* 1974–1983.

Yi, J. (2008). The use of diaries as a qualitative research method to investigate teachers' perception and use of rating schemes. *Pan-Pacific Association of Applied Linguistics, 12*(1), 1–10.

Yin, R. (2003). *Case study research: Design and methods* (3rd ed.). Thousand Oaks, CA: Sage.

Index

ABOUT THE AUTHOR

Rick A. Houser is currently Professor and Department Head in Educational Studies in Psychology, Research Methodology, and Counseling at the University of Alabama. He has been Associate Dean in the College of Education at the University of Massachusetts, Boston. Also, he was Professor and Department Chair for several years at the University of Massachusetts, Boston. Rick Houser has taught graduate-level research courses for more than 27 years. He received his doctorate from the University of Pittsburgh in rehabilitation counseling with a minor in research methodology. He conducts research in ethical decision making, stress and coping, educational neuroscience, and neuroscience and counseling.